OSCAR
WILDE

THE
BEDSIDE
WILDE

CLASSICS FOR PLEASURE

CHANCELLOR PRESS

The Picture of Dorian Gray
was first published in Great Britain in book form in 1891.
The Happy Prince and Other Tales
(which includes *The Happy Prince, The Nightingale and the Rose, The Selfish Giant* and *The Devoted Friend*)
was first published in Great Britain in 1888.
Lord Arthur Savile's Crime and Other Stories
(which includes *The Canterville Ghost*)
and *A House of Pomegranates*
(which includes *The Young King, The Birthday of the Infanta,
The Fisherman and his Soul* and *The Star-Child*)
were first published in Great Britain in 1891.
Lady Windermere's Fan
was first published in Great Britain in 1893.
A Woman of No Importance
was first published in Great Britain in 1894.
An Ideal Husband and *The Importance of Being Earnest*
were first published in Great Britain in 1899.
Vera, or *the Nihilists*
was first published in Great Britain in 1880.
The Duchess of Padua
was first published in Great Britain in 1883.

This edition published in Great Britain 1993
by Chancellor Press
an imprint of Reed Illustrated Books Limited
Michelin House, 81 Fulham Road, London SW3 6RB
and Auckland, Melbourne, Singapore and Toronto

ISBN 1 851 52359 6

A CIP catalogue record for this book is available
from the British Library

Printed by William Clowes, Beccles

ILLUSTRATIONS

The Happy Prince, The Nightingale and the Rose, The Selfish Giant and *The Devoted Friend*: illustrations by Walter Crane and Jacomb Hood from the first edition of *The Happy Prince and Other Tales* (1888) published by David Nutt.

The Young King, The Birthday of the Infanta, The Fisherman and his Soul and *The Star-Child*: illustrations by Charles Ricketts and Charles Shannon from the first edition of *A House of Pomegranates* (1891) published by Osgood McIlvaine.

CONTENTS

Extract

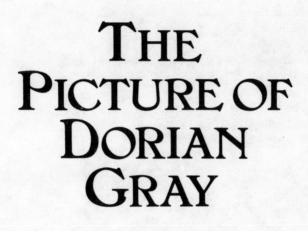

THE PICTURE OF DORIAN GRAY

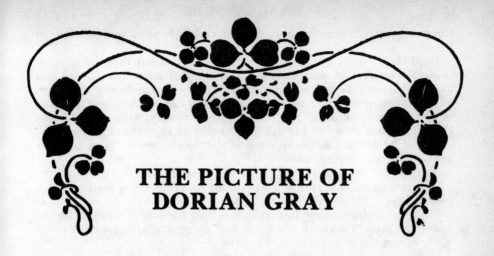

THE PICTURE OF
DORIAN GRAY

*Dorian Gray is greatly admired by the artist Basil Hallward who
has painted a portrait of him which perfectly reflects his physical
and moral beauty. Hallward has introduced Dorian to his friend
Sir Henry Wotton, a hedonistic and cynical roué who has come to
exercise a dangerous influence over the young man ...*

4

ONE AFTERNOON. A month later, Dorian Gray was reclining in a luxurious
arm-chair, in the little library of Lord Henry's house in Mayfair. It was, in its way,
a very charming room, with its high-panelled wainscoting of olive-stained oak,
its cream-coloured frieze and ceiling of raised plaster-work, and its brick-dust
felt carpet strewn with silk long-fringed Persian rugs. On a tiny satinwood table
stood a statuette by Clodion, and beside it lay a copy of *Les Cent Nouvelles*, bound
for Margaret of Valois by Clovis Eve, and powdered with the gilt daisies that
Queen had selected for her device. Some large blue china jars and parrot-tulips
were arranged on the mantelshelf, and through the small leaded panels of

the window streamed the apricot-coloured light of a summer day in London.

Lord Henry had not yet come in. He was always late on principle, his principle being that punctuality is the thief of time. So the lad was looking rather sulky, as with listless fingers he turned over the pages of an elaborately-illustrated edition of *Manon Lescaut* that he had found in one of the bookcases. The formal monotonous ticking of the Louis Quatorze clock annoyed him. Once or twice he thought of going away.

At last he heard a step outside, and the door opened. 'How late you are, Harry!' he murmured.

'I am afraid it is not Harry, Mr Gray,' answered a shrill voice.

He glanced quickly round, and rose to his feet. 'I beg your pardon. I thought—'

'You thought it was my husband. It is only his wife. You must let me introduce myself. I know you quite well by your photographs. I think my husband has got seventeen of them.'

'Not seventeen, Lady Henry?'

'Well, eighteen, then. And I saw you with him the other night at the Opera.' She laughed nervously as she spoke, and watched him with her vague forget-me-not eyes. She was a curious woman, whose dresses always looked as if they had been designed in a rage and put on in a tempest. She was usually in love with somebody, and, as her passion was never returned, she had kept all her illusions. She tried to look picturesque, but only succeeded in being untidy. Her name was Victoria, and she had a perfect mania for going to church.

'That was at *Lohengrin*, Lady Henry, I think?'

'Yes; it was at dear *Lohengrin*. I like Wagner's music better than anybody's. It is so loud that one can talk the whole time without other people hearing what one says. That is a great advantage; don't you think so, Mr Gray?'

The same nervous staccato laugh broke from her thin lips, and her fingers began to play with a long tortoise-shell paper-knife.

Dorian smiled, and shook his head. 'I am afraid I don't think so, Lady Henry. I never talk during music, at least during good music. If one hears bad music, it is one's duty to drown it in conversation.'

'Ah! that is one of Harry's views, isn't it, Mr Gray? I always hear Harry's views from his friends. It is the only way I get to know of them. But you must not think I don't like good music. I adore it, but I am afraid of it. It makes me too romantic. I have simply worshipped pianists – two at a time, sometimes, Harry tells me. I don't know what it is about them. Perhaps it is that they are foreigners. They all are, ain't they? Even those that are born in England become foreigners after a time, don't they? It is so clever of them, and such a compliment to art. Makes it quite cosmopolitan, doesn't it? You have never been to any of my parties, have you, Mr Gray? You must come. I can't afford orchids, but I spare no expense in foreigners. They make one's rooms look so picturesque. But here is Harry! – Harry, I came in to look for you, to ask you something – I forget what it was – and I found Mr Gray here.

We have had such a pleasant chat about music. We have quite the same ideas. No; I think our ideas are quite different. But he has been most pleasant. I am so glad I've seen him.'

'I am charmed, my love, quite charmed,' said Lord Henry, elevating his dark crescent-shaped eyebrows and looking at them both with an amused smile. 'So sorry I am late, Dorian. I went to look after a piece of old brocade in Wardour Street, and had to bargain for hours for it. Nowadays people know the price of everything, and the value of nothing.'

'I am afraid I must be going,' exclaimed Lady Henry, breaking an awkward silence with her silly sudden laugh. 'I have promised to drive with the Duchess. Good-bye, Mr Gray. Good-bye, Harry. You are dining out, I suppose? So am I. Perhaps I shall see you at Lady Thornbury's.'

'I dare say, my dear,' said Lord Henry, shutting the door behind her, as, looking like a bird of paradise that had been out all night in the rain, she flitted out of the room, leaving a faint odour of frangipani. Then he lit a cigarette, and flung himself down on the sofa.

'Never marry a woman with straw-coloured hair, Dorian,' he said, after a few puffs.

'Why, Harry?'

'Because they are so sentimental.'

'But I like sentimental people.'

'Never marry at all, Dorian. Men marry because they are tired; women, because they are curious; both are disappointed.'

'I don't think I am likely to marry, Harry. I am too much in love. That is one of your aphorisms. I am putting it into practice, as I do everything that you say.'

'Who are you in love with?' asked Lord Henry, after a pause.

'With an actress,' said Dorian Gray, blushing.

Lord Henry shrugged his shoulders. 'That is a rather commonplace début.'

'You would not say so if you saw her, Harry.'

'Who is she?'

'Her name is Sibyl Vane.'

'Never heard of her.'

'No one has. People will some day, however. She is a genius.'

'My dear boy, no woman is a genius. Women are a decorative sex. They never have anything to say, but they say it charmingly. Women represent the triumph of matter over mind, just as men represent the triumph of mind over morals.'

'Harry, how can you?'

'My dear Dorian, it is quite true. I am analysing women at the present, so I ought to know. The subject is not so abstruse as I thought it was. I find that, ultimately, there are only two kinds of women, the plain and the coloured. The plain women are very useful. If you want to gain a reputation for respectability, you have merely to take them down to supper. The other women are very charming. They commit one mistake, however. They paint in order to try and look young. Our grandmothers painted in order to try and talk brilliantly. *Rouge* and *esprit* used to go together. That is all over now. As long as a woman can look ten years younger than her own daughter, she is perfectly satisfied. As for conversation, there are only five women in London worth talking to, and two of these can't be admitted into decent society. However, tell me about your genius. How long have you known her?'

'Ah! Harry, your views terrify me.'

'Never mind that. How long have you known her?'

'About three weeks.'

'And where did you come across her?'

'I will tell you, Harry; but you mustn't be unsympathetic about it. After all, it never would have happened if I had not met you. You filled me with a wild desire to know everything about life. For days after I met you something seemed to throb in my veins. As I lounged in the Park, or strolled down Piccadilly, I used to look at everyone who passed me, and wonder, with a mad curiosity, what sort of lives they led. Some of them fascinated me. Others filled me with terror. There was an exquisite poison in the air. I had a passion for sensations. . . . Well, one evening about seven o'clock I determined to go out in search of some adventure. I felt that this grey, monstrous London of ours, with its myriads of people, its sordid sinners, and its splendid sins, as you once phrased it, must have something in store for me. I fancied a thousand things. The mere danger gave me a sense of delight. I remembered what you had said to me on that wonderful evening when we first dined together, about the search for beauty being the real secret of life. I don't know what I expected, but I went out and wandered eastward, soon losing my way in a labyrinth of grimy streets and black, grassless squares. About half-past eight I passed by an absurd little theatre, with great flaring gas-jets and gaudy play-bills. A hideous Jew, in the most amazing waistcoat I ever beheld in my life, was standing at the entrance, smoking a vile cigar. He had greasy ringlets, and an enormous diamond blazed in the centre of a soiled shirt. "Have a box, My Lord?" he said, when he saw me, and he took off his hat with an air of gorgeous servility. There was something about him, Harry, that amused me. He was such a monster. You will laugh at me, I know, but I really went in and paid a whole guinea for the stage-box. To the present day I can't make out why I did so; and yet if I hadn't – my dear Harry, if I hadn't, I should have missed the greatest romance of my life. I see you are laughing. It is horrid of you!'

'I am not laughing, Dorian; at least I am not laughing at you. But you should not say the greatest romance of your life. You should say the first romance of your life. You will always be loved, and you will always be in love with love. A *grande passion* is the privilege of people who have nothing to do. That is the one use of the idle classes of a country. Don't be afraid. There are exquisite things in store for you. This is merely the beginning.'

'Do you think my nature so shallow?' cried Dorian Gray, angrily.

'No; I think your nature so deep.'

'How do you mean?'

'My dear boy, the people who love only once in their lives are really the shallow people. What they call their loyalty, and their fidelity, I call either the lethargy of custom or their lack of imagination. Faithfulness is to the emotional life what consistency is to the life of the intellect – simply a confession of failures. Faithfulness! I must analyse it some day. The passion for property is in it. There are many things that we would throw away if we were not afraid that others might pick them up. But I don't want to interrupt you. Go on with your story.'

'Well, I found myself seated in a horrid little private box, with a vulgar drop-scene staring me in the face. I looked out from behind the curtain and surveyed the house. It was a tawdry affair, all Cupids and cornucopias, like a third-rate wedding cake. The gallery and pit were fairly full, but the two rows of dingy stalls were quite empty, and there was hardly a person in what I suppose they called the dress-circle. Women went about with oranges and ginger-beer, and there was a terrible consumption of nuts going on.'

'It must have been just like the palmy days of the British Drama.'

'Just like, I should fancy, and very depressing. I began to wonder what on earth I should do, when I caught sight of the play-bill. What do you think the play was, Harry?'

'I should think *The Idiot Boy or Dumb but Innocent.* Our fathers used to like that sort of piece, I believe. The longer I live, Dorian, the more keenly I feel that whatever was good enough for our fathers is not good enough for us. In art, as in politics, *les grandpères ont toujours tort.*'

'This play was good enough for us, Harry. It was *Romeo and Juliet.* I must admit that I was rather annoyed at the idea of seeing Shakespeare done in such a wretched hole of a place. Still, I felt interested, in a sort of way. At any rate, I determined to wait for the first act. There was a dreadful orchestra, presided over by a young Hebrew who sat at a cracked piano, that nearly drove me away, but at last the drop-scene was drawn up, and the play began. Romeo was a stout elderly gentleman, with corked eyebrows, a husky tragedy voice, and a figure like a beer-barrel. Mercutio was almost as bad. He was played by the low-comedian, who had introduced gags of his own and was on most friendly terms with the pit. They were both as grotesque as the scenery, and that looked as if it had come out of a country booth. But Juliet! Harry, imagine a girl, hardly seventeen years of age, with a little flower-like face, a small Greek head with plaited coils of dark-brown hair, eyes that were violet wells of passion, lips that were like the petals of a rose. She was the loveliest thing I had ever seen in my life. You said to me once that pathos left you unmoved, but that beauty, mere beauty, could fill your eyes with tears. I tell you, Harry, I could hardly see this girl for the mist of tears that came across me. And her voice – I never heard such a voice. It was very low at first, with deep, mellow notes, that seemed to fall singly upon one's ear. Then it became a little louder, and sounded like a flute or a distant hautbois. In the garden scene it had all the tremulous ecstasy that one hears just before dawn when

nightingales are singing. There were moments, later on, when it had
the wild passion of violets. You know how a voice can stir one. Your
voice and the voice of Sibyl Vane are two things that I shall never
forget. When I close my eyes, I hear them, and each of them says
something different. I don't know which to follow. Why should I not
love her? Harry, I do love her. She is everything to me in life. Night
after night I go to see her play. One evening she is Rosalind, and the
next evening she is Imogen. I have seen her die in the gloom of an
Italian tomb, sucking the poison from her lover's lips. I have watched
her wandering through the forest of Arden, disguised as a pretty boy
in hose and doublet and dainty cap. She has been mad, and has come
into the presence of a guilty king, and given him rue to wear, and bitter
herbs to taste of. She has been innocent, and the black hands of jealousy
have crushed her reed-like throat. I have seen her in every age and in
every costume. Ordinary women never appeal to one's imagination.
They are limited to their century. No glamour ever transfigures them.
One knows their minds as easily as one knows their bonnets. One can
always find them. There is no mystery in any of them. They ride in the
Park in the morning, and chatter at tea-parties in the afternoon. They
have their stereotyped smile, and their fashionable manner. They are
quite obvious. But an actress! How different an actress is! Harry! why
didn't you tell me that the only thing worth loving is an actress?'

'Because I have loved so many of them, Dorian.'

'Oh, yes, horrid people with dyed hair and painted faces.'

'Don't run down dyed hair and painted faces. There is an extraordinary charm in them, sometimes,' said Lord Henry.

'I wish now I had not told you about Sibyl Vane.'

'You could not have helped telling me, Dorian. All through your life
you will tell me everything you do.'

'Yes, Harry, I believe that is true. I cannot help telling you things.
You have a curious influence over me. If I ever did a crime, I would
come and confess it to you. You would understand me.'

'People like you – the wilful sunbeams of life – don't commit crimes,
Dorian. But I am much obliged for the compliment, all the same. And
now tell me – reach me the matches, like a good boy: thanks – what are
your actual relations with Sibyl Vane?'

Dorian Gray leaped to his feet, with flushed cheeks and burning eyes.
'Harry! Sibyl Vane is sacred!'

'It is only the sacred things that are worth touching, Dorian,' said
Lord Henry, with a strange touch of pathos in his voice. 'But why
should you be annoyed? I suppose she will belong to you some day.
When one is in love, one always begins by deceiving one's self, and one
always ends by deceiving others. That is what the world calls a romance.
You know her, at any rate, I suppose?'

'Of course I know her. On the first night I was at the theatre, the
horrid old Jew came round to the box after the performance was over,
and offered to take me behind the scenes and introduce me to her. I
was furious with him, and told him that Juliet had been dead for

hundreds of years, and that her body was lying in a marble tomb in Verona. I think, from his blank look of amazement, that he was under the impression that I had taken too much champagne, or something.'

'I am not surprised.'

'Then he asked me if I wrote for any of the newspapers. I told him I never even read them. He seemed terribly disappointed at that, and confided to me that all the dramatic critics were in a conspiracy against him, and that they were every one of them to be bought.'

'I should not wonder if he was quite right there. But, on the other hand, judging from their appearance, most of them cannot be at all expensive.'

'Well, he seemed to think they were beyond his means,' laughed Dorian. 'By this time, however, the lights were being put out in the theatre, and I had to go. He wanted me to try some cigars that he strongly recommended. I declined. The next night, of course, I arrived at the place again. When he saw me he made me a low bow, and assured me that I was a munificent patron of art. He was a most offensive brute, though he had an extraordinary passion for Shakespeare. He told me once, with an air of pride, that his five bankruptcies were entirely due to "The Bard," as he insisted on calling him. He seemed to think it a distinction.'

'It was a distinction, my dear Dorian – a great distinction. Most people become bankrupt through having invested too heavily in the prose of life. To have ruined oneself over poetry is an honour. But when did you first speak to Miss Sibyl Vane?'

'The third night. She had been playing Rosalind. I could not help going round. I had thrown her some flowers, and she had looked at me; at least I fancied that she had. The old Jew was persistent. He seemed determined to take me behind, so I consented. It was curious my not wanting to know her, wasn't it?'

'No; I don't think so.'

'My dear Harry, why?'

'I will tell you some other time. Now I want to know about the girl.'

'Sibyl? Oh, she was so shy, and so gentle. There is something of a child about her. Her eyes opened wide in exquisite wonder when I told her what I thought of her performance, and she seemed quite unconscious of her power. I think we were both rather nervous. The old Jew stood grinning at the doorway of the dusty green-room, making elaborate speeches about us both, while we stood looking at each other like children. He would insist on calling me "My Lord," so I had to assure Sibyl that I was not anything of the kind. She said quite simply to me, "You look more like a prince. I must call you Prince Charming."'

'Upon my word, Dorian, Miss Sibyl knows how to pay compliments.'

'You don't understand her, Harry. She regarded me merely as a person in a play. She knows nothing of life. She lives with her mother, a faded tired woman who played Lady Capulet in a sort of magenta dressing-wrapper on the first night, and looks as if she had seen better days.'

'I know that look. It depresses me,' murmured Lord Henry, examining his rings.

'The Jew wanted to tell me her history, but I said it did not interest me.'

'You were quite right. There is always something infinitely mean about other people's tragedies.'

'Sibyl is the only thing I care about. What is it to me where she came from? From her little head to her little feet, she is absolutely and entirely divine. Every night of my life I go to see her act, and every night she is more marvellous.'

'That is the reason, I suppose, that you never dine with me now. I thought you must have some curious romance on hand. You have; but it is not quite what I expected.'

'My dear Harry, we either lunch or sup together every day, and I have been to the Opera with you several times,' said Dorian, opening his blue eyes in wonder.

'You always come dreadfully late.'

'Well, I can't help going to see Sibyl play,' he cried, 'even if it is only for a single act. I get hungry for her presence; and when I think of the wonderful soul that is hidden away in that little ivory body, I am filled with awe.'

'You can dine with me to-night, Dorian, can't you?'

He shook his head. 'To-night she is Imogen,' he answered, 'and to-morrow night she will be Juliet.'

'When is she Sibyl Vane?'

'Never.'

'I congratulate you.'

'How horrid you are! She is all the great heroines of the world in one. She is more than an individual. You laugh, but I tell you she has genius. I love her, and I must make her love me. You, who know all the secrets of life, tell me how to charm Sibyl Vane to love me! I want to make Romeo jealous. I want the dead lovers of the world to hear our laughter, and grow sad. I want a breath of our passion to stir their dust into consciousness, to wake their ashes into pain. My God, Harry, how I worship her!' He was walking up and down the room as he spoke. Hectic spots of red burned in his cheeks. He was terribly excited.

Lord Henry watched him with a subtle sense of pleasure. How different he was now from the shy, frightened boy he had met in Basil Hallward's studio. His nature had developed like a flower, had borne blossoms of scarlet flame. Out of its secret hiding-place had crept his Soul, and Desire had come to meet it on the way.

'And what do you propose to do?' said Lord Henry at last.

'I want you and Basil to come with me some night and see her act. I have not the slightest fear of the result. You are certain to acknowledge her genius. Then we must get her out of the Jew's hands. She is bound to him for three years – at least for two years and eight months – from the present time. I shall have to pay him something, of course. When all that is settled, I shall take a West End theatre and bring her out properly. She will make the world as mad as she has made me.'

'That would be impossible, my dear boy!'

'Yes, she will. She has not merely art, consummate art-instinct, in her, but she has personality also; and you have often told me that it is personalities, not principles, that move the age.'

'Well, what night shall we go?'

'Let me see. To-day is Tuesday. Let us fix to-morrow. She plays Juliet to-morrow.'

'All right. The Bristol at eight o'clock; and I will get Basil.'

'Not eight, Harry, please. Half-past six. We must be there before the curtain rises. You must see her in the first act, where she meets Romeo.'

'Half-past six! What an hour! It will be like having a meat-tea, or reading an English novel. It must be seven. No gentleman dines before seven. Shall you see Basil between this and then? Or shall I write to him?'

'Dear Basil! I have not laid eyes on him for a week. It is rather horrid of me, as he has sent me my portrait in the most wonderful frame, specially designed by himself, and, though I am a little jealous of the picture for being a whole month younger than I am, I must admit that I delight in it. Perhaps you had better write to him. I don't want to see him alone. He says things that annoy me. He gives me good advice.'

Lord Henry smiled. 'People are very fond of giving away what they need most themselves. It is what I call the depth of generosity.'

'Oh, Basil is the best of fellows, but he seems to me to be just a bit of a Philistine. Since I have known you, Harry, I have discovered that.'

'Basil, my dear boy, puts everything that is charming in him into his work. The consequence is that he has nothing left for life but his prejudices, his principles, and his common sense. The only artists I have ever known, who are personally delightful, are bad artists. Good artists exist simply in what they make, and consequently are perfectly uninteresting in what they are. A great poet, a really great poet, is the most unpoetical of all creatures. But inferior poets are absolutely fascinating. The worse their rhymes are, the more picturesque they look. The mere fact of having published a book of second-rate sonnets makes a man quite irresistible. He lives the poetry that he cannot write. The others write the poetry that they dare not realise.'

'I wonder is that really so, Harry?' said Dorian Gray, putting some perfume on his handkerchief out of a large gold-topped bottle that stood on the table. 'It must be, if you say it. And now I am off. Imogen is waiting for me. Don't forget about tomorrow. Good-bye.'

As he left the room, Lord Henry's heavy eyelids drooped, and he began to think. Certainly few people had ever interested him so much as Dorian Gray, and yet the lad's mad adoration of some one else caused him not the slightest pang of annoyance or jealousy. He was pleased by it. It made him a more interesting study. He had been always enthralled by the methods of natural science, but the ordinary subject-matter of that science had seemed to him trivial and of no import. And so he had begun by vivisecting himself, as he had ended by vivisecting others. Human life – that appeared to him the one thing worth investigating.

Compared to it there was nothing else of any value. It was true that as one watched life in its curious crucible of pain and pleasure, one could not wear over one's face a mask of glass, nor keep the sulphurous fumes from troubling the brain, and making the imagination turbid with monstrous fancies and misshapen dreams. There were poisons so subtle that to know their properties one had to sicken of them. There were maladies so strange that one had to pass through them if one sought to understand their nature. And, yet, what a great reward one received! How wonderful the whole world became to one! To note the curious hard logic of passion, and the emotional coloured life of the intellect – to observe where they met, and where they separated, at what point they were in unison, and at what point they were at discord – there was a delight in that! What matter what the cost was? One could never pay too high a price for any sensation.

He was conscious – and the thought brought a gleam of pleasure into his brown agate eyes – that it was through certain words of his, musical words said with musical utterance, that Dorian Gray's soul had turned to this white girl and bowed in worship before her. To a large extent the lad was his own creation. He had made him premature. That was something. Ordinary people waited till life disclosed to them its secrets, but to the few, to the elect, the mysteries of life were revealed before the veil was drawn away. Sometimes this was the effect of art, and chiefly of the art of literature, which dealt immediately with the passions and the intellect. But now and then a complex personality took the place and assumed the office of art; was indeed, in its way, a real work of art, Life having its elaborate masterpieces, just as poetry has, or sculpture, or painting.

Yes; the lad was premature. He was gathering his harvest while it was yet spring. The pulse and passion of youth were in him, but he was becoming self-conscious. It was delightful to watch him. With his beautiful face, and his beautiful soul, he was a thing to wonder at. It was no matter how it all ended, or was destined to end. He was like one of those gracious figures in a pageant or a play, whose joys seem to be remote from one, but whose sorrows stir one's sense of beauty and whose wounds are like red roses.

Soul and body, body and soul – how mysterious they were! There was animalism in the soul, and the body had its moments of spirituality. The senses could refine, and the intellect could degrade. Who could say where the fleshly impulse ceased, or the psychical impulse began? How shallow were the arbitrary definitions of ordinary psychologists! And yet how difficult to decide between the claims of the various schools! Was the soul a shadow seated in the house of sin? Or was the body really in the soul, as Giordano Bruno thought? The separation of spirit from matter was a mystery, and the union of spirit with matter was a mystery also.

He began to wonder whether we could ever make psychology so absolute a science that each little spring of life would be revealed to us. As it was, we always misunderstood ourselves, and rarely understood others. Experience was of no ethical value. It was merely the name men gave to their mistakes. Moralists had, as a rule, regarded it as a mode of warning, had claimed for it a certain ethical efficacy in the formation of character, had praised it as something that taught us what to follow and showed us what to avoid. But there was no motive power in experience. It was as little of an active cause as conscience itself. All that it really demonstrated was that our future would be the same as our past, and that the sin we had done once, and with loathing, we would do many times, and with joy.

It was clear to him that the experimental method was the only method by which one could arrive at any scientific analysis of the passions; and certainly Dorian Gray was a subject made to his hand and seemed to promise rich and fruitful results. His sudden mad love for Sibyl Vane was a psychological phenomenon of no small interest. There was no doubt that curiosity had much to do with it, curiosity and the desire for new experiences; yet it was not a simple but rather a very complex passion. What there was in it of the purely sensuous instinct of boyhood had been transformed by the workings of the imagination, changed into something that seemed to the lad himself to be remote from sense, and was for that very reason all the more dangerous. It was the passions about whose origin we deceived ourselves that tyrannised most strongly over us. Our weakest motives were those of whose nature we were conscious. It often happened that when we thought we were experimenting on others we were really experimenting on ourselves.

While Lord Henry sat dreaming on these things, a knock came to the door, and his valet entered, and reminded him it was time to dress for dinner. He got up and looked out into the street. The sunset had smitten into scarlet gold the upper windows of the houses opposite. The panes glowed like plates of heated metal. The sky above was like a faded rose. He thought of his friend's young fiery-coloured life, and wondered how it was all going to end.

When he arrived home, about half-past twelve o'clock, he saw a telegram lying on the hall table. He opened it, and found it was from Dorian Gray. It was to tell him that he was engaged to be married to Sibyl Vane.

5

'MOTHER, MOTHER, I am so happy!' whispered the girl, burying her face in the lap of the faded, tired-looking woman who, with back turned to the shrill intrusive light, was sitting in the one arm-chair that their dingy sitting-room contained. 'I am so happy!' she repeated, 'and you must be happy too!'

Mrs Vane winced, and put her thin bismuth-whitened hands on her daughter's head. 'Happy!' she echoed. 'I am only happy, Sibyl, when I see you act. You must not think of anything but your acting. Mr Isaacs has been very good to us, and we owe him money.'

The girl looked up and pouted. 'Money, mother?' she cried, 'what does money matter? Love is more than money.'

'Mr Isaacs has advanced us fifty pounds to pay off our debts, and to get a proper outfit for James. You must not forget that, Sibyl. Fifty pounds is a very large sum. Mr Isaacs has been most considerate.'

'He is not a gentleman, mother, and I hate the way he talks to me,' said the girl, rising to her feet, and going over to the window.

'I don't know how we could manage without him,' answered the elder woman, querulously.

Sibyl Vane tossed her head and laughed. 'We don't want him any more, mother. Prince Charming rules life for us now.' Then she paused. A rose shook in her blood, and shadowed her cheeks. Quick breath parted the petals of her lips. They trembled. Some southern wind of passion swept over her, and stirred the dainty folds of her dress. 'I love him,' she said, simply.

'Foolish child! foolish child!' was the parrot-phrase flung in answer. The waving of crooked, false-jewelled fingers gave grotesqueness to the words.

The girl laughed again. The joy of a caged bird was in her voice. Her eyes caught the melody, and echoed it in radiance; then closed for a moment, as though to hide their secret. When they opened the mist of a dream had passed across them.

Thin-lipped wisdom spoke at her from the worn chair, hinted at prudence, quoted from that book of cowardice whose author apes the name of common sense. She did not listen. She was free in her prison of passion. Her prince, Prince Charming, was with her. She had called on Memory to remake him. She had sent her soul to search for him, and it had brought him back. His kiss burned again upon her mouth. Her eyelids were warm with his breath.

Then Wisdom altered its method and spoke of espial and discovery. This young man might be rich. If so, marriage should be thought of. Against the shell of her ear broke the waves of worldly cunning. The arrows of craft shot by her. She saw the thin lips moving, and smiled.

Suddenly she felt the need to speak. The wordy silence troubled her. 'Mother, mother,' she cried, 'why does he love me so much? I know why I love him. I love him because he is like what Love himself should be. But what does he see in me? I am not worthy of him. And yet – why, I cannot tell – though I feel so much beneath him, I don't feel humble. I feel proud, terribly proud. Mother, did you love my father as I love Prince Charming?'

The elder woman grew pale beneath the coarse powder that daubed her cheeks, and her dry lips twitched with a spasm of pain. Sibyl rushed to her, flung her arms round her neck, and kissed her. 'Forgive me, mother, I know it pains you to talk about our father. But it only pains you because you loved him so much. Don't look so sad. I am as happy to-day as you were twenty years ago. Ah! let me be happy for ever!'

'My child, you are far too young to think of falling in love. Besides, what do you know of this young man? You don't even know his name.

The whole thing is most inconvenient, and really, when James is going away to Australia, and I have so much to think of, I must say that you should have shown more consideration. However, as I said before, if he is rich . . .'

'Ah! Mother, mother, let me be happy!'

Mrs Vane glanced at her, and, with one of those false theatrical gestures that so often became a mode of second nature to a stage-player, clasped her in her arms. At this moment the door opened, and a young lad with rough brown hair came into the room. He was thick-set of figure, and his hands and feet were large, and somewhat clumsy in movement. He was not so finely bred as his sister. One would hardly have guessed the close relationship that existed between them. Mrs Vane fixed her eyes on him, and intensified the smile. She mentally elevated her son to the dignity of an audience. She felt sure that the *tableau* was interesting.

'You might keep some of your kisses for me, Sibyl, I think,' said the lad, with a good-natured grumble.

'Ah! but you don't like being kissed, Jim,' she cried. 'You are a dreadful old bear.' And she ran across the room and hugged him.

James Vane looked into his sister's face with tenderness. 'I want you to come out with me for a walk, Sibyl. I don't suppose I shall ever see this horrid London again. I am sure I don't want to.'

'My son, don't say such dreadful things,' murmured Mrs Vane, taking up a tawdry theatrical dress, with a sigh, and beginning to patch it. She felt a little disappointed that he had not joined the group. It would have increased the theatrical picturesqueness of the situation.

'Why not, mother? I mean it.'

'You pain me, my son. I trust you will return from Australia in a position of affluence. I believe there is no society of any kind in the Colonies, nothing that I would call society; so when you have made your fortune you must come back and assert yourself in London.'

'Society!' muttered the lad. 'I don't want to know anything about that. I should like to make some money to take you and Sibyl off the stage. I hate it!'

'Ah, Jim!' said Sibyl, laughing, 'how unkind of you! But are you really going for a walk with me? That will be nice! I was afraid you were going to say good-bye to some of your friends – to Tom Hardy, who gave you that hideous pipe, or Ned Langton, who makes fun of you for smoking it. It is very sweet of you to let me have your last afternoon. Where shall we go? Let us go to the Park.'

'I am too shabby,' he answered, frowning. 'Only swell people go to the Park.'

'Nonsense, Jim,' she whispered, stroking the sleeve of his coat.

He hesitated for a moment. 'Very well,' he said at last, 'but don't be too long dressing.' She danced out of the door. One could hear her singing as she ran upstairs. Her little feet pattered overhead.

He walked up and down the room two or three times. Then he turned to the still figure in the chair. 'Mother, are my things ready?' he asked.

'Quite ready, James,' she answered, keeping her eyes on her work. For some months past she had felt ill at ease when she was alone with this rough, stern son of hers. Her shallow secret nature was troubled when their eyes met. She used to wonder if he suspected anything. The silence, for he made no other observation, became intolerable to her. She began to complain. Women defend themselves by attacking, just as they attack by sudden and strange surrenders. 'I hope you will be contented, James, with your sea-faring life,' she said. 'You must remember that it is your own choice. You might have entered a solicitor's office. Solicitors are a very respectable class, and in the country often dine with the best families.'

'I hate offices, and I hate clerks,' he replied. 'But you are quite right. I have chosen my own life. All I say is, watch over Sibyl. Don't let her come to any harm. Mother, you must watch over her.'

'James, you really talk very strangely. Of course I watch over Sibyl.' 'I hear a gentleman comes every night to the theatre, and goes behind to talk to her. Is that right? What about that?'

'You are speaking about things you don't understand, James. In the profession we are accustomed to receive a great deal of most gratifying attention. I myself used to receive many bouquets at one time. That was when acting was really understood. As for Sibyl, I do not know at present whether her attachment is serious or not. But there is no doubt that the young man in question is a perfect gentleman. He is always most polite to me. Besides, he has the appearance of being rich, and the flowers he sends are lovely.'

'You don't know his name, though,' said the lad, harshly.

'No,' answered his mother, with a placid expression in her face. 'He has not yet revealed his real name. I think it is quite romantic of him. He is probably a member of the aristocracy.'

James Vane bit his lip. 'Watch over Sibyl, mother,' he cried; 'watch over her.'

'My son, you distress me very much. Sibyl is always under my special care. Of course, if this gentleman is wealthy, there is no reason why she should not contract an alliance with him. I trust he is one of the aristocracy. He has all the appearance of it, I must say. It might be a most brilliant marriage for Sibyl. They would make a charming couple. His good looks are really quite remarkable; everybody notices them.'

The lad muttered something to himself, and drummed on the window-pane with his coarse fingers. He had just turned round to say something, when the door opened, and Sibyl ran in.

'How serious you both are!' she cried. 'What is the matter?'

'Nothing,' he answered. 'I suppose one must be serious sometimes. Good-bye, mother; I will have my dinner at five o'clock. Everything is packed, except my shirts, so you need not trouble.'

'Good-bye, my son,' she answered, with a bow of strained stateliness.

She was extremely annoyed at the tone he had adopted with her, and there was something in his look that had made her feel afraid.

'Kiss me, mother,' said the girl. Her flower-like lips touched the withered cheek and warmed its frost.

'My child! my child!' cried Mrs Vane, looking up to the ceiling in search of an imaginary gallery.

'Come, Sibyl,' said her brother, impatiently. He hated his mother's affectations.

They went out into the flickering wind-blown sunlight, and strolled down the dreary Euston Road. The passers-by glanced in wonder at the sullen, heavy youth, who, in coarse, ill-fitting clothes, was in the company of such a graceful, refined-looking girl. He was like a common gardener walking with a rose.

Jim frowned from time to time when he caught the inquisitive glance of some stranger. He had that dislike of being stared at which comes on geniuses late in life, and never leaves the commonplace. Sibyl, however, was quite unconscious of the effect she was producing. Her love was trembling in laughter on her lips. She was thinking of Prince Charming, and, that she might think of him all the more, she did not talk of him, but prattled on about the ship in which Jim was going to sail, about the gold he was certain to find, about the wonderful heiress whose life he was to save from the wicked, red-shirted bush-rangers. For he was not to remain a sailor, or a super-cargo, or whatever he was going to be. Oh, no! A sailor's existence was dreadful. Fancy being cooped up in a horrid ship, with the hoarse, hump-backed waves trying to get in, and a black wind blowing the masts down, and tearing the sails into long screaming ribbons! He was to leave the vessel at Melbourne, bid a polite good-bye to the captain, and go off at once to the gold-fields. Before a week was over he was to come across a large nugget of pure gold, the largest nugget that had ever been discovered, and bring it down to the coast in a wagon guarded by six mounted policemen. The bushrangers were to attack them three times, and be defeated with immense slaughter. Or, no. He was not to go to the gold-fields at all. They were horrid places, where men got intoxicated, and shot each other in bar-rooms, and used bad language. He was to be a nice sheep-farmer, and one evening, as he was riding home, he was to see the beautiful heiress being carried off by a robber on a black horse, and give chase, and rescue her. Of course she would fall in love with him, and he with her, and they would get married, and come home, and live in an immense house in London. Yes, there were delightful things in store for him. But he must be very good, and not lose his temper, or spend his money foolishly. She was only a year older than he was, but she knew so much more of life. He must be sure, also, to write to her by every mail, and to say his prayers each night before he went to sleep. God was very good, and would watch over him. She would pray for him, too, and in a few years he would come back quite rich and happy.

The lad listened sulkily to her, and made no answer. He was heart-sick at leaving home.

Yet it was not this alone that made him gloomy and morose. Inexperienced though he was, he had still a strong sense of the danger of Sibyl's position. This young dandy who was making love to her could mean her no good. He was a gentleman, and he hated him for that, hated him through some curious race-instinct for which he could not account, and which for that reason was all the more dominant within him. He was conscious also of the shallowness and vanity of his mother's nature, and in that saw infinite peril for Sibyl and Sibyl's happiness. Children begin by loving their parents; as they grow older they judge them; sometimes they forgive them.

His mother! He had something on his mind to ask of her, something that he had brooded on for many months of silence. A chance phrase that he had heard at the theatre, a whispered sneer that had reached his ears one night as he waited at the stage-door, had set loose a train of horrible thoughts. He remembered it as if it had been the lash of a hunting-crop across his face. His brows knit together into a wedge-like furrow, and with a twitch of pain he bit his underlip.

'You are not listening to a word I am saying, Jim,' cried Sibyl, 'and I am making the most delightful plans for your future. Do say something.'

'What do you want me to say?'

'Oh! that you will be a good boy, and not forget us,' she answered, smiling at him.

He shrugged his shoulders. 'You are more likely to forget me, than I am to forget you, Sibyl.'

She flushed. 'What do you mean, Jim?' she asked.

'You have a new friend, I hear. Who is he? Why have you not told me about him? He means you no good.'

'Stop, Jim!' she exclaimed. 'You must not say anything against him. I love him.'

'Why, you don't even know his name,' answered the lad. 'Who is he? I have a right to know.'

'He is called Prince Charming. Don't you like the name? Oh! you silly boy! you should never forget it. If you only saw him, you would think him the most wonderful person in the world. Some day you will meet him: when you come back from Australia. You will like him so much. Everybody likes him, and I . . . love him. I wish you could come to the theatre to-night. He is going to be there, and I am to play Juliet. Oh! how I shall play it! Fancy, Jim, to be in love and play Juliet! To have him sitting there! To play for his delight! I am afraid I may frighten the company, frighten or enthral them. To be in love is to surpass oneself. Poor dreadful Mr Isaacs will be shouting "genius" to his loafers at the bar. He has preached me as a dogma; to-night he will announce me as a revelation. I feel it. And it is all his, his only, Prince Charming, my wonderful lover, my god of graces. But I am poor beside him. Poor? What does that matter? When poverty creeps in at the door, love flies in through the window. Our proverbs want rewriting. They were made in winter, and it is summer now; springtime for me, I think, a very dance of blossoms in blue skies.'

'He is a gentleman,' said the lad, sullenly.

'A prince!' she cried, musically. 'What more do you want?'

'He wants to enslave you.'

'I shudder at the thought of being free.'

'I want you to beware of him.'

'To see him is to worship him, to know him is to trust him.'

'Sibyl, you are mad about him.'

She laughed and took his arm. 'You dear old Jim, you talk as if you were a hundred. Some day you will be in love yourself. Then you will know what it is. Don't look so sulky. Surely you should be glad to think that, though you are going away, you leave me happier than I have ever been before. Life has been hard for us both, terribly hard and difficult. But it will be different now. You are going to a new world, and I have found one. Here are two chairs; let us sit down and see the smart people go by.'

They took their seats amidst a crowd of watchers. The tulip-beds across the road flamed like throbbing rings of fire. A white dust, tremulous cloud of orrisroot it seemed, hung in the panting air. The brightly coloured parasols danced and dipped like monstrous butterflies.

She made her brother talk of himself, his hopes, his prospects. He spoke slowly and with effort. They passed words to each other as players at a game pass counters. Sibyl felt oppressed. She could not communicate her joy. A faint smile curving that sullen mouth was all the echo she could win. After some time she became silent. Suddenly she caught a glimpse of golden hair and laughing lips, and in an open carriage with two ladies Dorian Gray drove past.

She started to her feet. 'There he is!' she cried.

'Who?' said Jim Vane.

'Prince Charming,' she answered, looking after the victoria.

He jumped up, and seized her roughly by the arm. 'Show him to me. Which is he? Point him out. I must see him!' he exclaimed; but at that moment the Duke of Berwick's four-in-hand came between, and when it had left the space clear, the carriage had swept out of the Park.

'He is gone,' murmured Sibyl sadly. 'I wish you had seen him.'

'I wish I had for as sure as there is a God in heaven, if he ever does you any wrong I shall kill him.'

She looked at him in horror. He repeated his words. They cut the air like a dagger. The people round began to gape. A lady standing close to her tittered.

'Come away, Jim; come away,' she whispered. He followed her doggedly, as she passed through the crowd. He felt glad at what he had said.

When they reached the Achilles Statue she turned round. There was pity in her eyes that became laughter on her lips. She shook her head at him. 'You are foolish, Jim, utterly foolish; a bad-tempered boy, that is all. How can you say such horrible things? You don't know what you are talking about. You are simply jealous and unkind. Ah! I wish you would fall in love. Love makes people good, and what you said was wicked.'

'I am sixteen,' he answered, 'and I know what I am about. Mother is no help to you. She doesn't understand how to look after you. I wish now that I was not going to Australia at all. I have a great mind to chuck the whole thing up. I would, if my articles hadn't been signed.'

'Oh, don't be so serious, Jim. You are like one of the heroes of those silly melodramas mother used to be so fond of acting in. I am not going to quarrel with you. I have seen him, and oh! to see him is perfect happiness. We won't quarrel. I know you would never harm anyone I love, would you?'

'Not as long as you love him, I suppose,' was the sullen answer.

'I shall love him for ever!' she cried.

'And he?'

'For ever, too!'

'He had better.'

She shrank from him. Then she laughed and put her hand on his arm. He was merely a boy.

At the Marble Arch they hailed an omnibus, which left them close to their shabby home in the Euston Road. It was after five o'clock, and Sibyl had to lie down for a couple of hours before acting. Jim insisted that she should do so. He said that he would sooner part with her when their mother was not present. She would be sure to make a scene, and he detested scenes of every kind.

In Sibyl's own room they parted. There was jealousy in the lad's heart, and a fierce, murderous hatred of the stranger who, as it seemed to him, had come between them. Yet, when her arms were flung round his neck, and her fingers strayed through his hair, he softened, and kissed her with real affection. There were tears in his eyes as he went downstairs.

His mother was waiting for him below. She grumbled at his unpunctuality, as he entered. He made no answer, but sat down to his meagre meal. The flies buzzed round the table and crawled over the stained cloth. Through the rumble of omnibuses, and the clatter of street-cabs, he could hear the droning voice devouring each minute that was left to him.

After some time, he thrust away his plate, and put his head in his hands. He felt that he had a right to know. It should have been told to him before, if it was as he suspected. Leaden with fear, his mother watched him. Words dropped mechanically from her lips. A tattered lace handkerchief twitched in her fingers. When the clock struck six, he got up, and went to the door. Then he turned back, and looked at her. Their eyes met. In hers he saw a wild appeal for mercy. It enraged him.

'Mother, I have something to ask you,' he said. Her eyes wandered vaguely about the room. She made no answer. 'Tell me the truth. I have a right to know. Were you married to my father?'

She heaved a deep sigh. It was a sigh of relief. The terrible moment, the moment that night and day, for weeks and months, she had dreaded, had come at last, and yet she felt no terror. Indeed in some measure it was a disappointment to her. The vulgar directness of the question called for a direct answer. The situation had not been gradually led up to. It was crude. It reminded her of a bad rehearsal.

'No,' she answered, wondering at the harsh simplicity of life.

'My father was a scoundrel then?' cried the lad, clenching his fists.

She shook her head. 'I knew he was not free. We loved each other very much. If he had lived, he would have made provision for us. Don't speak against him, my son. He was your father, and a gentleman. Indeed he was highly connected.'

An oath broke from his lips. 'I don't care for myself,' he exclaimed, 'but don't let Sibyl . . . It is a gentleman, isn't it, who is in love with her, or says he is? Highly connected, too, I suppose.'

For a moment a hideous sense of humiliation came over the woman. Her head drooped. She wiped her eyes with shaking hands. 'Sibyl has a mother,' she murmured; 'I had none.'

The lad was touched. He went towards her, and stooping down he kissed her. 'I am sorry if I have pained you by asking about my father,' he said, 'but I could not help it. I must go now. Good-bye. Don't forget that you will only have one child now to look after, and believe me that if this man wrongs my sister, I will find out who he is, track him down, and kill him like a dog. I swear it.'

The exaggerated folly of the threat, the passionate gesture that accompanied it, the mad melodramatic words, made life seem more vivid to her. She was familiar with the atmosphere. She breathed more freely, and for the first time for many months she really admired her son. She would have liked to continue the scene on the same emotional scale, but he cut her short. Trunks had to be carried down, and mufflers looked for. The lodging-house drudge bustled in and out. There was the bargaining with the cabman. The moment was lost in vulgar details. It was with a renewed feeling of disappointment that she waved the tattered lace handkerchief from the window, as her son drove away. She was conscious that a great opportunity had been wasted. She consoled herself by telling Sibyl how desolate she felt her life would be, now that she had only one child to look after. She remembered the phrase. It had pleased her. Of the threat she said nothing. It was vividly and dramatically expressed. She felt that they would all laugh at it some day.

6

'I SUPPOSE YOU HAVE heard the news, Basil?' said Lord Henry, that evening, as Hallward was shown into a little private room at the Bristol, where dinner had been laid for three.

'No, Harry,' answered the artist, giving his hat and coat to the bowing waiter. 'What is it? Nothing about politics, I hope? They don't interest me. There is hardly a single person in the House of Commons worth painting; though many of them would be the better for a little white-washing.'

'Dorian Gray is engaged to be married,' said Lord Henry, watching him as he spoke.

Hallward started, and then frowned. 'Dorian engaged to be married!' he cried. 'Impossible!'

'It is perfectly true.'

'To whom?'

'To some little actress or other.'

'I can't believe it. Dorian is far too sensible.'

'Dorian is far too wise not to do foolish things now and then, my dear Basil.'

'Marriage is hardly a thing that one can do now and then, Harry.'

'Except in America,' rejoined Lord Henry, languidly. 'But I didn't say he was married. I said he was engaged to be married. There is a great difference. I have a distinct remembrance of being married, but I have no recollection at all of being engaged. I am inclined to think that I never was engaged.'

'But think of Dorian's birth, and position, and wealth. It would be absurd for him to marry so much beneath him.'

'If you want to make him marry this girl tell him that, Basil. He is sure to do it, then. Whenever a man does a thoroughly stupid thing, it is always from the noblest motives.'

'I hope the girl is good, Harry. I don't want to see Dorian tied to some vile creature, who might degrade his nature and ruin his intellect.'

'Oh, she is better than good – she is beautiful,' murmured Lord Henry, sipping a glass of vermouth and orange bitters. 'Dorian says she is beautiful; and he is not often wrong about things of that kind. Your portrait of him has quickened his appreciation of the personal appearance of other people. It has had that excellent effect, amongst others. We are to see her to-night, if that boy doesn't forget his appointment.'

'Are you serious?'

'Quite serious, Basil. I should be miserable if I thought I should ever be more serious than I am at the present moment.'

'But do you approve of it, Harry?' asked the painter, walking up and down the room, and biting his lip. 'You can't approve of it, possibly. It is some silly infatuation.'

'I never approve, or disapprove, of anything now. It is an absurd attitude to take towards life. We are not sent into the world to air our moral prejudices. I never take any notice of what common people say, and I never interfere with what charming people do. If a personality fascinates me, whatever mode of expression that personality selects is absolutely delightful to me. Dorian Gray falls in love with a beautiful girl who acts Juliet, and proposes to marry her. Why not? If he wedded Messalina he would be none the less interesting. You know I am not a champion of marriage. The real drawback to marriage is that it makes one unselfish. And unselfish people are colourless. They lack individuality. Still, there are certain temperaments that marriage makes more complex. They retain their egotism, and add to it many other egos. They are forced to have more than one life. They become more highly organised, and to be highly organised is, I should fancy, the object of man's existence. Besides, every experience is of value, and, whatever one may say against marriage, it is certainly an experience. I hope that

Dorian Gray will make this girl his wife, passionately adore her for six months, and then suddenly become fascinated by someone else. He would be a wonderful study.'

'You don't mean a single word of all that, Harry; you know you don't. If Dorian Gray's life were spoiled, no one would be sorrier than yourself. You are much better than you pretend to be.'

Lord Henry laughed. 'The reason we all like to think so well of others is that we are all afraid for ourselves. The basis of optimism is sheer terror. We think that we are generous because we credit our neighbour with the possession of those virtues that are likely to be a benefit to us. We praise the banker that we may overdraw our account, and find good qualities in the highwayman in the hope that he may spare our pockets. I mean everything that I have said. I have the greatest contempt for optimism. As for a spoiled life, no life is spoiled but one whose growth is arrested. If you want to mar a nature, you have merely to reform it. As for marriage, of course that would be silly, but there are other and more interesting bonds between men and women. I will certainly encourage them. They have the charm of being fashionable. But here is Dorian himself. He will tell you more than I can.'

'My dear Harry, my dear Basil, you must both congratulate me!' said the lad, throwing off his evening cape with its satin-lined wings and shaking each of his friends by the hand in turn. 'I have never been so happy. Of course it is sudden; all really delightful things are. And yet it seems to me to be the one thing I have been looking for all my life.' He was flushed with excitement and pleasure, and looked extraordinarily handsome.

'I hope you will always be very happy, Dorian,' said Hallward, 'but I don't quite forgive you for not having let me know of your engagement. You let Harry know.'

'And I don't forgive you for being late for dinner,' broke in Lord Henry, putting his hand on the lad's shoulder, and smiling as he spoke. 'Come, let us sit down and try what the new chef here is like, and then you will tell us how it all came about.'

'There is really not much to tell,' cried Dorian, as they took their seats at the small round table. 'What happened was simply this. After I left you yesterday evening, Harry, I dressed, had some dinner at that little Italian restaurant in Rupert Street you introduced me to, and went down at eight o'clock to the theatre. Sibyl was playing Rosalind. Of course the scenery was dreadful, and the Orlando absurd. But Sibyl! You should have seen her! When she came on in her boy's clothes she was perfectly wonderful. She wore a moss-coloured velvet jerkin with cinnamon sleeves, slim brown cross-gartered hose, a dainty little green cap with a hawk's feather caught in a jewel, and a hooded cloak lined with dull red. She had never seemed to me more exquisite. She had all the delicate grace of that Tanagra figurine that you have in your studio, Basil. Her hair clustered round her face like dark leaves round a pale rose. As for her acting – well, you shall see her to-night. She is simply a born artist. I sat in the dingy box absolutely enthralled. I forgot that

I was in London, and in the nineteenth century. I was away with my love in a forest that no man had ever seen. After the performance was over I went behind, and spoke to her. As we were sitting together, suddenly there came into her eyes a look that I had never seen there before. My lips moved towards hers. We kissed each other. I can't describe to you what I felt at that moment. It seemed to me that all my life had been narrowed to one perfect point of rose-coloured joy. She trembled all over, and shook like a white narcissus. Then she flung herself on her knees and kissed my hands. I feel that I should not tell you all this, but I can't help it. Of course our engagement is a dead secret. She had not even told her own mother. I don't know what my guardians will say. Lord Radley is sure to be furious. I don't care. I shall be of age in less than a year, and then I can do what I like. I have been right, Basil, haven't I, to take my love out of poetry, and to find my wife in Shakespeare's plays? Lips that Shakespeare taught to speak have whispered their secret in my ear. I have had the arms of Rosalind around me, and kissed Juliet on the mouth.'

'Yes, Dorian, I suppose you were right.' said Hallward, slowly.

'Have you seen her to-day?' asked Lord Henry.

Dorian Gray shook her head. 'I left her in the forest of Arden, I shall find her in an orchard in Verona.'

Lord Henry sipped his champagne in a meditative manner. 'At what particular point did you mention the word marriage, Dorian? And what did she say in answer? Perhaps you forgot all about it.'

'My dear Harry, I did not treat it as a business transaction, and I did not make any formal proposal. I told her that I loved her, and she said she was not worthy to be my wife. Not worthy! Why, the whole world is nothing to me compared with her.'

'Women are wonderfully practical,' murmured Lord Henry – 'much more practical than we are. In situations of that kind we often forget to say anything about marriage, and they always remind us.'

Hallward laid his hand upon his arm. 'Don't, Harry. You have annoyed Dorian. He is not like other men. He would never bring misery upon anyone. His nature is too fine for that.'

Lord Henry looked across the table. 'Dorian is never annoyed with me,' he answered. 'I asked the question for the best reason possible, for the only reason, indeed, that excuses one for asking any question – simply curiosity. I have a theory that it is always the women who propose to us, and not we who propose to the women. Except, of course, in middle-class life. But then the middle classes are not modern.'

Dorian Gray laughed and tossed his head. 'You are quite incorrigible, Harry; but I don't mind. It is impossible to be angry with you. When you see Sibyl Vane you will feel that the man who could wrong her would be a beast, a beast without a heart. I cannot understand how anyone can wish to shame the thing he loves. I love Sibyl Vane. I want to place her on a pedestal of gold, and to see the world worship the woman who is mine. What is marriage? An irrevocable vow. You mock at it for that. Ah! don't mock. It is an irrevocable vow that I want to take. Her trust makes me faithful, her belief makes me good. When I am with her, I regret all that you have taught me. I become different from what you have known me to be. I am changed, and the mere touch of Sibyl Vane's hand makes me forget you and all your wrong, fascinating, poisonous, delightful theories.'

'And those are . . .?' asked Lord Henry, helping himself to some salad.

'Oh, your theories about life, your theories about love, your theories about pleasure. All your theories, in fact, Harry.'

'Pleasure is the only thing worth having a theory about,' he answered, in his slow, melodious voice. 'But I am afraid I cannot claim my theory as my own. It belongs to Nature, not to me. Pleasure is Nature's test, her sign of approval. When we are happy we are always good, but when we are good we are not always happy.'

'Ah! but what do you mean by good?' cried Basil Hallward.

'Yes,' echoed Dorian, leaning back in his chair, and looking at Lord Henry over the heavy clusters of purple-lipped irises that stood in the centre of the table, 'what do you mean by good, Harry?'

'To be good is to be in harmony with oneself,' he replied, touching the thin stem of his glass with his pale, fine-pointed fingers. 'Discord is to be forced to be in harmony with others. One's own life – that is the important thing. As for the lives of one's neighbours, if one wishes to be a prig or a Puritan, one can flaunt one's moral views about them, but they are not one's concern. Besides, Individualism has really the higher aim. Modern morality consists in accepting the standard of one's age. I consider that for any man of culture to accept the standard of his age is a form of the grossest immorality.'

'But, surely, if one lives merely for oneself, Harry, one pays a terrible price for doing so?' suggested the painter.

'Yes, we are overcharged for everything nowadays. I should fancy that the real tragedy of the poor is that they can afford nothing but self-denial. Beautiful sins, like beautiful things, are the privilege of the rich.'

'One has to pay in other ways but money.'

'What sort of ways, Basil?'

'Oh! I should fancy in remorse, in suffering, in . . . well, in the consciousness of degradation.'

Lord Henry shrugged his shoulders. 'My dear fellow, mediæval art is charming, but mediæval emotions are out of date. One can use them in fiction, of course. But then the only things that one can use in fiction are the things that one has ceased to use in fact. Believe me, no civilised man ever regrets a pleasure, and no uncivilised man ever knows what a pleasure is.'

'I know what pleasure is,' cried Dorian Gray. 'It is to adore someone.'

'That is certainly better than being adored,' he answered, toying with some fruits. 'Being adored is a nuisance. Women treat us just as Humanity treats its gods. They worship us, and are always bothering us to do something for them.'

'I should have said that whatever they ask for they had first given to us,' murmured the lad, gravely. 'They create Love in our natures. They have a right to demand it back.'

'That is quite true, Dorian,' cried Hallward.

'Nothing is ever quite true,' said Lord Henry.

'This is,' interrupted Dorian. 'You must admit, Harry, that women give to men the very gold of their lives.'

'Possibly,' he sighed, 'but they invariably want it back in such very small change. That is the worry. Women, as some witty Frenchman once put it, inspire us with the desire to do masterpieces, and always prevent us from carrying them out.'

'Harry, you are dreadful! I don't know why I like you so much.'

'You will always like me, Dorian,' he replied. 'Will you have some coffee, you fellows? – Waiter, bring coffee, and *fine-champagne*, and some cigarettes. No: don't mind the cigarettes; I have some. Basil, I can't allow you to smoke cigars. You must have a cigarette. A cigarette is the perfect type of a perfect pleasure. It is exquisite, and it leaves one unsatisfied. What more can one want? Yes, Dorian, you will always be fond of me. I represent to you all the sins you have never had the courage to commit.'

'What nonsense you talk, Harry!' cried the lad, taking a light from a fire-breathing silver dragon that the waiter had placed on the table. 'Let us go down to the theatre. When Sibyl comes on the stage you will have a new ideal of life. She will represent something to you that you have never known.'

'I have known everything,' said Lord Henry, with a tired look in his eyes, 'but I am always ready for a new emotion. I am afraid, however, that, for me at any rate, there is no such thing. Still, your wonderful girl may thrill me. I love acting. It is so much more real than life. Let us go. Dorian, you will come with me. I am so sorry, Basil, but there is only room for two in the brougham. You must follow us in a hansom.'

They got up and put on their coats, sipping their coffee standing. The painter was silent and preoccupied. There was a gloom over him. He could not bear this marriage, and yet it seemed to him to be better than many other things that might have happened. After a few minutes they all passed downstairs. He drove off by himself, as had been arranged, and watched the flashing lights of the little brougham in front of him. A strange sense of loss came over him. He felt that Dorian Gray would never again be to him all that he had been in the past. Life had come between them. . . . His eyes darkened, and the crowded, flaring streets became blurred to his eyes. When the cab drew up at the theatre, it seemed to him that he had grown years older.

7

FOR SOME REASON OR other, the house was crowded that night, and the fat Jew manager who met them at the door was beaming from ear to ear with an oily, tremulous smile. He escorted them to their box with a sort of pompous humility, waving his fat jewelled hands, and talking at the top of his voice. Dorian Gray loathed him more than ever. He felt as if he had come to look for Miranda and had been met by Caliban. Lord Henry, upon the other hand, rather liked him. At least he declared he did, and insisted on shaking him by the hand, and assuring him that he was proud to meet a man who had discovered a real genius and gone bankrupt over a poet. Hallward amused himself with watching the faces in the pit. The heat was terribly oppressive, and the huge sunlight flamed like a monstrous dahlia with petals of yellow fire. The youths in the gallery had taken off their coats and waistcoats and hung them over the side. They talked to each other across the theatre, and shared their oranges with the tawdry girls who sat beside them. Some women were laughing in the pit. Their voices were horribly shrill and discordant. The sound of the popping of corks came from the bar.

'What a place to find one's divinity in!' said Lord Henry.

'Yes!' answered Dorian Gray. 'It was here I found her, and she is divine beyond all living things. When she acts you will forget everything. These common, rough people, with their coarse faces and brutal gestures, become quite different when she is on the stage. They sit silently and watch her. They weep and laugh as she wills them to do. She makes them as responsive as a violin. She spiritualises them, and one feels that they are of the same flesh and blood as oneself.'

'The same flesh and blood as oneself! Oh, I hope not!' exclaimed Lord Henry, who was scanning the occupants of the gallery through his opera-glass.

'Don't pay any attention to him, Dorian,' said the painter. 'I understand what you mean, and I believe in this girl. Anyone you love must be marvellous, and any girl that has the effect you describe must be fine and noble. To spiritualise one's age – that is something worth doing. If this girl can give a soul to those who have lived without one, if she can create the sense of beauty in people whose lives have been sordid and ugly, if she can strip them of their selfishness and lend them tears for sorrows that are not their own, she is worthy of all your adoration, worthy of the adoration of the world. This marriage is quite right. I did not think so at first, but I admit it now. The gods made Sibyl Vane for you. Without her you would have been incomplete.'

'Thanks, Basil,' answered Dorian Gray, pressing his hand. 'I knew that you would understand me. Harry is so cynical, he terrifies me. But here is the orchestra. It is quite dreadful, but it only lasts for about five minutes. Then the curtain rises, and you will see the girl to whom I am going to give all my life, to whom I have given everything that is good in me.'

A quarter of an hour afterwards, amidst an extraordinary turmoil of applause, Sibyl Vane stepped on to the stage. Yes, she was certainly lovely to look at – one of the loveliest creatures, Lord Henry thought, that he had ever seen. There was something of the fawn in her shy grace and startled eyes. A faint blush, like the shadow of a rose in a mirror of silver, came to her cheeks as she glanced at the crowded, enthusiastic house. She stepped back a few paces, and her lips seemed to tremble. Basil Hallward leaped to his feet and began to applaud.

Motionless, and as one in a dream, sat Dorian Gray, gazing at her. Lord Henry peered through his glasses, murmuring, 'Charming! Charming!'

The scene was the hall of Capulet's house, and Romeo in his pilgrim's dress had entered with Mercutio and his other friends. The band, such as it was, struck up a few bars of music, and the dance began.

Through the crowd of ungainly, shabbily dressed actors, Sibyl Vane moved like a creature from a finer world. Her body swayed, while she danced, as a plant sways in the water. The curves of her throat were the curves of a white lily. Her hands seemed to be made of cool ivory.

Yet she was curiously listless. She showed no sign of joy when her eyes rested on Romeo. The few words she had to speak—

> 'Good pilgrim, you do wrong your hand too much,
> Which mannerly devotion shows in this;
> For saints have hands that pilgrim's hands do touch,
> And palm to palm is holy palmers' kiss—'

with the brief dialogue that follows, were spoken in a thoroughly artificial manner. The voice was exquisite, but from the point of view of tone it was absolutely false. It was wrong in colour. It took away all the life from the verse. It made the passion unreal.

Dorian Gray grew pale as he watched her. He was puzzled and anxious. Neither of his friends dared to say anything to him. She seemed to them to be absolutely incompetent. They were horribly disappointed.

Yet they felt that the true test of any Juliet is the balcony scene of the second act. They waited for that. If she failed there, there was nothing in her.

She looked charming as she came out in the moonlight. That could not be denied. But the staginess of her acting was unbearable, and grew worse as she went on. Her gestures became absurdly artificial. She over-emphasised everything that she had to say. The beautiful passage—

> 'Thou knowest the mask of night is on my face,
> Else would a maiden blush bepaint my cheek
> For that which thou hast heard me speak tonight—'

was declaimed with the painful precision of a schoolgirl who has been taught to recite by some second-rate professor of elocution. When she leaned over the balcony and came to those wonderful lines—

> 'Although I joy in thee,
> I have no joy of this contract to-night;
> It is too rash, too unadvised, too sudden;
> Too like the lightning, which doth cease to be
> Ere one can say, "It lightens." Sweet, good-night!
> This bud of love by summer's ripening breath
> May prove a beauteous flower when next we meet—'

she spoke the words as though they conveyed no meaning to her. It was not nervousness. Indeed, so far from being nervous, she was absolutely self-contained. It was simply bad art. She was a complete failure.

Even the common, uneducated audience of the pit and gallery lost their interest in the play. They got restless, and began to talk loudly and to whistle. The Jew manager, who was standing at the back of the dress-circle, stamped and swore with rage. The only person unmoved was the girl herself.

When the second act was over there came a storm of hisses, and Lord Henry got up from his chair and put on his coat. 'She is quite beautiful, Dorian,' he said. 'but she can't act. Let us go.'

'I am going to see the play through,' answered the lad, in a hard, bitter voice. 'I am awfully sorry that I have made you waste an evening, Harry. I apologise to you both.'

'My dear Dorian, I should think Miss Vane was ill,' interrupted Hallward. 'We will come some other night.'

'I wish she were ill,' he rejoined. 'But she seems to me to be simply callous and cold. She was entirely altered. Last night she was a great artist. This evening she is merely a commonplace, mediocre actress.'

'Don't talk like that about anyone you love, Dorian. Love is a more wonderful thing than Art.'

'They are both simply forms of imitation,' remarked Lord Henry. 'But do let us go. Dorian, you must not stay here any longer. It is not good for one's morals to see bad acting. Besides, I don't suppose you will want your wife to act. So what does it matter if she plays Juliet like a wooden doll? She is very lovely, and if she knows as little about life as she does about acting, she will be a delightful experience. There are only two kinds of people who are really fascinating – people who know absolutely everything, and people who know absolutely nothing. Good heavens, my dear boy, don't look so tragic! The secret of remaining young is never to have an emotion that is unbecoming. Come to the club with Basil and myself. We will smoke cigarettes and drink to the beauty of Sibyl Vane. She is beautiful. What more can you want?'

'Go away, Harry,' cried the lad. 'I want to be alone. Basil, you must go. Ah! can't you see that my heart is breaking?' The hot tears came to his eyes. His lips trembled, and, rushing to the back of the box, he leaned up against the wall, hiding his face in his hands.

'Let us go, Basil,' said Lord Henry, with a strange tenderness in his voice; and the two young men passed out together.

A few moments afterwards the footlights flared up, and the curtain rose on the third act. Dorian Gray went back to his seat. He looked pale, and proud, and indifferent. The play dragged on, and seemed interminable. Half of the audience went out, tramping in heavy boots, and laughing. The whole thing was a fiasco. The last act was played to almost empty benches. The curtain went down on a titter, and some groans.

As soon as it was over, Dorian Gray rushed behind the scenes into the green-room. The girl was standing there alone, with a look of triumph on her face. Her eyes were lit with an exquisite fire. There was a radiance about her. Her parted lips were smiling over some secret of their own.

When he entered, she looked at him, and an expression of infinite joy came over her. 'How badly I acted to-night, Dorian!' she cried.

'Horribly!' he answered, gazing at her in amazement – 'horribly! It was dreadful. Are you ill? You have no idea what it was. You have no idea what I suffered.'

The girl smiled. 'Dorian,' she answered, lingering over his name with long-drawn music in her voice, as though it were sweeter than honey to the red petals of her mouth – 'Dorian, you should have understood. But you understand now, don't you?'

'Understand what?' he asked, angrily.

'Why I was so bad to-night. Why I shall always be bad. Why I shall never act well again.'

He shrugged his shoulders. 'You are ill, I suppose. When you are ill you shouldn't act. You make yourself ridiculous. My friends were bored. I was bored.'

She seemed not to listen to him. She was transfigured with joy. An ecstasy of happiness dominated her.

'Dorian, Dorian,' she cried, 'before I knew you, acting was the one reality of my life. It was only in the theatre that I lived. I thought that it was all true. I was Rosalind one night, and Portia the other. The joy of Beatrice was my joy, and the sorrows of Cordelia were mine also. I believed in everything. The common people who acted with me seemed to me to be godlike. The painted scenes were my world. I knew nothing but shadows, and I thought them real. You came – oh, my beautiful love! – and you freed my soul from prison. You taught me what reality really is. To-night, for the first time in my life, I saw through the hollowness, the sham, the silliness of the empty pageant in which I had always played. To-night, for the first time, I became conscious that the Romeo was hideous, and old, and painted, that the moonlight in the orchard was false, that the scenery was vulgar, and that the words I had to speak were unreal, were not my words, were not what I wanted to say. You had brought me something higher, something of which all art is but a reflection. You had made me understand what love really is. My love! my love! Prince Charming! Prince of life! I have grown sick of shadows. You are more to me than all art can ever be. What have I to do with the puppets of a play? When I came on to-night, I could not understand how it was that everything had gone from me. I thought that I was going to be wonderful. I found that I could do nothing. Suddenly it dawned on my soul what it all meant. The knowledge was exquisite to me. I heard them hissing, and I smiled. What could they know of love such as ours? Take me away, Dorian – take me away with you, where we can be quite alone. I hate the stage. I might mimic a passion that I do not feel, but I cannot mimic one that burns me like fire. Oh, Dorian, Dorian, you understand now what it signifies? Even if I could do it, it would be profanation for me to play at being in love. You have made me see that.'

He flung himself down on the sofa, and turned away his face. 'You have killed my love,' he muttered.

She looked at him in wonder, and laughed. He made no answer. She came across to him, and with her little fingers stroked his hair. She knelt down and pressed his hands to her lips. He drew them away, and a shudder ran through him.

Then he leaped up, and went to the door. 'Yes,' he cried, 'you have killed my love. You used to stir my imagination. Now you don't even stir my curiosity. You simply produce no effect. I loved you because you were marvellous, because you had genius and intellect, because you realised the dreams of great poets and gave shape and substance to the shadows of art. You have thrown it all away. You are shallow and stupid. My God! how mad I was to love you! What a fool I have been! You are nothing to me now. I will never see you again. I will never think of you. I will never mention your name. You don't know what you were to me, once. Why, once . . . Oh, I can't bear to think of it! I wish I had never laid eyes upon you! You have spoiled the romance of my life. How little you can know of love, if you say it mars your art! Without your art you are nothing. I would have made you famous, splendid, magnificent. The world would have worshipped you, and you would have borne my name. What are you now? A third-rate actress with a pretty face.'

The girl grew white, and trembled. She clenched her hands together, and her voice seemed to catch in her throat. 'You are not serious, Dorian?' she murmured. 'You are acting.'

'Acting! I leave that to you. You do it so well,' he answered bitterly.

She rose from her knees, and, with a piteous expression of pain in her face, came across the room to him. She put her hand upon his arm, and looked into his eyes. He thrust her back. 'Don't touch me!' he cried.

A low moan broke from her, and she flung herself at his feet, and lay there like a trampled flower. 'Dorian, Dorian, don't leave me!' she whispered. 'I am so sorry I didn't act well. I was thinking of you all the time. But I will try – indeed, I will try. It came so suddenly across me, my love for you. I think I should never have known it if you had not kissed me – if we had not kissed each other. Kiss me again, my love. Don't go away from me. I couldn't bear it. Oh! don't go away from me. My brother. . . . No; never mind. He didn't mean it. He was in jest. . . . But you, oh! can't you forgive me for to-night? I will work so hard, and try to improve. Don't be cruel to me because I love you better than anything in the world. After all, it is only once that I have not pleased you. But you are quite right, Dorian. I should have shown myself more of an artist. It was foolish of me; and yet I couldn't help it. Oh, don't leave me, don't leave me.' A fit of passionate sobbing choked her. She crouched on the floor like a wounded thing, and Dorian Gray, with his beautiful eyes, looked down at her, and his chiselled lips curled in exquisite disdain. There is always something ridiculous about the emotions of people whom one has ceased to love. Sibyl Vane to him seemed to be absurdly melodramatic. Her tears and sobs annoyed him.

'I am going,' he said at last, in his calm, clear voice. 'I don't wish to be unkind, but I can't see you again. You have disappointed me.'

She wept silently, and made no answer, but crept nearer. Her little hands stretched blindly out, and appeared to be seeking for him. He turned on his heel, and left the room. In a few moments he was out of the theatre.

Where he went to he hardly knew. He remembered wandering through dimly-lit streets, past gaunt black-shadowed archways and evil-looking houses. Women with hoarse voices and harsh laughter had called after him. Drunkards had reeled by cursing, and chattering to themselves like monstrous apes. He had seen grotesque children huddled upon doorsteps, and heard shrieks and oaths from gloomy courts.

As the dawn was just breaking he found himself close to Covent Garden. The darkness lifted, and flushed with faint fires, the sky hollowed itself into a perfect pearl. Huge carts filled with nodding lilies rumbled slowly down the polished empty street. The air was heavy with the perfume of the flowers, and their beauty seemed to bring him an anodyne for his pain. He followed into the market, and watched the men unloading their wagons. A white-smocked carter offered him some cherries. He thanked him, and wondered why he refused to accept any money for them, and began to eat them listlessly. They had been plucked at midnight, and the coldness of the moon had entered into them. A long line of boys carrying crates of striped tulips, and of yellow and red roses, defiled in front of him, threading their way through the huge jade-green piles of vegetables. Under the portico, with its grey sun-bleached pillars, loitered a troop of draggled bare-headed girls, waiting for the auction to be over. Others crowded round the swinging doors of the coffee-house in the Plazza. The heavy carthorses slipped and stamped upon the rough stones, shaking their bells and trappings. Some of the drivers were lying asleep on a pile of sacks. Iris-necked, and pink-footed, the pigeons ran about picking up seeds.

After a little while, he hailed a hansom, and drove home. For a few moments he loitered upon the doorstep, looking round at the silent Square with its blank, close-shuttered windows, and its staring blinds. The sky was pure opal now, and the roofs of the houses glistened like silver against it. From some chimney opposite a thin wreath of smoke was rising. It curled, a violet ribbon, through the nacre-coloured air.

In the huge gilt Venetian lantern, spoil of some Doge's barge, that hung from the ceiling of the great oak-panelled hall of entrance, lights were still burning from three flickering jets: thin blue petals of flame they seemed, rimmed with white fire. He turned them out, and having thrown his hat and cape on the table, passed through the library towards the door of his bedroom, a large octagonal chamber on the ground floor that, in his new-born feeling for luxury, he had just had decorated for himself, and hung with some curious Renaissance tapestries that had been discovered stored in a disused attic at Selby Royal. As he was turning the handle of the door, his eye fell upon the portrait Basil Hallward had painted of him. He started back as if in surprise. Then he went on into his own room, looking somewhat puzzled. After he had taken the buttonhole out of his coat, he seemed to hesitate. Finally he came back, went over to the picture, and examined it. In the dim arrested light that struggled through the cream-coloured silk blinds, the face appeared to him to be a little changed. The expression looked different. One would have said that there was a touch of cruelty in the mouth. It was certainly strange.

He turned round, and, walking to the window, drew up the blind. The bright dawn flooded the room, and swept the fantastic shadows into dusky corners, where they lay shuddering. But the strange expression that he had noticed in the face of the portrait seemed to linger there, to be more intensified even. The quivering, ardent sunlight showed him the lines of cruelty round the mouth as clearly as if he had been looking into a mirror after he had done some dreadful thing.

He winced, and taking up from the table an oval glass framed in ivory Cupids, one of Lord Henry's many presents to him, glanced hurriedly into its polished depths. No line like that warped his red lips. What did it mean?

He rubbed his eyes, and came close to the picture, and examined it again. There were no signs of any change when he looked into the actual painting, and yet there was no doubt that the whole expression had altered. It was not a mere fancy of his own. The thing was horribly apparent.

He threw himself into a chair, and began to think. Suddenly there flashed across his mind what he had said in Basil Hallward's studio the day the picture had been finished. Yes, he remembered it perfectly. He had uttered a mad wish that he himself might remain young, and the portrait grow old; that his own beauty might be untarnished, and the face on the canvas bear the burden of his passions and his sins; that the painted image might be seared with the lines of suffering and thought, and that he might keep all the delicate bloom and loveliness of his then just conscious boyhood. Surely his wish had not been fulfilled? Such things were impossible. It seemed monstrous even to think of them. And, yet, there was the picture before him, with the touch of cruelty in the mouth.

Cruelty! Had he been cruel? It was the girl's fault, not his. He had dreamed of her as a great artist, had given his love to her because he had thought her great. Then she had disappointed him. She had been shallow and unworthy. And, yet, a feeling of infinite regret came over him, as he thought of her lying at his feet sobbing like a little child. He remembered with what callousness he had watched her. Why had he been made like that? Why had such a soul been given to him? But he had suffered also. During the three terrible hours that the play had lasted, he had lived centuries of pain, æon upon æon of torture. His life was well worth hers. She had marred him for a moment, if he had wounded her for an age. Besides, women were better suited to bear sorrow than men. They lived on their emotions. They only thought of their emotions. When they took lovers, it was merely to have some one with whom they could have scenes. Lord Henry had told him that, and Lord Henry knew what women were. Why should he trouble about Sibyl Vane? She was nothing to him now.

But the picture? What was he to say of that? It held the secret of his life, and told his story. It had taught him to love his own beauty. Would it teach him to loathe his own soul? Would he ever look at it again?

No; it was merely an illusion wrought on the troubled senses. The horrible night that he had passed had left phantoms behind it. Suddenly there had fallen upon his brain that tiny scarlet speck that makes men mad. The picture had not changed. It was folly to think so.

Yet it was watching him, with its beautiful marred face and its cruel smile. Its bright hair gleamed in the early sunlight. Its blue eyes met his own. A sense of infinite pity, not for himself, but for the painted image of himself, came over him. It had altered already, and would alter more. Its gold would wither into grey. Its red and white roses would die. For every sin that he committed a stain would fleck and wreck its fairness. But he would not sin. The picture, changed or unchanged, would be to him the visible emblem of conscience. He would resist temptation. He would not see Lord Henry any more – would not, at any rate, listen to those subtle poisonous theories that in Basil Hallward's garden had first stirred within him the passion for impossible things. He would go back to Sibyl Vane, make her amends, marry her, try to love her again. Yes, it was his duty to do so. She must have suffered more than he had. Poor child! He had been selfish and cruel to her. The fascination that she had exercised over him would return. They would be happy together. His life with her would be beautiful and pure.

He got up from his chair, and drew a large screen right in front of the portrait, shuddering as he glanced at it. 'How horrible!' he murmured to himself, and he walked across to the window and opened it. When he stepped out on to the grass, he drew a deep breath. The fresh morning air seemed to drive away all his sombre passions. He thought only of Sibyl. A faint echo of his love came back to him. He repeated her name over and over again. The birds that were singing in the dew-drenched garden seemed to be telling the flowers about her.

8

IT WAS LONG PAST NOON when he awoke. His valet had crept several times on tiptoe into the room to see if he was stirring, and had wondered what made his young master sleep so late. Finally his bell sounded, and Victor came softly in with a cup of tea, and a pile of letters, on a small tray of old Sèvres china, and drew back the olive-satin curtains, with their shimmering blue lining, that hung in front of the three tall windows.

'Monsieur has slept well this morning.' he said, smiling.

'What o'clock is it, Victor?' asked Dorian Gray, drowsily.

'One hour and a quarter, Monsieur.'

How late it was! He sat up, and, having sipped some tea, turned over his letters. One of them was from Lord Henry, and had been brought by hand that morning. He hesitated for a moment, and then put it aside. The others he opened listlessly. They contained the usual collection of cards, invitations to dinner, tickets for private views, programmes of charity concerts, and the like, that are showered on fashionable young men every morning during the season. There was a rather heavy bill, for a chased silver Louis-Quinze toilet-set, that he had not yet had the courage to send on to his guardians, who were extremely old-fashioned people and did not realise that we live in an age when unnecessary things are our only necessities; and there were several very courteously worded communications from Jermyn Street money-lenders offering to advance any sum of money at a moment's notice and at the most reasonable rates of interest.

After about ten minutes he got up, and, throwing on an elaborate dressing-gown of silk-embroidered cashmere wool, passed into the onyx-paved bathroom. The cool water refreshed him after his long sleep. He seemed to have forgotten all that he had gone through. A dim sense of having taken part in some strange tragedy came to him once or twice, but there was the unreality of a dream about it.

As soon as he was dressed, he went into the library and sat down to a light French breakfast, that had been laid out for him on a small round table close to the open window. It was an exquisite day. The warm air seemed laden with spices. A bee flew in, and buzzed round the blue-dragon bowl that, filled with sulphur-yellow roses, stood before him. He felt perfectly happy.

Suddenly his eye fell on the screen that he had placed in front of the portrait, and he started.

'Too cold for Monsieur?' asked his valet, putting an omelette on the table. 'I'll shut the window?'

Dorian shook his head. 'I am not cold,' he murmured.

Was it all true? Had the portrait really changed? Or had it been simply his own imagination that had made him see a look of evil where there had been a look of joy? Surely a painted canvas could not alter? The thing was absurd. It would serve as a tale to tell Basil some day. It would make him smile.

And, yet, how vivid was his recollection of the whole thing! First in the dim twilight, and then in the bright dawn, he had seen the touch of cruelty round the warped lips. He almost dreaded his valet leaving the room. He knew that when he was alone he would have to examine the portrait. He was afraid of certainty. When the coffee and cigarettes had been brought and the man turned to go, he felt a wild desire to tell him to remain. As the door was closing behind him he called him back. The man stood waiting for his orders. Dorian looked at him for a moment. 'I am not at home to anyone, Victor,' he said, with a sigh. The man bowed and retired.

Then he rose from the table, lit a cigarette, and flung himself down on a luxuriously-cushioned couch that stood facing the screen. The screen was an old one, of gilt Spanish leather, stamped and wrought with a rather florid Louis-Quatorze pattern. He scanned it curiously, wondering if ever before it had concealed the secret of a man's life.

Should he move it aside, after all? Why not let it stay there? What was the use of knowing? If the thing was true, it was terrible. If it was not true, why trouble about it? But what if, by some fate or deadlier chance, eyes other than his spied behind, and saw the horrible change? What should he do if Basil Hallward came and asked to look at his own picture? Basil would be sure to do that. No; the thing had to be examined, and at once. Anything would be better than this dreadful state of doubt.

He got up, and locked both doors. At least he would be alone when he looked upon the mask of his shame. Then he drew the screen aside, and saw himself face to face. It was perfectly true. The portrait had altered.

As he often remembered afterwards, and always with no small wonder, he found himself at first gazing at the portrait with a feeling of almost scientific interest. That such a change should have taken place was incredible to him. And yet it was a fact. Was there some subtle affinity between the chemical atoms, that shaped themselves into form and colour on the canvas, and the soul that was within him? Could it be that what that soul thought, they realised? – that what it dreamed, they made true? Or was there some other, more terrible reason? He shuddered, and felt afraid, and, going back to the couch, lay there, gazing at the picture in sickened horror.

One thing, however, he felt that it had done for him. It had made him conscious how unjust, how cruel, he had been to Sibyl Vane. It was not too late to make reparation for that. She could still be his wife. His unreal and selfish love would yield to some higher influence, would be transformed into some nobler passion, and the portrait that Basil Hallward had painted of him would be a guide to him through life, would be to him what holiness is to some, and conscience to others, and the fear of God to us all. There were opiates for remorse, drugs that could lull the moral sense to sleep. But here was a visible symbol of the degradation of sin. Here was an ever-present sign of the ruin men brought upon their souls.

Three o'clock struck, and four, and the half-hour rang its double chime, but Dorian Gray did not stir. He was trying to gather up the scarlet threads of life, and to weave them into a pattern; to find his way through the sanguine labyrinth of passion through which he was wandering. He did not know what to do, or what to think. Finally, he went over to the table, and wrote a passionate letter to the girl he had loved, imploring her forgiveness, and accusing himself of madness. He covered page after page with wild words of sorrow, and wilder words of pain. There is a luxury in self-reproach. When we blame ourselves we feel that no one else has a right to blame us. It is the confession, not the priest, that gives us absolution. When Dorian had finished the letter, he felt that he had been forgiven.

Suddenly there came a knock at the door, and he heard Lord Henry's voice outside. 'My dear boy, I must see you. Let me in at once. I can't bear your shutting yourself up like this.'

He made no answer at first, but remained quite still. The knocking still continued, and grew louder. Yes, it was better to let Lord Henry in, and to explain to him the new life he was going to lead, to quarrel with him if it became necessary to quarrel, to part if parting was inevitable. He jumped up, drew the screen hastily across the picture, and unlocked the door.

'I am so sorry for it all, Dorian,' said Lord Henry, as he entered. 'But you must not think too much about it.'

'Do you mean about Sibyl Vane?' asked the lad.

'Yes, of course,' answered Lord Henry, sinking into a chair, and slowly pulling off his yellow gloves. 'It is dreadful, from one point of view, but it was not your fault. Tell me, did you go behind and see her, after the play was over?'

'Yes.'

'I felt sure you had. Did you make a scene with her?'

'I was brutal, Harry – perfectly brutal. But it is all right now. I am not sorry for anything that has happened. It has taught me to know myself better.'

'Ah, Dorian, I am so glad you take it in that way! I was afraid I would find you plunged in remorse, and tearing that nice curly hair of yours.'

'I have got through all that,' said Dorian, shaking his head, and smiling. 'I am perfectly happy now. I know what conscience is, to begin with. It is not what you told me it was. It is the divinest thing in us. Don't sneer at it, Harry, any more – at least not before me. I want to be good. I can't bear the idea of my soul being hideous.'

'A very charming artistic basis for ethics, Dorian! I congratulate you on it. But how are you going to begin?'

'By marrying Sibyl Vane.'

'Marrying Sibyl Vane!' cried Lord Henry, standing up, and looking at him in perplexed amazement. 'But, my dear Dorian—'

'Yes, Harry, I know what you are going to say. Something dreadful about marriage. Don't say it. Don't ever say things of that kind to me again. Two days ago I asked Sibyl to marry me. I am not going to break my word to her. She is to be my wife!'

'Your wife! Dorian! . . . Didn't you get my letter? I wrote to you this morning, and sent the note down, by my own man.'

'Your letter? Oh, yes, I remember. I have not read it yet, Harry. I was afraid there might be something in it that I wouldn't like. You cut life to pieces with your epigrams.'

'You know nothing then?'

'What do you mean?'

Lord Henry walked across the room, and, sitting down by Dorian Gray, took both his hands in his own, and held them tightly. 'Dorian,' he said, 'my letter – don't be frightened – was to tell you that Sibyl Vane is dead.'

A cry of pain broke from the lad's lips, and he leaped to his feet, tearing his hands away from Lord Henry's grasp. 'Dead! Sibyl dead! It is not true! It is a horrible lie! How dare you say it?'

'It is quite true, Dorian,' said Lord Henry, gravely. 'It is in all the morning papers. I wrote down to you to ask you not to see anyone till I came. There will have to be an inquest, of course, and you must not be mixed up in it. Things like that make a man fashionable in Paris. But in London people are so prejudiced. Here, one should never make one's début with a scandal. One should reserve that to give an interest to one's old age. I suppose they don't know your name at the theatre? If they don't, it is all right. Did anyone see you going round to her room? That is an important point.'

Dorian did not answer for a few moments. He was dazed with horror. Finally he stammered in a stifled voice. 'Harry, did you say an inquest? What did you mean by that? Did Sibyl – ? Oh, Harry, I can't bear it! But be quick. Tell me everything at once.'

'I have no doubt it was not an accident, Dorian, though it must be put in that way to the public. It seems that as she was leaving the theatre with her mother, about half-past twelve or so, she said she had forgotten something upstairs. They waited some time for her, but she did not come down again. They ultimately found her lying dead on the floor of her dressing-room. She had swallowed something by mistake, some dreadful thing they use at theatres. I don't know what it was, but it had either prussic acid or white lead in it. I should fancy it was prussic acid, as she seems to have died instantaneously.'

'Harry, Harry, it is terrible!' cried the lad.

'Yes; it is very tragic, of course, but you must not get yourself mixed up in it. I see by *The Standard* that she was seventeen. I should have thought she was almost younger than that. She looked such a child, and seemed to know so little about acting. Dorian, you mustn't let this thing get on your nerves. You must come and dine with me, and afterwards we will look in at the Opera. It is a Patti night, and everybody will be there. You can come to my sister's box. She has got some smart women with her.'

'So I have murdered Sibyl Vane,' said Dorian Gray, half to himself – 'murdered her as surely as if I had cut her little throat with a knife. Yet the roses are not less lovely for all that. The birds sing just as happily in my garden. And to-night I am to dine with you, and then go on to the Opera, and sup somewhere, I suppose, afterwards. How extraordinarily dramatic life is! If I had read all this in a book, Harry, I think I would have wept over it. Somehow, now that it has happened actually, and to me, it seems far too wonderful for tears. Here is the first passionate love-letter I have ever written in my life. Strange, that my first passionate love-letter should have been addressed to a dead girl. Can they feel, I wonder, those white silent people we call the dead? Sibyl! Can she feel, or know, or listen? Oh, Harry, how I loved her once! It seems years ago to me now. She was everything to me. Then came that dreadful night – was it really only last night? – when she played so badly, and my heart almost broke. She explained it all to me. It was terribly pathetic. But I was not moved a bit. I thought her shallow. Suddenly something happened that made me afraid. I can't tell you what it was, but it was terrible. I said I would go back to her. I felt I had done wrong. And now she is dead. My God! My God! Harry, what shall I do? You don't know the danger I am in, and there is nothing to keep me straight. She would have done that for me. She had no right to kill herself. It was selfish of her.'

'My dear Dorian,' answered Lord Henry, taking a cigarette from his case, and producing a gold-latten match-box, 'the only way a woman can ever reform a man is by boring him so completely that he loses all possible interest in life. If you had married this girl you would have been wretched. Of course, you would have treated her kindly. One can always be kind to people about whom one cares nothing. But she would have soon found out that you were absolutely indifferent to her. And when a woman finds that out about her husband, she either becomes dreadfully dowdy, or wears very smart bonnets that some other woman's husband has to pay for. I say nothing about the social mistake, which would have been abject, which, of course, I would not have allowed, but I assure you that in any case the whole thing would have been an absolute failure.'

'I suppose it would,' muttered the lad, walking up and down the room, and looking horribly pale. 'But I thought it was my duty. It is not my fault that this terrible tragedy has prevented my doing what was right. I remember your saying once that there is a fatality about good resolutions – that they are always made too late. Mine certainly were.'

'Good resolutions are useless attempts to interfere with scientific laws. Their origin is pure vanity. Their result is absolutely nil. They give us, now and then, some of those luxurious sterile emotions that have a certain charm for the weak. That is all that can be said for them. They are simply cheques that men draw on a bank where they have no account.'

'Harry,' cried Dorian Gray, coming over and sitting down beside him, 'why is it that I cannot feel this tragedy as much as I want to? I don't think I am heartless. Do you?'

'You have done too many foolish things during the last fortnight to be entitled to give yourself that name, Dorian,' answered Lord Henry, with his sweet, melancholy smile.

The lad frowned. 'I don't like that explanation, Harry,' he rejoined, 'but I am glad you don't think I am heartless. I am nothing of the kind. I know I am not. And yet I must admit that this thing that has happened does not affect me as it should. It seems to me to be simply like a wonderful ending to a wonderful play. It has all the terrible beauty of a Greek tragedy, a tragedy in which I took a great part, but by which I have not been wounded.'

'It is an interesting question,' said Lord Henry, who found an exquisite pleasure in playing on the lad's unconscious egotism – 'an extremely interesting question. I fancy that the true explanation is this. It often happens that the real tragedies of life occur in such an inartistic manner that they hurt us by their crude violence, their absolute incoherence, their absurd want of meaning, their entire lack of style. They affect us just as vulgarity affects us. They give us an impression of sheer brute force, and we revolt against that. Sometimes, however, a tragedy that possesses artistic elements of beauty crosses our lives. If these elements of beauty are real, the whole thing simply appeals to our sense of dramatic effect. Suddenly we find that we are no longer the actors, but the spectators of the play. Or rather we are both. We watch ourselves, and the mere wonder of the spectacle enthrals us. In the present case, what is it that has really happened? Someone has killed herself for love of you. I wish that I had ever had such an experience. It would have made me in love with love for the rest of my life. The people who have adored me – there have not been very many, but there have been some – have always insisted on living on, long after I had ceased to care for them, or they to care for me. They have become stout and tedious, and when I meet them they go in at once for reminiscences. That awful memory of woman! What a fearful thing it is. And what an utter intellectual stagnation it reveals! One should absorb the colour of life, but one should never remember its details. Details are always vulgar.'

'I must sow poppies in my garden,' sighed Dorian.

'There is no necessity,' rejoined his companion. 'Life has always poppies in her hands. Of course, now and then things linger. I once wore nothing but violets all through one season, as a form of artistic mourning for a romance that would not die. Ultimately, however, it did die. I forget what killed it. I think it was her proposing to sacrifice the whole world for me. That is always a dreadful moment. It fills one with the terror of eternity. Well – would you believe it? – a week ago, at Lady Hampshire's, I found myself seated at dinner next the lady in question, and she insisted on going over the whole thing again, and digging up the past, and raking up the future. I had buried my romance in a bed of asphodel. She dragged it out again, and assured me that I had spoiled her life. I am bound to state that she ate an enormous dinner, so I did not feel any anxiety. But what a lack of taste she showed! The one charm of the past is that it is the past. But women never know when the curtain has fallen. They always want a sixth act, and as soon as the interest of the play is entirely over they propose to continue it. If they were allowed their own way, every comedy would have a tragic ending, and every tragedy would culminate in a farce. They are charmingly artificial, but they have no sense of art. You are more fortunate than I am. I assure you, Dorian, that not one of the women I have known would have done for me what Sibyl Vane did for you. Ordinary women always console themselves. Some of them do it by going in for sentimental colours. Never trust a woman who wears mauve, whatever her age may be, or a woman over thirty-five who is fond of pink ribbons. It always means that they have a history. Others find a great consolation in suddenly discovering the good qualities of their husbands. They flaunt their conjugal felicity in one's face, as if it were the most fascinating of sins. Religion consoles some. Its mysteries have all the charm of a flirtation, a woman once told me; and I can quite understand it. Besides, nothing makes one so vain as being told that one is a sinner. Conscience makes egotists of us all. Yes; there is really no end to the consolations that women find in modern life. Indeed, I have not mentioned the most important one.'

'What is that, Harry?' said the lad, listlessly.

'Oh, the obvious consolation. Taking someone else's admirer when one loses one's own. In good society that always whitewashes a woman. But really, Dorian, how different Sibyl Vane must have been from all the women one meets! There is something to me quite beautiful about her death. I am glad I am living in a century when such wonders happen. They make one believe in the reality of the things we all play with, such as romance, passion, and love.'

'I was terribly cruel to her. You forget that.'

'I am afraid that women appreciate cruelty, downright cruelty, more than anything else. They have wonderfully primitive instincts. We have emancipated them, but they remain slaves looking for their masters, all the same. They love being dominated. I am sure you were splendid. I have never seen you really and absolutely angry, but I can fancy how delightful you looked. And, after all, you said something to me the day before yesterday that seemed to me at the time to be merely fanciful, but that I see now was absolutely true, and it holds the key to everything.'

'What was that, Harry?'

'You said to me that Sibyl Vane represented to you all the heroines of romance – that she was Desdemona one night, and Ophelia the other; that if she died as Juliet, she came to life as Imogen.'

'She will never come to life again now,' muttered the lad, burying his face in his hands.

'No, she will never come to life. She has played her last part. But you must think of that lonely death in the tawdry dressing-room simply as a strange lurid fragment from some Jacobean tragedy, as a wonderful scene from Webster, or Ford, or Cyril Tourneur. The girl never really lived, and so she has never really died. To you at least she was always a dream, a phantom that flitted through Shakespeare's plays and left them lovelier for its presence, a reed through which Shakespeare's music sounded richer and more full of joy. The moment she touched actual life, she marred it, and it marred her, and so she passed away. Mourn for Ophelia, if you like. Put ashes on your head because Cordelia was strangled. Cry out against Heaven because the daughter of Brabantio died. But don't waste your tears over Sibyl Vane. She was less real than they are.'

There was a silence. The evening darkened in the room. Noiselessly, and with silver feet, the shadows crept in from the garden. The colours faded wearily out of things.

After some time Dorian Gray looked up. 'You have explained me to myself, Harry,' he murmured, with something of a sigh of relief. 'I felt all that you have said, but somehow I was afraid of it, and I could not express it to myself. How well you know me! But we will not talk again of what has happened. It has been a marvellous experience. That is all. I wonder if life has still in store for me anything as marvellous.'

'Life has everything in store for you, Dorian. There is nothing that you, with your extraordinary good looks, will not be able to do.'

'But suppose, Harry, I became haggard, and old, and wrinkled? What then?'

'Ah, then,' said Lord Henry, rising to go – 'then, my dear Dorian, you would have to fight for your victories. As it is, they are brought to you. No, you must keep your good looks. We live in an age that reads too much to be wise, and that thinks too much to be beautiful. We cannot spare you. And now you had better dress, and drive down to the club. We are rather late, as it is.'

'I think I shall join you at the Opera, Harry. I feel too tired to eat anything. What is the number of your sister's box?'

'Twenty-seven, I believe. It is on the grand tier. You will see her name on the door. But I am sorry you won't come and dine.'

'I don't feel up to it,' said Dorian, listlessly. 'But I am awfully obliged to you for all that you have said to me. You are certainly my best friend. No one has ever understood me as you have.'

'We are only at the beginning of our friendship, Dorian,' answered Lord Henry, shaking him by the hand. 'Good-bye. I shall see you before nine-thirty, I hope. Remember, Patti is singing.'

As he closed the door behind him, Dorian Gray touched the bell, and in a few minutes Victor appeared with the lamps and drew the blinds down.

He waited impatiently for him to go. The man seemed to take an interminable time over everything.

As soon as he had left, he rushed to the screen, and drew it back. No; there was no further change in the picture. It had received the news of Sibyl Vane's death before he had known of it himself. It was conscious of the events of life as they occurred. The vicious cruelty that marred the fine lines of the mouth had, no doubt, appeared at the very moment that the girl had drunk the poison, whatever it was. Or was it indifferent to results? Did it merely take cognizance of what passed within the soul? He wondered, and hoped that some day he would see the change taking place before his very eyes, shuddering as he hoped it.

Poor Sibyl! What a romance it had all been! She had often mimicked death on the stage. Then Death himself had touched her, and taken her with him. How had she played that dreadful last scene? Had she cursed him, as she died? No; she had died for love of him, and love would always be a sacrament to him now. She had atoned for everything, by the sacrifice she had made of her life. He would not think any more of what she had made him go through, on that horrible night at the theatre. When he thought of her, it would be as a wonderful tragic figure sent on to the world's stage to show the supreme reality of Love. A wonderful tragic figure? Tears came to his eyes as he remembered her child-like look, and winsome fanciful ways, and shy tremulous grace. He brushed them away hastily, and looked again at the picture.

He felt that the time had really come for making his choice. Or had his choice already been made? Yes, life had decided that for him – life, and his own infinite curiosity about life. Eternal youth, infinite passion, pleasures subtle and secret, wild joys and wilder sins – he was to have all these things. The portrait was to bear the burden of his shame: that was all.

A feeling of pain crept over him, as he thought of the desecration that was in store for the fair face on the canvas. Once, in boyish mockery of Narcissus, he had kissed, or feigned to kiss, those painted lips that now smiled so cruelly at him. Morning after morning he had sat before the portrait, wondering at its beauty, almost enamoured of it, as it seemed to him at times. Was it to alter now with every mood to which he yielded? Was it to become a monstrous and loathsome thing, to be hidden away in a locked room, to be shut out from the sunlight that had so often touched to brighter gold the waving wonder of its hair? The pity of it! The pity of it!

For a moment he thought of praying that the horrible sympathy that existed between him and the picture might cease. It had changed in answer to a prayer; perhaps in answer to a prayer it might remain unchanged. And, yet, who, that knew anything about Life, would surrender the chance of remaining always young, however fantastic that chance might be, or with what fateful consequences it might be fraught? Besides, was it really under his control? Had it indeed been prayer that had produced the substitution? Might there not be some curious scientific reason for it all? If thought could exercise its influence upon a living organism, might not thought exercise an influence upon dead and inorganic things? Nay, without thought or conscious desire, might not things external to ourselves vibrate in unison with our moods and passions, atom calling to atom in secret love of strange affinity? But the reason was of no importance. He would never again tempt by a prayer any terrible power. If the picture was to alter, it was to alter. That was all. Why inquire too closely into it?

For there would be a real pleasure in watching it. He would be able to follow his mind into its secret places. This portrait would be to him the most magical of mirrors. As it had revealed to him his own body, so it would reveal to him his own soul. And when winter came upon it, he would still be standing where spring trembles on the verge of summer. When the blood crept from its face, and left behind a pallid mask of chalk with leaden eyes, he would keep the glamour of boyhood. Not one blossom of his loveliness would ever fade. Not one pulse of his life would ever weaken. Like the gods of the Greeks, he would be strong, and fleet, and joyous. What did it matter what happened to the coloured image on the canvas? He would be safe. That was everything.

He drew the screen back into its former place in front of the picture, smiling as he did so, and passed into his bedroom, where his valet was already waiting for him. An hour later he was at the Opera, and Lord Henry was leaning over his chair.

STORIES

THE HAPPY PRINCE

HIGH ABOVE THE CITY, ON A TALL column, stood the statue of the Happy Prince. He was gilded all over with thin leaves of fine gold, for eyes he had two bright sapphires, and a large red ruby glowed on his sword-hilt.

He was very much admired indeed. 'He is as beautiful as a weather-cock,' remarked one of the Town Councillors who wished to gain a reputation for having artistic tastes; 'only not quite so useful,' he added, fearing lest people should think him unpractical, which he really was not.

'Why can't you be like the Happy Prince?' asked a sensible mother of her little boy who was crying for the moon. 'The Happy Prince never dreams of crying for anything.'

'I am glad there is some one in the world who is quite happy,' muttered a disappointed man as he gazed at the wonderful statue.

'He looks just like an angel,' said the Charity Children as they came out of the cathedral in their bright scarlet cloaks and their clean white pinafores.

'How do you know?' said the Mathematical Master, 'you have never seen one.'

'Ah! but we have, in our dreams,' answered the children; and the Mathematical Master frowned and looked very severe, for he did not approve of children dreaming.

One night there flew over the city a little Swallow. His friends had gone away to Egypt six weeks before, but he had stayed behind, for he was in love with the most beautiful Reed. He had met her early in the spring as he was flying down the river after a big yellow moth, and had been so attracted by her slender waist that he had stopped to talk to her.

'Shall I love you?' said the Swallow, who liked to come to the point at once, and the Reed made him a low bow. So he flew round and round her, touching the water with his wings, and making silver ripples. This was his courtship, and it lasted all through the summer.

'It is a ridiculous attachment,' twittered the other Swallows; 'she has no money, and far too many relations;' and indeed the river was quite full of Reeds. Then, when the autumn came they all flew away.

After they had gone he felt lonely, and began to tire of his lady-love. 'She has no conversation,' he said, 'and I am afraid that she is a coquette, for she is always flirting with the wind.' And certainly, whenever the wind blew, the Reed made the most graceful curtseys. 'I admit that she is domestic,' he continued, 'but I love travelling, and my wife, consequently, should love travelling also.'

'Will you come away with me?' he said finally to her, but the Reed shook her head, she was so attached to her home.

'You have been trifling with me,' he cried. 'I am off to the Pyramids. Good-bye!' and he flew away.

All day long he flew, and at night-time he arrived at the city. 'Where shall I put up?' he said; 'I hope the town has made preparations.'

Then he saw the statue on the tall column.

'I will put up there,' he cried; 'it is a fine position, with plenty of fresh air.' So he alighted just between the feet of the Happy Prince.

'I have a golden bedroom,' he said softly to himself as he looked round, and he prepared to go to sleep; but just as he was putting his head under his wing a large drop of water fell on him. 'What a curious thing!' he cried; 'there is not a single cloud in the sky, the stars are quite clear and bright, and yet it is raining. The climate in the north of Europe is really dreadful. The Reed used to like the rain, but that was merely her selfishness.'

Then another drop fell.

'What is the use of a statue if it cannot keep the rain off?' he said; 'I must look for a good chimney-pot,' and he determined to fly away.

But before he had opened his wings, a third drop fell, and he looked up, and saw – Ah! what did he see?

The eyes of the Happy Prince were filled with tears, and tears were running down his golden cheeks. His face was so beautiful in the moonlight that the little Swallow was filled with pity.

'Who are you?' he said.

'I am the Happy Prince.'

'Why are you weeping then?' asked the Swallow; 'you have quite drenched me.'

'When I was alive and had a human heart,' answered the statue, 'I did not know what tears were, for I lived in the Palace of Sans-Souci, where sorrow is not allowed to enter. In the daytime I played with my companions in the garden, and in the evening I led the dance in the Great Hall. Round the garden ran a very lofty wall, but I never cared to ask what lay beyond it, everything about me was so beautiful. My courtiers called me the Happy Prince, and happy indeed I was, if pleasure be happiness. So I lived, and so I died. And now that I am dead they have set me up here so high that I can see all the ugliness and all the misery of my city, and though my heart is made of lead yet I cannot choose but weep.'

'What! is he not solid gold?' said the Swallow to himself. He was too polite to make any personal remarks out loud.

'Far away,' continued the statue in a low musical voice, 'far away in a little street there is a poor house. One of the windows is open, and through it I can see a woman seated at a table. Her face is thin and worn, and she has coarse, red hands, all pricked by the needle, for she is a seamstress. She is embroidering passion-flowers on a satin gown for the loveliest of the Queen's maids-of-honour to wear at the next Court-ball. In a bed in the corner of the room her little boy is lying ill. He has a fever, and is asking for oranges. His mother has nothing to give him but river water, so he is crying. Swallow, Swallow, little Swallow, will you not bring her the ruby out of my sword-hilt? My feet are fastened to this pedestal and I cannot move.'

'I am waited for in Egypt,' said the Swallow. 'My friends are flying up and down the Nile, and talking to the large lotus-flowers. Soon they will go to sleep in the tomb of the great King. The King is there himself in his painted coffin. He is wrapped in yellow linen, and embalmed with spices. Round his neck is a chain of pale green jade, and his hands are like withered leaves.'

'Swallow, Swallow, little Swallow,' said the Prince, 'will you not stay with me for one night, and be my messenger? The boy is so thirsty, and the mother so sad.'

'I don't think I like boys,' answered the Swallow. 'Last summer, when I was staying on the river, there were two rude boys, the miller's sons, who were always throwing stones at me. They never hit me, of course; we swallows fly far too well for that, and besides I come of a family famous for its agility; but still, it was a mark of disrespect.'

But the Happy Prince looked so sad that the little Swallow was sorry. 'It is very cold here,' he said; 'but I will stay with you for one night, and be your messenger.'

'Thank you, little Swallow,' said the Prince.

So the Swallow picked out the great ruby from the Prince's sword, and flew away with it in his beak over the roofs of the town.

He passed by the cathedral tower, where the white marble angels were sculptured. He passed by the palace and heard the sound of dancing. A beautiful girl came out on the balcony with her lover. 'How wonderful the stars are,' he said to her, 'and how wonderful is the power of love!'

'I hope my dress will be ready in time for the State-ball,' she answered; 'I have ordered passion-flowers to be embroidered on it: but the seamstresses are so lazy.'

He passed over the river, and saw the lanterns hanging to the masts of the ships. He passed over the Ghetto, and saw the old Jews bargaining with each other, and weighing out money in copper scales. At last he came to the poor house and looked in. The boy was tossing feverishly on his bed, and the mother had fallen asleep, she was so tired. In he hopped, and laid the great ruby on the table beside the woman's thimble. Then he flew gently round the bed, fanning the boy's forehead with his wings. 'How cool I feel!' said the boy, 'I must be getting better;' and he sank into a delicious slumber.

Then the Swallow flew back to the Happy Prince, and told him what he had done. 'It is curious,' he remarked, 'but I feel quite warm now, although it is so cold.'

'That is because you have done a good action,' said the Prince. And the little Swallow began to think, and then he fell asleep. Thinking always made him sleepy.

When day broke he flew down to the river and had a bath. 'What a remarkable phenomenon!' said the Professor of Ornithology as he was passing over the bridge. 'A swallow in winter!' And he wrote a long letter about it to the local newspaper. Every one quoted it, it was full of so many words that they could not understand.

'To-night I go to Egypt,' said the Swallow, and he was in high spirits at the prospect. He visited all the public monuments, and sat a long time on top of the church steeple. Wherever he went the Sparrows chirruped, and said to each other, 'What a distinguished stranger!' so he enjoyed himself very much.

When the moon rose he flew back to the Happy Prince. 'Have you any commissions for Egypt?' he cried; 'I am just starting.'

'Swallow, Swallow, little Swallow,' said the Prince, 'will you not stay with me one night longer?'

'I am waited for in Egypt,' answered the Swallow. 'To-morrow my friends will fly up to the Second Cataract. The river-horse couches there among the bulrushes, and on a great granite throne sits the God Memnon. All night long he watches the stars, and when the morning star shines he utters one cry of joy, and then he is silent. At noon the yellow lions come down to the water's edge to drink. They have eyes like green beryls, and their roar is louder than the roar of the cataract.'

'Swallow, Swallow, little Swallow,' said the Prince, 'far away across the city I see a young man in a garret. He is leaning over a desk covered with papers, and in a tumbler by his side there is a bunch of withered violets. His hair is brown and crisp, and his lips are red as a pomegranate, and he has large and dreamy eyes. He is trying to finish a play for the Director of the Theatre, but he is too cold to write any more. There is no fire in the grate, and hunger has made him faint.'

'I will wait with you one night longer,' said the Swallow, who really had a good heart. 'Shall I take him another ruby?'

'Alas! I have no ruby now,' said the Prince: 'my eyes are all that I have left. They are made of rare sapphires, which were brought out of India a thousand years ago. Pluck out one of them and take it to him. He will sell it to the jeweller, and buy firewood, and finish his play.'

'Dear Prince,' said the Swallow, 'I cannot do that;' and he began to weep.

'Swallow, Swallow, little Swallow,' said the Prince, 'do as I command you.'

So the Swallow plucked out the Prince's eye, and flew away to the student's garret. It was easy enough to get in, as there was a hole in the roof. Through this he darted, and came into the room. The young man had his head buried in his hands, so he did not hear the flutter of the bird's wings, and when he looked up he found the beautiful sapphire lying on the withered violets.

'I am beginning to be appreciated,' he cried; 'this is from some great admirer. Now I can finish my play,' and he looked quite happy.

The next day the Swallow flew down to the harbour. He sat on the mast of a large vessel and watched the sailors hauling big chests out of the hold with ropes. 'Heave a-hoy!' they shouted as each chest came up. 'I am going to Egypt!' cried the Swallow, but nobody minded, and when the moon rose he flew back to the Happy Prince.

'I am come to bid you good-bye,' he cried.

'Swallow, Swallow, little Swallow,' said the Prince, 'will you not stay with me one night longer?'

'It is winter,' answered the Swallow, 'and the chill snow will soon be here. In Egypt the sun is warm on the green palm-trees, and the crocodiles lie in the mud and look lazily about them. My companions are building a nest in the Temple of Baalbec, and the pink and white doves are watching them, and cooing to each other. Dear Prince, I must leave you, but I will never forget you, and next spring I will bring you back two beautiful jewels in place of those you have given away. The ruby shall be redder than a red rose, and the sapphire shall be as blue as the great sea.'

'In the square below,' said the Happy Prince, 'there stands a little match-girl. She has let her matches fall in the gutter, and they are all spoiled. Her father will beat her if she does not bring home some money, and she is crying. She has no shoes or stockings, and her little head is bare. Pluck out my other eye, and give it to her, and her father will not beat her.'

'I will stay with you one night longer,' said the Swallow, 'but I cannot pluck out your eye. You would be quite blind then.'

'Swallow, Swallow, little Swallow,' said the Prince, 'do as I command you.'

So he plucked out the Prince's other eye, and darted down with it. He swooped past the match-girl, and slipped the jewel into the palm of her hand. 'What a lovely bit of glass!' cried the little girl; and she ran home, laughing.

Then the Swallow came back to the Prince, 'You are blind now,' he said, 'so I will stay with you always.'

'No, little Swallow,' said the poor Prince, 'you must go away to Egypt.'

'I will stay with you always,' said the Swallow, and he slept at the Prince's feet.

All the next day he sat on the Prince's shoulder, and told him stories of what he had seen in strange lands. He told him of the red ibises, who stand in long rows on the banks of the Nile, and catch goldfish in their beaks; of the Sphinx, who is as old as the world itself, and lives in the desert, and knows everything; of the merchants, who walk slowly by the side of their camels and carry amber beads in their hands; of the King of the Mountains of the Moon, who is as black as ebony, and worships a large crystal; of the great green snake that sleeps in a palm-tree, and has twenty priests to feed it with honey-cakes; and of the pygmies who sail over a big lake on large flat leaves, and are always at war with the butterflies.

'Dear little Swallow,' said the Prince, 'you tell me of marvellous things, but more marvellous than anything is the suffering of men and of women. There is no Mystery so great as Misery. Fly over my city, little Swallow, and tell me what you see there.'

So the Swallow flew over the great city, and saw the rich making merry in their beautiful houses, while the beggars were sitting at the gates. He flew into dark lanes, and saw the white faces of starving children looking out listlessly at the black streets. Under the archway of a bridge two little boys were lying in one another's arms to try and keep themselves warm. 'How hungry we are!' they said. 'You must not lie here', shouted the watchman, and they wandered out into the rain.

Then he flew back and told the Prince what he had seen.

'I am covered with fine gold,' said the Prince, 'you must take it off, leaf by leaf, and give it to my poor; the living always think that gold can make them happy.'

Leaf after leaf of the fine gold the Swallow picked off, till the Happy Prince looked quite dull and grey. Leaf after leaf of the fine gold he brought to the poor, and the children's faces grew rosier, and they laughed and played games in the street. 'We have bread now!' they cried.

Then the snow came, and after the snow came the frost. The streets looked as if they were made of silver, they were so bright and glistening; long icicles like crystal daggers hung down from the eaves of the houses, everybody went about in furs, and the little boys wore scarlet caps and skated on the ice.

The poor little Swallow grew colder and colder, but he would not leave the Prince, he loved him too well. He picked up crumbs outside the baker's door when the baker was not looking, and tried to keep himself warm by flapping his wings.

But at last he knew that he was going to die. He had just enough strength to fly up to the Prince's shoulder once more. 'Good-bye, dear Prince!' he murmured, 'will you let me kiss your hand?'

'I am glad that you are going to Egypt at last, little Swallow,' said the Prince, 'you have stayed too long here; but you must kiss me on the lips, for I love you.'

'It is not to Egypt that I am going,' said the Swallow. 'I am going to the House of Death. Death is the brother of Sleep, is he not?'

And he kissed the Happy Prince on the lips, and fell down dead at his feet.

At that moment a curious crack sounded inside the statue, as if something had broken. The fact is that the leaden heart had snapped right in two. It certainly was a dreadfully hard frost.

Early the next morning the Mayor was walking in the square below in company with the Town Councillors. As they passed the column he looked up at the statue: 'Dear me! how shabby the Happy Prince looks!' he said.

'How shabby, indeed!' cried the Town Councillors, who always agreed with the Mayor: and they went up to look at it.

'The ruby has fallen out of his sword, his eyes are gone, and he is golden no longer,' said the Mayor; 'in fact, he is little better than a beggar!'

'Little better than a beggar,' said the Town Councillors.

'And here is actually a dead bird at his feet!' continued the Mayor. 'We must really issue a proclamation that birds are not to be allowed to die here.' And the Town Clerk made a note of the suggestion.

So they pulled down the statue of the Happy Prince. 'As he is no longer beautiful he is no longer useful,' said the Art Professor at the University.

Then they melted the statue in a furnace, and the Mayor held a meeting of the Corporation to decide what was to be done with the metal. 'We must have another statue, of course,' he said, 'and it shall be a statue of myself.'

'Of myself,' said each of the Town Councillors, and they quarrelled. When I last heard of them they were quarrelling still.

'What a strange thing!' said the overseer of the workmen at the foundry. 'This broken lead heart will not melt in the furnace. We must throw it away.' So they threw it on a dust-heap where the dead Swallow was also lying.

'Bring me the two most precious things in the city,' said God to one of His Angels; and the Angel brought Him the leaden heart and the dead bird.

'You have rightly chosen,' said God, 'for in my garden of Paradise this little bird shall sing for evermore, and in my city of gold the Happy Prince shall praise me.'

THE
NIGHTINGALE
AND THE ROSE

'SHE SAID THAT SHE WOULD DANCE with me if I brought her red roses,' cried the young Student, 'but in all my garden there is no red rose.'

From her nest in the holm-oak tree the Nightingale heard him, and she looked out through the leaves and wondered.

'No red rose in all my garden!' he cried, and his beautiful eyes filled with tears. 'Ah, on what little things does happiness depend! I have read all that the wise men have written, and all the secrets of philosophy are mine, yet for want of a red rose is my life made wretched.'

'Here at last is a true lover,' said the Nightingale. 'Night after night have I sung of him though I knew him not: night after night have I told his story to the stars and now I see him. His hair is dark as the hyacinth-blossom, and his lips are red as the rose of his desire, but passion has made his face like pale ivory and sorrow has set her seal upon his brow.'

'The Prince gives a ball to-morrow night,' murmured the young Student, 'and my love will be of the company. If I bring her a red rose she will dance with me till dawn. If I bring her a red rose, I shall hold her in my arms, and she will lean her head upon my shoulder and her hand will be clasped in mine. But there is no red rose in my garden, so I shall sit lonely and she will pass me by. She will have no heed of me, and my heart will break.'

'Here, indeed, is the true lover,' said the Nightingale. 'What I sing of, he suffers: what is joy to me, to him is pain. Surely love is a wonderful thing. It is more precious than emeralds and dearer than fine opals. Pearls and pomegranates cannot buy it, nor is it set forth in the market-place. It may not be purchased of the merchants, nor can it be weighed out in the balance for gold.'

'The musicians will sit in their gallery,' said the young Student, 'and play upon their stringed instruments, and my love will dance to the sound of the harp and the violin. She will dance so lightly that her feet will not touch the floor, and the courtiers in their gay dresses will throng round her. But with me she will not dance, for I have no red rose to give her;' and he flung himself down on the grass, and buried his face in his hands, and wept.

'Why is he weeping?' asked a little Green Lizard, as he ran past him with his tail in the air.

'Why, indeed?' said a Butterfly, who was fluttering about after a sunbeam.

'Why, indeed?' whispered a Daisy to his neighbour, in a soft, low voice.

'He is weeping for a red rose,' said the Nightingale.

'For a red rose?' they cried; 'how very ridiculous!' and the little Lizard, who was something of a cynic, laughed outright.

But the Nightingale understood the secret of the Student's sorrow, and she sat silent in the oak-tree, and thought about the mystery of Love.

Suddenly she spread her brown wings for flight, and soared into the air. She passed through the grove like a shadow, and like a shadow she sailed across the garden.

In the centre of the grass-plot was standing a beautiful rose-tree, and when she saw it she flew over to it, and lit upon a spray.

'Give me a red rose,' she cried, 'and I will sing you my sweetest song.'

But the Tree shook its head.

'My roses are white,' it answered; 'as white as the foam of the sea, and whiter than the snow on the mountain. But go to my brother who grows round the old sun-dial, and perhaps he will give you what you want.'

So the Nightingale flew over to the Rose-tree that was growing round the old sun-dial.

'Give me a red rose,' she cried, 'and I will sing you my sweetest song.'

But the Tree shook its head.

'My roses are yellow,' it answered; 'as yellow as the hair of the mermaiden who sits upon an amber throne, and yellower than the daffodil that blooms in the meadow before the mower comes with his scythe. But go to my brother who grows beneath the Student's window, and perhaps he will give you what you want.'

So the Nightingale flew over to the Rose-tree that was growing beneath the Student's window.

'Give me a red rose,' she cried, 'and I will sing you my sweetest song.'

But the Tree shook its head.

'My roses are red,' it answered; 'as red as the feet of the dove, and redder than the great fans of coral that wave and wave in the ocean-cavern. But the winter has chilled my veins, and the frost has nipped my buds, and the storm has broken my branches, and I shall have no roses at all this year.'

'One red rose is all I want,' cried the Nightingale, 'only one red rose! Is there no way by which I can get it?'

'There is a way,' answered the Tree; 'but it is so terrible that I dare not tell it to you.'

'Tell it to me,' said the Nightingale, 'I am not afraid.'

'If you want a red rose,' said the Tree, 'you must build it out of music by moonlight, and stain it with your own heart's-blood. You must sing to me with your breast against a thorn. All night long you must sing to me, and the thorn must pierce your heart, and your life-blood must flow into my veins, and become mine.'

'Death is a great price to pay for a red rose,' cried the Nightingale, 'and Life is very dear to all. It is pleasant to sit in the green wood, and to watch the Sun in his chariot of gold, and the Moon in her chariot of pearl. Sweet is the scent of the hawthorn, and sweet are the bluebells that hide in the valley, and the heather that blows on the hill. Yet Love is better than Life, and what is the heart of a bird compared to the heart of a man?'

So she spread her brown wings for flight, and soared into the air. She swept over the garden like a shadow, and like a shadow she sailed through the grove.

The young Student was still lying on the grass, where she had left him, and the tears were not yet dry in his beautiful eyes.

'Be happy,' cried the Nightingale, 'be happy; you shall have your red rose. I will build it out of music by moonlight, and stain it with my own heart's-blood. All that I ask of you in return is that you will be a true lover, for Love is wiser than Philosophy, though he is wise, and mightier than Power, though he is mighty. Flame-coloured are his wings, and coloured like flame is his body. His lips are sweet as honey, and his breath is like frankincense.'

The Student looked up from the grass, and listened, but he could not understand what the Nightingale was saying to him, for he only knew the things that are written down in books.

But the Oak-tree understood, and felt sad, for he was very fond of the little Nightingale who had built her nest in his branches.

'Sing me one last song,' he whispered; 'I shall feel lonely when you are gone.'

So the Nightingale sang to the Oak-tree, and her voice was like water bubbling from a silver jar.

When she had finished her song, the Student got up, and pulled a note-book and a lead-pencil out of his pocket.

'She has form,' he said to himself, as he walked away through the grove – 'that cannot be denied to her; but has she got feeling? I am afraid not. In fact, she is like most artists; she is all style without any sincerity. She would not sacrifice herself for others. She thinks merely of music, and everybody knows that the arts are selfish. Still, it must be admitted that she has some beautiful notes in her voice. What a pity it is that they do not mean anything, or do any practical good!' And he went into his room, and lay down on his little pallet-bed, and began to think of his love; and, after a time, he fell asleep.

And when the moon shone in the heavens the Nightingale flew to the Rose-tree, and set her breast against the thorn. All night long she sang, with her breast against the thorn, and the cold crystal Moon leaned down and listened. All night long she sang, and the thorn went deeper and deeper into her breast, and her life-blood ebbed away from her.

She sang first of the birth of love in the heart of a boy and a girl. And on the topmost spray of the Rose-tree there blossomed a marvellous rose, petal following petal, as song followed song. Pale was it, at first, as the mist that hangs over the river – pale as the feet of the morning, and silver as the wings of the dawn. As the shadow of a rose in a mirror of silver, as the shadow of a rose in a water-pool, so was the rose that blossomed on the topmost spray of the Tree.

But the Tree cried to the Nightingale to press closer against the thorn. 'Press closer, little Nightingale,' cried the Tree, 'or the Day will come before the rose is finished.'

So the Nightingale pressed closer against the thorn, and louder and louder grew her song, for she sang of the birth of passion in the soul of a man and a maid.

And a delicate flush of pink came into the leaves of the rose, like the flush in the face of the bridegroom when he kisses the lips of the bride. But the thorn had not yet reached her heart, so the rose's heart remained white, for only a Nightingale's heart's-blood can crimson the heart of a rose.

And the Tree cried to the Nightingale to press closer against the thorn. 'Press closer, little Nightingale,' cried the Tree, 'or the Day will come before the rose is finished.'

So the Nightingale pressed closer against the thorn, and the thorn touched her heart, and a fierce pang of pain shot through her. Bitter, bitter was the pain, and wilder and wilder grew her song, for she sang of the Love that is perfected by Death, of the Love that dies not in the tomb.

And the marvellous rose became crimson, like the rose of the eastern sky. Crimson was the girdle of petals, and crimson as a ruby was the heart.

But the Nightingale's voice grew fainter, and her little wings began to beat, and a film came over her eyes. Fainter and fainter grew her song, and she felt something choking in her throat.

Then she gave one last burst of music. The white Moon heard it, and she forgot the dawn, and lingered on in the sky. The red rose heard it, and it trembled all over with ecstasy, and opened its petals to the cold morning air. Echo bore it to her purple cavern in the hills, and woke the sleeping shepherds from their dreams. It floated through the reeds of the river, and they carried its message to the sea.

'Look, look!' cried the Tree, 'the rose is finished now;' but the Nightingale made no answer, for she was lying dead in the long grass, with the thorn in her heart.

And at noon the Student opened his window and looked out.

'Why, what a wonderful piece of luck!' he cried; 'here is a red rose! I have never seen any rose like it in all my life. It is so beautiful that I am sure it has a long Latin name;' and he leaned down and plucked it.

Then he put on his hat, and ran up to the Professor's house with the rose in his hand.

The daughter of the Professor was sitting in the doorway winding blue silk on a reel, and her little dog was lying at her feet.

'You said that you would dance with me if I brought you a red rose,' cried the Student. 'Here is the reddest rose in all the world. You will wear it to-night next your heart, and as we dance together it will tell you how I love you.'

But the girl frowned.

'I am afraid it will not go with my dress,' she answered; 'and, besides, the Chamberlain's nephew has sent me some real jewels, and everybody knows that jewels cost far more than flowers.'

'Well upon my word, you are very ungrateful,' said the Student angrily; and he threw the rose into the street, where it fell into the gutter, and a cart-wheel went over it.

'Ungrateful!' said the girl. 'I tell you what, you are very rude; and, after all, who are you? Only a Student. Why, I don't believe you have even got silver buckles to your shoes as the Chamberlain's nephew has;' and she got up from her chair and went into the house.

'What a silly thing Love is!' said the Student as he walked away. 'It is not half as useful as Logic, for it does not prove anything, and it is always telling one of things that are not going to happen, and making one believe things that are not true. In fact, it is quite unpractical, and, as in this age to be practical is everything, I shall go back to Philosophy and study Metaphysics.'

So he returned to his room and pulled out a great dusty book, and began to read.

THE SELFISH GIANT

EVERY AFTERNOON, AS THEY WERE coming from school, the children used to go and play in the Giant's garden.

It was a large lovely garden, with soft green grass. Here and there over the grass stood beautiful flowers like stars, and there were twelve peach-trees that in the spring-time broke out into delicate blossoms of pink and pearl, and in the autumn bore rich fruit. The birds sat on the trees and sang so sweetly that the children used to stop their games in order to listen to them. 'How happy we are here!' they cried to each other.

One day the Giant came back. He had been to visit his friend the Cornish ogre, and had stayed with him for seven years. After the seven years were over he had said all that he had to say, for his conversation was limited, and he determined to return to his own castle. When he arrived he saw the children playing in the garden.

'What are you doing here?' he cried in a very gruff voice, and the children ran away.

'My own garden is my own garden,' said the Giant; 'any one can understand that, and I will allow nobody to play in it but myself.' So he built a high wall all round it, and put up a notice-board.

> TRESPASSERS
> WILL BE
> PROSECUTED

He was a very selfish Giant.

The poor children had now nowhere to play. They tried to play on the road, but the road was very dusty and full of hard stones, and they did not like it. They used to wander round the high walls when their lessons were over, and talk about the beautiful garden inside. 'How happy we were there!' they said to each other.

Then the Spring came, and all over the country there were little blossoms and little birds. Only in the garden of the Selfish Giant it was still winter. The birds did not care to sing in it as there were no children, and the trees forgot to blossom. Once a beautiful flower put its head out from the grass, but when it saw the notice-board it was so sorry for the children that it slipped back into the ground again, and went off to sleep. The only people who were pleased were the Snow and the Frost. 'Spring has forgotten this garden,' they cried, 'so we will live here all the year round.' The Snow covered up the grass with her great white cloak, and the Frost painted all the trees silver. Then they invited the North Wind to stay with them, and he came. He was wrapped in furs, and he roared all day about the garden, and blew the chimney-pots down. 'This is a delightful spot,' he said, 'we must ask the Hail on a visit.' So the Hail came. Every day for three hours he rattled on the roof of the castle till he broke most of the slates, and then he ran round and round the garden as fast as he could go. He was dressed in grey, and his breath was like ice.

'I cannot understand why the Spring is so late in coming,' said the Selfish Giant, as he sat at the window and looked out at his cold, white garden; 'I hope there will be a change in the weather.'

But the Spring never came, nor the Summer. The Autumn gave golden fruit to every garden, but to the Giant's garden she gave none. 'He is too selfish,' she said. So it was always Winter there, and the North Wind and the Hail, and the Frost, and the Snow danced about through the trees.

One morning the Giant was lying awake in bed when he heard some lovely music. It sounded so sweet to his ears that he thought it must be the King's musicians passing by. It was really only a little linnet singing outside his window, but it was so long since he had heard a bird sing in his garden that it seemed to him to be the most beautiful music in the world. Then the Hail stopped dancing over his head, and the North Wind ceased roaring, and a delicious perfume came to him through the open casement. 'I believe the Spring has come at last,' said the Giant; and he jumped out of bed and looked out.

What did he see?

He saw a most wonderful sight. Through a little hole in the wall the children had crept in, and they were sitting in the branches of the trees. In every tree that he could see there was a little child. And the trees were so glad to have the children back again that they had covered themselves with blossoms, and were waving their arms gently above the children's heads. The birds were flying about and twittering with delight, and the flowers were looking up through the green grass and laughing. It was a lovely scene, only in one corner it was still winter. It was the farthest corner of the garden, and in it was standing a little boy. He was so small that he could not reach up to the branches of the tree, and he was wandering all round it, crying bitterly. The poor tree was still covered with frost and snow, and the North Wind was blowing and roaring above it. 'Climb up! little boy,' said the Tree, and it bent its branches down as low at it could; but the boy was too tiny.

And the Giant's heart melted as he looked out. 'How selfish I have been!' he said: 'now I know why the Spring would not come here. I will put that poor little boy on the top of the tree, and then I will knock down the wall, and my garden shall be the children's playground for ever and ever.' He was really very sorry for what he had done.

So he crept downstairs and opened the front door quite softly, and went out into the garden. But when the children saw him they were so frightened that they all ran away, and the garden became winter again. Only the little boy did not run for his eyes were so full of tears that he did not see the Giant coming. And the Giant stole up behind him and took him gently in his hand, and put him up into the tree. And the tree broke at once into blossom, and the birds came and sang on it, and the little boy stretched out his two arms and flung them round the Giant's neck, and kissed him. And the other children when they saw that the Giant was not wicked any longer, came running back, and with them came the Spring. 'It is your garden now, little children,' said the Giant, and he took a great axe and knocked down the wall. And when the people were going to market at twelve o'clock they found the Giant playing with the children in the most beautiful garden they had ever seen.

All day long they played, and in the evening they came to the Giant to bid him good-bye.

'But where is your little companion?' he said: 'the boy I put into the tree.' The Giant loved him the best because he had kissed him.

'We don't know,' answered the children: 'he has gone away.'

'You must tell him to be sure and come to-morrow,' said the Giant. But the children said that they did not know where he lived and had never seen him before; and the Giant felt very sad.

Every afternoon, when school was over, the children came and played with the Giant. But the little boy whom the Giant loved was never seen again. The Giant was very kind to all the children, yet he longed for his first little friend, and often spoke of him. 'How I would like to see him!' he used to say.

Years went over, and the Giant grew very old and feeble. He could not play about any more, so he sat in a huge arm-chair, and watched the children at their games, and admired his garden. 'I have many beautiful flowers,' he said; 'but the children are the most beautiful flowers of all.'

One winter morning he looked out of his window as he was dressing. He did not hate the Winter now, for he knew that it was merely the Spring asleep, and that the flowers were resting.

Suddenly he rubbed his eyes in wonder and looked and looked. It certainly was a marvellous sight. In the farthest corner of the garden was a tree quite covered with lovely white blossoms. Its branches were golden, and silver fruit hung down from them, and underneath it stood the little boy he had loved.

Downstairs ran the Giant in great joy, and out into the garden. He hastened across the grass, and came near to the child. And when he came quite close his face grew red with anger, and he said, 'Who hath dared to wound thee?' For on the palms of the child's hands were the prints of two nails, and the prints of two nails were on the little feet.

'Who hath dared to wound thee?' cried the Giant, 'tell me, that I may take my big sword and slay him.'

'Nay,' answered the child: 'but these are the wounds of Love.'

'Who art thou?' said the Giant, and a strange awe fell on him, and he knelt before the little child.

And the child smiled on the Giant, and said to him, 'You let me play once in your garden, to-day you shall come with me to my garden, which is Paradise.'

And when the children ran in that afternoon, they found the Giant lying dead under the tree, all covered with white blossoms.

THE DEVOTED
FRIEND

ONE MORNING THE OLD WATER-RAT put his head out of his hole. He had bright beady eyes and stiff grey whiskers, and his tail was like a long bit of black indiarubber. The little ducks were swimming about in the pond, looking just like a lot of yellow canaries, and their mother, who was pure white with real red legs, was trying to teach them how to stand on their heads in the water.

'You will never be in the best society unless you can stand on your heads,' she kept saying to them; and every now and then she showed them how it was done. But the little ducks paid no attention to her. They were so young that they did not know what an advantage it is to be in society at all.

'What disobedient children!' cried the old Water-rat; 'they really deserve to be drowned.'

'Nothing of the kind,' answered the Duck; 'every one must make a beginning, and parents cannot be too patient.'

'Ah! I know nothing about the feelings of parents,' said the Water-rat: 'I am not a family man. In fact, I have never been married, and I never intend to be. Love is all very well in its way, but friendship is much higher. Indeed, I know of nothing in the world that is either nobler or rarer than a devoted friendship.'

'And what, pray, is your idea of the duties of a devoted friend?' asked a green Linnet, who was sitting on a willow-tree hard by, and had overheard the conversation.

'Yes, that is just what I want to know,' said the Duck; and she swam away to the end of the pond, and stood upon her head, in order to give her children a good example.

'What a silly question!' cried the Water-rat. 'I should expect my devoted friend to be devoted to me, of course.'

'And what would you do in return?' said the little bird, swinging upon a silver spray, and flapping his tiny wings.

'I don't understand you,' answered the Water-rat.

'Let me tell you a story on the subject,' said the Linnet.

'Is the story about me?' asked the Water-rat. 'If so, I will listen to it, for I am extremely fond of fiction.'

'It is applicable to you,' answered the Linnet; and he flew down, and alighting upon the bank, he told the story of The Devoted Friend.

'Once upon a time,' said the Linnet, 'there was an honest little fellow named Hans.'

'Was he very distinguished?' asked the Water-rat.

'No,' answered the Linnet, 'I don't think he was distinguished at all, except for his kind heart, and his funny, round, good-humoured face. He lived in a tiny cottage all by himself, and every day he worked in his garden. In all the country-side there was no garden so lovely as his. Sweet-Williams grew there, and Gilly-flowers, and Shepherds'-purses, and Fair-maids of France. There were damask Roses, and yellow Roses, lilac Crocuses and gold, purple Violets and white. Columbine and Ladysmock, Marjoram and Wild Basil, the Cowslip and the Flower-de-luce, the Daffodil and the Clove-Pink bloomed or blossomed in their proper order as the months went by, one flower taking another flower's place, so that there were always beautiful things to look at, and pleasant odours to smell.

'Little Hans had a great many friends, but the most devoted friend of all was big Hugh the Miller. Indeed, so devoted was the rich Miller to little Hans, that he would never go by his garden without leaning over the wall and plucking a large nosegay, or a handful of sweet herbs, or filling his pockets with plums and cherries if it was the fruit season.

' "Real friends should have everything in common," the Miller used to say, and little Hans nodded and smiled, and felt very proud of having a friend with such noble ideas.

'Sometimes, indeed, the neighbours thought it strange that the rich Miller never gave little Hans anything in return, though he had a hundred sacks of flour stored away in his mill, and six milch cows, and a large flock of woolly sheep; but Hans never troubled his head about these things, and nothing gave him greater pleasure than to listen to all the wonderful things the Miller used to say about the unselfishness of true friendship.

'So little Hans worked away in his garden. During the spring, the summer, and the autumn he was very happy, but when the winter came, and he had no fruit or flowers to bring to the market, he suffered a good deal from cold and hunger, and often had to go to bed without any supper but a few dried pears or some hard nuts. In the winter, also, he was extremely lonely, as the Miller never came to see him then.

' "There is no good in my going to see little Hans as long as the snow lasts," the Miller used to say to his wife, "for when people are in trouble they should be left alone and not be bothered by visitors. That at least is my idea about friendship, and I am sure I am right. So I shall wait till the spring comes, and then I shall pay him a visit, and he will be able to give me a large basket of primroses, and that will make him so happy."

' "You are certainly very thoughtful about others," answered the
Wife, as she sat in her comfortable armchair by the big pinewood fire;
"very thoughtful indeed. It is quite a treat to hear you talk about
friendship. I am sure the clergyman himself could not say such beautiful
things as you do, though he does live in a three-storied house, and wear
a gold ring on his little finger."

' "But could we not ask little Hans up here?" said the Miller's youngest
son. "If poor Hans is in trouble I will give him half my porridge, and
show him my white rabbits."

' "What a silly boy you are!" cried the Miller; "I really don't know
what is the use of sending you to school. You seem not to learn anything.
Why, if little Hans came up here, and saw our warm fire, and our good
supper, and our great cask of red wine, he might get envious, and envy
is a most terrible thing, and would spoil anybody's nature. I certainly
will not allow Hans' nature to be spoiled. I am his best friend, and I
will always watch over him, and see that he is not led into any temptations. Besides, if Hans came here, he might ask me to let him have some
flour on credit, and that I could not do. Flour is one thing, and
friendship is another, and they should not be confused. Why, the words
are spelt differently, and mean quite different things. Everybody can
see that."

' "How well you talk!" said the Miller's Wife, pouring herself out a
large glass of warm ale; "really I feel quite drowsy. It is just like being
in church."

' "Lots of people act well," answered the Miller; "but very few people
talk well, which shows that talking is much the more difficult thing of
the two, and much the finer thing also;" and he looked sternly across
the table at his little son, who felt so ashamed of himself that he hung
his head down, and grew quite scarlet and began to cry into his tea.
However, he was so young that you must excuse him.'

'Is that the end of the story?' asked the Water-rat.

'Certainly not,' answered the Linnet, 'that is the beginning.'

'Then you are quite behind the age,' said the Water-rat. 'Every good
storyteller nowadays starts with the end, and then goes on to the
beginning, and concludes with the middle. That is the new method. I
heard all about it the other day from a critic who was walking round
the pond with a young man. He spoke of the matter at great length,
and I am sure he must have been right, for he had blue spectacles and
a bald head, and whenever the young man made any remark, he always
answered "Pooh!" But pray go on with your story. I like the Miller
immensely. I have all kinds of beautiful sentiments myself, so there is a
great sympathy between us.'

'Well,' said the Linnet, hopping now on one leg and now on the
other, 'as soon as the winter was over, and the primroses began to open
their pale yellow stars, the Miller said to his wife that he would go down
and see little Hans.

' "Why, what a good heart you have!" cried his Wife; "you are always
thinking of others. And mind you take the big basket with you for the
flowers."

'So the Miller tied the sails of the windmill together with a strong iron chain, and went down the hill with the basket on his arm.

' "Good morning, little Hans," said the Miller.

' "Good morning," said Hans, leaning on his spade, and smiling from ear to ear.

' "And how have you been all the winter?" said the Miller.

' "Well, really," cried Hans, "it is very good of you to ask, very good indeed. I am afraid I had rather a hard time of it, but now the spring has come, and I am quite happy, and all my flowers are doing well."

' "We often talked of you during the winter, Hans," said the Miller, "and wondered how you were getting on."

' "That was kind of you," said Hans; "I was half afraid you had forgotten me."

' "Hans, I am surprised at you," said the Miller; "friendship never forgets. That is the wonderful thing about it, but I am afraid you don't understand the poetry of life. How lovely your primroses are looking, by-the-bye!"

' "They are certainly very lovely," said Hans, "and it is a most lucky thing for me that I have so many. I am going to bring them into the market and sell them to the Burgomaster's daughter, and buy back my wheelbarrow with the money."

' "Buy back your wheelbarrow? You don't mean to say you have sold it? What a very stupid thing to do!"

' "Well, the fact is," said Hans, "that I was obliged to. You see the winter was a very bad time for me, and I really had no money at all to buy bread with. So I first sold the silver buttons off my Sunday coat, and then I sold my silver chain, and then I sold my big pipe, and at last I sold my wheelbarrow. But I am going to buy them all back again now."

' "Hans," said the Miller, "I will give you my wheelbarrow. It is not in very good repair, indeed, one side is gone, and there is something wrong with the wheel-spokes, but in spite of that I will give it to you. I know it is very generous of me, and a great many people would think me extremely foolish for parting with it, but I am not like the rest of the world. I think that generosity is the essence of friendship, and, besides, I have got a new wheelbarrow for myself. Yes, you may set your mind at ease, I will give you my wheelbarrow."

' "Well, really, that is generous of you," said little Hans, and his funny round face glowed all over with pleasure. "I can easily put it in repair, as I have a plank of wood in the house."

' "A plank of wood!" said the Miller; "why, that is just what I want for the roof of my barn. There is a very large hole in it, and the corn will all get damp if I don't stop it up. How lucky you mentioned it! It is quite remarkable how one good action always breeds another. I have given you my wheelbarrow, and now you are going to give me your plank. Of course, the wheelbarrow is worth far more than the plank, but true friendship never notices things like that. Pray get it at once, and I will set to work at my barn this very day."

' "Certainly," cried little Hans, and he ran into the shed and dragged the plank out.

' "It is not a very big plank," said the Miller, looking at it, "and I am afraid that after I have mended my barn-roof there won't be any left for you to mend the wheelbarrow with; but, of course, that is not my fault. And now, as I have given you my wheelbarrow, I am sure you would like to give me some flowers in return. Here is the basket, and mind you fill it quite full."

' "Quite full?" said little Hans, rather sorrowfully, for it was really a very big basket, and he knew that if he filled it he would have no flowers left for the market, and he was very anxious to get his silver buttons back.

' "Well, really," answered the Miller, "as I have given you my wheelbarrow, I don't think that it is much to ask you for a few flowers. I may be wrong, but I should have thought that friendship, true friendship, was quite free from selfishness of any kind."

' "My dear friend, my best friend," cried little Hans, "you are welcome to all the flowers in my garden. I would much sooner have your good opinion than my silver buttons, any day;" and he ran and plucked all his pretty primroses, and filled the Miller's basket.

' "Good-bye, little Hans," said the Miller, and he went up the hill with the plank on his shoulder, and the big basket in his hand.

' "Good-bye," said little Hans, and he began to dig away quite merrily, he was so pleased about the wheelbarrow.

'The next day he was nailing up some honeysuckle against the porch, when he heard the Miller's voice calling to him from the road. So he jumped off the ladder, and ran down the garden, and looked over the wall.

'There was the Miller with a large sack of flour on his back.

' "Dear little Hans," said the Miller, "would you mind carrying this sack of flour for me to market?"

' "Oh, I am so sorry," said Hans, "but I am really very busy to-day. I have got all my creepers to nail up, and all my flowers to water, and all my grass to roll."

' "Well, really," said the Miller, "I think, that considering that I am going to give you my wheelbarrow it is rather unfriendly of you to refuse."

' "Oh, don't say that," cried little Hans, "I wouldn't be unfriendly for the whole world;" and he ran in for his cap, and trudged off with the big sack on his shoulders.

'It was a very hot day, and the road was terribly dusty, and before Hans had reached the sixth milestone he was so tired that he had to sit down and rest. However, he went on bravely, and at last he reached the market. After he had waited there for some time, he sold the sack of flour for a very good price, and then he returned home at once, for he was afraid that if he stopped too late he might meet some robbers on the way.

' "It has certainly been a hard day," said little Hans to himself as he was going to bed, "but I am glad I did not refuse the Miller, for he is my best friend and, besides, he is going to give me his wheelbarrow."

'Early the next morning the Miller came down to get the money for his sack of flour, but little Hans was so tired that he was still in bed.

' "Upon my word," said the Miller, "you are very lazy. Really, considering that I am going to give you my wheelbarrow, I think you might work harder. Idleness is a great sin, and I certainly don't like any of my friends to be idle or sluggish. You must not mind my speaking quite plainly to you. Of course I should not dream of doing so if I were not your friend. But what is the good of friendship if one cannot say exactly what one means? Anybody can say charming things and try to please and to flatter, but a true friend always says unpleasant things, and does not mind giving pain. Indeed, if he is a really true friend he prefers it, for he knows that then he is doing good."

' "I am very sorry," said little Hans, rubbing his eyes and pulling off his nightcap, "but I was so tired that I thought I would lie in bed for a little time, and listen to the birds singing. Do you know that I always work better after hearing the birds sing?"

' "Well, I am glad of that," said the Miller, clapping little Hans on the back, "for I want you to come up to the mill as soon as you are dressed and mend my barn-roof for me."

'Poor little Hans was very anxious to go and work in his garden, for his flowers had not been watered for two days, but he did not like to refuse the Miller, as he was such a good friend to him.

' "Do you think it would be unfriendly of me if I said I was busy?" he enquired in a shy and timid voice.

' "Well, really," answered the Miller, "I do not think it is much to ask of you, considering that I am going to give you my wheelbarrow; but, of course, if you refuse I will go and do it myself."

' "Oh! on no account," cried little Hans; and he jumped out of bed, and dressed himself, and went up to the barn.

'He worked there all day long, till sunset, and at sunset the Miller came to see how he was getting on.

' "Have you mended the hole in the roof yet, little Hans?" cried the Miller in a cheery voice.

' "It is quite mended," answered little Hans, coming down the ladder.

' "Ah!" said the Miller, "there is no work so delightful as the work one does for others."

' "It is certainly a great privilege to hear you talk," answered little Hans, sitting down and wiping his forehead, "a very great privilege. But I am afraid I shall never have such beautiful ideas as you have."

' "Oh! they will come to you," said the Miller, "but you must take more pains. At present you have only the practice of friendship; some day you will have the theory also."

' "Do you really think I shall?" asked little Hans.

' "I have no doubt of it," answered the Miller, "but now that you have mended the roof, you had better go home and rest, for I want you to drive my sheep to the mountain to-morrow."

'Poor little Hans was afraid to say anything to this, and early the next morning the Miller brought his sheep round to the cottage, and Hans started off with them to the mountain. It took him the whole day to get there and back; and when he returned he was so tired that he went off to sleep in his chair, and did not wake up till it was broad daylight.

' "What a delightful time I shall have in my garden!" he said, and he went to work at once.

'But somehow he was never able to look after his flowers at all, for his friend the Miller was always coming round and sending him off on long errands, or getting him to help at the mill. Little Hans was very much distressed at times, as he was afraid his flowers would think he had forgotten them, but he consoled himself by the reflection that the Miller was his best friend. "Besides," he used to say, "he is going to give me his wheelbarrow, and that is an act of pure generosity."

'So little Hans worked away for the Miller, and the Miller said all kinds of beautiful things about friendship, which Hans took down in a notebook, and used to read over at night, for he was a very good scholar.

'Now it happened that one evening little Hans was sitting by his fireside when a loud rap came at the door. It was a very wild night, and the wind was blowing and roaring round the house so terribly that at first he thought it was merely the storm. But a second rap came, and then a third, louder than any of the others.

' "It is some poor traveller," said little Hans to himself, and he ran to the door.

'There stood the Miller with a lantern in one hand and a big stick in the other.

' "Dear little Hans," cried the Miller, "I am in great trouble. My little boy has fallen off a ladder and hurt himself, and I am going for the Doctor. But he lives so far away, and it is such a bad night, that it has just occurred to me that it would be much better if you went instead of me. You know I am going to give you my wheelbarrow, and so it is only fair that you should do something for me in return."

' "Certainly," cried little Hans, "I take it quite as a compliment your coming to me, and I will start off at once. But you must lend me your lantern, as the night is so dark that I am afraid I might fall into the ditch."

' "I am very sorry," answered the Miller, "but it is my new lantern, and it would be a great loss to me if anything happened to it."

' "Well, never mind, I will do without it," cried little Hans, and he took down his great fur coat, and his warm scarlet cap, and tied a muffler round his throat, and started off.

'What a dreadful storm it was! The night was so black that little Hans could hardly see, and the wind was so strong that he could hardly stand. However, he was very courageous, and after he had been walking about three hours, he arrived at the Doctor's house, and knocked at the door.

' "Who is there?" cried the Doctor, putting his head out of his bedroom window.

' "Little Hans, Doctor."

' "What do you want, little Hans?"

' "The Miller's son has fallen from a ladder, and has hurt himself, and the Miller wants you to come at once."

' "All right!" said the Doctor; and he ordered his horse, and his big boots, and his lantern, and came downstairs, and rode off in the direction of the Miller's house, little Hans trudging behind him.

'But the storm grew worse and worse, and the rain fell in torrents, and little Hans could not see where he was going, or keep up with the horse. At last he lost his way, and wandered off on the moor, which was a very dangerous place, as it was full of deep holes, and there poor little Hans was drowned. His body was found the next day by some goatherds, floating in a great pool of water, and was brought back by them to the cottage.

'Everybody went to little Hans' funeral, as he was so popular, and the Miller was the chief mourner.

' "As I was his best friend," said the Miller, "it is only fair that I should have the best place;" so he walked at the head of the procession in a long black cloak, and every now and then he wiped his eyes with a big pocket-handkerchief.

' "Little Hans is certainly a great loss to everyone," said the Blacksmith, when the funeral was over, and they were all seated comfortably in the inn, drinking spiced wine and eating sweet cakes.

' "A great loss to me at any rate," answered the Miller; "why, I had as good as given him my wheelbarrow, and now I really don't know what to do with it. It is very much in my way at home, and it is in such bad repair that I could not get anything for it if I sold it. I will certainly take care not to give away anything again. One certainly suffers for being generous.'"

'Well?' said the Water-rat, after a long pause.

'Well, that is the end,' said the Linnet.

'But what became of the Miller?' asked the Water-rat.

'Oh! I really don't know,' replied the Linnet; 'and I am sure that I don't care.'

'It is quite evident then that you have no sympathy in your nature,' said the Water-rat.

'I am afraid you don't quite see the moral of the story,' remarked the Linnet.

'The what?' screamed the Water-rat.

'The moral.'

'Do you mean to say that the story has a moral?'

'Certainly,' said the Linnet.

'Well, really,' said the Water-rat, in a very angry manner, 'I think you should have told me that before you began. If you had done so, I certainly would not have listened to you; in fact, I should have said "Pooh," like the critic. However, I can say it now;' so he shouted out 'Pooh,' at the top of his voice, gave a whisk with his tail, and went back into his hole.

'And how do you like the Water-rat?' asked the Duck, who came paddling up some minutes afterwards. 'He has a great many good points, but for my own part I have a mother's feelings, and I can never look at a confirmed bachelor without the tears coming into my eyes.'

'I am rather afraid that I have annoyed him,' answered the Linnet. 'The fact is that I told him a story with a moral.'

'Ah! that is always a very dangerous thing to do,' said the Duck.

And I quite agree with her.

THE CANTERVILLE GHOST

A Hylo-Idealistic Romance

When the American minister, Mr Hiram B. Otis, bought Canterville Chase, Lord Canterville warned him that the house was haunted by a ghost who had struck terror into the hearts of its occupants for three centuries. However, the American and his exuberant family are unimpressed and unafraid ...

2

THE STORM RAGED FIERCELY ALL that night, but nothing of particular note occurred. The next morning, however, when they came down to breakfast, they found the terrible stain of blood once again on the floor. 'I don't think it can be the fault of the Paragon Detergent,' said Washington, 'for I have tried it with everything. It must be the ghost.' He accordingly rubbed out the stain a second time, but the second morning it appeared again. The third morning also it was there, though the library had been locked up at night by Mr Otis himself, and the key carried upstairs. The whole family were now quite interested; Mr Otis began to suspect that he had been too dogmatic in his denial of the existence of ghosts, Mrs Otis expressed her intention of joining the Psychical Society, and Washington prepared a long letter to Messrs Myers and Podmore on the subject of the Permanence of Sanguineous Stains when connected with crime. That night all doubts about the objective existence of phantasmata were removed for ever.

The day had been warm and sunny; and, in the cool of the evening, the whole family went out for a drive. They did not return home till nine o'clock, when they had a light supper. The conversation in no way turned upon ghosts, so there were not even those primary conditions of receptive expectation which so often precede the presentation of psychical phenomena. The subjects discussed, as I have since learned from Mr Otis, were merely such as form the ordinary conversation of cultured Americans of the better class, such as the immense superiority of Miss Fanny Davenport over Sarah Bernhardt as an actress; the difficulty of obtaining green corn, buckwheat cakes, and hominy, even in the best English houses; the importance of Boston in the development of the world-soul; the advantages of the baggage check system in railway travelling; and the sweetness of the New York accent as compared to the London drawl. No mention at all was made of the supernatural, nor was Sir Simon de Canterville alluded to in any way. At eleven o'clock the family retired, and by half past all the lights were out. Some time after, Mr Otis was awakened by a curious noise in the corridor, outside his room. It sounded like the clank of metal, and seemed to be coming nearer every moment. He got up at once, struck a match, and looked at the time. It was exactly one o'clock. He was quite calm, and felt his pulse, which was not at all feverish. The strange noise still continued, and with it he heard distinctly the sound of footsteps. He put on his slippers, took a small oblong phial out of his dressing-case, and opened the door. Right in front of him he saw, in the wan moonlight, an old man of terrible aspect. His eyes were as red as burning coals; long grey hair fell over his shoulders in matted coils; his garments, which were of antique cut, were soiled and ragged, and from his wrists and ankles hung heavy manacles and rusty gyves.

'My dear sir,' said Mr Otis, 'I really must insist on your oiling those chains, and have brought you for that purpose a small bottle of the Tammany Rising Sun Lubricator. It is said to be completely efficacious upon one application, and there are several testimonials to that effect on the wrapper from some of our most eminent native divines. I shall leave it here for you by the bedroom candles, and will be happy to supply you with more should you require it.' With these words the United States Minister laid the bottle down on a marble table, and, closing his door, retired to rest.

For a moment the Canterville ghost stood quite motionless in natural indignation; then, dashing the bottle violently upon the polished floor, he fled down the corridor, uttering hollow groans, and emitting a ghastly green light. Just, however, as he reached the top of the great oak staircase, a door was flung open, two little white-robed figures appeared, and a large pillow whizzed past his head! There was evidently no time to be lost, so, hastily adopting the Fourth Dimension of Space as a means of escape, he vanished through the wainscoting, and the house became quite quiet.

On reaching a small secret chamber in the left wing, he leaned up against a moonbeam to recover his breath, and began to try and realise his position. Never, in a brilliant and uninterrupted career of three hundred years, had he been so grossly insulted. He thought of the Dowager Duchess, whom he had frightened into a fit as she stood before the glass in her lace and diamonds; of the four housemaids, who had gone off into hysterics when he merely grinned at them through the curtains of one of the spare bedrooms; of the rector of the parish, whose candle he had blown out as he was coming late one night from the library, and who had been under the care of Sir William Gull ever since, a perfect martyr to nervous disorders; and of old Madame de Tremouillac, who, having wakened up one morning early and seen a skeleton seated in an arm-chair by the fire reading her diary, had been confined to her bed for six weeks with an attack of brain fever, and, on her recovery, had become reconciled to the Church, and had broken off her connection with that notorious sceptic Monsieur de Voltaire. He remembered the terrible night when the wicked Lord Canterville was found choking in his dressing-room, with the knave of diamonds half-way down his throat, and confessed, just before he died, that he had cheated Charles James Fox out of £50,000 at Crockford's by means of that very card, and swore that the ghost had made him swallow it. All his great achievements came back to him again, from the butler who had shot himself in the pantry because he had seen a green hand tapping at the window pane, to the beautiful Lady Stutfield, who was always obliged to wear a black velvet band round her throat to hide the mark of five fingers burnt upon her white skin, and who drowned herself at last in the carp-pond at the end of the King's Walk. With the enthusiastic egotism of the true artist he went over his most celebrated performances, and smiled bitterly to himself as he recalled to mind his last appearance as 'Red Ruben, or the Strangled Babe', his début as 'Gaunt Gibeon, the Blood-sucker of Bexley Moor', and the furore he had excited one lovely June evening by merely playing ninepins with his own bones upon the lawn-tennis ground. And after all this, some wretched modern Americans were to come and offer him the Rising Sun Lubricator, and throw pillows at his head! It was quite unbearable. Besides, no ghosts in history had ever been treated in this manner. Accordingly, he determined to have vengeance, and remained till daylight in an attitude of deep thought.

3

THE NEXT MORNING WHEN THE Otis family met at breakfast, they discussed the ghost at some length. The United States Minister was naturally a little annoyed to find that his present had not been accepted. 'I have no wish,' he said, 'to do the ghost any personal injury, and I must say that, considering the length of time he has been in the house, I don't think it is at all polite to throw pillows at him' – a very just remark, at which, I am sorry to say, the twins burst into shouts of laughter. 'Upon the other hand,' he continued, 'if he really declines to use the Rising

Sun Lubricator, we shall have to take his chains from him. It would be quite impossible to sleep, with such a noise going on   outside the bedrooms.'

For the rest of the week, however, they were undisturbed, the only thing that excited any attention being the continual renewal of the blood-stain on the library floor. This certainly was very strange, as the door was always locked at night by Mr Otis, and the windows kept closely barred. The chameleon-like colour, also, of the stain excited a good deal of comment. Some mornings it was a dull (almost Indian) red, then it would be vermilion, then a rich purple, and once when they came down for family prayers, according to the simple rites of the Free American Reformed Episcopalian Church, they found it a bright emerald-green. These kaleidoscopic changes naturally amused the party very much, and bets on the subject were freely made every evening. The only person who did not enter into the joke was little Virginia, who, for some unexplained reason, was always a good deal distressed at the sight of the blood-stain, and very nearly cried the morning it was emerald-green.

The second appearance of the ghost was on Sunday night. Shortly after they had gone to bed they were suddenly alarmed by a fearful crash in the hall. Rushing downstairs, they found that a large suit of old armour had become detached from its stand, and had fallen on the stone floor, while, seated in a high-backed chair, was the Canterville ghost, rubbing his knees with an expression of acute agony on his face. The twins, having brought their peashooters with them, at once discharged two pellets on him, with that accuracy of aim which can only be attained by long and careful practice on a writing-master, while the United States Minister covered him with his revolver, and called upon him, in accordance with Californian etiquette, to hold up his hands! The ghost started up with a wild shriek of rage, and swept through them like a mist, extinguishing Washington Otis's candle as he passed, and so leaving them all in total darkness. On reaching the top of the staircase he recovered himself, and determined to give his celebrated peal of demoniac laughter. This he had on more than one occasion found extremely useful. It was said to have turned Lord Raker's wig grey in a single night, and had certainly made three of Lady Canterville's French governesses   give warning before their month was up. He accordingly laughed his most horrible laugh, till the old vaulted roof rang and rang again, but hardly had the fearful echo died away when a door opened, and Mrs Otis came out in a light blue dressing-gown. 'I am afraid you are far from well,' she said, 'and have brought you a bottle of Dr Dobell's tincture. If it is indigestion, you will find it a most excellent remedy.' The ghost glared at her in fury, and began at once to make preparations for turning himself into a large black dog, an accomplishment for which he was justly renowned, and to which the family doctor always attributed the permanent idiocy of Lord Canterville's uncle, the Hon Thomas Horton. The sound of approaching footsteps, however, made him hesitate in his fell purpose, so he contented himself with becoming faintly phosphorescent, and vanished with a deep churchyard groan, just as the twins had come up to him.

On reaching his room he entirely broke down, and became a prey to the most violent agitation. The vulgarity of the twins, and the gross materialism of Mrs Otis, were naturally extremely annoying, but what really distressed him most was, that he had been unable to wear the suit of mail. He had hoped that even modern Americans would be thrilled by the sight of a Spectre In Armour, if for no more sensible reason, at least out of respect for their national poet Longfellow, over whose graceful and attractive poetry he himself had whiled away many a weary hour when the Cantervilles were up in town. Besides, it was his own suit. He had worn it with success at the Kenilworth tournament, and had been highly complimented on it by no less a person than the Virgin Queen herself. Yet when he had put it on, he had been completely overpowered by the weight of the huge breastplate and steel casque, and had fallen heavily on the stone pavement, barking both his knees severely, and bruising the knuckles of his right hand.

For some days after this he was extremely ill, and hardly stirred out of his room at all, except to keep the blood-stain in proper repair. However, by taking great care of himself, he recovered, and resolved to make a third attempt to frighten the United States Minister and his family. He selected Friday, the 17th of August, for his appearance, and spent most of that day in looking over his wardrobe, ultimately deciding in favour of a large slouched hat with a red feather, a winding-sheet frilled at the wrists and neck, and a rusty dagger. Towards evening a violent storm of rain came on, and the wind was so high that all the windows and doors in the old house shook and rattled. In fact, it was just such weather as he loved. His plan of action was this. He was to make his way quietly to Washington Otis's room, gibber at him from the foot of the bed, and stab himself three times in the throat to the sound of slow music. He bore Washington a special grudge, being quite aware that it was he who was in the habit of removing the famous Canterville blood-stain, by means of Pinkerton's Paragon Detergent. Having reduced the reckless and foolhardy youth to a condition of abject terror, he was then to proceed to the room occupied by the United States Minister and his wife, and there to place a clammy hand on Mrs Otis's forehead, while he hissed into her trembling husband's ear the awful secrets of the charnel-house. With regard to little Virginia, he had not quite made up his mind. She had never insulted him in any way, and was pretty and gentle. A few hollow groans from the wardrobe, he thought, would be more than sufficient, or, if that failed to wake her, he might grabble at the counterpane with palsy-twitching fingers. As for the twins, he was quite determined to teach them a lesson. The first thing to be done was, of course, to sit upon their chests, so as to produce the stifling sensation of nightmare. Then, as their beds were quite close to each other, to stand between them in the form of a green icy-cold corpse, till they became paralysed with fear, and finally, to throw off the winding-sheet, and crawl round the room, with white bleached bones and one rolling eyeball, in the character of 'Dumb Daniel, or the Suicide's Skeleton', a rôle in which he had on more than one occasion produced a great effect, and which he considered quite equal to his famous part of 'Martin the Maniac, or the Masked Mystery'.

At half past ten he heard the family going to bed. For some time he was disturbed by wild shrieks of laughter from the twins, who, with the light-hearted gaiety of schoolboys, were evidently amusing themselves before they retired to rest, but at a quarter past eleven all was still, and, as midnight sounded, he sallied forth. The owl beat against the window panes, the raven croaked from the old yew-tree, and the wind wandered moaning round the house like a lost soul; but the Otis family slept unconscious of their doom, and high above the rain and storm he could hear the steady snoring of the Minister for the United States. He stepped stealthily out of the wainscoting, with an evil smile on his cruel, wrinkled mouth, and the moon hid her face in a cloud as he stole past the great oriel window, where his own arms and those of his murdered wife were blazoned in azure and gold. On and on he glided, like an evil shadow, the very darkness seeming to loathe him as he passed. Once he thought he heard something call, and stopped; but it was only the baying of a dog from the Red Farm, and he went on, muttering strange sixteenth-century curses, and ever and anon brandishing the rusty dagger in the midnight air. Finally he reached the corner of the passage that led to luckless Washington's room. For a moment he paused there, the wind blowing his long grey locks about his head, and twisting into grotesque and fantastic folds the nameless horror of the dead man's shroud. Then the clock struck the quarter, and he felt the time was come. He chuckled to himself, and turned the corner; but no sooner had he done so, than, with a piteous wail of terror, he fell back, and hid his blanched face in his long, bony hands. Right in front of him was standing a horrible spectre, motionless as a carven image, and monstrous as a madman's dream! Its head was bald and burnished; its face round, and fat, and white; and hideous laughter seemed to have writhed its features into an eternal grin. From the eyes streamed rays of scarlet light, the mouth was a wide well of fire, and a hideous garment, like to his own, swathed with its silent snows the Titan form. On its breast was a placard with strange writing in antique characters, some scroll of shame it seemed, some record of wild sins, some awful calendar of crime, and, with its right hand, it bore aloft a falchion of gleaming steel.

Never having seen a ghost before, he naturally was terribly frightened, and, after a second hasty glance at the awful phantom, he fled back to his room, tripping up in his long winding-sheet as he sped down the corridor, and finally dropping the rusty dagger into the Minister's jack-boots, where it was found in the morning by the butler. Once in the privacy of his own apartment, he flung himself down on a small pallet-bed, and hid his face under the clothes. After a time, however, the brave old Canterville spirit asserted itself, and he determined to go and speak to the other ghost as soon as it was daylight. Accordingly, just as the dawn was touching the hills with silver, he returned towards the spot where he had first laid eyes on the grisly phantom, feeling that, after all, two ghosts were better than one, and that, by the aid of his new friend, he might safely grapple with the twins. On reaching the spot, however, a terrible sight met his gaze. Something had evidently happened to the spectre, for the light had entirely faded from its hollow eyes, the gleaming falchion had fallen from its hand, and it was leaning up against the wall in a strained and uncomfortable attitude. He rushed foward and seized it in his arms, when, to his horror, the head slipped off and rolled on the floor, the body assumed a recumbent posture, and he found himself clasping a white dimity bed-curtain, with a sweeping-brush, a kitchen cleaver, and a hollow turnip lying at his feet! Unable to understand this curious transformation, he clutched the placard with feverish haste, and there, in the grey morning light, he read these fearful words:

> # YE OTIS GHOSTE.
> ## Ye Onlie True and Originale Spook.
> ## Beware of Ye Imitations.
> ### All others are
> ### Counterfeite.

The whole thing flashed across him. He had been tricked, foiled, and outwitted! The old Canterville look came into his eyes; he ground his toothless gums together; and, raising his withered hands high above his head, swore, according to the picturesque phraseology of the antique school, that when Chanticleer had sounded twice his merry horn, deeds of blood would be wrought, and Murder walk abroad with silent feet.

Hardly had he finished this awful oath when, from the red-tiled roof of a distant homestead, a cock crew. He laughed a long, low, bitter laugh, and waited. Hour after hour he waited, but the cock, for some strange reason, did not crow again. Finally, at half past seven, the arrival of the housemaids made him give up his fearful vigil, and he stalked back to his room, thinking of his vain hope and baffled purpose. There he consulted several books of ancient chivalry, of which he was exceedingly fond, and found that, on every occasion on which his oath had been used, Chanticleer had always crowed a second time. 'Perdition seize the naughty fowl,' he muttered, 'I have seen the day when, with my stout spear, I would have run him through the gorge, and made him crow for me an 'twere in death!' He then retired to a comfortable lead coffin, and stayed there till evening.

4

THE NEXT DAY THE GHOST was very weak and tired. The terrible excitement of the last four weeks was beginning to have its effect. His nerves were completely shattered, and he started at the slightest noise. For five days he kept his room, and at last made up his mind to give up the point of the blood-stain on the library floor. If the Otis family did not want it, they clearly did not deserve it. They were evidently people on a low, material plane of existence, and quite incapable of appreciating the symbolic value of sensuous phenomena. The question of phantasmic apparitions, and the development of astral bodies, was of course quite a different matter, and really not under his control. It was his solemn duty to appear in the corridor once a week, and to gibber from the large oriel window on the first and third Wednesday in every month, and he did not see how he could honourably escape from his obligations. It is quite true that his life had been very evil, but, upon the other hand, he was most conscientious in all things connected with the supernatural. For the next three Saturdays, accordingly, he traversed the corridor as usual between midnight and three o'clock, taking every possible precaution against being either heard or seen. He removed his boots, trod as lightly as possible on the old worm-eaten boards, wore a large black velvet cloak, and was careful to use the Rising Sun Lubricator for oiling his chains. I am bound to acknowledge that it was with a good deal of difficulty that he brought himself to adopt this last mode of protection. However, one night, while the family were at dinner, he slipped into Mr Otis's bedroom and carried off the bottle. He felt a little humiliated at first, but afterwards was sensible enough to see that there was a great deal to be said for the invention, and, to a certain degree, it served his purpose. Still, in spite of everything, he was not left unmolested. Strings were continually being stretched across the corridor, over which he tripped in the dark, and on one occasion, while dressed for the part of 'Black Isaac, or the Huntsman of Hogley Woods', he met with a severe fall, through treading on a butter-slide, which the twins had constructed from the entrance of the Tapestry Chamber to the top of the oak staircase. This last insult so enraged him, that he resolved to assert his dignity, and determined to visit the insolent young Etonians the next night in his celebrated character of 'Reckless Rupert, or the Headless Earl'.

He had not appeared in this disguise for more than seventy years; in fact, not since he had so frightened pretty Lady Barbara Modish by means of it, that she suddenly broke off her engagement with the present Lord Canterville's grandfather, and ran away to Gretna Green with handsome Jack Castleton, declaring that nothing in the world would induce her to marry into a family that allowed such a horrible phantom to walk up and down the terrace at twilight. Poor Jack was afterwards shot in a duel by Lord Canterville on Wandsworth Common, and Lady Barbara died of a broken heart at Tunbridge Wells before the year was out, so, in every way, it had been a great success. It was, however, an extremely difficult 'make-up', if I may use such a theatrical expression in connection with one of the greatest mysteries of the supernatural, or, to employ a more scientific term, the higher-natural world and it took him fully three hours to make his preparations. At last everything was ready, and he was very pleased with his appearance.

The big leather riding-boots that went with the dress were just a little too large for him, and he could only find one of the two horse-pistols, but, on the whole, he was quite satisfied, and at a quarter past one he glided out of the wainscoting and crept down the corridor. On reaching the room occupied by the twins, which I should mention was called the Blue Bed Chamber, on account of the colour of its hangings, he found the door just ajar. Wishing to make an effective entrance, he flung it wide open, when a heavy jug of water fell right down on him, wetting him to the skin, and just missing his left shoulder by a couple of inches. At the same moment he heard stifled shrieks of laughter proceeding from the four-post bed. The shock to his nervous system was so great that he fled back to his room as hard as he could go, and the next day he was laid up with a severe cold. The only thing that at all consoled him in the whole affair was the fact that he had not brought his head with him, for, had he done so, the consequences might have been very serious.

He now gave up all hope of ever frightening this rude American family, and contented himself, as a rule, with creeping about the passages in list slippers, with a thick red muffler round his throat for fear of draughts, and a small arquebuse, in case he should be attacked by the twins. The final blow he received occurred on the 19th of September. He had gone downstairs to the great entrance-hall, feeling sure that there, at any rate, he would be quite unmolested, and was amusing himself by making satirical remarks on the large Saroni photographs of the United States Minister and his wife, which had now taken the place of the Canterville family pictures. He was simply but neatly clad in a long shroud, spotted with churchyard mould, had tied up his jaw with a strip of yellow linen, and carried a small lantern and a sexton's spade. In fact, he was dressed for the character of 'Jonas the Graveless, or the Corpse-Snatcher of Chertsey Barn', one of his most remarkable impersonations, and one which the Cantervilles had every reason to remember, as it was the real origin of their quarrel with their neighbour, Lord Rufford. It was about a quarter past two o'clock in the morning, and, as far as he could ascertain, no one was stirring. As he was strolling towards the library, however, to see if there were any traces left of the bloodstain, suddenly there leaped out on him from a dark corner two figures, who waved their arms wildly above their heads, and shrieked out 'BOO!' in his ear.

Seized with a panic, which, under the circumstances, was only natural, he rushed for the staircase, but found Washington Otis waiting for him there with the big garden-syringe; and being thus hemmed in by his enemies on every side, and driven almost to bay, he vanished into the great iron stove, which, fortunately for him, was not lit, and had to make his way home through the flues and chimneys, arriving at his own room in a terrible state of dirt, disorder, and despair.

After this he was not seen again on any nocturnal expedition. The twins lay in wait for him on several occasions, and strewed the passages with nutshells every night to the great annoyance of their parents and the servants, but it was of no avail. It was quite evident that his feelings were so wounded that he would not appear. Mr Otis consequently resumed his great work on the history of the Democratic Party, on which he had been engaged for some years; Mrs Otis organised a wonderful clambake, which amazed the whole county; the boys took to lacrosse, euchre, poker, and other American national games; and Virginia rode about the lanes on her pony, accompanied by the young Duke of Cheshire, who had come to spend the last week of his holidays at Canterville Chase. It was generally assumed that the ghost had gone away, and, in fact, Mr Otis wrote a letter to that effect to Lord Canterville, who, in reply, expressed his great pleasure at the news, and sent his best congratulations to the Minister's worthy wife.

The Otises, however, were deceived, for the ghost was still in the house, and though now almost an invalid, was by no means ready to let matters rest, particularly as he heard that among the guests was the young Duke of Cheshire, whose grand-uncle, Lord Francis Stilton, had once bet a hundred guineas with Colonel Carbury that he would play dice with the Canterville ghost, and was found the next morning lying on the floor of the card-room in such a helpless paralytic state, that though he lived on to a great age, he was never able to say anything again but 'Double Sixes'. The story was well known at the time, though, of course, out of respect to the feelings of the two noble families, every attempt was made to hush it up; and a full account of all the circumstances connected with it will be found in the third volume of Lord Tattle's *Recollections of the Prince Regent and his Friends*. The ghost, then, was naturally very anxious to show that he had not lost his influence over the Stiltons, with whom, indeed, he was distantly connected, his own first cousin having been married *en secondes noces* to the Sieur de Bulkeley, from whom, as everyone knows, the Dukes of Cheshire are lineally descended. Accordingly, he made arrangements for appearing to Virginia's little lover in his celebrated impersonation of 'The Vampire Monk, or, the Bloodless Benedictine', a performance so horrible that when old Lady Startup saw it, which she did on one fatal New Year's Eve, in the year 1764, she went off into the most piercing shrieks, which culminated in violent apoplexy, and died in three days, after disinheriting the Cantervilles, who were her nearest relations, and leaving all her money to her London apothecary. At the last moment, however, his terror of the twins prevented his leaving his room, and the little Duke slept in peace under the great feathered canopy in the Royal Bedchamber, and dreamed of Virginia.

5

A FEW DAYS AFTER THIS, Virginia and her curly-haired cavalier went out riding on Brockley meadows, where she tore her habit so badly in getting through a hedge, that, on her return home, she made up her mind to go up by the back staircase so as not to be seen. As she was running past the Tapestry Chamber, the door of which happened to be open, she fancied she saw some one inside, and thinking it was her mother's maid, who sometimes used to bring her work there, looked in to ask her to mend her habit. To her immense surprise, however, it was the Canterville Ghost himself! He was sitting by the window, watching the ruined gold of the yellow trees fly through the air, and the red leaves dancing madly down the long avenue. His head was leaning on his hand, and his whole attitude was one of extreme depression. Indeed, so forlorn, and so much out of repair did he look, that little Virginia, whose first idea had been to run away and lock herself in her room, was filled with pity, and determined to try and comfort him. So light was her footfall, and so deep his melancholy, that he was not aware of her presence till she spoke to him.

'I am so sorry for you,' she said, 'but my brothers are going back to Eton tomorrow, and then, if you behave yourself, no one will annoy you.'

'It is absurd asking me to behave myself,' he answered, looking round in astonishment at the pretty little girl who had ventured to address him, 'quite absurd. I must rattle my chains, and groan through keyholes, and walk about at night, if that is what you mean. It is my only reason for existing.'

'It is no reason at all for existing, and you know you have been very wicked. Mrs Umney told us, the first day we arrived here, that you had killed your wife.'

'Well, I quite admit it,' said the Ghost petulantly, 'but it was a purely family matter, and concerned no one else.'

'It is very wrong to kill any one,' said Virginia, who at times had a sweet Puritan gravity, caught from some old New England ancestor.

'Oh, I hate the cheap severity of abstract ethics! My wife was very plain, never had my ruffs properly starched, and knew nothing about cookery. Why, there was a buck I had shot in Hogley Woods, a magnificent pricket, and do you know how she had it sent up to table? However, it is no matter now, for it is all over, and I don't think it was very nice of her brothers to starve me to death, though I did kill her.'

'Starve you to death? Oh, Mr Ghost, I mean Sir Simon, are you hungry? I have a sandwich in my case. Would you like it?'

'No, thank you, I never eat anything now; but it is very kind of you, all the same, and you are much nicer than the rest of your horrid, rude, vulgar, dishonest family.'

'Stop!' cried Virginia, stamping her foot, 'it is you who are rude, and horrid, and vulgar; and as for dishonesty, you know you stole the paints out of my box to try and furbish up that ridiculous bloodstain in the library. First you took all my reds, including the vermilion, and I couldn't do any more sunsets, then you took the emerald-green and the chrome-yellow, and finally I had nothing left but indigo and Chinese white, and could only do moonlight scenes, which are always depressing to look at, and not at all easy to paint. I never told on you, though I was very much annoyed, and it was most ridiculous, the whole thing; for who ever heard of emerald-green blood?'

'Well, really,' said the Ghost, rather meekly, 'what was I to do? It is a very difficult thing to get real blood nowadays, and, as your brother began it all with his Paragon Detergent, I certainly saw no reason why I should not have your paints. As for colour, that is always a matter of taste: the Cantervilles have blue blood, for instance, the very bluest in England; but I know you Americans don't care for things of this kind.'

'You know nothing about it, and the best thing you can do is to emigrate and improve your mind. My father will be only too happy to give you a free passage, and though there is a heavy duty on spirits of every kind, there will be no difficulty about the Custom House, as the officers are all Democrats. Once in New York, you are sure to be a great success. I know lots of people there who would give a hundred thousand dollars to have a grandfather, and much more than that to have a family Ghost.'

'I don't think I should like America.'

'I suppose because we have no ruins and no curiosities,' said Virginia satirically.

'No ruins! no curiosities!' answered the Ghost; 'you have your navy and your manners.'

'Good evening; I will go and ask papa to get the twins an extra week's holiday.'

'Please don't go, Miss Virginia,' he cried; 'I am so lonely and so unhappy, and I really don't know what to do. I want to go to sleep and I cannot.'

'That's quite absurd. You have merely to go to bed and blow out the candle. It is very difficult sometimes to keep awake, especially at church, but there is no difficulty at all about sleeping. Why, even babies know how to do that, and they are not very clever.'

'I have not slept for three hundred years,' he said sadly, and Virginia's beautiful blue eyes opened in wonder; 'for three hundred years I have not slept, and I am so tired.'

Virginia grew quite grave, and her little lips trembled like rose-leaves. She came towards him, and kneeling down at his side, looked up into his old withered face.

'Poor, poor Ghost,' she murmured; 'have you no place where you can sleep?'

'Far away beyond the pine-woods,' he answered, in a low dreamy voice, 'there is a little garden. There the grass grows long and deep, there are the great white stars of the hemlock flower, there the nightingale sings all night long. All night long he sings, and the cold, crystal moon looks down, and the yew-tree spreads out its giant arms over the sleepers.'

Virginia's eyes grew dim with tears, and she hid her face in her hands.

'You mean the Garden of Death,' she whispered.

'Yes, Death. Death must be so beautiful. To lie in the soft brown earth, with the grasses waving above one's head, and listen to silence. To have no yesterday, and no tomorrow. To forget time, to forgive life, to be at peace. You can help me. You can open for me the portals of Death's house, for Love is always with you, and Love is stronger than Death is.'

Virginia trembled, a cold shudder ran through her, and for a few moments there was silence. She felt as if she was in a terrible dream.

Then the Ghost spoke again, and his voice sounded like the sighing of the wind.

'Have you ever read the old prophecy on the library window?'

'Oh, often,' cried the little girl, looking up; 'I know it quite well. It is painted in curious black letters, and it is difficult to read. There are only six lines:

> *When a golden girl can win*
> *Prayer from out the lips of sin,*
> *When the barren almond bears,*
> *And a little child gives away its tears,*
> *Then shall all the house be still*
> *And peace come to Canterville.*

But I don't know what they mean.'

'They mean,' he said sadly, 'that you must weep for me for my sins, because I have no tears, and pray with me for my soul, because I have no faith, and then, if you have always been sweet, and good, and gentle, the Angel of Death will have mercy on me. You will see fearful shapes in darkness, and wicked voices will whisper in your ear, but they will not harm you, for against the purity of a little child the powers of Hell cannot prevail.'

Virginia made no answer, and the Ghost wrung his hands in wild despair as he looked down at her bowed golden head. Suddenly she stood up, very pale, and with a strange light in her eyes. 'I am not afraid,' she said firmly, 'and I will ask the Angel to have mercy on you.'

He rose from his seat with a faint cry of joy, and taking her hand bent over it with old-fashioned grace and kissed it. His fingers were as cold as ice, and his lips burned like fire, but Virginia did not falter, as he led her across the dusky room. On the faded green tapestry were broidered little huntsmen. They blew their tasselled horns and with their tiny hands waved to her to go back. 'Go back! little Virginia,' they cried, 'go back!' but the Ghost clutched her hand more tightly, and she shut her eyes against them. Horrible animals with lizard tails, and goggle eyes, blinked at her from the carven chimney-piece, and murmured 'Beware! little Virginia, beware! we may never see you again,' but the Ghost glided on more swiftly, and Virginia did not listen. When they reached the end of the room he stopped, and muttered some words she could not understand. She opened her eyes, and saw the wall slowly fading away like a mist, and a great black cavern in front of her. A bitter cold wind swept round them, and she felt something pulling at her dress. 'Quick, quick,' cried the Ghost, 'or it will be too late,' and, in a moment, the wainscoting had closed behind them, and the Tapestry Chamber was empty.

ABOUT TEN MINUTES LATER, THE bell rang for tea, and, as Virginia did not come down, Mrs Otis sent up one of the footmen to tell her. After a little time he returned and said that he could not find Miss Virginia anywhere. As she was in the habit of going out to the garden every evening to get flowers for the dinner-table, Mrs Otis was not at all alarmed at first, but when six o'clock struck, and Virginia did not appear, she became really agitated, and sent the boys out to look for her, while she herself and Mr Otis searched every room in the house. At half-past six the boys came back and said that they could find no trace of their sister anywhere. They were all now in the greatest state of excitement, and did not know what to do, when Mr Otis suddenly remembered that, some few days before, he had given a band of gypsies permission to camp in the park. He accordingly at once set off for Blackfell Hollow, where he knew they were, accompanied by his eldest son and two of the farm-servants. The little Duke of Cheshire, who was perfectly frantic with anxiety, begged hard to be allowed to go too, but Mr Otis would not allow him, as he was afraid there might be a scuffle. On arriving at the spot, however, he found that the gypsies had gone, and it was evident that their departure had been rather sudden, as the fire was still burning, and some plates were lying on the grass. Having sent off Washington and the two men to scour the district, he ran home, and despatched telegrams to all the police inspectors in the county, telling them to look out for a little girl who had been kidnapped by tramps or gypsies. He then ordered his horse to be brought round, and, after insisting on his wife and the three boys sitting down to dinner, rode off down the Ascot Road with a groom. He had hardly, however, gone a couple of miles when he heard somebody galloping after him, and, looking round, saw the little Duke coming up on his pony, with his face very flushed and no hat. 'I'm awfully sorry, Mr Otis,' gasped out the boy, 'but I can't eat any dinner as long as Virginia is lost. Please, don't be angry with me; if you had let us be engaged last year, there would never have been all this trouble. You won't send me back, will you? I can't go! I won't go!'

The Minister could not help smiling at the handsome young scapegrace, and was a good deal touched at his devotion to Virginia, so leaning down from his horse, he patted him kindly on the shoulders, and said, 'Well, Cecil, if you won't go back I suppose you must come with me, but I must get you a hat at Ascot.'

'Oh, bother my hat! I want Virginia!' cried the little Duke, laughing, and they galloped on to the railway station. There Mr Otis inquired of the station-master if any one answering the description of Virginia had been seen on the platform, but could get no news of her. The station-master, however, wired up and down the line, and assured him that a strict watch would be kept for her, and, after having bought a hat for the little Duke from a linen-draper, who was just putting up his shutters, Mr Otis rode off to Bexley, a village about four miles away, which he was told was a well-known haunt of the gypsies, as there was a large common next to it. Here they roused up the rural policeman, but could get no information from him, and, after riding all over the common, they turned their horses' heads homewards, and reached the Chase about eleven o'clock, dead-tired and almost heart-broken. They found Washington and the twins waiting for them at the gate-house with lanterns, as the avenue was very dark. Not the slightest trace of Virginia had been discovered. The gypsies had been caught on Broxley meadows, but she was not with them, and they had explained their sudden departure by saying that they had mistaken the date of Chorton Fair, and had gone off in a hurry for fear they might be late. Indeed, they had been quite distressed at hearing of Virginia's disappearance, as they were very grateful to Mr Otis for having allowed them to camp in his park, and four of their number had stayed behind to help in the search. The carp-pond had been dragged, and the whole Chase thoroughly gone over, but without any result. It was evident that, for that night at any rate, Virginia was lost to them; and it was in a state of the deepest depression that Mr Otis and the boys walked up to the house, the groom following behind with the two horses and the pony. In the hall they found a group of frightened servants, and lying on a sofa in the library was poor Mrs Otis, almost out of her mind with terror and anxiety, and having her forehead bathed with eau-de-cologne by the old house-keeper. Mr Otis at once insisted on her having something to eat, and ordered up supper for the whole party. It was a melancholy meal, as hardly any one spoke, and even the twins were awestruck and subdued, as they were very fond of their sister. When they had finished, Mr Otis, in spite of the entreaties of the little Duke, ordered them all to bed, saying that nothing more could be done that night, and that he would telegraph in the morning to Scotland Yard for some detectives to be sent down immediately. Just as they were passing out of the dining-room, midnight began to boom from the clock tower, and when the last stroke sounded they heard a crash and a sudden shrill cry; a dreadful peal of thunder shook the house, a strain of unearthly music floated through the air, a panel at the top of the staircase flew back with a loud noise, and out on the landing, looking very pale and white, with a little casket in her hand, stepped Virginia. In a moment they had all rushed up to her. Mrs Otis clasped her passionately in her arms, the Duke smothered her with violent kisses, and the twins executed a wild war-dance round the group.

'Good heavens! child, where have you been?' said Mr Otis, rather angrily, thinking that she had been playing some foolish trick on them. 'Cecil and I have been riding all over the country looking for you, and your mother has been frightened to death. You must never play these practical jokes any more.'

'Except on the Ghost! except on the Ghost!' shrieked the twins, as they capered about.

'My own darling, thank God you are found; you must never leave my side again,' murmured Mrs Otis, as she kissed the trembling child, and smoothed the tangled gold of her hair.

'Papa,' said Virginia quietly, 'I have been with the Ghost. He is dead, and you must come and see him. He had been very wicked, but he was really sorry for all that he had done, and he gave me this box of beautiful jewels before he died.'

The whole family gazed at her in mute astonishment, but she was quite grave and serious; and, turning round, she led them through the opening in the wainscoting down a narrow secret corridor, Washington following with a lighted candle, which he had caught up from the table. Finally, they came to a great oak door, studded with rusty nails. When Virginia touched it, it swung back on its heavy hinges, and they found themselves in a little low room, with a vaulted ceiling, and one tiny grated window. Imbedded in the wall was a huge iron ring, and chained to it was a gaunt skeleton, that was stretched out at full length on the stone floor, and seemed to be trying to grasp with its long fleshless fingers an old-fashioned trencher and ewer, that were placed just out of its reach. The jug had evidently been once filled with water, as it was covered inside with green mould. There was nothing on the trencher but a pile of dust. Virginia knelt down beside the skeleton, and, folding her little hands together, began to pray silently, while the rest of the party looked on in wonder at the terrible tragedy whose secret was now disclosed to them.

'Hallo!' suddenly exclaimed one of the twins, who had been looking out of the window to try and discover in what wing of the house the room was situated. 'Hallo! the old withered almond-tree has blossomed. I can see the flowers quite plainly in the moonlight.'

'God has forgiven him,' said Virginia gravely, as she rose to her feet, and a beautiful light seemed to illumine her face.

'What an angel you are!' cried the young Duke, and he put his arm round her neck and kissed her.

7

FOUR DAYS AFTER THESE curious incidents a funeral started from Canterville Chase at about eleven o'clock at night. The hearse was drawn by eight black horses, each of which carried on its head a great tuft of nodding ostrich-plumes, and the leaden coffin was covered by a rich purple pall, on which was embroidered in gold the Canterville coat-of-arms. By the side of the hearse and the coaches walked the servants with lighted torches, and the whole procession was wonderfully impressive. Lord Canterville was the chief mourner, having come up specially from Wales to attend the funeral, and sat in the first carriage along with little Virginia. Then came the United States Minister and his wife, then Washington and the three boys, and in the last carriage was Mrs Umney. It was generally felt that, as she had been frightened by the ghost for more than fifty years of her life, she had a right to see the last of him. A deep grave had been dug in the corner of the churchyard, just under the old yew-tree, and the service was read in the most impressive manner by the Rev Augustus Dampier. When the ceremony was over, the servants, according to an old custom observed in the Canterville family, extinguished their torches, and, as the coffin was being lowered into the grave, Virginia stepped forward and laid on it a large cross made of white and pink almond-blossoms. As she did so, the moon came out from behind a cloud, and flooded with its silent silver the little churchyard, and from a distant copse a nightingale began to sing. She thought of the ghost's description of the Garden of Death, her eyes became dim with tears, and she hardly spoke a word during the drive home.

The next morning, before Lord Canterville went up to town, Mr Otis had an interview with him on the subject of the jewels the ghost had given to Virginia. They were perfectly magnificent, especially a certain ruby necklace with old Venetian setting, which was really a superb specimen of sixteenth-century work, and their value was so great that Mr Otis felt considerable scruples about allowing his daughter to accept them.

'My Lord,' he said, 'I know that in this country mortmain is held to apply to trinkets as well as to land, and it is quite clear to me that these jewels are, or should be, heirlooms in your family. I must beg you, accordingly, to take them to London with you, and to regard them simply as a portion of your property which has been restored to you under certain strange conditions. As for my daughter, she is merely a child, and has as yet, I am glad to say, but little interest in such appurtenances of idle luxury. I am also informed by Mrs Otis, who, I may say, is no mean authority upon Art – having had the privilege of spending several winters in Boston when she was a girl – that these gems are of great monetary worth, and if offered for sale would fetch a tall price. Under these circumstances, Lord Canterville, I feel sure that you will recognise how impossible it would be for me to allow them to remain in the possession of any member of my family; and, indeed, all such vain gauds and toys, however suitable or necessary to the dignity of the British aristocracy, would be completely out of place among those who have been brought up on the severe, and I believe immortal, principles of republican simplicity. Perhaps I should mention that Virginia is very anxious that you should allow her to retain the box as a memento of your unfortunate but misguided ancestor. As it is extremely old, and consequently a good deal out of repair, you may perhaps think fit to comply with her request. For my own part, I confess I am a good deal surprised to find a child of mine expressing sympathy with medievalism in any form, and can only account for it by the fact that Virginia was born in one of your London suburbs shortly after Mrs Otis had returned from a trip to Athens.'

Lord Canterville listened very gravely to the worthy Minister's speech, pulling his grey moustache now and then to hide an involuntary smile, and when Mr Otis had ended, he shook him cordially by the hand, and said, 'My dear sir, your charming little daughter rendered my unlucky ancestor, Sir Simon, a very important service, and I and my family are much indebted to her for her marvellous courage and pluck. The jewels are clearly hers, and, egad, I believe that if I were heartless enough to take them from her, the wicked old fellow would be out of his grave in a fortnight, leading me the devil of a life. As for their being heirlooms, nothing is an heirloom that is not so mentioned in a will or legal document, and the existence of these jewels has been quite unknown. I assure you I have no more claim on them than your butler, and when Miss Virginia grows up I daresay she will be pleased to have pretty things to wear. Besides, you forget, Mr Otis, that you took the furniture and the ghost at a valuation, and anything that belonged to the ghost passed at once into your possession, as, whatever activity Sir Simon may have shown in the corridor at night, in point of law he was really dead, and you acquired his property by purchase.'

Mr Otis was a good deal distressed at Lord Canterville's refusal, and begged him to reconsider his decision, but the good-natured peer was quite firm, and finally induced the Minister to allow his daughter to retain the present the ghost had given her, and when, in the spring of 1890, the young Duchess of Cheshire was presented at the Queen's first drawing-room on the occasion of her marriage, her jewels were the universal theme of admiration. For Virginia received the coronet, which is the reward of all good little American girls, and was married to her boy-lover as soon as he came of age. They were both so charming, and they loved each other so much, that every one was delighted at the match, except the old Marchioness of Dumbleton, who had tried to catch the Duke for one of her seven unmarried daughters, and had given no less than three expensive dinner-parties for that purpose, and, strange to say, Mr Otis himself. Mr Otis was extremely fond of the young Duke personally, but, theoretically, he objected to titles, and, to use his own words, 'was not without apprehension lest, amid the ener-vating influences of a pleasure-loving aristocracy, the true principles of republican simplicity should be forgotten.' His objections, however, were completely overruled, and I believe that when he walked up the aisle of St George's, Hanover Square, with his daughter leaning on his arm, there was not a prouder man in the whole length and breadth of England.

The Duke and Duchess, after the honeymoon was over, went down to Canterville Chase, and on the day after their arrival they walked over in the afternoon to the lonely churchyard by the pine-woods. There had been a great deal of difficulty at first about the inscription on Sir Simon's tombstone, but finally it had been decided to engrave on it simply the initials of the old gentleman's name, and the verse from the library window. The Duchess had brought with her some lovely roses, which she strewed upon the grave, and after they had stood by it for some time they strolled into the ruined chancel of the old abbey. There the Duchess sat down on a fallen pillar, while her husband lay at her feet smoking a cigarette and looking up at her beautiful eyes. Suddenly he threw his cigarette away, took hold of her hand, and said to her, 'Virginia, a wife should have no secrets from her husband.'

'Dear Cecil! I have no secrets from you.'

'Yes, you have,' he answered, smiling, 'you have never told me what happened to you when you were locked up with the ghost.'

'I have never told any one, Cecil,' said Virginia gravely.

'I know that, but you might tell me.'

'Please don't ask me, Cecil. I cannot tell you. Poor Sir Simon! I owe him a great deal. Yes, don't laugh, Cecil, I really do. He made me see what Life is, and what Death signifies, and why Love is stronger than both.'

The Duke rose and kissed his wife lovingly.

'You can have your secret as long as I have your heart,' he murmured.

'You have always had that, Cecil.'

'And you will tell our children some day, won't you?'

Virginia blushed.

THE YOUNG KING

IT WAS THE NIGHT BEFORE THE DAY fixed for his coronation, and the young King was sitting alone in his beautiful chamber. His courtiers had all taken their leave of him, bowing their heads to the ground, according to the ceremonious usage of the day, and had retired to the Great Hall of the Palace, to receive a few last lessons from the Professor of Etiquette; there being some of them who had still quite natural manners, which in a courtier is, I need hardly say, a very grave offence.

The lad – for he was only a lad, being but sixteen years of age – was not sorry at their departure, and had flung himself back with a deep sigh of relief on the soft cushions of his embroidered couch, lying there, wild-eyed and open-mouthed, like a brown woodland Faun, or some young animal of the forest newly snared by the hunters.

And, indeed, it was the hunters who had found him, coming upon him almost by chance as, bare-limbed and pipe in hand, he was following the flock of the poor goat-herd who had brought him up, and whose son he had always fancied himself to be. The child of the old King's only daughter by a secret marriage with one much beneath her in station – a stranger, some said, who, by the wonderful magic of his lute-playing, had made the young Princess love him; while others spoke of an artist from Rimini, to whom the Princess had shown much, perhaps too much honour, and who had suddenly disappeared from the city, leaving his work in the Cathedral unfinished – he had been, when but a week old, stolen away from his mother's side, as she slept, and given into the charge of a common peasant and his wife, who were without children of their own, and lived in a remote part of the forest, more than a day's ride from the town. Grief, or the plague, as the court physician stated, or, as some suggested, a swift Italian poison administered in a cup of spiced wine, slew, within an hour of her wakening, the white girl who had given him birth, and as the trusty messenger who bare the child across his saddle-bow stooped from his weary horse and knocked at the rude door of the goatherd's hut, the body of the Princess was being lowered into an open grave that had been dug in a

deserted churchyard, beyond the city gates, a grave where it was said that another body was also lying, that of a young man of marvellous and foreign beauty, whose hands were tied behind him with a knotted cord, and whose breast was stabbed with many red wounds.

Such, at least, was the story that men whispered to each other. Certain it was that the old King, when on his death-bed, whether moved by remorse for his great sin, or merely desiring that the kingdom should not pass away from his line, had had the lad sent for, and, in the presence of the Council, had acknowledged him as his heir.

And it seems that from the very first moment of his recognition he had shown signs of that strange passion for beauty that was destined to have so great an influence over his life. Those who accompanied him to the suite of rooms set apart for his service, often spoke of the cry of pleasure that broke from his lips when he saw the delicate raiment and rich jewels that had been prepared for him, and of the almost fierce joy with which he flung aside his rough leathern tunic and coarse sheepskin cloak. He missed, indeed, at times the freedom of the forest life, and was always apt to chafe at the tedious Court ceremonies that occupied so much of each day, but the wonderful palace – *Joyeuse*, as they called it – of which he now found himself lord, seemed to him to be a new world fresh-fashioned for his delight; and as soon as he could escape from the council-board or audience-chamber, he would run down the great staircase, with its lions of gilt bronze and its steps of bright porphyry, and wander from room to room, and from corridor to corridor, like one who was seeking to find in beauty an anodyne from pain, a sort of restoration from sickness.

Upon these journeys of discovery, as he would call them – and, indeed, they were to him real voyages through a marvellous land, he would sometimes be accompanied by the slim, fair-haired Court pages, with their floating mantles, and gay fluttering ribands; but more often he would be alone, feeling through a certain quick instinct, which was almost a divination, that the secrets of art are best learned in secret, and that Beauty, like Wisdom, loves the lonely worshipper.

Many curious stories were related about him at this period. It was said that a stout Burgomaster, who had come to deliver a florid oratorical address on behalf of the citizens of the town, had caught sight of him kneeling in real adoration before a great picture that had just been brought from Venice, and that seemed to herald the worship of some new gods. On another occasion he had been missed for several hours, and after a lengthened search had been discovered in a little chamber in one of the northern turrets of the palace gazing, as one in a trance, at a Greek gem carved with the figure of Adonis. He had been seen, so the tale ran, pressing his warm lips to the marble brow of an antique statue that had been discovered in the bed of the river on the occasion of the building of the stone bridge, and was inscribed with the name of the Bithynian slave of Hadrian. He had passed a whole night in noting the effect of the moonlight on a silver image of Endymion.

All rare and costly materials had certainly a great fascination for him, and in his eagerness to procure them he had sent away many merchants, some to traffic for amber with the rough fisher-folk of the north seas, some to Egypt to look for that curious green turquoise which is found only in the tombs of kings, and is said to possess magical properties, some to Persia for silken carpets and painted pottery, and others to India to buy gauze and stained ivory, moonstones and bracelets of jade, sandalwood and blue enamel and shawls of fine wool.

But what had occupied him most was the robe he was to wear at his coronation, the robe of tissued gold, and the ruby-studded crown, and the sceptre with its rows and rings of pearls. Indeed, it was of this that he was thinking to-night, as he lay back on his luxurious couch, watching the great pinewood log that was burning itself out on the open hearth. The designs, which were from the hands of the most famous artists of the time, had been submitted to him many months before, and he had given orders that the artificers were to toil night and day to carry them out, and that the whole world was to be searched for jewels that would be worthy of their work. He saw himself in fancy standing at the high altar of the cathedral in the fair raiment of a King, and a smile played and lingered about his boyish lips, and lit up with a bright lustre his dark woodland eyes.

After some time he rose from his seat, and leaning against the carved penthouse of the chimney, looked round at the dimly-lit room. The walls were hung with rich tapestries representing the Triumph of Beauty. A large press, inlaid with agate and lapis-lazuli, filled one corner, and facing the window stood a curiously wrought cabinet with lacquer panels of powdered and mosaiced gold, on which were placed some delicate goblets of Venetian glass, and a cup of dark-veined onyx. Pale poppies were broidered on the silk coverlet of the bed, as though they had fallen from the tired hands of sleep, and tall reeds of fluted ivory bare up the velvet canopy, from which great tufts of ostrich plumes sprang, like white foam, to the pallid silver of the fretted ceiling. A laughing Narcissus in green bronze held a polished mirror above its head. On the table stood a flat bowl of amethyst.

Outside he could see the huge dome of the cathedral, looming like a bubble over the shadowy houses, and the weary sentinels pacing up and down on the misty terrace by the river. Far away, in an orchard, a nightingale was singing. A faint perfume of jasmine came through the open window. He brushed his brown curls back from his forehead, and taking up a lute, let his fingers stray across the cords. His heavy eyelids drooped, and a strange languor came over him. Never before had he felt so keenly, or with such exquisite joy, the magic and mystery of beautiful things.

When midnight sounded from the clock-tower he touched a bell, and his pages entered and disrobed him with much ceremony, pouring rose-water over his hands, and strewing flowers on his pillow. A few moments after that they had left the room, he fell asleep.

And as he slept he dreamed a dream, and this was his dream. He thought that he was standing in a long, low attic, amidst the whir and clatter of many looms. The meagre daylight peered in through the grated windows, and showed him the gaunt figures of the weavers bending over their cases. Pale, sickly-looking children were crouched on the huge crossbeams. As the shuttles dashed through the warp they lifted up the heavy battens, and when the shuttles stopped they let the battens fall and pressed the threads together. Their faces were pinched with famine, and their thin hands shook and trembled. Some haggard women were seated at a table sewing. A horrible odour filled the place. The air was foul and heavy, and the walls dripped and streamed with damp.

The young King went over to one of the weavers, and stood by him and watched him.

And the weaver looked at him angrily and said, 'Why art thou watching me? Art thou a spy set on us by our master?'

'Who is thy master?' asked the young King.

'Our master!' cried the weaver, bitterly. 'He is a man like myself. Indeed, there is but this difference between us – that he wears fine clothes while I go in rags, and that while I am weak from hunger he suffers not a little from over-feeding.'

'The land is free,' said the young King, 'and thou art no man's slave.'

'In war,' answered the weaver, 'the strong make slaves of the weak, and in peace the rich make slaves of the poor. We must work to live, and they give us such mean wages that we die. We toil for them all day long, and they heap up gold in their coffers, and our children fade away before their time, and the faces of those we love become hard and evil. We tread out the grapes, and another drinks the wine. We sow the corn, and our own board is empty. We have chains, though no eye beholds them; and we are slaves, though men call us free.'

'Is it so with all?' he asked.

'It is so with all,' answered the weaver, 'with the young as well as with the old, with the women as well as with the men, with the little children as well as with those who are stricken in years. The merchants grind us down, and we must needs do their bidding. The priest rides by and tells his beads, and no man has care of us. Through our sunless lanes creeps Poverty with her hungry eyes, and Sin with his sodden face follows close behind her. Misery wakes us in the morning, and Shame sits with us at night. But what are these things to thee? Thou art not one of us. Thy face is too happy.' And he turned away scowling, and threw the shuttle across the loom, and the young King saw that it was threaded with a thread of gold.

And a great terror seized upon him, and he said to the weaver, 'What robe is this that thou art weaving?'

'It is the robe for the coronation of the young King,' he answered; 'what is that to thee?'

And the young King gave a loud cry and woke, and lo! he was in his own chamber, and through the window he saw the great honey-coloured moon hanging in the dusky air.

And he fell asleep again, and dreamed, and this was his dream. He thought that he was lying on the deck of a huge galley that was being rowed by a hundred slaves. On a carpet by his side the master of the galley was seated. He was black as ebony, and his turban was of crimson silk. Great ear-rings of silver dragged down the thick lobes of his ears, and in his hands he had a pair of ivory scales.

The slaves were naked, but for a ragged loincloth, and each man was chained to his neighbour. The hot sun beat brightly upon them, and the negroes ran up and down the gangway and lashed them with whips of hide. They stretched out their lean arms and pulled the heavy oars through the water. The salt spray flew from the blades.

At last they reached a little bay, and began to take soundings. A light wind blew from the shore, and covered the deck and the great lateen sail with a fine red dust. Three Arabs mounted on wild asses rode out and threw spears at them. The master of the galley took a painted bow in his hand and shot one of them in the throat. He fell heavily into the surf, and his companions galloped away. A woman wrapped in a yellow veil followed slowly on a camel, looking back now and then at the dead body.

As soon as they had cast anchor and hauled down the sail, the negroes went into the hold and brought up a long rope-ladder, heavily weighted with lead. The master of the galley threw it over the side, making the ends fast to two iron stanchions. Then the negroes seized the youngest of the slaves and knocked his gyves off, and filled his nostrils and his ears with wax, and tied a big stone round his waist. He crept wearily down the ladder, and disappeared into the sea. A few bubbles rose where he sank. Some of the other slaves peered curiously over the side. At the prow of the galley sat a shark-charmer beating monotonously upon a drum.

After some time the diver rose up out of the water, and clung panting to the ladder with a pearl in his right hand. The negroes seized it from him, and thrust him back. The slaves fell asleep over their oars.

Again and again he came up, and each time that he did so he brought with him a beautiful pearl. The master of the galley weighed them, and put them into a little bag of green leather.

The young King tried to speak, but his tongue seemed to cleave to the roof of his mouth, and his lips refused to move. The negroes chattered to each other, and began to quarrel over a string of bright beads. Two cranes flew round and round the vessel.

Then the diver came up for the last time, and the pearl that he brought with him was fairer than all the pearls of Ormuz, for it was shaped like the full moon, and whiter than the morning star. But his face was strangely pale, and as he fell upon the deck the blood gushed from his ears and nostrils. He quivered for a little, and then he was still. The negroes shrugged their shoulders, and threw the body overboard.

And the master of the galley laughed, and, reaching out, he took the pearl, and when he saw it he pressed it to his forehead and bowed. 'It shall be,' he said, 'for the sceptre of the young King,' and he made a sign to the negroes to draw up the anchor.

And when the young King heard this he gave a great cry and woke, and through the window he saw the long grey fingers of the dawn clutching at the fading stars.

And he fell asleep again, and dreamed, and this was his dream. He thought that he was wandering through a dim wood, hung with strange fruits and with beautiful poisonous flowers. The adders hissed at him as he went by, and the bright parrots flew screaming from branch to branch. Huge tortoises lay asleep upon the hot mud. The trees were full of apes and peacocks.

On and on he went, till he reached the outskirts of the wood, and there he saw an immense multitude of men toiling in the bed of a dried-up river. They swarmed up the crag like ants. They dug deep pits in the ground and went down into them. Some of them cleft the rocks with great axes; others grabbled in the sand. They tore up the cactus by its roots, and trampled on the scarlet blossoms. They hurried about, calling to each other, and no man was idle.

From the darkness of a cavern Death and Avarice watched them, and Death said, 'I am weary; give me a third of them and let me go.'

But Avarice shook her head. 'They are my servants,' she answered.

And Death said to her, 'What hast thou got in thy hand?'

'I have three grains of corn,' she answered; 'what is that to thee?'

'Give me one of them,' cried Death, 'to plant in my garden; only one of them, and I will go away.'

'I will not give thee anything,' said Avarice, and she hid her hand in the fold of her raiment.

And Death laughed, and took a cup, and dipped it into a pool of water, and out of the cup rose Ague. She passed through the great multitude, and a third of them lay dead. A cold mist followed her, and the water-snakes ran by her side.

And when Avarice saw that a third of the multitude was dead she beat her breast and wept. She beat her barren bosom, and cried aloud. 'Thou hast slain a third of my servants,' she cried, 'get thee gone. There is war in the mountains of Tartary, and the kings of each side are calling to thee. The Afghans have slain the black ox, and are marching to battle. They have beaten upon their shields with their spears, and have put on their helmets of iron. What is my valley to thee, that thou shouldst tarry in it? Get thee gone, and come here no more.'

'Nay,' answered Death, 'but till thou hast given me a grain of corn I will not go.'

But Avarice shut her hand, and clenched her teeth. 'I will not give thee anything,' she muttered.

And Death laughed, and took up a black stone, and threw it into the forest, and out of a thicket of wild hemlock came Fever in a robe of flame. She passed through the multitude, and touched them, and each man that she touched died. The grass withered beneath her feet as she walked.

And Avarice shuddered, and put ashes on her head. 'Thou art cruel,' she cried; 'thou art cruel. There is famine in the walled cities of India, and the cisterns of Samarcand have run dry. There is famine in the walled cities of Egypt, and the locusts have come up from the desert. The Nile has not overflowed its banks, and the priests have nursed Isis and Osiris. Get thee gone to those who need thee, and leave me my servants.'

'Nay,' answered Death, 'but till thou hast given me a grain of corn I will not go.'

'I will not give thee anything,' said Avarice.

And Death laughed again, and he whistled through his fingers, and a woman came flying through the air. Plague was written upon her forehead, and a crowd of lean vultures wheeled round her. She covered the valley with her wings, and no man was left alive.

And Avarice fled shrieking through the forest, and Death leaped upon his red horse and galloped away, and his galloping was faster than the wind.

And out of the slime at the bottom of the valley crept dragons and horrible things with scales, and the jackals came trotting along the sand, sniffing up the air with their nostrils.

And the young King wept, and said: 'Who were these men, and for what were they seeking?'

'For rubies for a king's crown,' answered one who stood behind him.

And the young King started, and, turning round, he saw a man habited as a pilgrim and holding in his hand a mirror of silver.

And he grew pale, and said: 'For what king?'

And the pilgrim answered: 'Look in this mirror, and thou shalt see him.'

And he looked in the mirror, and, seeing his own face, he gave a great cry and woke, and the bright sunlight was streaming into the room, and from the trees of the garden and pleasaunce the birds were singing.

And the Chamberlain and the high officers of State came in and made obeisance to him, and the pages brought him the robe of tissued gold, and set the crown and the sceptre before him.

And the young King looked at them, and they were beautiful. More beautiful were they than aught that he had ever seen. But he remembered his dreams, and he said to his lords: 'Take these things away, for I will not wear them.'

And the courtiers were amazed, and some of them laughed, for they thought that he was jesting.

But he spake sternly to them again, and said: 'Take these things away, and hide them from me. Though it be the day of my coronation, I will not wear them. For on the loom of sorrow, and by the white hands of Pain, has this my robe been woven. There is Blood in the heart of the ruby, and Death in the heart of the pearl.' And he told them of his three dreams.

And when the courtiers heard them they looked at each other and whispered, saying: 'Surely he is mad; for what is a dream but a dream, and a vision but a vision? They are not real things that one should heed them. And what have we to do with the lives of those who toil for us? Shall a man not eat bread till he has seen the sower, nor drink wine till he has talked with the vine-dresser?'

And the Chamberlain spake to the young King, and said, 'My lord, I pray thee set aside these black thoughts of thine, and put on this fair robe, and set this crown upon thy head. For how shall the people know that thou art a king, if thou hast not a king's raiment?'

And the young King looked at him. 'Is it so, indeed?' he questioned. 'Will they not know me for a king if I have not a king's raiment?'

'They will not know thee, my lord,' cried the Chamberlain.

'I had thought that there had been men who were kinglike,' he answered, 'but it may be as thou sayest. And yet I will not wear this robe, nor will I be crowned with this crown, but even as I came to the palace so will I go forth from it.'

And he bade them all leave him, save one page whom he kept as his companion, a lad a year younger than himself. Him he kept for his service, and when he had bathed himself in clear water, he opened a great painted chest, and from it he took the leathern tunic and rough sheepskin cloak that he had worn when he had watched on the hillside the shaggy goats of the goatherd. These he put on, and in his hand he took his rude shepherd's staff.

And the little page opened his big blue eyes in wonder, and said smiling to him, 'My lord, I see thy robe and thy sceptre, but where is thy crown?'

And the young King plucked a spray of wild briar that was climbing over the balcony, and bent it, and made a circlet of it, and set it on his own head.

'This shall be my crown,' he answered.

And thus attired he passed out of his chamber into the Great Hall, where the nobles were waiting for him.

And the nobles made merry, and some of them cried out to him, 'My lord, the people wait for their king, and thou showest them a beggar,' and others were wroth and said, 'He brings shame upon our state, and is unworthy to be our master.' But he answered them not a word, but passed on, and went down the bright porphyry staircase, and out through the gates of bronze, and mounted upon his horse, and rode towards the cathedral, the little page running beside him.

And the people laughed and said, 'It is the King's fool who is riding by,' and they mocked him.

And he drew rein and said, 'Nay, but I am the King.' And he told them his three dreams.

And a man came out of the crowd and spake bitterly to him, and said, 'Sir, knowest thou not that out of the luxury of the rich cometh the life of the poor? By your pomp we are nurtured, and your vices give us bread. To toil for a master is bitter, but to have no master to toil for is more bitter still. Thinkest thou that the ravens will feed us? And what cure hast thou for these things? Wilt thou say to the buyer, "Thou shalt buy for so much," and to the seller, "Thou shalt sell at this price"? I trow not. Therefore go back to thy Palace and put on thy purple and fine linen. What hast thou to do with us, and what we suffer?'

'Are not the rich and the poor brothers?' asked the young King.

'Ay,' answered the man, 'and the name of the rich brother is Cain.'

And the young King's eyes filled with tears, and he rode on through the murmurs of the people, and the little page grew afraid and left him.

And when he reached the great portal of the cathedral, the soldiers thrust their halberts out and said, 'What dost thou seek here? None enters by this door but the King.'

And his face flushed with anger, and he said to them, 'I am the King,' and waved their halberts aside and passed in.

And when the old bishop saw him coming in his goatherd's dress, he rose up in wonder from his throne, and went to meet him, and said to him, 'My son, is this a king's apparel? And with what crown shall I crown thee, and what sceptre shall I place in thy hand? Surely this should be to thee a day of joy, and not a day of abasement.'

'Shall Joy wear what Grief has fashioned?' said the young King. And he told him his three dreams.

And when the Bishop had heard them he knit his brows, and said,

'My son, I am an old man, and in the winter of my days, and I know
that many evil things are done in the wide world. The fierce robbers
come down from the mountains, and carry off the little children, and
sell them to the Moors. The lions lie in wait for the caravans, and leap
upon the camels. The wild boar roots up the corn in the valley, and the
foxes gnaw the vines upon the hill. The pirates lay waste the sea-coast
and burn the ships of the fishermen, and take their nets from them. In
the salt-marshes live the lepers; they have houses of wattled reeds, and
none may come nigh them. The beggars wander through the cities, and
eat their food with the dogs. Canst thou make these things not to be?
Will thou take the leper for thy bedfellow, and set the beggar at thy
board? Shall the lion do thy bidding, and the wild boar obey thee? Is
not He who made misery wiser than thou art? Wherefore I praise thee
not for this that thou hast done, but I bid thee ride back to the Palace
and make thy face glad, and put on the raiment that beseemeth a king,
and with the crown of gold I will crown thee, and the sceptre of pearl
will I place in thy hand. And as for thy dreams, think no more of them.
The burden of this world is too great for one man to bear, and the
world's sorrow too heavy for one heart to suffer.'

'Sayest thou that in this house?' said the young King, and he strode
past the Bishop, and climbed up the steps of the altar, and stood before
the image of Christ.

He stood before the image of Christ, and on his right hand and on
his left were the marvellous vessels of gold, the chalice with the yellow
wine, and the vial with the holy oil. He knelt before the image of Christ,
and the great candles burned brightly by the jewelled shrine, and the
smoke of the incense curled in thin blue wreaths through the dome.
He bowed his head in prayer, and the priests in their stiff copes crept
away from the altar.

And suddenly a wild tumult came from the street outside, and in
entered the nobles with drawn swords and nodding plumes, and shields
of polished steel. 'Where is this dreamer of dreams?' they cried. 'Where
is this King, who is apparelled like a beggar – this boy who brings shame
upon our state? Surely we will slay him, for he is unworthy to rule over
us.'

And the young King bowed his head again, and prayed, and when he
had finished his prayer he rose up, and turning round he looked at
them sadly.

And lo! through the painted windows came the sunlight streaming
upon him, and the sunbeams wove round him a tissued robe that was
fairer than the robe that had been fashioned for his pleasure. The dead
staff blossomed, and bare lilies that were whiter than pearls. The dry
thorn blossomed, and bare roses that were redder than rubies. Whiter
than fine pearls were the lilies, and their stems were of bright silver.
Redder than male rubies were the roses, and their leaves were of beaten
gold.

He stood there in the raiment of a king, and the gates of the jewelled
shrine flew open and from the crystal of the many-rayed monstrance

shone a marvellous and mystical light. He stood there in a king's raiment, and the Glory of God filled the place, and the saints in their carven niches seemed to move. In the fair raiment of a king he stood before them, and the organ pealed out its music, and the trumpeters blew upon their trumpets, and the singing boys sang.

And the people fell upon their knees in awe, and the nobles sheathed their swords and did homage, and the Bishop's face grew pale, and his hands trembled. 'A greater than I hath crowned thee,' he cried, and he knelt before him.

And the young King came down from the high altar, and passed home through the midst of the people. But no man dared look upon his face, for it was like the face of an angel.

THE BIRTHDAY
OF THE INFANTA

IT WAS THE BIRTHDAY OF THE INFANTA. She was just twelve years of age, and the sun was shining brightly in the gardens of the palace.

Although she was a real Princess and the Infanta of Spain, she had only one birthday every year, just like the children of quite poor people, so it was naturally a matter of great importance to the whole country that she should have a really fine day for the occasion. And a really fine day it certainly was. The tall striped tulips stood straight up upon their stalks, like long rows of soldiers, and looked defiantly across the grass at the roses, and said: 'We are quite as splendid as you are now.' The purple butterflies fluttered about with gold dust on their wings, visiting each flower in turn; the little lizards crept out of the crevices of the wall, and lay basking in the white glare; and the pomegranates split and cracked with the heat, and showed their bleeding red hearts. Even the pale yellow lemons, that hung in such profusion from the mouldering trellis and along the dim arcades, seemed to have caught a richer colour from the wonderful sunlight, and the magnolia trees opened their great globe-like blossoms of folded ivory, and filled the air with a sweet heavy perfume.

The little Princess herself walked up and down the terrace with her companions, and played at hide and seek round the stone vases and the old moss-grown statues. On ordinary days she was only allowed to play with children of her own rank, so she had always to play alone, but her birthday was an exception, and the King had given orders that she was to invite any of her young friends whom she liked to come and amuse themselves with her. There was a stately grace about these slim Spanish children as they glided about, the boys with their large-plumed hats and short fluttering cloaks, the girls holding up the trains of their long brocade gowns, and shielding the sun from their eyes with huge fans of black and silver. But the Infanta was the most graceful of all, and the most tastefully attired, after the somewhat cumbrous fashion of the day. Her robe was of grey satin, the skirt and the wide puffed sleeves heavily embroidered with silver, and the stiff corset studded with rows of fine pearls. Two tiny slippers with big pink rosettes peeped out beneath her dress as she walked. Pink and pearl was her great gauze fan, and in her hair, which like an aureole of faded gold stood out stiffly round her pale little face, she had a beautiful white rose.

From a window in the palace the sad melancholy King watched them. Behind him stood his brother, Don Pedro of Aragon, whom he hated, and his confessor, the Grand Inquisitor of Granada, sat by his side. Sadder even than usual was the King, for as he looked at the Infanta bowing with childish gravity to the assembling courtiers, or laughing behind the fan at the grim Duchess of Albuquerque who always accompanied her, he thought of the young Queen, her mother, who but a short time before – so it seemed to him – had come from the gay country of France, and had withered away in the sombre splendour of the Spanish court, dying just six months after the birth of her child, and before she had seen the almonds blossom twice in the orchard, or plucked the second year's fruit from the old gnarled fig-tree that stood in the centre of the now grass-grown courtyard. So great had been his love for her that he had not suffered even the grave to hide her from him. She had been embalmed by a Moorish physician, who in return for this service had been granted his life, which for heresy and suspicion of magical practices had been already forfeited, men said, to the Holy Office, and her body was still lying on its tapestried bier in the black marble chapel of the Palace, just as the monks had borne her on that windy March day nearly twelve years before. Once every month the King, wrapped in a dark cloak and with a muffled lantern in his hand, went in and knelt by her side calling out, 'Mi reina! Mi reina!' and sometimes breaking through the formal etiquette that in Spain governs every separate action of life, and sets limits even to the sorrow of a King, he would clutch at the pale jewelled hands in a wild agony of grief, and try to wake by his mad kisses the cold painted face.

To-day he seemed to see her again, as he had seen her first at the Castle of Fontainebleau, when he was but fifteen years of age, and she still younger. They had been formally betrothed on that occasion by the Papal Nuncio in the presence of the French King and all the Court, and he had returned to the Escurial bearing with him a little ringlet of yellow hair, and the memory of two childish lips bending down to kiss his hand as he stepped into his carriage. Later on had followed the marriage, hastily performed at Burgos, a small town on the frontier between the two countries, and the grand public entry into Madrid with the customary celebration of high mass at the Church of La Atocha, and a more than usually solemn *auto-da-fé*, in which nearly three hundred heretics, amongst whom were many Englishmen, had been delivered over to the secular arm to be burned.

Certainly he had loved her madly, and to the ruin, many thought, of his country, then at war with England for the possession of the empire of the New World. He had hardly ever permitted her to be out of his sight; for her, he had forgotten, or seemed to have forgotten, all grave affairs of State; and, with that terrible blindness that passion brings upon its servants, he had failed to notice that the elaborate ceremonies by which he sought to please her did but aggravate the strange malady from which she suffered. When she died he was, for a time, like one bereft of reason. Indeed, there is no doubt but that he would have formally abdicated and retired to the great Trappist monastery at Granada, of which he was already titular Prior, had he not been afraid to leave the little Infanta at the mercy of his brother, whose cruelty, even in Spain, was notorious, and who was suspected by many of having caused the Queen's death by means of a pair of poisoned gloves that he had presented to her on the occasion of her visiting his castle in Aragon. Even after the expiration of the three years of public mourning that he had ordained throughout his whole dominions by royal edict, he would never suffer his ministers to speak about any new alliance, and when the Emperor himself sent to him, and offered him the hand of the lovely Archduchess of Bohemia, his niece, in marriage, he bade the ambassadors tell their master that the King of Spain was already wedded to Sorrow, and that though she was but a barren bride he loved her better than Beauty; an answer that cost his crown the rich provinces of the Netherlands, which soon after, at the Emperor's instigation, revolted against him under the leadership of some fanatics of the Reformed Church.

His whole married life, with its fierce, fiery-coloured joys and the terrible agony of its sudden ending, seemed to come back to him to-day as he watched the Infanta playing on the terrace. She had all the Queen's pretty petulance of manner, the same wilful way of tossing her head, the same proud, curved, beautiful mouth, the same wonderful smile – *vrai sourire de France* indeed – as she glanced up now and then at the window, or stretched out her little hand for the stately Spanish gentlemen to kiss. But the shrill laughter of the children grated on his ears, and the bright pitiless sunlight mocked his sorrow, and a dull odour of strange spices such as embalmers use, seemed to taint – or was it fancy? – the clear morning air. He buried his face in his hands, and when the Infanta looked up again the curtains had been drawn, and the King had retired.

She made a little *moue* of disappointment, and shrugged her shoulders. Surely he might have stayed with her on her birthday. What did the stupid State-affairs matter? Or had he gone to that gloomy chapel, where the candles were always burning, and where she was never allowed to enter? How silly of him, when the sun was shining so brightly, and everybody was so happy! Besides, he would miss the sham bull-fight for which the trumpet was already sounding, to say nothing of the puppet-show and the other wonderful things. Her uncle and the Grand Inquisitor were much more sensible. They had come out on the terrace, and paid her nice compliments. So she tossed her pretty head, and taking Don Pedro by the hand, she walked slowly down the steps towards a long pavilion of purple silk that had been erected at the end of the garden, the other children following in strict order of precedence, those who had the longest names going first.

A procession of noble boys, fantastically dressed as *toreadors*, came out to meet her, and the young Count of Tierra-Nueva, a wonderfully handsome lad of about fourteen years of age, uncovering his head with all the grace of a born hidalgo and grandee of Spain, led her solemnly in to a little gilt and ivory chair that was placed on a raised dais above the arena. The children grouped themselves all round, fluttering their big fans and whispering to each other, and Don Pedro and the Grand Inquisitor stood laughing at the entrance. Even the Duchess – the Camerera-Mayor as she was called – a thin, hard-featured woman with a yellow ruff, did not look quite so bad-tempered as usual, and something like a chill smile flitted across her wrinkled face and twitched her thin bloodless lips.

It certainly was a marvellous bull-fight, and much nicer, the Infanta thought, than the real bull-fight that she had been brought to see at Seville, on the occasion of the visit of the Duke of Parma to her father. Some of the boys pranced about on richly-caparisoned hobby-horses brandishing long javelins with gay streamers of bright ribands attached to them; others went on foot waving their scarlet cloaks before the bull, and vaulting lightly over the barrier when he charged them; and as for the bull himself, he was just like a live bull, though he was only made of wickerwork and stretched hide, and sometimes insisted on running round the arena on his hind legs, which no live bull ever dreams of doing. He made a splendid fight of it too, and the children got so excited that they stood up upon the benches, and waved their lace handkerchiefs and cried out: *Bravo toro! Bravo toro!* just as sensibly as if they had been grown-up people. At last, however, after a prolonged combat, during which several of the hobby-horses were gored through and through, and their riders dismounted, the young Count of Tierra-Nueva brought the bull to his knees, and having obtained permission from the Infanta to give the *coup de grâce*, he plunged his wooden sword into the neck of the animal with such violence that the head came right off, and disclosed the laughing face of little Monsieur de Lorraine, the son of the French Ambassador at Madrid.

The arena was then cleared amidst applause, and the dead hobby-horses dragged solemnly away by two Moorish pages in yellow and black liveries, and after a short interlude, during which a French posture-master performed upon a tight-rope, some Italian puppets appeared in the semi-classical tragedy of *Sophonisba* on the stage of a small theatre that had been built up for the purpose. They acted so well, and their gestures were so extremely natural, that at the close of the play the eyes of the Infanta were quite dim with tears. Indeed some of the children really cried, and had to be comforted with sweetmeats, and the Grand Inquisitor himself was so affected that he could not help saying to Don Pedro that it seemed to him intolerable that things made simply out of wood and coloured wax, and worked mechanically by wires, should be so unhappy and meet with such terrible misfortunes.

An African juggler followed, who brought in a large flat basket covered with a red cloth, and having placed it in the centre of the arena, he took from his turban a curious reed pipe, and blew through it. In a few moments the cloth began to move, and as the pipe grew shriller and shriller two green and gold snakes put out their strange wedge-shaped heads and rose slowly up, swaying to and fro with the music as a plant sways in the water. The children, however, were rather frightened at their spotted hoods and quick darting tongues, and were much more pleased when the juggler made a tiny orange-tree grow out of the sand and bear pretty white blossoms and clusters of real fruit; and when he took the fan of the little daughter of the Marquess de Las-Torres, and changed it into a blue bird that flew all round the pavilion and sang, their delight and amazement knew no bounds. The solemn minuet, too, performed by the dancing boys from the church of Nuestra Senora Del Pilar, was charming. The Infanta had never before seen this wonderful ceremony which takes place every year at Maytime in front of the high altar of the Virgin, and in her honour; and indeed none of the royal family of Spain had entered the great cathedral of Saragossa since a mad priest, supposed by many to have been in the pay of Elizabeth of England, had tried to administer a poisoned wafer to the Prince of the Asturias. So she had known only by hearsay of 'Our Lady's Dance', as it was called, and it certainly was a beautiful sight. The boys wore old-fashioned court dresses of white velvet, and their curious three-cornered hats were fringed with silver and surmounted with huge plumes of ostrich feathers, the dazzling whiteness of their costumes, as they moved about in the sunlight, being still more accentuated by their swarthy faces and long black hair. Everybody was fascinated by the grave dignity with which they moved through the intricate figures of the dance, and by the elaborate grace of their slow gestures, and stately bows, and when they had finished their performance and doffed their great plumed hats to the Infanta, she acknowledged their reverence with much courtesy, and made a vow that she would send a large wax candle to the shrine of Our Lady of Pilar in return for the pleasure that she had given her.

A troop of handsome Egyptians – as the gipsies were termed in those days – then advanced into the arena, and sitting down cross-legs, in a circle, began to play softly upon their zithers, moving their bodies to the tune, and humming, almost below their breath, a low dreamy air. When they caught sight of Don Pedro they scowled at him, and some of them looked terrified, for only a few weeks before he had had two of their tribe hanged for sorcery in the market-place at Seville, but the pretty Infanta charmed them as she leaned back peeping over her fan with her great blue eyes, and they felt sure that one so lovely as she was could never be cruel to anybody. So they played on very gently and just touched the cords of the zithers with their long pointed nails, and their heads began to nod as though they were falling asleep. Suddenly, with a cry so shrill that all the children were startled, and Don Pedro's hand clutched at the agate pommel of his dagger, they leapt to their feet and whirled madly round the enclosure beating their tambourines, and chanting some wild love-song in their strange guttural language. Then at another signal, they all flung themselves again to the ground and lay there quite still, the dull strumming of the zithers being the only sound that broke the silence. After they had done this several times, they disappeared for a moment and came back leading a brown shaggy bear by a chain, and carrying on their shoulders some little Barbary apes. The bear stood upon his head with the utmost gravity, and the wizened apes played all kinds of amusing tricks with two gipsy boys who seemed to be their masters, and fought with tiny swords, and fired off guns, and went through a regular soldier's drill just like the King's own bodyguard. In fact the gipsies were a great success.

But the funniest part of the whole morning's entertainment, was undoubtedly the dancing of the little Dwarf. When he stumbled into the arena, waddling on his crooked legs and wagging his huge misshapen head from side to side, the children went off into a loud shout of delight, and the Infanta herself laughed so much that the Camerera was obliged to remind her that although there were many precedents in Spain for a King's daughter weeping before her equals, there were none for a Princess of the blood royal making so merry before those who were her inferiors in birth. The Dwarf, however, was really quite irresistible, and even at the Spanish Court, always noted for its cultivated passion for the horrible, so fantastic a little monster had never been seen. It was his first appearance, too. He had been discovered only the day before, running wild through the forest, by two of the nobles who happened to have been hunting in a remote part of the great cork-wood that surrounded the town, and had been carried off by them to the Palace as a surprise for the Infanta; his father, who was a poor charcoal-burner, being but too well pleased to get rid of so ugly and useless a child. Perhaps the most amusing thing about him was his complete unconsciousness of his own grotesque appearance. Indeed he seemed quite happy and full of the highest spirits. When the children laughed, he laughed as freely and as joyously as any of them, and at the close of each dance he made them each the funniest of bows, smiling and nodding at them just as if he was really one of themselves, and not a little misshapen thing that Nature, in some humorous mood, had fashioned for others to mock at. As for the Infanta, she absolutely fascinated him. He could not keep his eyes off her, and seemed to dance for her alone, and when at the close of the performance, remembering how she had seen the great ladies of the Court throw bouquets to Caffarelli, the famous Italian treble, whom the Pope had sent from his own chapel to Madrid that he might cure the King's melancholy by the sweetness of his voice, she took out of her hair the beautiful white rose, and partly for a jest and partly to tease the Camerera, threw it to him across the arena with her sweetest smile, he took the whole matter quite seriously, and pressing the flower to his rough coarse lips he put his hand upon his heart, and sank on one knee before her, grinning from ear to ear, and with his little bright eyes sparkling with pleasure.

This so upset the gravity of the Infanta that she kept on laughing long after the little Dwarf had run out of the arena, and expressed a desire to her uncle that the dance should be immediately repeated. The Camerera, however, on the plea that the sun was too hot, decided that it would be better that her Highness should return without delay to the Palace, where a wonderful feast had been already prepared for her, including a real birthday cake with her own initials worked all over it in painted sugar and a lovely silver flag waving from the top. The Infanta accordingly rose up with much dignity, and having given orders that the little Dwarf was to dance again for her after the hour of siesta, and conveyed her thanks to the young Count of Tierra-Nueva for his charming reception, she went back to her apartments, the children following in the same order in which they had entered.

Now when the little Dwarf heard that he was to dance a second time before the Infanta, and by her own express command, he was so proud that he ran out into the garden, kissing the white rose in an absurd ecstasy of pleasure, and making the most uncouth and clumsy gestures of delight.

The Flowers were quite indignant at his daring to intrude into their beautiful home, and when they saw him capering up and down the walks, and waving his arms above his head in such a ridiculous manner, they could not restrain their feelings any longer.

'He is really far too ugly to be allowed to play in any place where we are,' cried the Tulips.

'He should drink poppy-juice, and go to sleep for a thousand years,' said the great scarlet Lilies, and they grew quite hot and angry.

'He is a perfect horror!' screamed the Cactus. 'Why, he is twisted and stumpy, and his head is completely out of proportion with his legs. Really he makes me feel prickly all over, and if he comes near me I will sting him with my thorns.'

'And he has actually got one of my best blooms,' exclaimed the White Rose-Tree. 'I gave it to the Infanta this morning myself, as a birthday present, and he has stolen it from her.' And she called out: 'Thief, thief, thief!' at the top of her voice.

Even the red Geraniums, who did not usually give themselves airs, and were known to have a great many poor relations themselves, curled up in disgust when they saw him, and when the Violets meekly remarked that though he was certainly extremely plain, still he could not help it, they retorted with a good deal of justice that that was his chief defect, and that there was no reason why one should admire a person because he was incurable; and, indeed, some of the Violets themselves felt that the ugliness of the little Dwarf was almost ostentatious, and that he would have shown much better taste if he had looked sad, or at least pensive, instead of jumping about merrily, and throwing himself into such grotesque and silly attitudes.

As for the old Sundial, who was an extremely remarkable individual, and had told the time of day to no less a person than the Emperor Charles V himself, he was so taken aback by the little Dwarf's appearance, that

he almost forgot to mark two whole minutes with his long shadowy finger, and could not help saying to the great milk-white Peacock, who was sunning herself on the balustrade, that every one knew that the children of Kings were Kings, and that the children of charcoal-burners were charcoal-burners, and that it was absurd to pretend that it wasn't so; a statement with which the Peacock entirely agreed, and indeed screamed out, 'Certainly, certainly,' in such a loud, harsh voice, that the Gold-fish who lived in the basin of the cool splashing fountain put their heads out of the water, and asked the huge stone Tritons what on earth was the matter.

But somehow the Birds liked him. They had seen him often in the forest, dancing about like an elf after the eddying leaves, or crouched up in the hollow of some old oak-tree, sharing his nuts with the squirrels. They did not mind his being ugly a bit. Why, even the Nightingale herself, who sang so sweetly in the orange groves at night that sometimes the Moon leaned down to listen, was not much to look at after all; and, besides, he had been kind to them, and during that terribly bitter winter, when there were no berries on the trees, and the ground was as hard as iron, and the wolves had come down to the very gates of the city to look for food, he had never once forgotten them, but had always given them crumbs out of his little hunch of black bread, and divided with them whatever poor breakfast he had.

So they flew round and round him, just touching his cheek with their wings as they passed, and chattered to each other, and the little Dwarf was so pleased that he could not help showing them the beautiful white rose, and telling them that the Infanta herself had given it to him because she loved him.

They did not understand a single word of what he was saying, but that made no matter, for they put their heads on one side, and looked wise, which is quite as good as understanding a thing, and very much easier.

The Lizards also took an immense fancy to him, and when he grew tired of running about and flung himself down on the grass to rest, they played and romped all over him, and tried to amuse him in the best way they could. 'Every one cannot be as beautiful as a lizard,' they cried; 'that would be too much to expect. And, though it sounds absurd to say so, he is really not so ugly after all, provided, of course, that one shuts one's eyes, and does not look at him.' The Lizards were extremely philosophical by nature, and often sat thinking for hours and hours together, when there was nothing else to do, or when the weather was too rainy for them to go out.

The Flowers, however, were excessively annoyed at their behaviour, and at the behaviour of the Birds. 'It only shows,' they said, 'what a vulgarising effect this incessant rushing and flying about has. Well-bred people always stay exactly in the same place as we do. No one ever saw us hopping up and down the walks, or galloping madly through the grass after dragon-flies. When we want a change of air, we send for the gardener, and he carries us to another bed. This is dignified, and as it should be. But birds and lizards have no sense of repose, and indeed birds have not even a permanent address. They are mere vagrants like the gipsies, and should be treated in exactly the same manner.' So they put their noses in the air, and looked very haughty, and were quite delighted when after some time they saw the little Dwarf scramble up from the grass, and make his way across the terrace to the palace.

'He should certainly be kept indoors for the rest of his natural life,' they said. 'Look at his hunched back, and his crooked legs,' and they began to titter.

But the little Dwarf knew nothing of all this. He liked the birds and the lizards immensely, and thought that the flowers were the most marvellous things in the whole world, except of course the Infanta, but then she had given him the beautiful white rose, and she loved him, and that made a great difference. How he wished that he had gone back with her! She would have put him on her right hand, and smiled at him, and he would have never left her side, but would have made her his playmate, and taught her all kinds of delightful tricks. For though he had never been in a palace before, he knew a great many wonderful things. He could make little cages out of rushes for the grasshoppers to sing in, and fashion the long-jointed bamboo into the pipe that Pan loves to hear. He knew the cry of every bird, and could call the starlings from the tree-top, or the heron from the mere. He knew the trail of every animal, and could track the hare by its delicate footprints, and the boar by the trampled leaves. All the wild-dances he knew, the mad dance in red raiment with the autumn, the light dance in blue sandals over the corn, the dance with white snow-wreaths in winter, and the blossom-dance, through the orchards in spring. He knew where the wood-pigeons built their nests, and once when a fowler had snared the parent birds, he had brought up the young ones himself, and had built a little dovecot for them in the cleft of a pollard elm. They were quite tame, and used to feed out of his hands every morning. She would like them, and the rabbits that scurried about in the long fern, and the jays with their steely feathers and black bills, and the hedgehogs that could curl themselves up into prickly balls, and the great wise tortoises that crawled slowly about, shaking their heads and nibbling at the young leaves. Yes, she must certainly come to the forest and play with him. He would give her his own little bed, and would watch outside the window till dawn, to see that the wild, horned cattle did not harm her, nor the gaunt wolves creep too near the hut. And at dawn he would tap at the shutters and wake her, and they would go out and dance together all the day long. It was really not a bit lonely in the forest. Sometimes a Bishop rode through on his white mule, reading out of a painted book. Sometimes in their green velvet caps, and their jerkins of tanned deerskin, the falconers passed by, with hooded hawks on their wrists. At vintage-time came the grape-treaders, with purple hands and feet, wreathed with glossy ivy and carrying dripping skins of wine; and the charcoal-burners sat round their huge braziers at night, watching the dry logs charring slowly in the fire, and roasting chestnuts in the ashes, and the robbers came out of their caves and made merry with them. Once, too, he had seen a beautiful procession winding up the long dusty road to Toledo. The monks went in front singing sweetly, and carrying bright banners and crosses of gold, and then, in silver armour, with matchlocks and pikes, came the soldiers, and in their midst walked three barefooted men, in strange yellow dresses painted all over with wonderful figures, and carrying lighted candles in their hands. Certainly there was a great deal to look at in the forest, and when she was tired he would find a soft bank of moss for her, or carry her in his arms, for he was very strong, though he knew that he was not tall. He would make her a necklace of red bryony berries, that would be quite as pretty as the white berries that she wore on her dress, and when she was tired of them, she could throw them away, and he would find her others. He would bring her acorn-cups and dew-drenched anemones, and tiny glow-worms to be stars in the pale gold of her hair.

But where was she? He asked the white rose, and it made him no answer. The whole palace seemed asleep, and even where the shutters had not been closed, heavy curtains had been drawn across the windows to keep out the glare. He wandered all round looking for some place through which he might gain an entrance, and at last he caught sight of a little private door that was lying open. He slipped through, and found himself in a splendid hall, far more splendid, he feared, than the forest, there was so much more gilding everywhere, and even the floor was made of great coloured stones, fitted together into a sort of geometrical pattern. But the little Infanta was not there, only some wonderful white statues that looked down on him from their jasper pedestals, with sad blank eyes and strangely smiling lips.

At the end of the hall hung a richly embroidered curtain of black velvet, powdered with suns and stars, the King's favourite devices, and broidered on the colour he loved best. Perhaps she was hiding behind that? He would try at any rate.

So he stole quietly across, and drew it aside. No; there was only another room, though a prettier room, he thought, than the one he had just left. The walls were hung with a many-figured green arras of needle-wrought tapestry representing a hunt, the work of some Flemish artists who had spent more than seven years in its composition. It had once been the chamber of *Jean le Fou*, as he was called, that mad King who was so enamoured of the chase, that he had often tried in his delirium to mount the huge rearing horses, and to drag down the stag on which the great hounds were leaping, sounding his hunting horn, and stabbing with his dagger at the pale flying deer. It was now used as the council-room, and on the centre table were lying the red portfolios of the ministers, stamped with the gold tulips of Spain, and with the arms and emblems of the house of Hapsburg.

The little Dwarf looked in wonder all round him, and was half-afraid to go on. The strange silent horsemen that galloped so swiftly through the long glades without making any noise, seemed to him like those terrible phantoms of whom he had heard the charcoal-burners speaking – the Comprachos, who hunt only at night, and if they meet a man, turn him into a hind, and chase him. But he thought of the pretty Infanta, and took courage. He wanted to find her alone, and to tell her that he too loved her. Perhaps she was in the room beyond.

He ran across the soft Moorish carpets, and opened the door. No! She was not here either. The room was quite empty.

It was a throne-room, used for the reception of foreign ambassadors, when the King, which of late had not been often, consented to give them a personal audience; the same room in which, many years before, envoys had appeared from England to make arrangements for the marriage of their Queen, then one of the Catholic sovereigns of Europe, with the Emperor's eldest son. The hangings were of gilt Cordovan leather, and a heavy gilt chandelier with branches for three hundred wax lights hung down from the black and white ceiling. Underneath a great canopy of gold cloth, on which the lions and towers of Castile were broidered in seed pearls, stood the throne itself, covered with a rich pall of black velvet studded with silver tulips and elaborately fringed with silver and pearls. On the second step of the throne was placed the kneeling-stool of the Infanta, with its cushion of cloth of silver tissue, and below that again, and beyond the limit of the canopy, stood the chair for the Papal Nuncio, who alone had the right to be seated in the King's presence on the occasion of any public ceremonial, and whose Cardinal's hat, with its tangled scarlet tassels, lay on a purple *tabouret* in front. On the wall facing the throne, hung a life-sized portrait of Charles V in hunting dress, with a great mastiff by his side, and a picture of Philip II receiving the homage of the Netherlands, occupied the centre of the other wall. Between the windows stood a black ebony cabinet, inlaid with plates of ivory, on which the figures from Holbein's Dance of Death had been graved – by the hand, some said, of that famous master himself.

But the little Dwarf cared nothing for all this magnificence. He would not have given his rose for all the pearls on the canopy, nor one white petal of his rose for the throne itself. What he wanted was to see the Infanta before she went down to the pavilion, and to ask her to come away with him when he had finished his dance. Here, in the Palace, the air was close and heavy, but in the forest the wind blew free, and the sunlight with wandering hands of gold moved the tremulous leaves aside. There were flowers, too, in the forest, not so splendid, perhaps, as the flowers in the garden, but more sweetly scented for all that; hyacinths in early spring that flooded with waving purple the cool glens, and grassy knolls; yellow primroses that nestled in little clumps round the gnarled roots of the oak-trees; bright celandine, and blue speedwell, and irises lilac and gold. There were grey catkins on the hazels, and the foxgloves drooped with the weight of their dappled bee-haunted cells. The chestnut had its spires of white stars, and the hawthorn its pallid moons of beauty. Yes: surely she would come if he could only find her! She would come with him to the fair forest, and all day long he would dance for her delight. A smile lit up his eyes at the thought, and he passed into the next room.

Of all the rooms this was the brightest and the most beautiful. The walls were covered with a pink-flowered Lucca damask, patterned with birds and dotted with dainty blossoms of silver; the furniture was of massive silver, festooned with florid wreaths, and swinging Cupids; in front of the two large fire-places stood great screens broidered with parrots and peacocks, and the floor, which was of sea-green onyx, seemed to stretch far away into the distance. Nor was he alone. Standing under the shadow of the doorway, at the extreme end of the room, he saw a little figure watching him. His heart trembled, a cry of joy broke from his lips, and he moved out into the sunlight. As he did so, the figure moved out also, and he saw it plainly.

The Infanta! It was a monster, the most grotesque monster he had ever beheld. Not properly shaped as all other people were, but hunchbacked, and crooked-limbed, with huge lolling head and mane of black hair. The little Dwarf frowned, and the monster frowned also. He laughed, and it laughed with him, and held its hands to its sides, just as he himself was doing. He made it a mocking bow, and it returned him a low reverence. He went towards it, and it came to meet him, copying each step that he made, and stopping when he stopped himself. He shouted with amusement, and ran forward, and reached out his hand, and the hand of the monster touched his, and it was as cold as ice. He grew afraid, and moved his hand across, and the monster's hand followed it quickly. He tried to press on, but something smooth and hard stopped him. The face of the monster was now close to his own, and seemed full of terror. He brushed his hair off his eyes. It imitated him. He struck at it, and it returned blow for blow. He loathed it, and it made hideous faces at him. He drew back, and it retreated.

What is it? He thought for a moment, and looked round at the rest of the room. It was strange, but everything seemed to have its double in this invisible wall of clear water. Yes, picture for picture was repeated, and couch for couch. The sleeping Faun that lay in the alcove by the doorway had its twin brother that slumbered, and the silver Venus that stood in the sunlight held out her arms to a Venus as lovely as herself.

Was it Echo? He had called to her once in the valley, and she had answered him word for word. Could she mock the eye, as she mocked the voice? Could she make a mimic world just like the real world? Could the shadows of things have colour and life and movement? Could it be that—?

He started, and taking from his breast the beautiful white rose, he turned round, and kissed it. The monster had a rose of its own, petal for petal the same! It kissed it with like kisses, and pressed it to its heart with horrible gestures.

When the truth dawned upon him, he gave a wild cry of despair, and fell sobbing to the ground. So it was he who was misshapen and hunchbacked, foul to look at and grotesque. He himself was the monster, and it was at him that all the children had been laughing, and the little Princess who he had thought loved him – she, too, had been merely mocking at his ugliness, and making merry over his twisted limbs. Why had they not left him in the forest, where there was no mirror to tell him how loathsome he was? Why had his father not killed him, rather than sell him to his shame? The hot tears poured down his cheeks, and he tore the white rose to pieces. The sprawling monster did the same, and scattered the faint petals in the air. It grovelled on the ground, and, when he looked at it, it watched him with a face drawn with pain. He crept away, lest he should see it, and covered his eyes with his hands. He crawled, like some wounded thing, into the shadow, and lay there moaning.

And at that moment the Infanta herself came in with her companions through the open window, and when they saw the ugly little dwarf lying on the ground and beating the floor with his clenched hands, in the most fantastic and exaggerated manner, they went off into shouts of happy laughter, and stood all round him and watched him.

'His dancing was funny,' said the Infanta; 'but his acting is funnier still. Indeed, he is almost as good as the puppets, only, of course, not quite so natural.' And she fluttered her big fan and applauded.

But the little Dwarf never looked up, and his sobs grew fainter and fainter, and suddenly he gave a curious gasp, and clutched his side. And then he fell back again, and lay quite still.

'That is capital,' said the Infanta, after a pause; 'but now you must dance for me.'

'Yes,' cried all the children, 'you must get up and dance, for you are as clever as the Barbary apes, and much more ridiculous.'

But the little Dwarf made no answer.

And the Infanta stamped her foot, and called out to her uncle, who was walking on the terrace with the Chamberlain, reading some despatches that had just arrived from Mexico, where the Holy Office had recently been established. 'My funny little dwarf is sulking,' she cried, 'you must wake him up and tell him to dance for me.'

They smiled at each other, and sauntered in, and Don Pedro stooped down, and slapped the Dwarf on the cheek with his embroidered glove. 'You must dance,' he said, '*petit monstre*. You must dance. The Infanta of Spain and the Indies wishes to be amused.'

But the little Dwarf never moved.

'A whipping master should be sent for,' said Don Pedro wearily, and he went back to the terrace. But the Chamberlain looked grave, and he knelt beside the little Dwarf, and put his hand upon his heart. And after a few moments he shrugged his shoulders, and rose up, and having made a low bow to the Infanta, he said—

'*Mi bella Princesa*, your funny little dwarf will never dance again. It is a pity, for he is so ugly that he might have made the King smile.'

'But why will he not dance again?' asked the Infanta laughing.

'Because his heart is broken,' answered the Chamberlain.

And the Infanta frowned, and her dainty rose-leaf lips curled in pretty disdain. 'For the future let those who come to play with me have no hearts,' she cried, and she ran out into the garden.

THE FISHERMAN
AND HIS SOUL

EVERY EVENING THE YOUNG FISHERMAN went out upon the sea, and threw his nets into the water.

When the wind blew from the land he caught nothing, or but little at best, for it was a bitter and black-winged wind, and rough waves rose up to meet it. But when the wind blew to the shore, the fish came in from the deep, and swam into the meshes of his nets, and he took them to the market-place and sold them.

Every evening he went out upon the sea, and one evening the net was so heavy that hardly could he draw it into the boat. And he laughed, and said to himself, 'Surely I have caught all the fish that swim, or snared some dull monster that will be a marvel to men, or some thing of horror that the great Queen will desire,' and putting forth all his strength, he tugged at the coarse ropes till, like lines of blue enamel round a vase of bronze, the long veins rose up on his arms. He tugged at the thin ropes, and nearer and nearer came the circle of flat corks, and the net rose at last to the top of the water.

But no fish at all was in it, nor any monster or thing of horror, but only a little Mermaid lying fast asleep.

Her hair was a wet fleece of gold, and each separate hair as a thread of fine gold in a cup of glass. Her body was as white ivory, and her tail was of silver and pearl. Silver and pearl was her tail, and the green weeds of the sea coiled round it; and like sea-shells were her ears, and her lips were like sea-coral. The cold waves dashed over her cold breasts, and the salt glistened upon her eyelids.

So beautiful was she that when the young Fisherman saw her he was filled with wonder, and he put out his hand and drew the net close to him, and leaning over the side he clasped her in his arms. And when he touched her, she gave a cry like a startled sea-gull, and woke, and looked at him in terror with her mauve-amethyst eyes, and struggled that she might escape. But he held her tightly to him and would not suffer her to depart.

And when she saw that she could in no way escape from him, she

began to weep, and said, 'I pray thee let me go, for I am the only daughter of a King, and my father is aged and alone.'

But the young Fisherman answered, 'I will not let thee go save thou makest me a promise that whenever I call thee, thou wilt come and sing to me, for the fish delight to listen to the song of the Sea-folk, and so shall my nets be full.'

'Wilt thou in very truth let me go, if I promise thee this?' cried the Mermaid.

'In very truth I will let thee go,' said the young Fisherman.

So she made him the promise he desired, and sware it by the oath of the Sea-folk. And he loosened his arms from about her, and she sank down into the water, trembling with a strange fear.

Every morning the young Fisherman went out upon the sea, and called to the Mermaid, and she rose out of the water and sang to him. Round and round her swam the dolphins, and the wild gulls wheeled above her head.

And she sang a marvellous song. For she sang of the Sea-folk who drive their flocks from cave to cave, and carry the little calves on their shoulders; of the Tritons who have long green beards, and hairy breasts, and blow through twisted conches when the King passes by; of the palace of the King which is all of amber, with a roof of clear emerald, and a pavement of bright pearl; and of the gardens of the sea where the great filigrane fans of coral wave all day long, and the fish dart about like silver birds, and the anemones cling to the rocks, and the pinks bourgeon in the ribbed yellow sand. She sang of the big whales that come down from the north seas and have sharp icicles hanging to their fins; of the Sirens who tell of such wonderful things that the merchants have to stop their ears with wax lest they should hear them, and leap into the water and be drowned; of the sunken galleys with their tall masts, and the frozen sailors clinging to the rigging, and the mackerel swimming in and out of the open portholes; of the little barnacles who are great travellers, and cling to the keels of the ships, and go round and round the world; and of the cuttlefish who live in the sides of the cliffs and stretch out their long black arms, and can make night come when they will it. She sang of the nautilus who has a boat of her own that is carved out of an opal and steered with a silken sail; of the happy Mermen who play upon harps and can charm the great Kraken to sleep; of the little children who catch hold of the slippery porpoises and ride laughing upon their backs; of the Mermaids who lie in the white foam and hold out their arms to the mariners; and of the sea-lions with their curved tusks, and the sea-horses with their floating manes.

And as she sang, all the tunny-fish came in from the deep to listen to her, and the young Fisherman threw his nets round them and caught them, and others he took with a spear. And when his boat was well-laden, the Mermaid would sink down into the sea, smiling at him.

Yet would she never come near him that he might touch her. Oftentimes he called to her and prayed of her, but she would not; and when he sought to seize her she dived into the water as a seal might dive, nor did he see her again that day. And each day the sound of her voice became sweeter to his ears. So sweet was her voice that he forgot his nets and his cunning, and had no care of his craft. Vermilion-finned and with eyes of bossy gold, the tunnies went by in shoals, but he heeded them not. His spear lay by his side unused, and his baskets of plaited osier were empty. With lips parted, and eyes dim with wonder, he sat idle in his boat and listened, listening till the sea-mists crept round him, and the wandering moon stained his brown limbs with silver.

And one evening he called to her, and said: 'Little Mermaid, little Mermaid, I love thee. Take me for thy bridegroom for I love thee.'

But the Mermaid shook her head. 'Thou hast a human soul,' she answered. 'If only thou wouldst send away thy soul, then could I love thee.'

And the young Fisherman said to himself, 'Of what use is my soul to me? I cannot see it. I may not touch it. I do not know it. Surely I will send it away from me, and much gladness shall be mine.' And a cry of joy broke from his lips, and standing up in the painted boat, he held out his arms to the Mermaid. 'I will send my soul away,' he cried, 'and you shall be my bride, and I will be thy bridegroom, and in the depth of the sea we will dwell together, and all that thou hast sung of thou shalt show me, and all that thou desirest I will do, nor shall our lives be divided.'

And the little Mermaid laughed for pleasure and hid her face in her hands.

'But how shall I send my soul from me?' cried the young Fisherman. 'Tell me how I may do it, and lo! it shall be done.'

'Alas! I know not,' said the little Mermaid: 'the Sea-folk have no souls.' And she sank down into the deep, looking wistfully at him.

Now early on the next morning, before the sun was the span of a man's hand above the hill, the young Fisherman went to the house of the Priest and knocked three times at the door.

The novice looked out through the wicket, and when he saw who it was, he drew back the latch and said to him, 'Enter.'

And the young Fisherman passed in, and knelt down on the sweet-smelling rushes of the floor, and cried to the Priest who was reading out of the Holy Book and said to him, 'Father, I am in love with one of the Sea-folk, and my soul hindereth me from having my desire. Tell me how I can send my soul away from me, for in truth I have no need of it. Of what value is my soul to me? I cannot see it. I may not touch it. I do not know it.'

And the Priest beat his breast, and answered, 'Alack, alack, thou art mad, or hast eaten of some poisonous herb, for the soul is the noblest part of man, and was given to us by God that we should nobly use it. There is no thing more precious than a human soul, nor any earthly thing that can be weighed with it. It is worth all the gold that is in the world, and is more precious than the rubies of the kings. Therefore, my son, think not any more of this matter, for it is a sin that may not be forgiven. And as for the Sea-folk, they are lost, and they who would traffic with them are lost also. They are the beasts of the field that know not good from evil, and for them the Lord has not died.'

The young Fisherman's eyes filled with tears when he heard the bitter words of the Priest, and he rose up from his knees and said to him, 'Father, the Fauns live in the forest and are glad, and on the rocks sit the Mermen with their harps of gold. Let me be as they are, I beseech thee, for their days are as the days of flowers. And as for my soul, what doth my soul profit me, if it stand between me and the thing that I love?'

'The love of the body is vile,' cried the Priest, knitting his brows, 'and vile and evil are the pagan things God suffers to wander through His world. Accursed be the Fauns of the woodland, and accursed be the singers of the sea! I have heard them at night-time, and they have sought to lure me from my beads. They tap at the window and laugh. They whisper into my ears the tale of their perilous joys. They tempt me with temptations, and when I would pray they make mouths at me. They are lost, I tell thee, they are lost. For them there is no heaven nor hell, and in neither shall they praise God's name.'

'Father,' cried the young Fisherman, 'thou knowest not what thou sayest. Once in my net I snared the daughter of a King. She is fairer than the morning star, and whiter than the moon. For her body I would give my soul, and for her love I would surrender heaven. Tell me what I ask of thee, and let me go in peace.'

'Away! Away!' cried the Priest: 'thy leman is lost, and thou shalt be lost with her.' And he gave him no blessing, but drove him from his door.

And the young Fisherman went down into the market-place, and he walked slowly, and with bowed head, as one who is in sorrow.

And when the merchants saw him coming, they began to whisper to each other, and one of them came forth to meet him, and called him by name, and said to him, 'What hast thou to sell?'

'I will sell thee my soul,' he answered: 'I pray thee buy it of me, for I am weary of it. Of what use is my soul to me? I cannot see it. I may not touch it. I do not know it.'

But the merchants mocked at him, and said, 'Of what use is a man's soul to us? It is not worth a clipped piece of silver. Sell us thy body for a slave, and we will clothe thee in sea-purple, and put a ring upon thy finger, and make thee the minion of the great Queen. But talk not of the soul, for to us it is nought, nor has it any value for our service.'

And the young Fisherman said to himself: 'How strange a thing this is! The Priest telleth me that the soul is worth all the gold in the world, and the merchants say that it is not worth a clipped piece of silver.' And he passed out of the market-place, and went down to the shore of the sea, and began to ponder on what he should do.

And at noon he remembered how one of his companions, who was a gatherer of samphire, had told him of a certain young Witch who dwelt in a cave at the head of the bay and was very cunning in her witcheries. And he set to and ran, so eager was he to get rid of his soul, and a cloud of dust followed him as he sped round the sand of the shore. By the itching of her palm the young Witch knew his coming, and she laughed and let down her red hair. With her red hair falling around her, she stood at the opening of the cave, and in her hand she had a spray of wild hemlock that was blossoming.

'What d'ye lack? What d'ye lack?' she cried, as he came panting up the steep, and bent down before her. 'Fish for thy net, when the wind is foul? I have a little reed-pipe, and when I blow on it the mullet come sailing into the bay. But it has a price, pretty boy, it has a price. What d'ye lack? What d'ye lack? A storm to wreck the ships, and wash the chests of rich treasure ashore? I have more storms than the wind has, for I serve one who is stronger than the wind, and with a sieve and a pail of water I can send the great galleys to the bottom of the sea. But I have a price, pretty boy, I have a price. What d'ye lack? What d'ye lack? I know a flower that grows in the valley, none knows it but I. It has purple leaves, and a star in its heart, and its juice is as white as milk. Shouldst thou touch with this flower the hard lips of the Queen, she would follow thee all over the world. Out of the bed of the King she would rise, and over the whole world she would follow thee. And it has a price, pretty boy, it has a price. What d'ye lack? What d'ye lack? I can pound a toad in a mortar, and make a broth of it, and stir the broth with a dead man's hand. Sprinkle it on thine enemy while he sleeps, and he will turn into a black viper, and his own mother will slay him. With a wheel I can draw the Moon from heaven, and in a crystal I can show thee Death. What d'ye lack? What d'ye lack? Tell me thy desire, and I will give it thee, and thou shalt pay me a price, pretty boy, thou shalt pay me a price.'

'My desire is but for a little thing,' said the young Fisherman, 'yet hath the Priest been wroth with me, and driven me forth. It is but for a little thing, and the merchants have mocked me, and denied me. Therefore am I come to thee, though men call thee evil, and whatever be thy price I shall pay it.'

'What wouldst thou?' asked the Witch, coming near to him.

'I would send my soul away from me,' answered the young Fisherman.

The Witch grew pale, and shuddered, and hid her face in her blue mantle. 'Pretty boy, pretty boy,' she muttered, 'that is a terrible thing to do.'

He tossed his brown curls and laughed. 'My soul is nought to me,' he answered. 'I cannot see it. I may not touch it. I do not know it.'

'What wilt thou give me if I tell thee?' asked the Witch, looking down at him with her beautiful eyes.

'Five pieces of gold,' he said, 'and my nets, and the wattled house where I live, and the painted boat in which I sail. Only tell me how to get rid of my soul, and I will give thee all that I possess.'

She laughed mockingly at him, and struck him with the spray of hemlock. 'I can turn the autumn leaves into gold,' she answered, 'and I can weave the pale moonbeams into silver if I will it. He whom I serve is richer than all the kings of this world, and has their dominions.'

'What then shall I give thee,' he cried, 'if thy price be neither gold nor silver?'

The Witch stroked his hair with her thin white hand. 'Thou must dance with me, pretty boy,' she murmured, and she smiled at him as she spoke.

'Nought but that?' cried the young Fisherman in wonder, and he rose to his feet.

'Nought but that,' she answered, and she smiled at him again.

'Then at sunset in some secret place we shall dance together,' he said, 'and after that we have danced thou shalt tell me the thing which I desire to know.'

She shook her head. 'When the moon is full, when the moon is full,' she muttered. Then she peered all round, and listened. A blue bird rose screaming from its nest and circled over the dunes, and three spotted birds rustled through the coarse grey grass and whistled to each other. There was no other sound save the sound of a wave fretting the smooth pebbles below. So she reached out her hand, and drew him near to her and put her dry lips close to his ear.

'To-night thou must come to the top of the mountain,' she whispered. 'It is a Sabbath, and He will be there.'

The young Fisherman started and looked at her, and she showed her white teeth and laughed. 'Who is He of whom thou speakest?' he asked. 'It matters not,' she answered. 'Go thou to-night, and stand under the branches of the hornbeam, and wait for my coming. If a black dog runs towards thee, strike it with a rod of willow, and it will go away. If an owl speak to thee, make it no answer. When the moon is full I shall be with thee, and we will dance together on the grass.'

'But wilt thou swear to me to tell me how I may send my soul from me?' he made question.

She moved out into the sunlight, and through her red hair rippled the wind. 'By the hoofs of the goat I swear it,' she made answer.

'Thou art the best of the witches,' cried the young Fisherman, 'and I will surely dance with thee to-night on the top of the mountain. I would indeed that thou hadst asked of me either gold or silver. But such as thy price is thou shalt have it, for it is but a little thing.' And he doffed his cap to her, and bent his head low, and ran back to the town filled with a great joy.

And the Witch watched him as he went, and when he had passed from her sight she entered her cave, and having taken a mirror from a box of carved cedarwood, she set it up on a frame, and burned vervain on lighted charcoal before it, and peered through the coils of the smoke. And after a time she clenched her hands in anger. 'He should have been mine,' she muttered, 'I am as fair as she is.'

And that evening, when the moon had risen, the young Fisherman climbed up to the top of the mountain, and stood under the branches of the hornbeam. Like a targe of polished metal the round sea lay at his feet, and the shadows of the fishing-boats moved in the little bay. A great owl, with yellow sulphurous eyes, called to him by his name, but he made it no answer. A black dog ran towards him and snarled. He struck it with a rod of willow, and it went away whining.

At midnight the witches came flying through the air like bats. 'Phew!' they cried, as they lit upon the ground, 'there is some one here we know not!' and they sniffed about, and chattered to each other, and made signs. Last of all came the young Witch, with her red hair streaming in the wind. She wore a dress of gold tissue embroidered with peacocks' eyes, and a little cap of green velvet was on her head.

'Where is he, where is he?' shrieked the witches when they saw her, but she only laughed, and ran to the hornbeam, and taking the Fisherman by the hand she led him out into the moonlight and began to dance.

Round and round they whirled, and the young Witch jumped so high that he could see the scarlet heels of her shoes. Then right across the dancers came the sound of the galloping of a horse, but no horse was to be seen, and he felt afraid.

'Faster,' cried the Witch, and she threw her arms about his neck, and her breath was hot upon his face. 'Faster, faster!' she cried, and the earth seemed to spin beneath his feet, and his brain grew troubled, and a great terror fell on him, as of some evil thing that was watching him, and at last he became aware that under the shadow of a rock there was a figure that had not been there before.

It was a man dressed in a suit of black velvet, cut in the Spanish fashion. His face was strangely pale, but his lips were like a proud red flower. He seemed weary, and was leaning back toying in a listless manner with the pommel of his dagger. On the grass beside him lay a plumed hat, and a pair of riding-gloves gauntleted with gilt lace, and sewn with seed-pearls wrought into a curious device. A short cloak lined with sables hung from his shoulder, and his delicate white hands were gemmed with rings. Heavy eye-lids drooped over his eyes.

The young Fisherman watched him, as one snared in a spell. At last their eyes met, and wherever he danced it seemed to him that the eyes of the man were upon him. He heard the Witch laugh, and caught her by the waist, and whirled her madly round and round.

Suddenly a dog bayed in the wood, and the dancers stopped, and going up two by two, knelt down, and kissed the man's hands. As they did so, a little smile touched his proud lips, as a bird's wing touches the water and makes it laugh. But there was disdain in it. He kept looking at the young Fisherman.

'Come! let us worship,' whispered the Witch, and she led him up, and a great desire to do as she besought him seized on him, and he followed her. But when he came close, and without knowing why he did it, he made on his breast the sign of the Cross, and called upon the holy name.

No sooner had he done so than the witches screamed like hawks and flew away, and the pallid face that had been watching him twitched with a spasm of pain. The man went over to a little wood, and whistled. A jennet with silver trappings came running to meet him. As he leapt upon the saddle he turned round, and looked at the young Fisherman sadly.

And the Witch with the red hair tried to fly away also, but the Fisherman caught her by her wrists, and held her fast.

'Loose me,' she cried, 'and let me go. For thou hast named what should not be named, and shown the sign that may not be looked at.'

'Nay,' he answered, 'but I will not let thee go till thou hast told me the secret.'

'What secret?' said the Witch, wrestling with him like a wild cat, and biting her foam-flecked lips.

'Thou knowest,' he made answer.

Her grass-green eyes grew dim with tears, and she said to the Fisherman, 'Ask me anything but that!'

He laughed, and held her all the more tightly.

And when she saw that she could not free herself, she whispered to him, 'Surely I am as fair as the daughter of the sea, and as comely as those that dwell in the blue waters,' and she fawned on him and put her face close to his.

But he thrust her back frowning, and said to her, 'If thou keepest not the promise that thou madest to me I will slay thee for a false witch.'

She grew grey as a blossom of the Judas tree, and shuddered. 'Be it so,' she muttered. 'It is thy soul and not mine. Do with it as thou wilt.' And she took from her girdle a little knife that had a handle of green viper's skin, and gave it to him.

'What shall this serve me?' he asked of her, wondering.

She was silent for a few moments, and a look of terror came over her face. Then she brushed her hair back from her forehead, and smiling strangely she said to him, 'What men call the shadow of the body is not the shadow of the body, but is the body of the soul. Stand on the sea-shore with thy back to the moon, and cut away from thy feet thy shadow, which is thy soul's body, and bid thy soul leave thee, and it will do so.'

The young Fisherman trembled. 'Is this true?' he murmured.

'It is true, and I would that I had not told thee of it,' she cried, and she clung to his knees weeping.

He put her from him and left her in the rank grass, and going to the edge of the mountain he placed the knife in his belt and began to climb down.

And his Soul that was within him called out to him and said, 'Lo! I have dwelt with thee for all these years, and have been thy servant. Send me not away from thee now, for what evil have I done thee?'

And the young Fisherman laughed. 'Thou hast done me no evil, but I have no need of thee,' he answered. 'The world is wide, and there is Heaven also, and Hell, and that dim twilight house that lies between. Go wherever thou wilt, but trouble me not, for my love is calling to me.'

And his Soul besought him piteously, but he heeded it not, but leapt from crag to crag, being sure-footed as a wild goat, and at last he reached the level ground and the yellow shore of the sea.

Bronze-limbed and well-knit, like a statue wrought by a Grecian, he stood on the sand with his back to the moon, and out of the foam came white arms that beckoned to him, and out of the waves rose dim forms that did him homage. Before him lay his shadow, which was the body of his soul, and behind him hung the moon in the honey-coloured air.

And his Soul said to him, 'If indeed thou must drive me from thee, send me not forth without a heart. The world is cruel, give me thy heart to take with me.'

He tossed his head and smiled. 'With what should I love my love if I gave thee my heart?' he cried.

'Nay, but be merciful,' said his Soul: 'give me thy heart, for the world is very cruel, and I am afraid.'

'My heart is my love's,' he answered, 'therefore tarry not, but get thee gone.'

'Should I not love also?' asked his Soul.

'Get thee gone, for I have no need of thee,' cried the young Fisherman, and he took the little knife with its handle of green viper's skin, and cut away his shadow from around his feet, and it rose up and stood before him, and looked at him, and it was even as himself.

He crept back, and thrust the knife into his belt, and a feeling of awe came over him. 'Get thee gone,' he murmured, 'and let me see thy face no more.' 'Nay, but we must meet again,' said the Soul. Its voice was low and flute-like, and its lips hardly moved while it spake.

'How shall we meet?' cried the young Fisherman. 'Thou wilt not follow me into the depths of the sea?'

'Once every year I will come to this place, and call to thee,' said the Soul. 'It may be that thou wilt have need of me.'

'What need should I have of thee?' cried the young Fisherman, 'but be it as thou wilt,' and he plunged into the water, and the Tritons blew their horns, and the little Mermaid rose up to meet him, and put her arms around his neck and kissed him on the mouth.

And the Soul stood on the lonely beach and watched them. And when they had sunk down into the sea, it went weeping away over the marshes.

And after a year was over the Soul came down to the shore of the sea and called to the young Fisherman, and he rose out of the deep, and said, 'Why dost thou call to me?'

And the Soul answered, 'Come nearer, that I may speak with thee, for I have seen marvellous things.'

So he came nearer, and couched in the shallow water, and leaned his head upon his hand and listened.

And the Soul said to him, 'When I left thee I turned my face to the East and journeyed. From the East cometh everything that is wise. Six days I journeyed, and on the morning of the seventh day I came to a hill that is in the country of the Tartars. I sat down under the shade of a tamarisk tree to shelter myself from the sun. The land was dry and burnt up with the heat. The people went to and fro over the plain like flies crawling upon a disk of polished copper.

'When it was noon a cloud of red dust rose up from the flat rim of the land. When the Tartars saw it, they strung their painted bows, and having leapt upon their little horses they galloped to meet it. The women fled screaming to the waggons, and hid themselves behind the felt curtains.

'At twilight the Tartars returned, but five of them were missing, and of those that came back not a few had been wounded. They harnessed their horses to the waggons and drove hastily away. Three jackals came out of a cave and peered after them. Then they sniffed up the air with their nostrils, and trotted off in the opposite direction.

'When the moon rose I saw a camp-fire burning on the plain, and went towards it. A company of merchants were seated round it on carpets. Their camels were picketed behind them, and the negroes who were their servants were pitching tents of tanned skin upon the sand, and making a high wall of the prickly pear.

'As I came near them, the chief of the merchants rose up and drew his sword and asked me my business.

'I answered that I was a Prince in my own land, and that I had escaped from the Tartars who had sought to make me their slave. The chief smiled, and showed me five heads fixed upon long reeds of bamboo.

'Then he asked me who was the prophet of God, and I answered him Mohammed.

'When he heard the name of the false prophet, he bowed and took me by the hand, and placed me by his side. A negro brought me some mare's milk in a wooden dish, and a piece of lamb's flesh roasted.

'At daybreak we started on our journey. I rode on a red-haired camel by the side of the chief, and a runner ran before us carrying a spear. The men of war were on either hand, and the mules followed with the merchandise. There were forty camels in the caravan, and the mules were twice forty in number.

'We went from the country of the Tartars into the country of those who curse the Moon. We saw the Gryphons guarding their gold on the white rocks, and the scaled Dragons sleeping in their caves. As we passed over the mountains we held our breath lest the snows might fall on us, and each man tied a veil of gauze before his eyes. As we passed through the valleys the Pygmies shot arrows at us from the hollows of the trees, and at night-time we heard the wild men beating on their drums. When we came to the Tower of Apes we set fruits before them, and they did not harm us. When we came to the Tower of Serpents we gave them warm milk in bowls of brass, and they let us go by. Three times in our journey we came to the banks of the Oxus. We crossed it on rafts of wood with great bladders of blown hide. The river-horses raged against us and sought to slay us. When the camels saw them they trembled.

'The kings of each city levied tolls on us, but they would not suffer us to enter their gates. They threw us bread over the walls, little maizecakes baked in honey and cakes of fine flour filled with dates. For every hundred baskets we gave them a bead of amber.

'When the dwellers in the villages saw us coming, they poisoned the wells and fled to the hill-summits. We fought with the Magadæ who are born old, and grow younger and younger every year, and die when they are little children; and with the Laktroi who say that they are the sons of tigers, and paint themselves yellow and black, and with the Aurantes who bury their dead on the tops of trees, and themselves live in dark caverns lest the Sun, who is their god, should slay them; and with the Krimnians who worship a crocodile, and give it earrings of green grass, and feed it with butter and fresh fowls; and with the Agazonbæ, who are dog-faced; and with the Sibans, who have horses' feet, and run more swiftly than horses. A third of our company died in battle, and a third died of want. The rest murmured against me, and said that I had brought them an evil fortune. I took a horned adder from beneath a stone and let it sting me. When they saw that I did not sicken they grew afraid.

'In the fourth month we reached the city of Illel. It was night-time when we came to the grove that is outside the walls, and the air was sultry, for the Moon was travelling in Scorpion. We took the ripe pomegranates from the trees, and brake them, and drank their sweet juices. Then we lay on our carpets and waited for the dawn.

'And at dawn we rose and knocked at the gate of the city. It was wrought out of red bronze, and carved with sea-dragons and dragons that have wings. The guards looked down from the battlements and asked us our business. The interpreter of the caravan answered that we had come from the island of Syria with much merchandise. They took hostages, and told us that they would open the gate to us at noon, and bade us tarry till then.

'When it was noon they opened the gate, and as we entered in the people came crowding out of the houses to look at us, and a crier went round the city crying through a shell. We stood in the market-place, and the negroes uncorded the bales of figured cloths and opened the carved chests of sycamore. And when they had ended their task, the merchants set forth their strange wares, the waxed linen from Egypt, and the painted linen from the country of the Ethiops, the purple sponges from Tyre and the blue hangings from Sidon, the cups of cold amber and the fine vessels of glass and the curious vessels of burnt clay. From the roof of a house a company of women watched us. One of them wore a mask of gilded leather.

'And on the first day the priests came and bartered with us, and on the second day came the nobles, and on the third day came the craftsmen and the slaves. And this is their custom with all merchants as long as they tarry in the city.

'And we tarried for a moon, and when the moon was waning, I wearied and wandered away through the streets of the city and came to the garden of its god. The priests in their yellow robes moved silently through the green trees, and on a pavement of black marble stood the rose-red house in which the god had his dwelling. Its doors were of powdered lacquer, and bulls and peacocks were wrought on them in raised and polished gold. The tilted roof was of sea-green porcelain and the jutting eaves were festooned with little bells. When the white doves flew past, they struck the bells with their wings and made them tinkle.

'In front of the temple was a pool of clear water paved with veined onyx. I lay down beside it, and with my pale fingers I touched the broad leaves. One of the priests came towards me and stood behind me. He had sandals on his feet, one of soft serpent-skin and the other of birds' plumage. On his head was a mitre of black felt decorated with silver crescents. Seven yellows were woven into his robe, and his frizzed hair was stained with antimony.

'After a little while he spake to me, and asked me my desire.

'I told him that my desire was to see the god.

' "The god is hunting," said the priest, looking strangely at me with his small slanting eyes.

' "Tell me in what forest, and I will ride with him," I answered.

'He combed out the soft fringes of his tunic with his long pointed nails. "The god is asleep," he murmured.

' "Tell me on what couch, and I will watch by him," I answered.

' "The god is at the feast," he cried.

' "If the wine be sweet I will drink it with him, and if it be bitter I will drink it with him also," was my answer.

'He bowed his head in wonder, and, taking me by the hand, he raised me up, and led me into the temple.

'And in the first chamber I saw an idol seated on a throne of jasper bordered with great orient pearls. It was carved out of ebony, and in stature was of the stature of a man. On its forehead was a ruby, and thick oil dripped from its hair on to its thighs. Its feet were red with the blood of a newly-slain kid, and its loins girt with a copper belt that was studded with seven beryls.

'And I said to the priest, "Is this the god?" And he answered me, "This is the god."

' "Show me the god," I cried, "or I will surely slay thee." And I touched his hand, and it became withered.

'And the priest besought me, saying, "Let my lord heal his servant, and I will show him the god."

'So I breathed with my breath upon his hand, and it became whole again, and he trembled and led me into the second chamber, and I saw an idol standing on a lotus of jade hung with great emeralds. It was carved out of ivory, and in stature was twice the stature of a man. On its forehead was a chrysolite, and its breasts were smeared with myrrh and cinnamon. In one hand it held a crooked sceptre of jade, and in the other a round crystal. It wore buskins of brass, and its thick neck was circled with a circle of selenites.

'And I said to the priest, "Is this the god?" And he answered me, "This is the god."

' "Show me the god," I cried, "or I will surely slay thee." And I touched his eyes, and they became blind.

'And the priest besought me, saying, "Let my lord heal his servant, and I will show him the god."

'So I breathed with my breath upon his eyes, and the sight came back to them, and he trembled again, and led me into the third chamber, and lo! there was no idol in it, nor image of any kind, but only a mirror of round metal set on an altar of stone.

'And I said to the priest, "Where is the god?"

'And he answered me: "There is no god but this mirror that thou seest, for this is the Mirror of Wisdom. And it reflecteth all things that are in heaven and on earth, save only the face of him who looketh into it. This it reflecteth not, so that he who looketh into it may be wise. Many other mirrors are there, but they are mirrors of Opinion. This only is the Mirror of Wisdom. And they who possess this mirror know everything, nor is there anything hidden from them. And they who possess it have not Wisdom. Therefore is it the god, and we worship it." And I looked into the mirror, and it was even as he had said to me.

'And I did a strange thing, but what I did matters not, for in a valley that is but a day's journey from this place have I hidden the Mirror of Wisdom. Do but suffer me to enter into thee again and be thy servant, and thou shalt be wiser than all the wise men, and Wisdom shall be thine. Suffer me to enter into thee, and none will be as wise as thou.'

But the young Fisherman laughed. 'Love is better than Wisdom,' he cried, 'and the little Mermaid loves me.'

'Nay, but there is nothing better than Wisdom,' said the Soul.

'Love is better,' answered the young Fisherman, and he plunged into the deep, and the Soul went weeping away over the marshes.

And after the second year was over, the Soul came down to the shore of the sea, and called to the young Fisherman, and he rose out of the deep and said, 'Why dost thou call to me?'

And the Soul answered, 'Come nearer, that I may speak with thee, for I have seen marvellous things.'

So he came nearer, and couched in the shallow water, and leaned his head upon his hand and listened.

And the Soul said to him, 'When I left thee, I turned my face to the South and journeyed. From the South cometh everything that is precious. Six days I journeyed along the highways that lead to the city of Ashter, along the dusty red-dyed highways by which the pilgrims are wont to go did I journey, and on the morning of the seventh day I lifted up my eyes, and lo! the city lay at my feet, for it is in a valley.

'There are nine gates to this city, and in front of each gate stands a bronze horse that neighs when the Bedouins come down from the mountains. The walls are cased with copper, and the watch-towers on the wall are roofed with brass. In every tower stands an archer with a bow in his hand. At sunrise he strikes with an arrow on a gong, and at sunset he blows through a horn of horn.

'When I sought to enter, the guards stopped me and asked of me who I was. I made answer that I was a Dervish and on my way to the city of Mecca, where there was a green veil on which the Koran was embroidered in silver letters by the hands of the angels. They were filled with wonder, and entreated me to pass in.

'Inside it is even as a bazaar. Surely thou shouldst have been with me. Across the narrow streets the gay lanterns of paper flutter like large butterflies. When the wind blows over the roofs they rise and fall as painted bubbles do. In front of their booths sit the merchants on silken carpets. They have straight black beards, and their turbans are covered with golden sequins, and long strings of amber and carved peach-stones glide through their cool fingers. Some of them sell galbanum and nard, and curious perfumes from the islands of the Indian Sea, and the thick oil of red roses, and myrrh and little nail-shaped cloves. When one stops to speak to them, they throw pinches of frankincense upon a charcoal brazier and make the air sweet. I saw a Syrian who held in his hands a thin rod like a reed. Grey threads of smoke came from it, and its odour as it burned was as the odour of the pink almond in spring. Others sell silver bracelets embossed all over with creamy blue turquoise stones, and anklets of brass wire fringed with little pearls, and tigers' claws set in gold, and the claws of that gilt cat, the leopard, set in gold also, and earrings of pierced emerald, and finger-rings of hollowed jade. From the tea-houses comes the sound of the guitar, and the opium-smokers with their white smiling faces look out at the passers-by.

'Of a truth thou shouldst have been with me. The wine-sellers elbow their way through the crowd with great black skins on their shoulders. Most of them sell the wine of Schiraz, which is as sweet as honey. They serve it in little metal cups and strew rose leaves upon it. In the market-place stand the fruit-sellers, who sell all kinds of fruit: ripe figs, with their bruised purple flesh, melons, smelling of musk and yellow as topazes, citrons and rose-apples and clusters of white grapes, round red-gold oranges, and oval lemons of green gold. Once I saw an elephant go by. Its trunk was painted with vermilion and turmeric, and over its ears it had a net of crimson silk cord. It stopped opposite one of the booths and began eating the oranges, and the man only laughed. Thou canst not think how strange a people they are. When they are glad they go to the bird-sellers and buy of them a caged bird, and set it free that their joy may be greater, and when they are sad they scourge themselves with thorns that their sorrow may not grow less.

'One evening I met some negroes carrying a heavy palanquin through the bazaar. It was made of gilded bamboo, and the poles were of vermilion lacquer studded with brass peacocks. Across the windows hung thin curtains of muslin embroidered with beetles' wings and with tiny seed-pearls, and as it passed by a pale-faced Circassian looked out and smiled at me. I followed behind, and the negroes hurried their steps and scowled. But I did not care. I felt a great curiosity come over me.

'At last they stopped at a square white house. There were no windows to it, only a little door like the door of a tomb. They set down the palanquin and knocked three times with a copper hammer. An Armenian in a caftan of green leather peered through the wicket, and when he saw them he opened, and spread a carpet on the ground, and the woman stepped out. As she went in, she turned round and smiled at me again. I had never seen any one so pale.

'When the moon rose I returned to the same place and sought for the house, but it was no longer there. When I saw that, I knew who the woman was, and wherefore she had smiled at me.

'Certainly thou shouldst have been with me. On the feast of the New Moon the young Emperor came forth from his palace and went into the mosque to pray. His hair and beard were dyed with rose-leaves, and his cheeks were powdered with a fine gold dust. The palms of his feet and hands were yellow with saffron.

'At sunrise he went forth from his palace in a robe of silver, and at sunset he returned to it again in a robe of gold. The people flung themselves on the ground and hid their faces, but I would not do so. I stood by the stall of a seller of dates and waited. When the Emperor saw me, he raised his painted eyebrows and stopped. I stood quite still, and made no obeisance. The people marvelled at my boldness, and counselled me to flee from the city. I paid no heed to them, but went and sat with the sellers of strange gods, who by reason of their craft are abominated. When I told them what I had done, each of them gave me a god and prayed me to leave them.

'That night, as I lay on a cushion in the tea-house that is in the Street of Pomegranates, the guards of the Emperor entered and led me to the palace. As I went in they closed each door behind me, and put a chain across it. Inside was a great court with an arcade running all round. The walls were of white alabaster, set here and there with blue and green tiles. The pillars were of green marble, and the pavement of a kind of peach-blossom marble. I had never seen anything like it before.

'As I passed across the court two veiled women looked down from a balcony and cursed me. The guards hastened on, and the butts of the lances rang upon the polished floor. They opened a gate of wrought ivory, and I found myself in a watered garden of seven terraces. It was planted with tulip-cups and moon-flowers, and silver-studded aloes. Like a slim reed of crystal a fountain hung in the dusky air. The cypress-trees were like burnt-out torches. From one of them a nightingale was singing.

'At the end of the garden stood a little pavilion. As we approached it two eunuchs came out to meet us. Their fat bodies swayed as they walked, and they glanced curiously at me with their yellow-lidded eyes. One of them drew aside the captain of the guard, and in a low voice whispered to him. The other kept munching scented pastilles, which he took with an affected gesture out of an oval box of lilac enamel.

'After a few moments the captain of the guard dismissed the soldiers. They went back to the palace, the eunuchs following slowly behind and plucking the sweet mulberries from the trees as they passed. Once the elder of the two turned round, and smiled at me with an evil smile.

'Then the captain of the guard motioned me towards the entrance of the pavilion. I walked on without trembling, and drawing the heavy curtain aside I entered in.

'The young Emperor was stretched on a couch of dyed lion skin, and a ger-falcon perched upon his wrist. Behind him stood a brass-turbaned Nubian, naked down to the waist, and with heavy earrings in his split ears. On a table by the side of the couch lay a mighty scimitar of steel.

'When the Emperor saw me he frowned, and said to me, "What is thy name? Knowest thou not that I am Emperor of this city?" But I made him no answer.

'He pointed with his finger at the scimitar, and the Nubian seized it, and rushing forward struck at me with great violence. The blade whizzed through me, and did me no hurt. The man fell sprawling on the floor, and when he rose up his teeth chattered with terror and he hid himself behind the couch.

'The Emperor leapt to his feet, and taking a lance from a stand of arms, he threw it at me. I caught it in its flight, and brake the shaft into two pieces. He shot at me with an arrow, but I held up my hands and it stopped in mid-air. Then he drew a dagger from a belt of white leather, and stabbed the Nubian in the throat lest the slave should tell of his dishonour. The man writhed like a trampled snake, and a red foam bubbled from his lips.

'As soon as he was dead the Emperor turned to me, and when he had wiped away the bright sweat from his brow with a little napkin of purfled and purple silk, he said to me, "Art thou a prophet, that I may not harm thee, or the son of a prophet, that I can do thee no hurt? I pray thee leave my city to-night, for while thou art in it I am no longer its lord."

'And I answered him, "I will go for half of thy treasure. Give me half of thy treasure, and I will go away."

'He took me by the hand, and led me out into the garden. When the captain of the guard saw me, he wondered. When the eunuchs saw me, their knees shook and they fell upon the ground in fear.

'There is a chamber in the palace that has eight walls of red porphyry, and a brass-scaled ceiling hung with lamps. The Emperor touched one of the walls and it opened, and we passed down a corridor that was lit with many torches. In niches upon each side stood great wine-jars filled to the brim with silver pieces. When we reached the centre of the corridor the Emperor spake the word that may not be spoken, and a granite door swung back on a secret spring, and he put his hands before his face lest his eyes should be dazzled.

'Thou couldst not believe how marvellous a place it was. There were huge tortoise-shells full of pearls, and hollowed moonstones of great size piled up with red rubies. The gold was stored in coffers of elephant-hide, and the gold-dust in leather bottles. There were opals and sapphires, the former in cups of crystal, and the latter in cups of jade. Round green emeralds were ranged in order upon thin plates of ivory, and in one corner were silk bags filled, some with turquoise-stones, and others with beryls. The ivory horns were heaped with purple amethysts, and the horns of brass with chalcedonies and sards. The pillars, which were of cedar, were hung with strings of yellow lynx-stones. In the flat oval shields, there were carbuncles, both wine-coloured and coloured like grass. And yet I have told thee but a tithe of what was there.

'And when the Emperor had taken away his hands from before his face he said to me: "This is my house of treasure, and half that is in it is thine, even as I promised to thee. And I will give thee camels and camel drivers, and they shall do thy bidding and take thy share of the treasure to whatever part of the world thou desirest to go. And the thing shall be done to-night, for I would not that the Sun, who is my father, should see that there is in my city a man whom I cannot slay."

'But I answered him, "The gold that is here is thine, and the silver also is thine, and thine are the precious jewels and the things of price. As for me, I have no need of these. Nor shall I take aught from thee but that little ring that thou wearest on the finger of thy hand."

'And the Emperor frowned. "It is but a ring of lead," he cried, "nor has it any value. Therefore take thy half of the treasure and go from my city."

' "Nay," I answered, "but I will take nought but that leaden ring, for I know what is written within it, and for what purpose."

'And the Emperor trembled, and besought me and said, "Take all the treasure and go from my city. The half that is mine shall be thine also."

'And I did a strange thing, but what I did matters not, for in a cave that is but a day's journey from this place have I hidden the Ring of Riches. It is but a day's journey from this place, and it waits for thy coming. He who has this Ring is richer than all the kings of the world. Come therefore and take it, and the world's riches shall be thine.'

But the young Fisherman laughed. 'Love is better than Riches,' he cried, 'and the little Mermaid loves me.'

'Nay, but there is nothing better than Riches,' said the Soul.

'Love is better,' answered the young Fisherman, and he plunged into the deep, and the Soul went weeping away over the marshes.

And after the third year was over, the Soul came down to the shore of the sea, and called to the young Fisherman, and he rose out of the deep and said, 'Why dost thou call to me?'

And the Soul answered, 'Come nearer, that I may speak with thee, for I have seen marvellous things.'

So he came nearer, and couched in the shallow water, and leaned his head upon his hand and listened.

And the Soul said to him: 'In a city that I know of there is an inn that standeth by a river. I sat there with sailors who drank of two different-coloured wines, and ate bread made of barley, and little salt fish served in bay leaves with vinegar. And as we sat and made merry, there entered to us an old man bearing a leathern carpet and a lute that had two horns of amber. And when he had laid out the carpet on the floor, he struck with a quill on the wire strings of his lute, and a girl whose face was veiled ran in and began to dance before us. Her face was veiled with a veil of gauze, but her feet were naked. Naked were her feet, and they moved over the carpet like little white pigeons. Never have I seen anything so marvellous, and the city in which she dances is but a day's journey from this place.'

Now when the young Fisherman heard the words of his Soul, he remembered that the little Mermaid had no feet and could not dance. And a great desire came over him, and he said to himself, 'It is but a day's journey, and I can return to my love,' and he laughed, and stood up in the shallow water, and strode towards the shore.

And when he had reached the dry shore he laughed again, and held out his arms to his Soul. And his Soul gave a great cry of joy and ran to meet him, and entered into him, and the young Fisherman saw stretched before him upon the sand that shadow of the body that is the body of the Soul.

And his Soul said to him, 'Let us not tarry, but get hence at once, for the Sea-gods are jealous, and have monsters that do their bidding.'

So they made haste, and all that night they journeyed beneath the moon, and all the next day they journeyed beneath the sun, and on the evening of the day they came to a city.

And the young Fisherman said to his Soul, 'Is this the city in which she dances of whom thou didst speak to me?'

And his Soul answered him, 'It is not this city, but another. Nevertheless let us enter in.'

So they entered in and passed through the streets, and as they passed through the Street of the Jewellers the young Fisherman saw a fair silver cup set forth in a booth. And his Soul said to him, 'Take that silver cup and hide it.'

So he took the cup and hid it in the fold of his tunic, and they went hurriedly out of the city.

And after that they had gone a league from the city, the young Fisherman frowned, and flung the cup away, and said to his Soul, 'Why didst thou tell me to take this cup and hide it, for it was an evil thing to do?'

But his Soul answered him, 'Be at peace, be at peace.'

And on the evening of the second day they came to a city, and the young Fisherman said to his Soul, 'Is this the city in which she dances of whom thou didst speak to me?'

And his Soul answered him, 'It is not this city, but another. Nevertheless let us enter in.'

So they entered in and passed through the streets, and as they passed through the Street of the Sellers of Sandals, the young Fisherman saw a child standing by a jar of water. And his Soul said to him, 'Smite that child.' So he smote the child till it wept, and when he had done this they went hurriedly out of the city.

And after that they had gone a league from the city the young Fisherman grew wroth, and said to his Soul, 'Why didst thou tell me to smite the child, for it was an evil thing to do?'

But his Soul answered him, 'Be at peace, be at peace.'

And on the evening of the third day they came to a city, and the young Fisherman said to his Soul, 'Is this the city in which she dances of whom thou didst speak to me?'

And his Soul answered him, 'It may be that it is in this city, therefore let us enter in.'

So they entered in and passed through the streets, but nowhere could the young Fisherman find the river or the inn that stood by its side. And the people of the city looked curiously at him, and he grew afraid and said to his Soul, 'Let us go hence, for she who dances with white feet is not here.'

But his Soul answered, 'Nay, but let us tarry, for the night is dark and there will be robbers on the way.'

So he sat him down in the market-place and rested, and after a time there went by a hooded merchant who had a cloak of cloth of Tartary, and bare a lantern of pierced horn at the end of a jointed reed. And the merchant said to him, 'Why dost thou sit in the market-place, seeing that the booths are closed and the bales corded?'

And the young Fisherman answered him, 'I can find no inn in this city, nor have I any kinsman who might give me shelter.'

'Are we not all kinsmen?' said the merchant. 'And did not one God make us? Therefore come with me, for I have a guest-chamber.'

So the young Fisherman rose up and followed the merchant to his house. And when he had passed through a garden of pomegranates and entered into the house, the merchant brought him rose-water in a copper dish that he might wash his hands, and ripe melons that he might quench his thirst, and set a bowl of rice and a piece of roasted kid before him.

And after that he had finished, the merchant led him to the guest-chamber, and bade him sleep and be at rest. And the young Fisherman gave him thanks, and kissed the ring that was on his hand, and flung himself down on the carpets of dyed goat's-hair. And when he had covered himself with a covering of black lamb's-wool he fell asleep.

And three hours before dawn, and while it was still night, his Soul waked him and said to him, 'Rise up and go to the room of the merchant, even to the room in which he sleepeth, and slay him, and take from him his gold, for we have need of it.'

And the young Fisherman rose up and crept towards the room of the merchant, and over the feet of the merchant there was lying a curved sword, and the tray by the side of the merchant held nine purses of gold. And he reached out his hand and touched the sword, and when he touched it the merchant started and awoke, and leaping up seized himself the sword and cried to the young Fisherman, 'Dost thou return evil for good, and pay with the shedding of blood for the kindness that I have shown thee?'

And his Soul said to the young Fisherman, 'Strike him,' and he struck him so that he swooned, and he seized then the nine purses of gold, and fled hastily through the garden of pomegranates, and set his face to the star that is the star of morning.

And when they had gone a league from the city, the young Fisherman beat his breast, and said to his Soul, 'Why didst thou bid me slay the merchant and take his gold? Surely thou art evil.'

But his Soul answered him, 'Be at peace, be at peace.'

'Nay,' cried the young Fisherman, 'I may not be at peace, for all that thou hast made me do I hate. Thee also I hate, and I bid thee tell me wherefore thou hast wrought with me in this wise.'

And his Soul answered him, 'When thou didst send me forth into the world thou gavest me no heart, so I learned to do all these things and love them.'

'What sayest thou?' murmured the young Fisherman.

'Thou knowest,' answered his Soul, 'thou knowest it well. Hast thou forgotten that thou gavest me no heart? I trow not. And so trouble not thyself nor me, but be at peace, for there is no pain that thou shalt not give away, nor any pleasure that thou shalt not receive.'

And when the young Fisherman heard these words he trembled and said to his Soul, 'Nay, but thou art evil, and hast made me forget my love, and hast tempted me with temptations, and hast set my feet in the ways of sins.'

And his Soul answered him, 'Thou hast not forgotten that when thou didst send me forth into the world thou gavest me no heart. Come, let us go to another city, and make merry, for we have nine purses of gold.'

But the young Fisherman took the nine purses of gold and flung them down, and trampled on them.

'Nay,' he cried, 'but I will have nought to do with thee, nor will I journey with thee anywhere, but even as I sent thee away before, so will I send thee away now, for thou hast wrought me no good.' And he turned his back to the moon, and with the little knife that had the handle of green viper's skin he strove to cut from his feet that shadow of the body which is the body of the Soul.

Yet his Soul stirred not from him, nor paid heed to his command, but said to him, 'The spell that the Witch told thee avails thee no more, for I may not leave thee, nor mayest thou drive me forth. Once in his life may a man send his Soul away, but he who receiveth back his Soul must keep it with him for ever, and this is his punishment and his reward.'

And the young Fisherman grew pale and clenched his hands and cried, 'She was a false Witch in that she told me not that.'

'Nay,' answered his Soul, 'but she was true to Him she worships, and whose servant she will be ever.'

And when the young Fisherman knew that he could no longer get rid of his Soul, and that it was an evil Soul, and would abide with him always, he fell upon the ground weeping bitterly.

And when it was day, the young Fisherman rose up and said to his Soul, 'I will bind my hands that I may not do thy bidding, and close my lips that I may not speak thy words, and I will return to the place where she whom I love has her dwelling. Even to the sea will I return, and to the little bay where she is wont to sing, and I will call to her and tell her the evil I have done and the evil thou hast wrought on me.'

And his Soul tempted him and said, 'Who is thy love, that thou shouldst return to her? The world has many fairer than she is. There are the dancing-girls of Samaris who dance in the manner of all kinds of birds and beasts. Their feet are painted with henna, and in their hands they have little copper bells. They laugh while they dance, and their laughter is as clear as the laughter of water. Come with me and I will show them to thee. For what is this trouble of thine about the things of sin? Is that which is pleasant to eat not made for the eater? Is there poison in that which is sweet to drink? Trouble not thyself, but come with me to another city. There is a little city hard by in which there is a garden of tulip-trees. And there dwell in this comely garden white peacocks and peacocks that have blue breasts. Their tails when they spread them to the sun are like disks of ivory and like gilt disks. And she who feeds them dances for pleasure, and sometimes she dances on her hands and at other times she dances with her feet. Her eyes are coloured with stibium, and her nostrils are shaped like the wings of a swallow. From a hook in one of her nostrils hangs a flower that is carved out of a pearl. She laughs while she dances, and the silver rings that are about her ankles tinkle like bells of silver. And so trouble not thyself any more, but come with me to this city.'

But the young Fisherman answered not his Soul, but closed his lips with the seal of silence and with a tight cord bound his hands, and journeyed back to the place from which he had come, even to the little bay where his love had been wont to sing. And ever did his Soul tempt him by the way, but he made it no answer, nor would he do any of the wickedness that it sought to make him do, so great was the power of the love that was within him.

And when he had reached the shore of the sea, he loosed the cord from his hands, and took the seal of silence from his lips, and called to the little Mermaid. But she came not to his call, though he called to her all day long and besought her.

And his Soul mocked him and said, 'Surely thou hast but little joy out of thy love. Thou art as one who in time of death pours water into a broken vessel. Thou givest away what thou hast, and nought is given to thee in return. It were better for thee to come with me, for I know where the Valley of Pleasure lies, and what things are wrought there.'

But the young Fisherman answered not his Soul, but in a cleft of the rock he built himself a house of wattles, and abode there for the space of a year. And every morning he called to the Mermaid, and every noon he called to her again, and at night-time he spake her name. Yet never did she rise out of the sea to meet him, nor in any place of the sea could he find her though he sought for her in the caves and in the green water, in the pools of the tide and in the wells that are at the bottom of the deep.

And ever did his Soul tempt him with evil, and whisper of terrible things. Yet did it not prevail against him, so great was the power of his love.

And after the year was over, the Soul thought within himself, 'I have tempted my master with evil, and his love is stronger than I am. I will tempt him now with good, and it may be that he will come with me.'

So he spake to the young Fisherman and said, 'I have told thee of the joy of the world, and thou hast turned a deaf ear to me. Suffer me now to tell thee of the world's pain, and it may be that thou wilt harken. For of a truth pain is the Lord of this world, nor is there any one who escapes from its net. There be some who lack raiment, and others who lack bread. There be widows who sit in purple, and widows who sit in rags. To and fro over the fens go the lepers, and they are cruel to each other. The beggars go up and down on the highways, and their wallets are empty. Through the streets of the cities walks Famine, and the Plague sits at their gates. Come, let us go forth and mend these things, and make them not to be. Wherefore shouldst thou tarry here calling to thy love, seeing she comes not to thy call? And what is love, that thou shouldst set this high store upon it?'

But the young Fisherman answered it nought, so great was the power of his love. And every morning he called to the Mermaid, and every noon he called to her again, and at night-time he spake her name. Yet never did she rise out of the sea to meet him, nor in any place of the sea could he find her, though he sought for her in the rivers of the sea, and in the valleys that are under the waves, in the sea that the night makes purple, and in the sea that the dawn leaves grey.

And after the second year was over, the Soul said to the young Fisherman at night-time, and as he sat in the wattled house alone, 'Lo! now I have tempted thee with evil, and I have tempted thee with good, and thy love is stronger than I am. Wherefore will I tempt thee no longer, but I pray thee to suffer me to enter thy heart, that I may be one with thee even as before.'

'Surely thou mayest enter,' said the young Fisherman, 'for in the days when with no heart thou didst go through the world thou must have much suffered.'

'Alas!' cried his Soul, 'I can find no place of entrance, so compassed about with love is this heart of thine.'

'Yet I would that I could help thee,' said the young Fisherman.

And as he spake there came a great cry of mourning from the sea, even the cry that men hear when one of the Sea-folk is dead. And the young Fisherman leapt up, and left his wattled house, and ran down to the shore. And the black waves came hurrying to the shore, bearing with them a burden that was whiter than silver. White as the surf it was, and like a flower it tossed on the waves. And the surf took it from the waves, and the foam took it from the surf, and the shore received it, and lying at his feet the young Fisherman saw the body of the little Mermaid. Dead at his feet it was lying.

Weeping as one smitten with pain he flung himself down beside it, and he kissed the cold red of the mouth, and toyed with the wet amber of the hair. He flung himself down beside it on the sand, weeping as one trembling with joy, and in his brown arms he held it to his breast. Cold were the lips, yet he kissed them. Salt was the honey of the hair, yet he tasted it with a bitter joy. He kissed the closed eyelids, and the wild spray that lay upon their cups was less salt than his tears.

And to the dead thing he made confession. Into the shells of its ears he poured the harsh wine of his tale. He put the little hands round his neck, and with his fingers he touched the thin reed of the throat. Bitter, bitter was his joy, and full of strange gladness was his pain.

The black sea came nearer, and the white foam moaned like a leper. With white claws of foam the sea grabbled at the shore. From the palace of the Sea-King came the cry of mourning again, and far out upon the sea the great Tritons blew hoarsely upon their horns.

'Flee away,' said his Soul, 'for ever doth the sea come nigher, and if thou tarriest it will slay thee. Flee away, for I am afraid, seeing that thy heart is closed against me by reason of the greatness of thy love. Flee away to a place of safety. Surely thou wilt not send me without a heart into another world?'

But the young Fisherman listened not to his Soul, but called on the little Mermaid and said, 'Love is better than wisdom, and more precious than riches, and fairer than the feet of the daughters of men. The fires cannot destroy it, nor can the waters quench it. I called on thee at dawn, and thou didst not come to my call. The moon heard thy name, yet

hadst thou no heed of me. For evilly had I left thee, and to my own hurt had I wandered away. Yet ever did thy love abide with me, and ever was it strong, nor did aught prevail against it, though I have looked upon evil and looked upon good. And now that thou art dead, surely I will die with thee also.'

And his Soul besought him to depart, but he would not, so great was his love. And the sea came nearer, and sought to cover him with its waves, and when he knew that the end was at hand he kissed with mad lips the cold lips of the Mermaid, and the heart that was within him brake. And as through the fullness of his love his heart did break, the Soul found an entrance and entered in, and was one with him even as before. And the sea covered the young Fisherman with its waves.

And in the morning the Priest went forth to bless the sea, for it had been troubled. And with him went the monks and the musicians, and the candle-bearers, and the swingers of censers, and a great company.

And when the Priest reached the shore he saw the young Fisherman lying drowned in the surf, and clasped in his arms was the body of the little Mermaid. And he drew back frowning, and having made the sign of the cross, he cried aloud and said, 'I will not bless the sea nor anything that is in it. Accursed be the Sea-folk, and accursed be all they who traffic with them. And as for him who for love's sake forsook God, and so lieth here with his leman slain by God's judgment, take up his body and the body of his leman, and bury them in the corner of the Field of the Fullers, and set no mark above them, nor sign of any kind, that none may know the place of their resting. For accursed were they in their lives, and accursed shall they be in their deaths also.'

And the people did as he commanded them, and in the corner of the Field of the Fullers, where no sweet herbs grew, they dug a deep pit, and laid the dead things within it.

And when the third year was over, and on a day that was a holy day, the Priest went up to the chapel, that he might show to the people the wounds of the Lord, and speak to them about the wrath of God.

And when he had robed himself with his robes, and entered in and bowed himself before the altar, he saw that the altar was covered with strange flowers that never had been seen before. Strange were they to look at, and of curious beauty, and their beauty troubled him, and their odour was sweet in his nostrils, and he felt glad, and understood not why he was glad.

And after that he had opened the tabernacle, and incensed the monstrance that was in it, and shown the fair wafer to the people, and hid it again behind the veil of veils, he began to speak to the people, desiring to speak to them of the wrath of God. But the beauty of the white flowers troubled him, and their odour was sweet in his nostrils, and there came another word into his lips, and he spake not of the wrath of God, but of the God whose name is Love. And why he so spake, he knew not.

And when he had finished his word the people wept, and the Priest went back to the sacristy, and his eyes were full of tears. And the deacons came in and began to unrobe him, and took from him the alb and the girdle, the maniple and the stole. And he stood as one in a dream.

And after that they had unrobed him, he looked at them and said, 'What are the flowers, that stand on the altar, and whence do they come?'

And they answered him, 'What flowers they are we cannot tell, but they come from the corner of the Fullers' Field.' And the Priest trembled, and returned to his own house and prayed.

And in the morning, while it was still dawn, he went forth with the monks and the musicians, and the candle-bearers and the swingers of censers, and a great company, and came to the shore of the sea, and blessed the sea, and all the wild things that are in it. The Fauns also he blessed, and the little things that dance in the woodland, and the bright-eyed things that peer through the leaves. All the things in God's world he blessed, and the people were filled with joy and wonder. Yet never again in the corner of the Fullers' Field grew flowers of any kind, but the field remained barren even as before. Nor came the Sea-folk into the bay as they had been wont to do, for they went to another part of the sea.

THE STAR–CHILD

ONCE UPON A TIME TWO POOR WOODCUTTERS were making their way home through a great pine-forest. It was winter, and a night of bitter cold. The snow lay thick upon the ground, and upon the branches of the trees: the frost kept snapping the little twigs on either side of them, as they passed: and when they came to the Mountain-Torrent she was hanging motionless in air, for the Ice-King had kissed her.

So cold was it that even the animals and the birds did not know what to make of it.

'Ugh!' snarled the Wolf, as he limped through the brushwood with his tail between his legs, 'this is perfectly monstrous weather. Why doesn't the Government look to it?'

'Weet! weet! weet!' twittered the green Linnets, 'the old Earth is dead, and they have laid her out in her white shroud.'

'The Earth is going to be married, and this is her bridal dress,' whispered the Turtle-doves to each other. Their little pink feet were quite frost-bitten, but they felt that it was their duty to take a romantic view of the situation.

'Nonsense!' growled the Wolf. 'I tell you that it is all the fault of the Government, and if you don't believe me I shall eat you.' The Wolf had a thoroughly practical mind, and was never at a loss for a good argument.

'Well, for my own part,' said the Woodpecker, who was a born philosopher, 'I don't care an atomic theory for explanations. If a thing is so, it is so, and at present it is terribly cold.'

Terribly cold it certainly was. The little Squirrels, who lived inside the tall fir-tree, kept rubbing each other's noses to keep themselves warm, and the Rabbits curled themselves up in their holes, and did not venture even to look out of doors. The only people who seemed to enjoy it were the great horned Owls. Their feathers were quite stiff with rime, but they did not mind, and they rolled their large yellow eyes, and called out to each other across the forest, 'Tu-whit! Tu-whoo! Tu-whit! Tu-whoo! what delightful weather we are having!'

On and on went the two Woodcutters, blowing lustily upon their fingers, and stamping with their huge iron-shod boots upon the caked snow. Once they sank into a deep drift, and came out as white as millers are, when the stones are grinding, and once they slipped on the hard smooth ice where the marsh-water was frozen, and their faggots fell out of their bundles, and they had to pick them up and bind them together again, and once they thought that they had lost their way, and a great terror seized on them, for they knew that the Snow is cruel to those who sleep in her arms. But they put their trust in the good Saint Martin who watches over all travellers, and retraced their steps, and went warily, and at last they reached the outskirts of the forest, and saw, far down in the valley beneath them, the lights of the village in which they dwelt.

So overjoyed were they at their deliverance that they laughed aloud, and the Earth seemed to them like a flower of silver, and the Moon like a flower of gold.

Yet, after that they had laughed they became sad, for they remembered their poverty, and one of them said to the other, 'Why did we make merry, seeing that life is for the rich, and not for such as we are? Better that we had died of cold in the forest, or that some wild beast had fallen upon us and slain us.'

'Truly,' answered his companion, 'much is given to some, and little is given to others. Injustice has parcelled out the world, nor is there equal division of aught save of sorrow.'

But as they were bewailing their misery to each other this strange thing happened. There fell from heaven a very bright and beautiful star. It slipped down the side of the sky, passing by the other stars in its course, and, as they watched it wondering, it seemed to them to sink behind a clump of willow-trees that stood hard by a little sheepfold no more than a stone's-throw away.

'Why! there is a crock of gold for whoever finds it,' they cried, and they set to and ran, so eager were they for the gold.

And one of them ran faster than his mate, and out-stripped him, and forced his way through the willows, and came out on the other side, and lo! there was indeed a thing of gold lying on the white snow. So he hastened towards it, and stooping down placed his hands upon it, and it was a cloak of golden tissue, curiously wrought with stars, and wrapped in many folds. And he cried out to his comrade that he had found the treasure that had fallen from the sky, and when his comrade had come up, they sat them down in the snow, and loosened the folds of the cloak that they might divide the pieces of gold. But, alas! no gold was in it, nor silver, nor, indeed, treasure of any kind, but only a little child who was asleep.

And one of them said to the other: 'This is a bitter ending to our hope, nor have we any good fortune, for what doth a child profit to a man? Let us leave it here, and go our way, seeing that we are poor men, and have children of our own whose bread we may not give to another.'

But his companion answered him: 'Nay, but it were an evil thing to

leave the child to perish here in the snow, and though I am as poor as thou art, and have many mouths to feed, and but little in the pot, yet will I bring it home with me, and my wife shall have care of it.'

So very tenderly he took up the child, and wrapped the cloak around it to shield it from the harsh cold, and made his way down the hill to the village, his comrade marvelling much at his foolishness and softness of heart.

And when they came to the village, his comrade said to him, 'Thou hast the child, therefore give me the cloak, for it is meet that we should share.'

But he answered him: 'Nay, for the cloak is neither mine nor thine, but the child's only,' and he bade him Godspeed, and went to his own house and knocked.

And when his wife opened the door and saw that her husband had returned safe to her, she put her arms round his neck and kissed him, and took from his back the bundle of faggots, and brushed the snow off his boots, and bade him come in.

But he said to her, 'I have found something in the forest, and I have brought it to thee to have care of it,' and he stirred not from the threshold.

'What is it?' she cried. 'Show it to me, for the house is bare, and we have need of many things.' And he drew the cloak back, and showed her the sleeping child.

'Alack, goodman!' she murmured, 'have we not children enough of our own, that thou must needs bring a changeling to sit by the hearth? And who knows if it will not bring us bad fortune? And how shall we tend it?' And she was wroth against him. .

'Nay, but it is a Star-Child,' he answered; and he told her the strange manner of the finding of it.

But she would not be appeased, but mocked at him, and spoke angrily, and cried: 'Our children lack bread, and shall we feed the child of another? Who is there who careth for us? And who giveth us food?'

'Nay, but God careth for the sparrows even, and feedeth them,' he answered.

'Do not the sparrows die of hunger in the winter?' she asked. 'And is it not winter now?' And the man answered nothing, but stirred not from the threshold.

And a bitter wind from the forest came in through the open door, and made her tremble, and she shivered, and said to him: 'Wilt thou not close the door? There cometh a bitter wind into the house, and I am cold.'

'Into a house where a heart is hard cometh there not always a bitter wind?' he asked. And the woman answered him nothing, but crept closer to the fire.

And after a time she turned round and looked at him, and her eyes were full of tears. And he came in swiftly, and placed the child in her arms, and she kissed it, and laid it in a little bed where the youngest of their own children was lying. And on the morrow the Woodcutter took the curious cloak of gold and placed it in a great chest, and a chain of amber that was round the child's neck his wife took and set it in the chest also.

So the Star-Child was brought up with the children of the Woodcutter, and sat at the same board with them, and was their playmate. And every year he became more beautiful to look at, so that all those who dwelt in the village were filled with wonder, for, while they were swarthy and black-haired, he was white and delicate as sawn ivory, and his curls were like the rings of the daffodil. His lips, also, were like the petals of a red flower, and his eyes were like violets by a river of pure water, and his body like the narcissus of a field where the mower comes not.

Yet did his beauty work him evil. For he grew proud, and cruel, and selfish. The children of the Woodcutter, and the other children of the village, he despised, saying that they were of mean parentage, while he was noble, being sprung from a Star, and he made himself master over them, and called them his servants. No pity had he for the poor, or for those who were blind or maimed or in any way afflicted, but would cast stones at them and drive them forth on to the highway, and bid them beg their bread elsewhere, so that none save the outlaws came twice to that village to ask for alms. Indeed, he was as one enamoured of beauty, and would mock at the weakly and ill-favoured, and make jest of them; and himself he loved, and in summer, when the winds were still, he would lie by the well in the priest's orchard and look down at the marvel of his own face, and laugh for the pleasure he had in his fairness.

Often did the Woodcutter and his wife chide him, and say: 'We did not deal with thee as thou dealest with those who are left desolate, and have none to succour them. Wherefore art thou so cruel to all who need pity?'

Often did the old priest send for him, and seek to teach him the love of living things, saying to him: 'The fly is thy brother. Do it no harm. The wild birds that roam through the forest have their freedom. Snare them not for thy pleasure. God made the blindworm and the mole, and each has its place. Who art thou to bring pain into God's world? Even the cattle of the field praise him.'

But the Star-Child heeded not their words, but would frown and flout, and go back to his companions, and lead them. And his companions followed him, for he was fair, and fleet of foot, and could dance and pipe, and make music. And wherever the Star-Child led them they followed, and whatever the Star-Child bade them do, that did they. And when he pierced with a sharp reed the dim eyes of the mole, they laughed, and when he cast stones at the leper they laughed also. And in all things he ruled them, and they became hard of heart even as he was.

Now there passed one day through the village a poor beggar-woman. Her garments were torn and ragged, and her feet were bleeding from the rough road on which she had travelled, and she was in very evil plight. And being weary she sat her down under a chestnut-tree to rest.

But when the Star-Child saw her, he said to his companions, 'See! There sitteth a foul beggar-woman under that fair and green-leaved tree. Come, let us drive her hence, for she is ugly and ill-favoured.'

So he came near and threw stones at her, and mocked her, and she looked at him with terror in her eyes, nor did she move her gaze from him. And when the Woodcutter, who was cleaving logs in a haggard hard by, saw what the Star-Child was doing, he ran up and rebuked him, and said to him, 'Surely thou art hard of heart and knowest not mercy, for what evil has this poor woman done to thee that thou shouldst treat her in this wise?'

And the Star-Child grew red with anger, and stamped his foot upon the ground, and said, 'Who art thou to question me what I do? I am no son of thine to do thy bidding.'

'Thou speakest truly,' answered the Woodcutter, 'yet did I show thee pity when I found thee in the forest.'

And when the woman heard these words she gave a loud cry and fell into a swoon. And the Woodcutter carried her to his own house, and his wife had care of her, and when she rose up from the swoon into which she had fallen, they set meat and drink before her, and bade her have comfort.

But she would neither eat nor drink, but said to the Woodcutter, 'Didst thou not say that the child was found in the forest? And was it not ten years, from this day?'

And the Woodcutter answered, 'Yea, it was in the forest that I found him, and it is ten years from this day.'

'And what signs didst thou find with him?' she cried. 'Bare he not upon his neck a chain of amber? Was not round him a cloak of gold tissue broidered with stars?'

'Truly,' answered the Woodcutter, 'it was even as thou sayest.' And he took the cloak and the amber chain from the chest where they lay, and showed them to her.

And when she saw them she wept for joy, and said, 'He is my little son whom I lost in the forest. I pray thee send for him quickly, for in search of him have I wandered over the whole world.'

So the Woodcutter and his wife went out and called to the Star-Child, and said to him, 'Go into the house, and there shalt thou find thy mother, who is waiting for thee.'

So he ran in, filled with wonder and great gladness. But when he saw her who was waiting there, he laughed scornfully and said, 'Why, where is my mother? For I see none here but this vile beggar-woman.'

And the woman answered him, 'I am thy mother.'

'Thou art mad to say so,' cried the Star-Child angrily. 'I am no son of thine, for thou art a beggar, and ugly, and in rags. Therefore get thee hence, and let me see thy foul face no more.'

'Nay, but thou art indeed my little son, whom I bare in the forest,' she cried, and she fell on her knees, and held out her arms to him. 'The robbers stole thee from me, and left thee to die,' she murmured, 'but I recognised thee when I saw thee, and the signs also have I recognised, the cloak of golden tissue and the amber chain. Therefore I pray thee come with me, for over the whole world have I wandered in search of thee. Come with me, my son, for I have need of thy love.'

But the Star-Child stirred not from his place, but shut the doors of his heart against her, nor was there any sound heard save the sound of the woman weeping for pain.

And at last he spoke to her, and his voice was hard and bitter. 'If in very truth thou art my mother,' he said, 'it had been better hadst thou stayed away, and not come here to bring me to shame, seeing that I thought I was the child of some Star, and not a beggar's child, as thou tellest me that I am. Therefore get thee hence, and let me see thee no more.'

'Alas! my son,' she cried, 'wilt thou not kiss me before I go? For I have suffered much to find thee.'

'Nay,' said the Star-Child, 'but thou art too foul to look at, and rather would I kiss the adder or the toad than thee.'

So the woman rose up, and went away into the forest weeping bitterly, and when the Star-Child saw that she had gone, he was glad, and ran back to his playmates that he might play with them.

But when they beheld him coming, they mocked him and said, 'Why, thou art as foul as the toad, and as loathsome as the adder. Get thee hence, for we will not suffer thee to play with us,' and they drave him out of the garden.

And the Star-Child frowned and said to himself, 'What is this that they say to me? I will go to the well of water and look into it, and it shall tell me of my beauty.'

So he went to the well of water and looked into it, and lo! his face was as the face of a toad, and his body was scaled like an adder. And he flung himself down on the grass and wept, and said to himself, 'Surely this has come upon me by reason of my sin. For I have denied my mother, and driven her away, and been proud, and cruel to her. Wherefore I will go and seek her through the whole world, nor will I rest till I have found her.'

And there came to him the little daughter of the Woodcutter, and she put her hand upon his shoulder and said, 'What doth it matter if thou hast lost thy comeliness? Stay with us, and I will not mock at thee.'

And he said to her, 'Nay, but I have been cruel to my mother, and as a punishment has this evil been sent to me. Wherefore I must go hence, and wander through the world till I find her, and she give me forgiveness.'

So he ran away into the forest and called out to his mother to come to him, but there was no answer. All day long he called to her, and when the sun set he lay down to sleep on a bed of leaves, and the birds and the animals fled from him, for they remembered his cruelty, and he was alone save for the toad that watched him, and the slow adder that crawled past.

And in the morning he rose up, and plucked some bitter berries from the trees and ate them, and took his way through the great wood, weeping sorely. And of everything that he met he made inquiry if perchance they had seen his mother.

He said to the Mole, 'Thou canst go beneath the earth. Tell me, is my mother there?'

And the Mole answered, 'Thou hast blinded mine eyes. How should I know?'

He said to the Linnet, 'Thou canst fly over the tops of the tall trees, and canst see the whole world. Tell me, canst thou see my mother?'

And the Linnet answered, 'Thou has clipt my wings for thy pleasure. How should I fly?'

And to the little Squirrel who lived in the fir-tree, and was lonely, he said, 'Where is my mother?'

And the Squirrel answered, 'Thou hast slain mine. Dost thou seek to slay thine also?'

And the Star-Child wept and bowed his head, and prayed forgiveness of God's things, and went on through the forest, seeking for the beggar-woman. And on the third day he came to the other side of the forest and went down into the plain.

And when he passed through the villages the children mocked him, and threw stones at him, and the carlots would not suffer him even to sleep in the byres lest he might bring mildew on the stored corn, so foul was he to look at, and their hired men drave him away, and there was none who had pity on him. Nor could he hear anywhere of the beggar-woman who was his mother, though for the space of three years he wandered over the world, and often seemed to see her on the road in front of him, and would call to her, and run after her till the sharp flints made his feet to bleed. But overtake her he could not, and those who dwelt by the way did ever deny that they had seen her, or any like to her, and they made sport of his sorrow.

For the space of three years he wandered over the world, and in the world there was neither love nor loving-kindness nor charity for him, but it was even such a world as he had made for himself in the days of his great pride.

And one evening he came to the gate of a strong-walled city that stood by a river, and, weary and footsore though he was, he made to enter in. But the soldiers who stood on guard dropped their halberts across the entrance, and said roughly to him, 'What is thy business in the city?'

'I am seeking for my mother,' he answered, 'and I pray ye to suffer me to pass, for it may be that she is in this city.'

But they mocked at him, and one of them wagged a black beard, and set down his shield and cried, 'Of a truth, thy mother will not be merry when she sees thee, for thou art more ill-favoured than the toad of the marsh, or the adder that crawls in the fen. Get thee gone. Get thee gone. Thy mother dwells not in this city.'

And another, who held a yellow banner in his hand, said to him, 'Who is thy mother, and wherefore art thou seeking for her?'

And he answered, 'My mother is a beggar even as I am, and I have treated her evilly, and I pray ye to suffer me to pass that she may give me her forgiveness, if it be that she tarrieth in this city.' But they would not, and pricked him with their spears.

And, as he turned away weeping, one whose armour was inlaid with gilt flowers, and on whose helmet crouched a lion that had wings, came up and made inquiry of the soldiers who it was who had sought entrance. And they said to him, 'It is a beggar and the child of a beggar, and we have driven him away.'

'Nay,' he cried, laughing, 'but we will sell the foul thing for a slave, and his price shall be the price of a bowl of sweet wine.'

And an old and evil-visaged man who was passing by called out, and said, 'I will buy him for that price,' and, when he had paid the price, he took the Star-Child by the hand and led him into the city.

And after that they had gone through many streets they came to a little door that was set in a wall that was covered with a pomegranate tree. And the old man touched the door with a ring of graved jasper and it opened, and they went down five steps of brass into a garden filled with black poppies and green jars of burnt clay. And the old man took then from his turban a scarf of figured silk, and bound with it the eyes of the Star-Child, and drave him in front of him. And when the scarf was taken off his eyes, the Star-Child found himself in a dungeon, that was lit by a lantern of horn.

And the old man set before him some mouldy bread on a trencher and said, 'Eat,' and some brackish water in a cup and said, 'Drink,' and when he had eaten and drunk, the old man went out, locking the door behind him and fastening it with an iron chain.

And on the morrow the old man, who was indeed the subtlest of the magicians of Libya and had learned his art from one who dwelt in the tombs of the Nile, came in to him and frowned at him, and said, 'In a wood that is nigh to the gate of this city of Giaours there are three pieces of gold. One is of white gold, and another is of yellow gold, and the gold of the third one is red. To-day thou shalt bring me the piece of white gold, and if thou bringest it not back, I will beat thee with a hundred stripes. Get thee away quickly, and at sunset I will be waiting for thee at the door of the garden. See that thou bringest the white gold, or it shall go ill with thee, for thou art my slave, and I have bought thee for the price of a bowl of sweet wine.' And he bound the eyes of the Star-Child with the scarf of figured silk, and led him through the house, and through the garden of poppies, and up the five steps of brass. And having opened the little door with his ring he set him in the street.

And the Star-Child went out of the gate of the city, and came to the wood of which the Magician had spoken to him.

Now this wood was very fair to look at from without, and seemed full of singing birds and of sweet-scented flowers, and the Star-Child entered it gladly. Yet did its beauty profit him little, for wherever he went harsh briars and thorns shot up from the ground and encompassed him, and evil nettles stung him, and the thistle pierced him with her daggers, so that he was in sore distress. Nor could he anywhere find the piece of white gold of which the Magician had spoken, though he sought for it from morn to noon, and from noon to sunset. And at sunset he set his face towards home, weeping bitterly, for he knew what fate was in store for him.

But when he had reached the outskirts of the wood, he heard from a thicket a cry as of some one in pain. And forgetting his own sorrow he ran back to the place, and saw there a little Hare caught in a trap that some hunter had set for it.

And the Star-Child had pity on it, and released it, and said to it, 'I am myself but a slave, yet may I give thee thy freedom.'

And the Hare answered him, and said: 'Surely thou hast given me freedom, and what shall I give thee in return?'

And the Star-Child said to it, 'I am seeking for a piece of white gold, nor can I anywhere find it, and if I bring it not to my master he will beat me.'

'Come thou with me,' said the Hare, 'and I will lead thee to it, for I know where it is hidden, and for what purpose.'

So the Star-Child went with the Hare, and lo! in the cleft of a great oak-tree he saw the piece of white gold that he was seeking. And he was filled with joy, and seized it, and said to the Hare, 'The

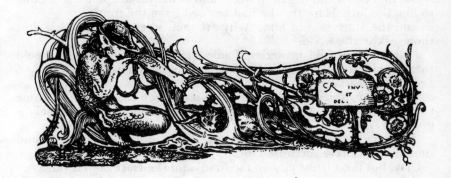

service that I did to thee thou hast rendered back again many times over, and the kindness that I showed thee thou has repaid a hundred-fold.'

'Nay,' answered the Hare, 'but as thou dealt with me, so I did deal with thee,' and it ran away swiftly, and the Star-Child went towards the city.

Now at the gate of the city there was seated one who was a leper. Over his face hung a cowl of grey linen, and through the eyelets his eyes gleamed like red coals. And when he saw the Star-Child coming, he struck upon a wooden bowl, and clattered his bell, and called out to him, and said, 'Give me a piece of money, or I must die of hunger. For they have thrust me out of the city, and there is no one who has pity on me.'

'Alas!' cried the Star-Child, 'I have but one piece of money in my wallet, and if I bring it not to my master he will beat me, for I am his slave.'

But the leper entreated him, and prayed of him, till the Star-Child had pity, and gave him the piece of white gold.

And when he came to the Magician's house, the Magician opened to him, and brought him in, and said to him, 'Hast thou the piece of white gold?' And the Star-Child answered, 'I have it not.' So the Magician fell upon him and beat him, and set before him an empty trencher, and said, 'Eat,' and an empty cup, and said, 'Drink,' and flung him again into the dungeon.

And on the morrow the Magician came to him, and said, 'If to-day thou bringest me not the piece of yellow gold, I will surely keep thee as my slave, and give thee three hundred stripes.'

So the Star-Child went to the wood, and all day long he searched for the piece of yellow gold, but nowhere could he find it. And at sunset he sat him down and began to weep, and as he was weeping there came to him the little Hare that he had rescued from the trap.

And the Hare said to him, 'Why art thou weeping? And what dost thou seek in the wood?'

And the Star-Child answered, 'I am seeking for a piece of yellow gold that is hidden here, and if I find it not my master will beat me, and keep me as a slave.'

'Follow me,' cried the Hare, and it ran through the wood till it came to a pool of water. And at the bottom of the pool the piece of yellow gold was lying.

'How shall I thank thee?' said the Star-Child, 'for lo! this is the second time that you have succoured me.'

'Nay, but thou hadst pity on me first,' said the Hare, and it ran away swiftly.

And the Star-Child took the piece of yellow gold, and put it in his wallet, and hurried to the city. But the leper saw him coming, and ran to meet him, and knelt down and cried, 'Give me a piece of money or I shall die of hunger.'

And the Star-Child said to him, 'I have in my wallet but one piece of yellow gold, and if I bring it not to my master he will beat me and keep me as his slave.'

But the leper entreated him sore, so that the Star-Child had pity on him and gave him the piece of yellow gold.

And when he came to the Magician's house, the Magician opened to him, and brought him in, and said to him, 'Hast thou the piece of yellow gold?' And the Star-Child said to him, 'I have not.' So the Magician fell upon him, and beat him, and loaded him with chains, and cast him again into the dungeon.

And on the morrow the Magician came to him, and said, 'If to-day thou bringest me the piece of red gold I will set thee free, but if thou bringest it not I will surely slay thee.'

So the Star-Child went to the wood, and all day long he searched for the piece of red gold, but nowhere could he find it. And at evening he sat him down and wept, and as he was weeping there came to him the little Hare.

And the Hare said to him, 'The piece of red gold that thou seekest is in the cavern that is behind thee. Therefore weep no more but be glad.'

'How shall I reward thee?' cried the Star-Child, 'for lo! this is the third time thou hast succoured me.'

'Nay, but thou hadst pity on me first,' said the Hare, and it ran away swiftly.

And the Star-Child entered the cavern, and in its farthest corner he

found the piece of red gold. So he put it in his wallet, and hurried to the city. And the leper seeing him coming, stood in the centre of the road, and cried out, and said to him, 'Give me the piece of red money, or I must die,' and the Star-Child had pity on him again, and gave him the piece of red gold, saying, 'Thy need is greater than mine.' Yet his heart was heavy, for he knew what evil fate awaited him.

But lo! as he passed through the gate of the city, the guards bowed down and made obeisance to him, saying, 'How beautiful is our lord!' and a crowd of citizens followed him, and cried out, 'Surely there is none so beautiful in the whole world!' so that the Star-Child wept, and said to himself, 'They are mocking me, and making light of my misery.' And so large was the concourse of the people, that he lost the threads of his way, and found himself at last in a great square, in which there was a palace of a King.

And the gate of the palace opened, and the priests and the high officers of the city ran forth to meet him, and they abased themselves before him, and said, 'Thou art our lord for whom we have been waiting, and the son of our King.'

And the Star-Child answered them and said, 'I am no king's son, but the child of a poor beggar-woman. And how say ye that I am beautiful, for I know that I am evil to look at?'

Then he, whose armour was inlaid with gilt flowers, and on whose helmet crouched a lion that had wings, held up a shield, and cried, 'How saith my lord that he is not beautiful?'

And the Star-Child looked, and lo! his face was even as it had been, and his comeliness had come back to him, and he saw that in his eyes which he had not seen there before.

And the priests and the high officers knelt down and said to him, 'It was prophesied of old that on this day should come he who was to rule over us. Therefore, let our lord take this crown and this sceptre, and be in his justice and mercy our King over us.'

But he said to them, 'I am not worthy, for I have denied the mother who bare me, nor may I rest till I have found her, and known her forgiveness. Therefore, let me go, for I must wander again over the world, and may not tarry here, though ye bring me the crown and the sceptre.' And as he spake he turned his face from them towards the street that led to the gate of the city, and lo! amongst the crowd that pressed round the soldiers, he saw the beggar-woman who was his mother, and at her side stood the leper, who had sat by the road.

And a cry of joy broke from his lips, and he ran over, and kneeling down he kissed the wounds on his mother's feet, and wet them with his tears. He bowed his head in the dust, and sobbing, as one whose heart might break, he said to her: 'Mother, I denied thee in the hour of my pride. Accept me in the hour of my humility. Mother, I gave thee hatred. Do thou give me love. Mother, I rejected thee. Receive thy child now.' But the beggar-woman answered him not a word.

And he reached out his hands, and clasped the white feet of the leper, and said to him: 'Thrice did I give thee of my mercy. Bid my mother speak to me once.' But the leper answered him not a word.

And he sobbed again and said: 'Mother, my suffering is greater than I can bear. Give me thy forgiveness, and let me go back to the forest.' And the beggar-woman put her hand on his head, and said to him, 'Rise,' and the leper put his hand on his head, and said to him, 'Rise,' also.

And he rose up from his feet, and looked at them, and lo! they were a King and a Queen.

And the Queen said to him, 'This is thy father whom thou hast succoured.'

And the King said, 'This is thy mother whose feet thou hast washed with thy tears.'

And they fell on his neck and kissed him, and brought him into the palace and clothed him in fair raiment, and set the crown upon his head, and the sceptre in his hand, and over the city that stood by the river he ruled, and was its lord. Much justice and mercy did he show to all, and the evil Magician he banished, and to the Wood-cutter and his wife he sent many rich gifts, and to their children he gave high honour. Nor would he suffer any to be cruel to bird or beast, but taught love and loving-kindness and charity, and to the poor he gave bread, and to the naked he gave raiment, and there was peace and plenty in the land.

Yet ruled he not long, so great had been his suffering, and so bitter the fire of his testing, for after the space of three years he died. And he who came after him ruled evilly.

PLAYS

LADY WINDERMERE'S FAN

The persons of the play

LORD WINDERMERE	MR HOPPER	LADY PLYMDALE
LORD DARLINGTON	PARKER, Butler	LADY STUTFIELD
LORD AUGUSTUS LORTON	LADY WINDERMERE	LADY JEDBURGH
MR DUMBY	THE DUCHESS OF BERWICK	MRS COWPER-COWPER
MR CECIL GRAHAM	LADY AGATHA CARLISLE	MRS ERLYNNE
		ROSALIE, Maid

Time: *the present,* Place: *London. The action of the play takes place within twenty-four hours, beginning on a Tuesday afternoon at five o'clock, and ending the next day at one-thirty p.m.*

Lady Windermere, a very moral young woman, suspects that her husband is having an affair with the notorious Mrs Erlynne. He has denied this and insisted that Mrs Erlynne be invited to his wife's twenty-first birthday dance. Lady Windermere has threatened that, if Mrs Erlynne attends, she will strike her across the face with the fan which is a birthday present from her husband ...

ACT TWO

Scene: Drawing-room in Lord Windermere's house. Door R.U. opening into ballroom, where band is playing. Door L. through which guests are entering. Door L.U. opens on to illuminated terrace. Palms, flowers, and brilliant lights. Room crowded with guests. Lady Windermere is receiving them.

DUCHESS OF BERWICK (*up C.*): So strange Lord Windermere isn't here. Mr Hopper is very late, too. You have kept those five dances for him, Agatha? (*Comes down.*)

LADY AGATHA: Yes, mamma.

DUCHESS OF BERWICK (*sitting on sofa*): Just let me see your card. I'm so glad Lady Windermere has revived cards. – They're a mother's only safeguard. You dear simple little thing! (*Scratches out two names.*) No nice girl should ever waltz with such particularly younger sons! It looks so fast! The last two dances you might pass on the terrace with Mr Hopper.

Enter Mr Dumby and Lady Plymdale from the ballroom.

LADY AGATHA: Yes, mamma.

DUCHESS OF BERWICK *(fanning herself)*: The air is so pleasant there.

PARKER: Mrs Cowper-Cowper. Lady Stutfield. Sir James Royston. Mr Guy Berkeley.

These people enter as announced.

DUMBY: Good evening, Lady Stutfield. I suppose this will be the last ball of the season?

LADY STUTFIELD: I suppose so, Mr Dumby. It's been a delightful season, hasn't it?

DUMBY: Quite delightful! Good evening, Duchess. I suppose this will be the last ball of the season?

DUCHESS OF BERWICK: I suppose so, Mr Dumby. It has been a very dull season, hasn't it?

DUMBY: Dreadfully dull! Dreadfully dull!

MRS COWPER-COWPER: Good evening, Mr Dumby. I suppose this will be the last ball of the season?

DUMBY: Oh, I think not. There'll probably be two more. *(Wanders back to Lady Plymdale.)*

PARKER: Mr Rufford. Lady Jedburgh and Miss Graham. Mr Hopper.

These people enter as announced.

HOPPER: How do you do, Lady Windermere? How do you do, Duchess? *(Bows to Lady Agatha.)*

DUCHESS OF BERWICK: Dear Mr Hopper, how nice of you to come so early. We all know how you are run after in London.

HOPPER: Capital place, London! They are not nearly so exclusive in London as they are in Sydney.

DUCHESS OF BERWICK: Ah! we know your value, Mr Hopper. We wish there were more like you. It would make life so much easier. Do you know, Mr Hopper, dear Agatha and I are so much interested in Australia. It must be so pretty with all the dear little kangaroos flying about. Agatha has found it on the map. What a curious shape it is! Just like a large packing case. However, it is a very young country, isn't it?

HOPPER: Wasn't it made at the same time as the others, Duchess?

DUCHESS OF BERWICK: How clever you are, Mr Hopper. You have a cleverness quite of your own. Now I mustn't keep you.

HOPPER: But I should like to dance with Lady Agatha, Duchess.

DUCHESS OF BERWICK: Well, I *hope* she has a dance left. Have you a dance left, Agatha?

LADY AGATHA: Yes, mamma.

DUCHESS OF BERWICK: The next one?

LADY AGATHA: Yes, mamma.

HOPPER: May I have the pleasure? *(Lady Agatha bows.)*

DUCHESS OF BERWICK: Mind you take great care of my little chatter-box, Mr Hopper.

Lady Agatha and Mr Hopper pass into ballroom.

Enter Lord Windermere L.

LORD WINDERMERE: Margaret, I want to speak to you.

LADY WINDERMERE: In a moment. (*The music stops.*)

PARKER: Lord Augustus Lorton.

Enter Lord Augustus.

LORD AUGUSTUS: Good evening, Lady Windermere.

DUCHESS OF BERWICK: Sir James, will you take me into the ballroom? Augustus has been dining with us to-night. I really have had quite enough of dear Augustus for the moment.

Sir James Royston gives the Duchess his arm and escorts her into the ballroom.

PARKER: Mr and Mrs Arthur Bowden. Lord and Lady Paisley. Lord Darlington.

These people enter as announced.

LORD AUGUSTUS (*coming up to Lord Windermere*): Want to speak to you particularly, dear boy. I'm worn to a shadow. Know I don't look it. None of us men do look what we really are. Demmed good thing, too. What I want to know is this. Who is she? Where does she come from? Why hasn't she got any demmed relations! Demmed nuisance, relations! But they make one so demmed respectable.

LORD WINDERMERE: You are talking of Mrs Erlynne, I suppose? I only met her six months ago. Till then, I never knew of her existence.

LORD AUGUSTUS: You have seen a good deal of her since then.

LORD WINDERMERE (*coldly*): Yes, I have seen a good deal of her since then. I have just seen her.

LORD AUGUSTUS: Egad! the women are very down on her. I have been dining with Arabella this evening! By Jove! you should have heard what she said about Mrs Erlynne. She didn't leave a rag on her. . . . (*Aside.*) Berwick and I told her that didn't matter much, as the lady in question must have an extremely fine figure. You should have seen Arabella's expression. . . . But, look here, dear boy. I don't know what to do about Mrs Erlynne. Egad! I might be married to her; she treats me with such demmed indifference. She's deuced clever, too! She explains everything. Egad! she explains you. She has got any amount of explanations for you – and all of them different.

LORD WINDERMERE: No explanations are necessary about my friendship with Mrs Erlynne.

LORD AUGUSTUS: Hem! Well, look here, dear old fellow. Do you think she will ever get into this demmed thing called Society? Would you introduce her to your wife? No use beating about the confounded bush. Would you do that?

LORD WINDERMERE: Mrs Erlynne is coming here to-night.

LORD AUGUSTUS: Your wife has sent her a card?

LORD WINDERMERE: Mrs Erlynne has received a card.

LORD AUGUSTUS: Then she's all right, dear boy. But why didn't you tell me that before? It would have saved me a heap of worry and demmed misunderstandings!

Lady Agatha and Mr Hopper cross and exit on terrace L.U.E.

PARKER: Mr Cecil Graham!

Enter Mr Cecil Graham.

CECIL GRAHAM (*bows to Lady Windermere, passes over and shakes hands with Lord Windermere*): Good evening, Arthur. Why don't you ask me how I am? I like people to ask me how I am. It shows a wide-spread interest in my health. Now, to-night I am not at all well. Been dining with my people. Wonder why it is one's people are always so tedious? My father would talk morality after dinner. I told him he was old enough to know better. But my experience is that as soon as people are old enough to know better, they don't know anything at all. Hullo, Tuppy! Hear you're going to be married again; thought you were tired of that game.

LORD AUGUSTUS: You're excessively trivial, my dear boy, excessively trivial!

CECIL GRAHAM: By the way, Tuppy, which is it? Have you been twice married and once divorced, or twice divorced and once married? I say you've been twice divorced and once married. It seems so much more probable.

LORD AUGUSTUS: I have a very bad memory. I really don't remember which. (*Moves away R.*)

LADY PLYMDALE: Lord Windermere, I've something most particular to ask you.

LORD WINDERMERE: I am afraid – if you will excuse me – I must join my wife.

LADY PLYMDALE: Oh, you mustn't dream of such a thing. It's most dangerous nowadays for a husband to pay any attention to his wife in public. It always makes people think that he beats her when they're alone. The world has grown so suspicious of anything that looks like a happy married life. But I'll tell you what it is at supper. (*Moves towards door of ballroom.*)

LORD WINDERMERE (*C*): Margaret! I must speak to you.

LADY WINDERMERE: Will you hold my fan for me, Lord Darlington? Thanks. (*Comes down to him.*)

LORD WINDERMERE (*crossing to her*): Margaret, what you said before dinner was, of course, impossible?

LADY WINDERMERE: That woman is not coming here to-night.

LORD WINDERMERE (*R.C.*): Mrs Erlynne is coming here, and if you in any way annoy or wound her, you will bring shame and sorrow on us both. Remember that! Ah, Margaret, only trust me! A wife should trust her husband!

LADY WINDERMERE (*C*): London is full of women who trust their husbands. One can always recognise them. They look so thoroughly unhappy. I am not going to be one of them (*Moves up.*) Lord Darlington, will you give me back my fan, please? Thanks. . . . A useful thing a fan, isn't it? . . . I want a friend to-night, Lord Darlington; I didn't know I would want one so soon.

LORD DARLINGTON: Lady Windermere! I knew the time would come some day; but why to-night?

LORD WINDERMERE: I will tell her. I must. It would be terrible if there were any scene. Margaret . . .

PARKER: Mrs Erlynne!

Lord Windermere starts. Mrs Erlynne enters, very beautifully dressed and very dignified. Lady Windermere clutches at her fan, then lets it drop on the floor. She bows coldly to Mrs Erlynne, who bows to her sweetly in turn, and sails into the room.

LORD DARLINGTON: You have dropped your fan, Lady Windermere. (*Picks it up and hands it to her.*)

MRS ERLYNNE (*C*): How do you do, again, Lord Windermere? How charming your sweet wife looks! Quite a picture!

LORD WINDERMERE (*in a low voice*): It was terribly rash of you to come!

MRS ERLYNNE (*smiling*): The wisest thing I ever did in my life. And, by the way, you must pay me a good deal of attention this evening. I am afraid of the women. You must introduce me to some of them. The men I can always manage. How do you do, Lord Augustus? You have quite neglected me lately. I have not seen you since yesterday. I am afraid you're faithless. Every one told me so.

LORD AUGUSTUS (*R*): Now really, Mrs Erlynne, allow me to explain.

MRS ERLYNNE (*R.C.*): No, dear Lord Augustus, you can't explain anything. It is your chief charm.

LORD AUGUSTUS: Ah! if you find charms in me, Mrs. Erlynne—

They converse together. Lord Windermere moves uneasily about the room watching Mrs Erlynne.

LORD DARLINGTON (*to Lady Windermere*): How pale you are!

LADY WINDERMERE: Cowards are always pale!

LORD DARLINGTON: You look faint. Come out on the terrace.

LADY WINDERMERE: Yes. (*To Parker*): Parker, send my cloak out.

MRS ERLYNNE (*crossing to her*): Lady Windermere, how beautifully your terrace is illuminated. Reminds me of Prince Doria's at Rome.

Lady Windermere bows coldly, and goes off with Lord Darlington.

Oh, how do you do, Mr Graham? Isn't that your aunt, Lady Jedburgh? I should so much like to know her.

CECIL GRAHAM (*after a moment's hesitation and embarrassment*): Oh, certainly, if you wish it. Aunt Caroline, allow me to introduce Mrs Erlynne.

MRS ERLYNNE: So pleased to meet you, Lady Jedburgh. (*Sits beside her on the sofa.*) Your nephew and I are great friends. I am so much interested in his political career. I think he's sure to be a wonderful success. He thinks like a Tory, and talks like a Radical, and that's so important nowadays. He's such a brilliant talker, too. But we all know from whom he inherits that. Lord Allandale was saying to me only yesterday, in the Park, that Mr Graham talks almost as well as his aunt.

LADY JEDBURGH (*R.*): Most kind of you to say these charming things to me! (*Mrs Erlynne smiles, and continues conversation.*)

DUMBY (*to Cecil Graham*): Did you introduce Mrs Erlynne to Lady Jedburgh?

CECIL GRAHAM: Had to, my dear fellow. Couldn't help it! That woman can make one do anything she wants. How, I don't know.

DUMBY: Hope to goodness she won't speak to me! (*Saunters towards Lady Plymdale.*)

MRS ERLYNNE (*C. To Lady Jedburgh*): On Thursday? With great pleasure. (*Rises, and speaks to Lord Windermere, laughing.*) What a bore it is to have to be civil to these old dowagers! But they always insist on it!

LADY PLYMDALE (*to Mr Dumby*): Who is that well-dressed woman talking to Windermere?

DUMBY: Haven't got the slightest idea! Looks like an *édition de luxe* of a wicked French novel, meant specially for the English market.

MRS ERLYNNE: So that is poor Dumby with Lady Plymdale? I hear she is frightfully jealous of him. He doesn't seem anxious to speak to me to-night. I suppose he is afraid of her. Those straw-coloured women have dreadful tempers. Do you know, I think I'll dance with you first, Windermere. (*Lord Windermere bites his lip and frowns.*) It will make Lord Augustus so jealous! Lord Augustus! (*Lord Augustus comes down.*) Lord Windermere insists on my dancing with him first; as it's his own house, I can't well refuse. You know I would much sooner dance with you.

LORD AUGUSTUS (*with a low bow*): I wish I could think so, Mrs Erlynne.

MRS ERLYNNE: You know it far too well. I can fancy a person dancing through life with you and finding it charming.

LORD AUGUSTUS (*placing his hand on his white waistcoat*): Oh, thank you, thank you. You are the most adorable of all ladies!

MRS ERLYNNE: What a nice speech! So simple and so sincere! Just the sort of speech I like. Well, you shall hold my bouquet. (*Goes towards ballroom on Lord Windermere's arm.*) Ah, Mr Dumby, how are you? I am so sorry I have been out the last three times you have called. Come and lunch on Friday.

DUMBY (*with perfect nonchalance*): Delighted!

Lady Plymdale glares with indignation at Mr Dumby. Lord Augustus follows Mrs Erlynne and Lord Windermere into the ballroom holding bouquet.

LADY PLYMDALE (*to Mr Dumby*): What an absolute brute you are! I never can believe a word you say! Why did you tell me you didn't know her? What do you mean by calling on her three times running? You are not to go to lunch there; of course you understand that?

DUMBY: My dear Laura, I wouldn't dream of going!

LADY PLYMDALE: You haven't told me her name yet! Who is she?

DUMBY (*coughs slightly and smooths his hair*): She's a Mrs Erlynne.

LADY PLYMDALE: That woman!

DUMBY: Yes; that is what every one calls her.

LADY PLYMDALE: How very interesting! How intensely interesting! I really must have a good stare at her. (*Goes to door of ballroom and looks in.*) I have heard the most shocking things about her. They say she is ruining poor Windermere. And Lady Windermere, who goes in for being so proper, invites her! How extremely amusing! It takes a thoroughly good woman to do a thoroughly stupid thing. You are to lunch there on Friday!

DUMBY: Why?

LADY PLYMDALE: Because I want you to take my husband with you. He has been so attentive lately, that he has become a perfect nuisance.

Now, this woman's just the thing for him. He'll dance attendance upon her as long as she lets him, and won't bother me. I assure you, women of that kind are most useful. They form the basis of other people's marriages.

DUMBY: What a mystery you are!

LADY PLYMDALE (*looking at him*): I wish *you* were!

DUMBY: I am – to myself. I am the only person in the world I should like to know thoroughly; but I don't see any chance of it just at present. *They pass into the ballroom, and Lady Windermere and Lord Darlington enter from the terrace.*

LADY WINDERMERE: Yes. Yes. Her coming here is monstrous, unbearable. I know now what you meant to-day at tea time. Why didn't you tell me right out? You should have!

LORD DARLINGTON: I couldn't! A man can't tell these things about another man! But if I had known he was going to make you ask her here to-night, I think I would have told you. That insult, at any rate, you would have been spared.

LADY WINDERMERE: I did not ask her. He insisted on her coming – against my entreaties – against my commands. Oh! the house is tainted for me! I feel that every woman here sneers at me as she dances by with my husband. What have I done to deserve this? I gave him all my life. He took it – used it – spoiled it! I am degraded in my own eyes, and I lack courage – I am a coward! (*Sits down on sofa.*)

LORD DARLINGTON: If I know you at all, I know that you can't live with a man who treats you like this! What sort of life would you have with him? You would feel that he was lying to you every moment of the day. You would feel that the look in his eyes was false, his voice false, his touch false, his passion false. He would come to you when he was weary of others; you would have to comfort him. He would come to you when he was devoted to others; you would have to charm him. You would have to be to him the mask of his real life, the cloak to hide his secret.

LADY WINDERMERE: You are right – you are terribly right. But where am I to turn? You said you would be my friend, Lord Darlington. – Tell me, what am I to do? Be my friend now.

LORD DARLINGTON: Between men and women there is no friendship possible. There is passion, enmity, worship, love, but no friendship. I love you—

LADY WINDERMERE: No, no! (*Rises.*)

LORD DARLINGTON: Yes, I love you! You are more to me than anything in the whole world. What does your husband give you? Nothing. Whatever is in him he gives to this wretched woman, whom he has thrust into your society, into your home, to shame you before every one. I offer you my life—

LADY WINDERMERE: Lord Darlington!

LORD DARLINGTON: My life – my whole life. Take it, and do with it what you will ... I love you – love you as I have never loved any living thing. From the moment I met you I loved you, loved you blindly, adoringly, madly! You did not know it then – you know it now! Leave this house to-night. I won't tell you that the world matters nothing, or the world's voice, or the voice of society. They matter a great deal. They matter far too much. But there are moments when one has to choose between living one's own life, fully, entirely, completely – or dragging out some false, shallow, degrading existence that the world in its hypocrisy demands. You have that moment now. Choose! Oh, my love, choose.

LADY WINDERMERE (*moving slowly away from him, and looking at him with startled eyes*): I have not the courage.

LORD DARLINGTON (*following her*): Yes; you have the courage. There may be six months of pain, of disgrace even, but when you no longer bear his name, when you bear mine, all will be well. Margaret, my love, my wife that shall be some day – yes, my wife! You know it! What are you now? This woman has the place that belongs by right to you. Oh! go – go out of this house, with head erect, with a smile upon your lips, with courage in your eyes. All London will know why you did it; and who will blame you? No one. If they do, what matter? Wrong? What is wrong? It's wrong for a man to abandon his wife for a shameless woman. It is wrong for a wife to remain with a man who so dishonours her. You said once you would make no compromise with things. Make none now. Be brave! Be yourself!

LADY WINDERMERE: I am afraid of being myself. Let me think. Let me wait! My husband may return to me. (*Sits down on sofa.*)

LORD DARLINGTON: And you would take him back! You are not what I thought you were. You are just the same as every other woman. You would stand anything rather than face the censure of a world whose praise you would despise. In a week you will be driving with this woman in the Park. She will be your constant guest – your dearest friend. You would endure anything rather than break with one blow this monstrous tie. You are right. You have no courage; none!

LADY WINDERMERE: Ah, give me time to think. I cannot answer you now. (*Passes her hand nervously over her brow.*)

LORD DARLINGTON: It must be now or not at all.

LADY WINDERMERE (*rising from the sofa*): Then, not at all! (*A pause.*)

LORD DARLINGTON: You break my heart!

LADY WINDERMERE: Mine is already broken. (*A pause.*)

LORD DARLINGTON: To-morrow I leave England. This is the last time I shall ever look on you. You will never see me again. For one moment our lives met – our souls touched. They must never meet or touch again. Good-bye, Margaret. (*Exit.*)

LADY WINDERMERE: How alone I am in life. How terribly alone!

The music stops. Enter the Duchess of Berwick and Lord Paisley laughing and talking. Other guests come in from ballroom.

DUCHESS OF BERWICK: Dear Margaret, I've just been having such a delightful chat with Mrs Erlynne. I am so sorry for what I said to you this afternoon about her. Of course, she must be all right if you invite her. A most attractive woman, and has such sensible views on life.

Told me she entirely disapproved of people marrying more than once, so I feel quite safe about poor Augustus. Can't imagine why people speak against her. It's those horrid nieces of mine – the Saville girls – they're always talking scandal. Still, I should go to Homburg, dear, I really should. She is just a little too attractive. But where is Agatha? Oh, there she is. (*Lady Agatha and Mr Hopper enter from terrace L.U.E.*) Mr Hopper, I am very, very angry with you. You have taken Agatha out on the terrace, and she is so delicate.

HOPPER (*L.C.*): Awfully sorry, Duchess. We went out for a moment and then got chatting together.

DUCHESS OF BERWICK (*C.*): Ah, about dear Australia, I suppose?

HOPPER: Yes!

DUCHESS OF BERWICK: Agatha, darling! (*Beckons her over.*)

LADY AGATHA: Yes, mamma!

DUCHESS OF BERWICK (*aside*): Did Mr Hopper definitely—

LADY AGATHA: Yes, mamma.

DUCHESS OF BERWICK: And what answer did you give him, dear child?

LADY AGATHA: Yes, mamma.

DUCHESS OF BERWICK (*affectionately*): My dear one! You always say the right thing. Mr Hopper! James! Agatha has told me everything. How cleverly you have both kept your secret.

HOPPER: You don't mind my taking Agatha off to Australia, then, Duchess?

DUCHESS OF BERWICK (*indignantly*): To Australia? Oh, don't mention that dreadful vulgar place.

HOPPER: But she said she'd like to come with me.

DUCHESS OF BERWICK (*severely*): Did you say that, Agatha?

LADY AGATHA: Yes, mamma.

DUCHESS OF BERWICK: Agatha, you say the most silly things possible. I think on the whole that Grosvenor Square would be a more healthy place to reside in. There are lots of vulgar people live in Grosvenor Square, but at any rate there are no horrid kangaroos crawling about. But we'll talk about that to-morrow. James, you can take Agatha down. You'll come to lunch, of course, James. At half-past one instead of two. The Duke will wish to say a few words to you, I am sure.

HOPPER: I should like to have a chat with the Duke, Duchess. He has not said a single word to me yet.

DUCHESS OF BERWICK: I think you'll find he will have a great deal to say to you to-morrow. (*Exit Lady Agatha with Mr Hopper.*) And now good-night, Margaret. I'm afraid it's the old, old story, dear. Love – well, not love at first sight, but love at the end of the season, which is so much more satisfactory.

LADY WINDERMERE: Good-night, Duchess.

Exit the Duchess of Berwick on Lord Paisley's arm.

LADY PLYMDALE: My dear Margaret, what a handsome woman your husband has been dancing with! I should be quite jealous if I were you! Is she a great friend of yours?

LADY WINDERMERE: No!

LADY PLYMDALE: Really? Good-night, dear. (*Looks at Mr Dumby and exit.*)

DUMBY: Awful manners young Hopper has!

CECIL GRAHAM: Ah! Hopper is one of Nature's gentlemen, the worst type of gentleman I know.

DUMBY: Sensible woman, Lady Windermere. Lots of wives would have objected to Mrs Erlynne coming. But Lady Windermere has that uncommon thing called common sense.

CECIL GRAHAM: And Windermere knows that nothing looks so like innocence as an indiscretion.

DUMBY: Yes; dear Windermere is becoming almost modern. Never thought he would. (*Bows to Lady Windermere and exit.*)

LADY JEDBURGH: Good-night, Lady Windermere. What a fascinating woman Mrs Erlynne is! She is coming to lunch on Thursday, won't you come too? I expect the Bishop and dear Lady Merton.

LADY WINDERMERE: I am afraid I am engaged, Lady Jedburgh.

LADY JEDBURGH: So sorry. Come, dear. (*Exeunt Lady Jedburgh and Miss Graham.*)

Enter Mrs Erlynne and Lord Windermere.

MRS ERLYNNE: Charming ball it has been! Quite reminds me of old days (*Sits on sofa.*) And I see that there are just as many fools in society as there used to be. So pleased to find that nothing has altered! Except Margaret. She's grown quite pretty. The last time I saw her – twenty years ago, she was a fright in flannel. Positive fright, I assure you. The dear Duchess! and that sweet Lady Agatha! Just the type of girl I like! Well, really, Windermere, if I am to be the Duchess's sister-in-law—

LORD WINDERMERE (*sitting L. of her*): But are you—?

Exit Mr Cecil Graham with rest of guests. Lady Windermere watches, with a look of scorn and pain, Mrs Erlynne and her husband. They are unconscious of her presence.

MRS ERLYNNE: Oh, yes! He's to call to-morrow at twelve o'clock. He wanted to propose to-night. In fact he did. He kept on proposing. Poor Augustus; you know how he repeats himself. Such a bad habit! But I told him I wouldn't give him an answer till to-morrow. Of course I am going to take him. And I dare say I'll make him an admirable wife, as wives go. And there is a great deal of good in Lord Augustus. Fortunately it is all on the surface. Just where good qualities should be. Of course you must help me in this matter.

LORD WINDERMERE: I am not called on to encourage Lord Augustus, I suppose?

MRS ERLYNNE: Oh, no! I do the encouraging. But you will make me a handsome settlement, Windermere, won't you?

LORD WINDERMERE (*frowning*): Is that what you want to talk to me about to-night?

MRS ERLYNNE: Yes.

LORD WINDERMERE (*with a gesture of impatience*): I will not talk of it here.

MRS ERLYNNE (*laughing*): Then we will talk of it on the terrace. Even business should have a picturesque background. Should it not, Windermere? With a proper background women can do anything.

LORD WINDERMERE: Won't to-morrow do as well?

MRS ERLYNNE: No; you see, to-morrow I am going to accept him. And I think it would be a good thing if I was able to tell him that I had – well, what shall I say? – £2000 a year left to me by a third cousin – or a second husband – or some distant relative of that kind. It would be an additional attraction, wouldn't it? You have a delightful opportunity now of paying me a compliment, Windermere. But you are not very clever at paying compliments. I am afraid Margaret doesn't encourage you in that excellent habit. It's a great mistake on her part. When men give up saying what is charming, they give up thinking what is charming. But seriously, what do you say to £2000? £2500, I think. In modern life margin is everything. Windermere, don't you think the world an intensely amusing place? I do!

Exit on terrace with Lord Windermere. Music strikes up in ballroom.

LADY WINDERMERE: To stay in this house any longer is impossible. To-night a man who loves me offered me his whole life. I refused it. It was foolish of me. I will offer him mine now. I will give him mine. I will go to him! (*Puts on cloak and goes to the door, then turns back. Sits down at table and writes a letter, puts it into an envelope, and leaves it on table.*) Arthur has never understood me. When he reads this, he will. He may do as he chooses now with his life. I have done with mine as I think best, as I think right. It is he who has broken the bond of marriage – not I. I only break its bondage. (*Exit.*)

Parker enters L. and crosses towards the ballroom R. Enter Mrs Erlynne.

MRS ERLYNNE: Is Lady Windermere in the ballroom?

PARKER: Her ladyship has just gone out.

MRS ERLYNNE: Gone out? She's not on the terrace?

PARKER: No, madam. Her ladyship has just gone out of the house.

MRS ERLYNNE (*starts, and looks at the servant with a puzzled expression in her face.*): Out of the house?

PARKER: Yes, madam – her ladyship told me she had left a letter for his lordship on the table.

MRS ERLYNNE: A letter for Lord Windermere?

PARKER: Yes, madam.

MRS ERLYNNE: Thank you.

Exit Parker. The music in the ballroom stops.

Gone out of her house! A letter addressed to her husband! (*Goes over to bureau and looks at letter. Takes it up and lays it down again with a shudder of fear.*) No, no! It would be impossible! Life doesn't repeat its tragedies like that! Oh, why does this horrible fancy come across me? Why do I remember now the one moment of my life I most wish to forget? Does life repeat its tragedies? (*Tears letter open and reads it, then sinks down into a chair with a gesture of anguish.*) Oh, how terrible! The same words that twenty years ago I wrote to her father! and how bitterly I have been punished for it! No; my punishment, my real punishment is to-night, is now! (*Still seated R.*)

Enter Lord Windermere L.U.E.

LORD WINDERMERE: Have you said good-night to my wife? (*Comes C.*)

MRS ERLYNNE (*crushing letter in her hand*): Yes.

LORD WINDERMERE: Where is she?

MRS ERLYNNE: She is very tired. She has gone to bed. She said she had a headache.

LORD WINDERMERE: I must go to her. You'll excuse me?

MRS ERLYNNE (*rising hurriedly*): Oh, no! It's nothing serious. She's only very tired, that is all. Besides, there are people still in the supper-room. She wants you to make her apologies to them. She said she didn't wish to be disturbed (*Drops letter.*) She asked me to tell you!

LORD WINDERMERE (*picks up letter*): You have dropped something.

MRS ERLYNNE: Oh yes, thank you, that is mine. (*Puts out her hand to take it.*)

LORD WINDERMERE (*still looking at letter*): But it's my wife's handwriting, isn't it?

MRS ERLYNNE (*takes the letter quickly*): Yes, it's – an address. Will you ask them to call my carriage, please?

LORD WINDERMERE: Certainly. (*Goes L. and Exit.*)

MRS ERLYNNE: Thanks! What can I do? What can I do? I feel a passion awakening within me that I never felt before. What can it mean? The daughter must not be like the mother – that would be terrible. How can I save her? How can I save my child? A moment may ruin a life. Who knows that better than I? Windermere must be got out of the house; that is absolutely necessary. (*Goes L.*) But how shall I do it? It must be done somehow. Ah!

Enter Lord Augustus R.U.E. carrying bouquet.

LORD AUGUSTUS: Dear lady, I am in such suspense! May I not have an answer to my request?

MRS ERLYNNE: Lord Augustus, listen to me. You are to take Lord Windermere down to your club at once, and keep him there as long as possible. You understand?

LORD AUGUSTUS: But you said you wished me to keep early hours!

MRS ERLYNNE (*nervously*): Do what I tell you. Do what I tell you.

LORD AUGUSTUS: And my reward?

MRS ERLYNNE: Your reward? Your reward? Oh! ask me that to-morrow. But don't let Windermere out of your sight to-night. If you do I will never forgive you. I will never speak to you again. I'll have nothing to do with you. Remember you are to keep Windermere at your club, and don't let him come back to-night. (*Exit L.*)

LORD AUGUSTUS: Well, really, I might be her husband already. Positively I might. (*Follows her in a bewildered manner.*)

ACT THREE

Scene: Lord Darlington's rooms. A large sofa is in front of fireplace R. At the back of the stage a curtain is drawn across the window. Doors L. and R. Table

*R. with writing materials. Table C. with siphons, glasses, and Tantalus frame.
Table L. with cigar and cigarette box. Lamps lit.*

LADY WINDERMERE (*standing by the fireplace*): Why doesn't he come? This waiting is horrible. He should be here. Why is he not here, to wake by passionate words some fire within me? I am cold – cold as a loveless thing. Arthur must have read my letter by this time. If he cared for me, he would have come after me, would have taken me back by force. But he doesn't care. He's entrammelled by this woman – fascinated by her – dominated by her. If a woman wants to hold a man, she has merely to appeal to what is worst in him. We make gods of men and they leave us. Others make brutes of them and they fawn and are faithful. How hideous life is! . . . Oh! it was mad of me to come here, horribly mad. And yet, which is the worst, I wonder, to be at the mercy of a man who loves one, or the wife of a man who in one's own house dishonours one? What woman knows? What woman in the whole world? But will he love me always, this man to whom I am giving my life? What do I bring him? Lips that have lost the note of joy, eyes that are blinded by tears, chill hands and icy heart. I bring him nothing. I must go back – no; I can't go back, my letter has put me in their power – Arthur would not take me back! That fatal letter! No! Lord Darlington leaves England to-morrow. I will go with him – I have no choice. (*Sits down for a few moments. Then starts up and puts on her cloak.*) No, no! I will go back, let Arthur do with me what he pleases. I can't wait here. It has been madness my coming. I must go at once. As for Lord Darlington. – Oh! here he is! What shall I do! What can I say to him? Will he let me go away at all? I have heard that men are brutal, horrible . . . Oh! (*Hides her face in her hands.*)
Enter Mrs Erlynne L.
MRS ERLYNNE: Lady Windermere! (*Lady Windermere starts and looks up. Then recoils in contempt.*) Thank Heaven I am in time. You must go back to your husband's house immediately.
LADY WINDERMERE: Must?
MRS ERLYNNE (*authoritatively*): Yes, you must! There is not a second to be lost. Lord Darlington may return at any moment.
LADY WINDERMERE: Don't come near me!
MRS ERLYNNE: Oh! You are on the brink of ruin, you are on the brink of a hideous precipice. You must leave this place at once; my carriage is waiting at the corner of the street. You must come with me and drive straight home.
Lady Windermere throws off her cloak and flings it on the sofa.
What are you doing?
LADY WINDERMERE: Mrs Erlynne – if you had not come here, I would have gone back. But now that I see you, I feel that nothing in the whole world would induce me to live under the same roof as Lord Windermere. You fill me with horror. There is something about you that stirs the wildest – rage within me. And I know why you are here.

My husband sent you to lure me back that I might serve as a blind to whatever relations exist between you and him.

MRS ERLYNNE: Oh! You don't think that – you can't.

LADY WINDERMERE: Go back to my husband, Mrs Erlynne. He belongs to you and not to me. I suppose he is afraid of a scandal. Men are such cowards. They outrage every law of the world, and are afraid of the world's tongue. But he had better prepare himself. He shall have a scandal. He shall have the worst scandal there has been in London for years. He shall see his name in every vile paper, mine on every hideous placard.

MRS ERLYNNE: No – no—

LADY WINDERMERE: Yes! he shall. Had he come himself, I admit I would have gone back to the life of degradation you and he had prepared for me – I was going back – but to stay himself at home, and to send you as his messenger – oh! it was infamous – infamous.

MRS ERLYNNE (*C.*): Lady Windermere, you wrong me horribly – you wrong your husband horribly. He doesn't know you are here – he thinks you are safe in your own house. He thinks you are asleep in your own room. He never read the mad letter you wrote to him!

LADY WINDERMERE (*R.*): Never read it!

MRS ERLYNNE: No – he knows nothing about it.

LADY WINDERMERE: How simple you think me! (*Going to her.*) You are lying to me!

MRS ERLYNNE (*restraining herself*): I am not. I am telling you the truth.

LADY WINDERMERE: If my husband didn't read my letter, how is it that you are here? Who told you I had left the house you were shameless enough to enter? Who told you where I had gone to? My husband told you, and sent you to decoy me back. (*Crosses L.*)

MRS ERLYNNE (*R.C.*): Your husband has never seen the letter. I – saw it, I opened it. I – read it.

LADY WINDERMERE (*turning to her*): You opened a letter of mine to my husband? You wouldn't dare!

MRS ERLYNNE: Dare! Oh! to save you from the abyss into which you are falling, there is nothing in the world I would not dare, nothing in the whole world. Here is the letter. Your husband has never read it. He never shall read it. (*Going to fireplace.*) It should never have been written. (*Tears it and throws it into the fire.*)

LADY WINDERMERE (*with infinite contempt in her voice and look*): How do I know that that was my letter after all? You seem to think that the commonest device can take me in!

MRS ERLYNNE: Oh! why do you disbelieve everything I tell you? What object do you think I have in coming here, except to save you from utter ruin, to save you from the consequence of a hideous mistake? That letter that is burnt now *was* your letter. I swear it to you!

LADY WINDERMERE (*slowly*): You took good care to burn it before I had examined it. I cannot trust you. You, whose whole life is a lie, how could you speak the truth about anything? (*Sits down.*)

MRS ERLYNNE (*hurriedly*): Think as you like about me – say what you choose against me, but go back, go back to the husband you love.

LADY WINDERMERE. (*sullenly*): I do *not* love him!

MRS ERLYNNE: You do, and you know that he loves you.

LADY WINDERMERE: He does not understand what love is. He understands it as little as you do – but I see what you want. It would be a great advantage for you to get me back. Dear Heaven! what a life I would have then! Living at the mercy of a woman who has neither mercy nor pity in her, a woman whom it is an infamy to meet, a degradation to know, a vile woman, a woman who comes between husband and wife!

MRS ERLYNNE (*with a gesture of despair*): Lady Windermere, Lady Windermere, don't say such terrible things. You don't know how terrible they are, how terrible and how unjust. Listen, you must listen! Only go back to your husband, and I promise you never to communicate with him again on any pretext – never to see him – never to have anything to do with his life or yours. The money that he gave me, he gave me not through love, but through hatred, not in worship, but in contempt. The hold I have over him—

LADY WINDERMERE (*rising*): Ah! you admit you have a hold!

MRS ERLYNNE: Yes, and I will tell you what it is. It is his love for you, Lady Windermere.

LADY WINDERMERE: You expect me to believe that?

MRS ERLYNNE: You must believe it! it is true. It is his love for you that has made him submit to – oh! call it what you like, tyranny, threats, anything you choose. But it is his love for you. His desire to spare you – shame, yes, shame and disgrace.

LADY WINDERMERE: What do you mean? You are insolent! What have I to do with you?

MRS ERLYNNE (*humbly*): Nothing. I know it – but I tell you that your husband loves you – that you may never meet with such love again in your whole life – that such love you will never meet – and that if you throw it away, the day may come when you will starve for love and it will not be given to you, beg for love and it will be denied you. – Oh! Arthur loves you!

LADY WINDERMERE: Arthur? And you tell me there is nothing between you?

MRS ERLYNNE: Lady Windermere, before Heaven your husband is guiltless of all offence towards you! And I – I tell you that had it ever occurred to me that such a monstrous suspicion would have entered your mind, I would have died rather than have crossed your life or his – oh! died, gladly died! (*Moves away to sofa R.*)

LADY WINDERMERE: You talk as if you had a heart. Women like you have no hearts. Heart is not in you. You are bought and sold. (*Sits L.C.*)

MRS ERLYNNE (*starts, with a gesture of pain. Then restrains herself, and comes over to where Lady Windermere is sitting. As she speaks, she stretches out her hands towards her, but does not dare to touch her*): Believe what you choose about me. I am not worth a moment's sorrow. But don't spoil your beautiful young life on my account! You don't know what may be in store for you, unless you leave this house at once. You don't know what it is to fall into the pit, to be despised, mocked, abandoned, sneered at – to be an outcast! to find the door shut against one, to have to creep in by hideous byways, afraid every moment lest the mask should be stripped from one's face, and all the while to hear the laughter, the horrible laughter of the world, a thing more tragic than all the tears the world has ever shed. You don't know what it is. One pays for one's sin, and then one pays again, and all one's life one pays. You must never know that. – As for me, if suffering be an expiation, then at this moment I have expiated all my faults, whatever they have been; for to-night you have made a heart in one who had it not, made it and broken it. – But let that pass. I may have wrecked my own life, but I will not let you wreck yours. You – why, you are a mere girl, you would be lost. You haven't got the kind of brains that enables a woman to get back. You have neither the wit nor the courage. You couldn't stand dishonour! No! Go back, Lady Windermere, to the husband who loves you, whom you love. You have a child, Lady Windermere. Go back to that child who even now, in pain or in joy, may be calling to you. (*Lady Windermere rises.*) God gave you that child. He will require from you that you make his life fine, that you watch over him. What answer will you make to God if his life is ruined through you? Back to your house, Lady Windermere – your husband loves you! He has never swerved for a moment from the love he bears you. But even if he had a thousand loves, you must stay with your child. If he was harsh to you, you must stay with your child. If he ill-treated you, you must stay with your child. If he abandoned you, your place is with your child.

Lady Windermere bursts into tears and buries her face in her hands.

(*Rushing to her*): Lady Windermere!

LADY WINDERMERE (*holding out her hands to her, helplessly, as a child might do*): Take me home. Take me home.

MRS ERLYNNE (*is about to embrace her. Then restrains herself. There is a look of wonderful joy in her face*): Come! Where is your cloak? (*Getting it from sofa*): Here. Put it on. Come at once!

They go to the door.

LADY WINDERMERE: Stop! Don't you hear voices?

MRS ERLYNNE: No, no! There is no one!

LADY WINDERMERE: Yes, there is! Listen! Oh! that is my husband's voice! He is coming in! Save me! Oh, it's some plot! You have sent for him. *Voices outside.*

MRS ERLYNNE: Silence! I'm here to save you, if I can. But I fear it is too late! There! (*Points to the curtain across the window.*) The first chance you have slip out, if you ever get a chance!

LADY WINDERMERE: But you!

MRS ERLYNNE: Oh! never mind me. I'll face them.

Lady Windermere hides herself behind the curtain.

LORD AUGUSTUS (*outside*): Nonsense, dear Windermere, you must not leave me!

MRS ERLYNNE: Lord Augustus! Then it is I who am lost! (*Hesitates for a moment, then looks round and sees door R., and exit through it.*)

Enter Lord Darlington, Mr Dumby, Lord Windermere, Lord Augustus Lorton, and Mr Cecil Graham.

DUMBY: What a nuisance their turning us out of the club at this hour! It's only two o'clock. (*Sinks into a chair.*) The lively part of the evening is only just beginning. (*Yawns and closes his eyes.*)

LORD WINDERMERE: It is very good of you, Lord Darlington, allowing Augustus to force our company on you, but I'm afraid I can't stay long.

LORD DARLINGTON: Really! I am so sorry! You'll take a cigar, won't you?

LORD WINDERMERE: Thanks! (*Sits down.*)

LORD AUGUSTUS (*to Lord Windermere*): My dear boy, you must not dream of going. I have a great deal to talk to you about, of demmed importance, too. (*Sits down with him at L. table.*)

CECIL GRAHAM: Oh! We all know what that is! Tuppy can't talk about anything but Mrs Erlynne.

LORD WINDERMERE: Well, that is no business of yours, is it, Cecil?

CECIL GRAHAM: None! That is why it interests me. My own business always bores me to death. I prefer other people's.

LORD DARLINGTON: Have something to drink, you fellows. Cecil, you'll have a whisky and soda?

CECIL GRAHAM: Thanks. (*Goes to table with Lord Darlington*): Mrs Erlynne looked very handsome to-night, didn't she?

LORD DARLINGTON: I am not one of her admirers.

CECIL GRAHAM: I usen't to be, but I am now. Why! she actually made me introduce her to poor dear Aunt Caroline. I believe she is going to lunch there.

LORD DARLINGTON (*in surprise*): No?

CECIL GRAHAM: She is, really.

LORD DARLINGTON: Excuse me, you fellows. I'm going away to-morrow. And I have to write a few letters. (*Goes to writing-table and sits down.*)

DUMBY: Clever woman, Mrs Erlynne.

CECIL GRAHAM: Hullo, Dumby! I thought you were asleep.

DUMBY: I am, I usually am!

LORD AUGUSTUS: A very clever woman. Knows perfectly well what a demmed fool I am – knows it as well as I do myself.

Cecil Graham comes towards him laughing.

Ah, you may laugh, my boy, but it is a great thing to come across a woman who thoroughly understands one.

DUMBY: It is an awfully dangerous thing. They always end by marrying one.

CECIL GRAHAM: But I thought, Tuppy, you were never going to see her again! Yes! you told me so yesterday evening at the club. You said you'd heard—

Whispering to him.

LORD AUGUSTUS: Oh, she's explained that.

CECIL GRAHAM: And the Wiesbaden affair?

LORD AUGUSTUS: She's explained that too.

DUMBY: And her income, Tuppy? Has she explained that?

LORD AUGUSTUS (*in a very serious voice*): She's going to explain that to-morrow.

Cecil Graham goes back to C. table.

DUMBY: Awfully commercial, women, nowadays. Our grandmothers threw their caps over the mills, of course, but, by Jove, their grand-daughters only throw their caps over mills that can raise the wind for them.

LORD AUGUSTUS: You want to make her out a wicked woman. She is not!

CECIL GRAHAM: Oh! Wicked women bother one. Good women bore one. That is the only difference between them.

LORD AUGUSTUS (*puffing a cigar*): Mrs Erlynne has a future before her.

DUMBY: Mrs Erlynne has a past before her.

LORD AUGUSTUS: I prefer women with a past. They're always so demmed amusing to talk to.

CECIL GRAHAM: Well, you'll have lots of topics of conversation with *her*, Tuppy. (*Rising and going to him.*)

LORD AUGUSTUS: You're getting annoying, dear boy; you're getting demmed annoying.

CECIL GRAHAM (*puts his hands on his shoulders*): Now, Tuppy, you've lost your figure and you've lost your character. Don't lose your temper; you have only got one.

LORD AUGUSTUS: My dear boy, if I wasn't the most good-natured man in London—

CECIL GRAHAM: We'd treat you with more respect, wouldn't we, Tuppy? (*Strolls away.*)

DUMBY: The youth of the present day are quite monstrous. They have absolutely no respect for dyed hair. (*Lord Augustus looks round angrily.*)

CECIL GRAHAM: Mrs Erlynne has a very great respect for dear Tuppy.

DUMBY: Then Mrs Erlynne sets an admirable example to the rest of her sex. It is perfectly brutal the way most women nowadays behave to men who are not their husbands.

LORD WINDERMERE: Dumby, you are ridiculous, and Cecil, you let your tongue run away with you. You must leave Mrs Erlynne alone. You don't really know anything about her, and you're always talking scandal against her.

CECIL GRAHAM (*coming towards him L.C.*): My dear Arthur, I never talk scandal. I only talk gossip.

LORD WINDERMERE: What is the difference between scandal and gossip?

CECIL GRAHAM: Oh! gossip is charming! History is merely gossip. But scandal is gossip made tedious by morality. Now, I never moralise. A man who moralises is usually a hypocrite, and a woman who moralises is invariably plain. There is nothing in the whole world so unbecoming to a woman as a Nonconformist conscience. And most women know it, I'm glad to say.

LORD AUGUSTUS: Just my sentiments, dear boy, just my sentiments.

CECIL GRAHAM: Sorry to hear it, Tuppy; whenever people agree with me, I always feel I must be wrong.

LORD AUGUSTUS: My dear boy, when I was your age—

CECIL GRAHAM: But you never were, Tuppy, and you never will be. (*Goes up to C.*) I say, Darlington, let us have some cards. You'll play, Arthur, won't you?

LORD WINDERMERE: No, thanks, Cecil.

DUMBY (*with a sigh*): Good heavens! how marriage ruins a man! It's as demoralising as cigarettes, and far more expensive.

CECIL GRAHAM: You'll play, of course, Tuppy?

LORD AUGUSTUS (*pouring himself out a brandy and soda at table*): Can't, dear boy. Promised Mrs Erlynne never to play or drink again.

CECIL GRAHAM: Now, my dear Tuppy, don't be led astray into the paths of virtue. Reformed, you would be perfectly tedious. That is the worst of women. They always want one to be good. And if we are good, when they meet us, they don't love us at all. They like to find us quite irretrievably bad, and to leave us quite unattractively good.

LORD DARLINGTON (*rising from R. Table, where he has been writing letters*): They always do find us bad!

DUMBY: I don't think we are bad. I think we are all good, except Tuppy.

LORD DARLINGTON: No, we are all in the gutter, but some of us are looking at the stars. (*Sits down at C. table*).

DUMBY: We are all in the gutter, but some of us are looking at the stars? Upon my word, you are very romantic to-night, Darlington.

CECIL GRAHAM: Too romantic! You must be in love. Who is the girl?

LORD DARLINGTON: The woman I love is not free, or thinks she isn't. (*Glances instinctively at Lord Windermere while he speaks.*)

CECIL GRAHAM: A married woman, then! Well, there's nothing in the world like the devotion of a married woman. It's a thing no married man knows anything about.

LORD DARLINGTON: Oh! she doesn't love me. She is a good woman. She is the only good woman I have ever met in my life.

CECIL GRAHAM: The only good woman you have ever met in your life?

LORD DARLINGTON: Yes!

CECIL GRAHAM (*lighting a cigarette*): Well, you are a lucky fellow! Why, I have met hundreds of good women. I never seem to meet any but good women. The world is perfectly packed with good women. To know them is a middle-class education.

LORD DARLINGTON: This woman has purity and innocence. She has everything we men have lost.

CECIL GRAHAM: My dear fellow, what on earth should we men do going about with purity and innocence? A carefully thought-out buttonhole is much more effective.

DUMBY: She doesn't really love you then?

LORD DARLINGTON: No, she does not!

DUMBY: I congratulate you, my dear fellow. In this world there are only two tragedies. One is not getting what one wants, and the other is getting it. The last is much the worst; the last is a real tragedy! But I am interested to hear she does not love you. How long could you love a woman who didn't love you, Cecil?

CECIL GRAHAM: A woman who didn't love me? Oh, all my life!

DUMBY: So could I. But it's so difficult to meet one.

LORD DARLINGTON: How can you be so conceited, Dumby?

DUMBY: I didn't say it as a matter of conceit. I said it as a matter of regret. I have been wildly, madly adored. I am sorry I have. It has been an immense nuisance. I should like to be allowed a little time to myself now and then.

LORD AUGUSTUS (*looking round*): Time to educate yourself, I suppose.

DUMBY: No, time to forget all I have learned. That is much more important, dear Tuppy. (*Lord Augustus moves uneasily in his chair.*)

LORD DARLINGTON: What cynics you fellows are!

CECIL GRAHAM: What is a cynic? (*Sitting on the back of the sofa.*)

LORD DARLINGTON: A man who knows the price of everything and the value of nothing.

CECIL GRAHAM: And a sentimentalist, my dear Darlington, is a man who sees an absurd value in everything, and doesn't know the market price of any single thing.

LORD DARLINGTON: You always amuse me, Cecil. You talk as if you were a man of experience.

CECIL GRAHAM: I am. (*Moves up to front of fireplace.*)

LORD DARLINGTON: You are far too young!

CECIL GRAHAM: That is a great error. Experience is a question of instinct about life. I have got it. Tuppy hasn't. Experience is the name Tuppy gives to his mistakes. That is all. (*Lord Augustus looks round indignantly.*)

DUMBY: Experience is the name every one gives to their mistakes.

CECIL GRAHAM (*standing with his back to the fireplace*): One shouldn't commit any. (*Sees Lady Windermere's fan on sofa.*)

DUMBY: Life would be very dull without them.

CECIL GRAHAM: Of course you are quite faithful to this woman you are in love with, Darlington, to this good woman?

LORD DARLINGTON: Cecil, if one really loves a woman, all other women in the world become absolutely meaningless to one. Love changes one – I am changed.

CECIL GRAHAM: Dear me! How very interesting! Tuppy, I want to talk to you. (*Lord Augustus takes no notice.*)

DUMBY: It's no use talking to Tuppy. You might just as well talk to a brick wall.

CECIL GRAHAM: But I like talking to a brick wall – it's the only thing in the world that never contradicts me! Tuppy!

LORD AUGUSTUS: Well, what is it? What is it? (*Rising and going over to Cecil Graham.*)

CECIL GRAHAM: Come over here. I want you particularly. (*Aside.*) Darlington has been moralising and talking about the purity of love, and that sort of thing, and he has got some woman in his rooms all the time.

LORD AUGUSTUS: No, really! really!

CECIL GRAHAM (*in a low voice*): Yes, here is her fan. (*Points to the fan.*)

LORD AUGUSTUS (*chuckling*): By Jove! By Jove!

LORD WINDERMERE (*up by door*): I am really off now, Lord Darlington. I am sorry you are leaving England so soon. Pray call on us when you come back! My wife and I will be charmed to see you!

LORD DARLINGTON (*up stage with Lord Windermere*); I am afraid I shall be away for many years. Good-night!

CECIL GRAHAM: Arthur!

LORD WINDERMERE: What?

CECIL GRAHAM: I want to speak to you for a moment. No, do come!

LORD WINDERMERE (*putting on his coat*): I can't – I'm off.

CECIL GRAHAM: It is something very particular. It will interest you enormously.

LORD WINDERMERE (*smiling*): It is some of your nonsense, Cecil.

CECIL GRAHAM: It isn't! It isn't really.

LORD AUGUSTUS (*going to him*): My dear fellow, you mustn't go yet. I have a lot to talk to you about. And Cecil has something to show you.

LORD WINDERMERE (*walking over*): Well, what is it?

CECIL GRAHAM: Darlington has got a woman here in his rooms. Here is her fan. Amusing, isn't it? (*A pause.*)

LORD WINDERMERE: Good God! (*Seizes the fan – Dumby rises.*)

CECIL GRAHAM: What is the matter?

LORD WINDERMERE: Lord Darlington!

LORD DARLINGTON (*turning round*): Yes!

LORD WINDERMERE: What is my wife's fan doing here in your rooms? Hands off, Cecil. Don't touch me.

LORD DARLINGTON: Your wife's fan?

LORD WINDERMERE: Yes, here it is?

LORD DARLINGTON (*walking towards him*): I don't know!

LORD WINDERMERE: You must know. I demand an explanation. Don't hold me, you fool. (*To Cecil Graham.*)

LORD DARLINGTON (*aside*): She is here after all!

LORD WINDERMERE: Speak, sir! Why is my wife's fan here? Answer me! By God! I'll search your rooms, and if my wife's here, I'll— (*Moves.*)

LORD DARLINGTON: You shall not search my rooms. You have no right to do so. I forbid you!

LORD WINDERMERE: You scoundrel! I'll not leave your room till I have searched every corner of it! What moves behind that curtain? (*Rushes towards the curtain C.*)

MRS ERLYNNE (*enters behind R.*): Lord Windermere!

LORD WINDERMERE: Mrs Erlynne!

Every one starts and turns round. Lady Windermere slips out from behind the curtain and glides from the room L.

MRS ERLYNNE: I am afraid I took your wife's fan in mistake for my own, when I was leaving your house to-night. I am so sorry. (*Takes fan from him. Lord Windermere looks at her in contempt. Lord Darlington in mingled astonishment and anger. Lord Augustus turns away. The other men smile at each other.*)

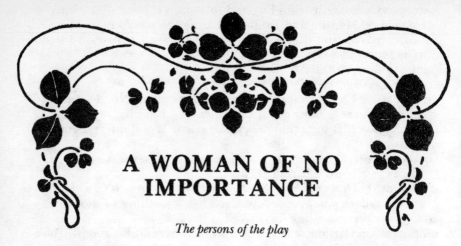

A WOMAN OF NO IMPORTANCE

The persons of the play

LORD ILLINGWORTH
SIR JOHN PONTEFRACT
LORD ALFRED RUFFORD
MR KELVIL, M.P.
THE VEN ARCHDEACON DAUBENY, D.D.
GERALD ARBUTHNOT
FARQUHAR, Butler
FRANCIS, Footman

LADY HUNSTANTON
LADY CAROLINE PONTEFRACT
LADY STUTFIELD
MRS ALLONBY
MISS HESTER WORSLEY
ALICE, Maid
MRS ARBUTHNOT

Time: *the present;* Place: *The Shires. The action of the play takes place within twenty-four hours.*

At a house party at Hunstanton Chase, Gerald Arbuthnot, a bank clerk who lives with his widowed mother, has announced that Lord Illingworth, one of the guests present, has offered him a post as his secretary. The young man is both excited and grateful ...

ACT TWO

Scene: Drawing-room at Hunstanton, after dinner, lamps lit. Door L.C. Door R.C. Ladies seated on sofa.

MRS ALLONBY: What a comfort it is to have got rid of the men for a little!
LADY STUTFIELD: Yes; men persecute us dreadfully, don't they?
MRS ALLONBY: Persecute us? I wish they did.

LADY HUNSTANTON: My dear!

MRS ALLONBY: The annoying thing is that the wretches can be perfectly happy without us. That is why I think it is every woman's duty never to leave them alone for a single moment, except during this short breathing space after dinner; without which, I believe, we poor women would be absolutely worn to shadows.

Enter Servants with coffee.

LADY HUNSTANTON: Worn to shadows, dear?

MRS ALLONBY: Yes, Lady Hunstanton. It is such a strain keeping men up to the mark. They are always trying to escape from us.

LADY STUTFIELD: It seems to me that it is we who are always trying to escape from them. Men are so very, very heartless. They know their power and use it.

LADY CAROLINE (*takes coffee from Servant*): What stuff and nonsense all this about men is! The thing to do is to keep men in their proper place.

MRS ALLONBY: But what is their proper place, Lady Caroline?

LADY CAROLINE: Looking after their wives, Mrs Allonby.

MRS ALLONBY (*takes coffee from Servant*): Really? And if they're not married?

LADY CAROLINE: If they are not married, they would be looking after a wife. It's perfectly scandalous the amount of bachelors who are going about society. There should be a law passed to compel them all to marry within twelve months.

LADY STUTFIELD (*refuses coffee*): But if they're in love with some one who, perhaps, is tied to another?

LADY CAROLINE: In that case, Lady Stutfield, they would be married off in a week to some plain respectable girl in order to teach them not to meddle with other people's property.

MRS ALLONBY: I don't think that we should ever be spoken of as other people's property. All men are married women's property. That is the only true definition of what married women's property really is. But we don't belong to any one.

LADY STUTFIELD: Oh, I am so very, very glad to hear you say so.

LADY HUNSTANTON: But do you really think, dear Caroline, that legislation would improve matters in any way? I am told that, nowadays, all the married men live like bachelors, and all the bachelors like married men.

MRS ALLONBY: I certainly never know one from the other.

LADY STUTFIELD: Oh, I think one can always know at once whether a man has home claims upon his life or not. I have noticed a very, very sad expression in the eyes of so many married men.

MRS ALLONBY: Ah, all that I have noticed is that they are horribly tedious when they are good husbands, and abominably conceited when they are not.

LADY HUNSTANTON: Well, I suppose the type of husband has completely changed since my young days, but I'm bound to state that poor dear Hunstanton was the most delightful of creatures, and as good as gold.

MRS ALLONBY: Ah, my husband is a sort of promissory note; I'm tired of meeting him.

LADY CAROLINE: But you renew him from time to time, don't you?

MRS ALLONBY: Oh no, Lady Caroline. I have only had one husband as yet. I suppose you look upon me as quite an amateur.

LADY CAROLINE: With your views on life I wonder you married at all.

MRS ALLONBY: So do I.

LADY HUNSTANTON: My dear child, I believe you are really very happy in your married life, but that you like to hide your happiness from others.

MRS ALLONBY: I assure you I was horribly deceived in Ernest.

LADY HUNSTANTON: Oh, I hope not, dear. I knew his mother quite well. She was a Stratton, Caroline, one of Lord Crowland's daughters.

LADY CAROLINE: Victoria Stratton? I remember her perfectly. A silly, fair-haired woman with no chin.

MRS ALLONBY: Ah, Ernest has a chin. He has a very strong chin, a square chin. Ernest's chin is far too square.

LADY STUTFIELD: But do you really think a man's chin can be too square? I think a man should look very, very strong, and that his chin should be quite, quite square.

MRS ALLONBY: Then you should certainly know Ernest, Lady Stutfield. It is only fair to tell you beforehand he has got no conversation at all.

LADY STUTFIELD: I adore silent men.

MRS ALLONBY: Oh, Ernest isn't silent. He talks the whole time. But he has got no conversation. What he talks about I don't know. I haven't listened to him for years.

LADY STUTFIELD: Have you never forgiven him then? How sad that seems! But all life is very, very sad, is it not?

MRS ALLONBY: Life, Lady Stutfield, is simply a *mauvais quart d'heure* made up of exquisite moments.

LADY STUTFIELD: Yes, there are moments, certainly. But was it something very, very wrong that Mr Allonby did? Did he become angry with you, and say anything that was unkind or true?

MRS ALLONBY: Oh, dear, no. Ernest is invariably calm. That is one of the reasons he always gets on my nerves. Nothing is so aggravating as calmness. There is something positively brutal about the good temper of most modern men. I wonder we women stand it as well as we do.

LADY STUTFIELD: Yes; men's good temper shows they are not so sensitive as we are, not so finely strung. It makes a great barrier often between husband and wife, does it not? But I would so much like to know what was the wrong thing Mr Allonby did.

MRS ALLONBY: Well, I will tell you, if you solemnly promise to tell everybody else.

LADY STUTFIELD: Thank you, thank you. I will make a point of repeating it.

MRS ALLONBY: When Ernest and I were engaged, he swore to me positively on his knees that he had never loved any one before in the whole course of his life. I was very young at the time, so I didn't believe him, I needn't tell you. Unfortunately, however, I made no inquiries of any kind till after I had been actually married four or five months. I found out then that what he had told me was perfectly true. And that sort of thing makes a man so absolutely uninteresting.

LADY HUNSTANTON: My dear!

MRS ALLONBY: Men always want to be a woman's first love. That is their clumsy vanity. We women have a more subtle instinct about things. What we like is to be a man's last romance.

LADY STUTFIELD: I see what you mean. It's very, very beautiful.

LADY HUNSTANTON: My dear child, you don't mean to tell me that you won't forgive your husband because he never loved any one else? Did you ever hear such a thing, Caroline? I am quite surprised.

LADY CAROLINE: Oh, women have become so highly educated, Jane, that nothing should surprise us nowadays, except happy marriages. They apparently are getting remarkably rare.

MRS ALLONBY: Oh, they're quite out of date.

LADY STUTFIELD: Except amongst the middle classes, I have been told.

MRS ALLONBY: How like the middle classes!

LADY STUTFIELD: Yes – is it not? – very, very like them.

LADY CAROLINE: If what you tell us about the middle classes is true, Lady Stutfield, it redounds greatly to their credit. It is much to be regretted that in our rank of life the wife should be so persistently frivolous, under the impression apparently that it is the proper thing to be. It is to that I attribute the unhappiness of so many marriages we all know of in society.

MRS ALLONBY: Do you know, Lady Caroline, I don't think the frivolity of the wife has ever anything to do with it. More marriages are ruined nowadays by the common sense of the husband than by anything else. How can a woman be expected to be happy with a man who insists on treating her as if she was a perfectly rational being?

LADY HUNSTANTON: My dear!

MRS ALLONBY: Man, poor, awkward reliable, necessary man belongs to a sex that has been rational for millions and millions of years. He can't help himself. It is in his race. The History of Woman is very different. We have always been picturesque protests against the mere existence of common sense. We saw its dangers from the first.

LADY STUTFIELD: Yes, the common sense of husbands is certainly most, most trying. Do tell me your conception of the Ideal Husband. I think it would be so very, very helpful.

MRS ALLONBY: The Ideal Husband? There couldn't be such a thing. The institution is wrong.

LADY STUTFIELD: The Ideal Man, then, in his relations to us. .

LADY CAROLINE: He would probably be extremely realistic.

MRS ALLONBY: The Ideal Man! Oh, the Ideal Man should talk to us as if we were goddesses, and treat us as if we were children. He should refuse all our serious requests, and gratify every one of our whims. He should encourage us to have caprices, and forbid us to have missions. He should always say much more than he means, and always mean much more than he says.

LADY HUNSTANTON: But how could he do both, dear?

MRS ALLONBY: He should never run down other pretty women. That would show he had no taste, or make one suspect that he had too much. No; he should be nice about them all, but say that somehow they don't attract him.

LADY STUTFIELD: Yes, that is always very, very pleasant to hear about other women.

MRS ALLONBY: If we ask him a question about anything, he should give us an answer all about ourselves. He should invariably praise us for whatever qualities he knows we haven't got. But he should be pitiless, quite pitiless, in reproaching us for the virtues that we have never dreamed of possessing. He should never believe that we know the use of useful things. That would be unforgivable. But he should shower on us everything we don't want.

LADY CAROLINE: As far as I can see, he is to do nothing but pay bills and compliments.

MRS ALLONBY: He should persistently compromise us in public, and treat us with absolute respect when we are alone. And yet he should be always ready to have a perfectly terrible scene, whenever we want one, and to become miserable, absolutely miserable, at a moment's notice, and to overwhelm us with just reproaches in less than twenty minutes, and to be positively violent at the end of half an hour, and to leave us for ever at a quarter to eight, when we have to go and dress for dinner. And when, after that, one has seen him for really the last time, and he has refused to take back the little things he has given one, and promised never to communicate with one again, or to write one any foolish letters, he should be perfectly broken-hearted, and telegraph to one all day long, and send one little notes every half-hour by a private hansom, and dine quite alone at the club, so that every one should know how unhappy he was. And after a whole dreadful week, during which one has gone about everywhere with one's husband, just to show how absolutely lonely one was, he may be given a third last parting, in the evening, and then, if his conduct has been quite irreproachable, and one has behaved really badly to him, he should be allowed to admit that he has been entirely in the wrong, and when he has admitted that, it becomes a woman's duty to forgive, and one can do it all over again from the beginning with variations.

LADY HUNSTANTON: How clever you are, my dear! You never mean a single word you say.

LADY STUTFIELD: Thank you, thank you. It has been quite, quite entrancing. I must try and remember it all. There are such a number of details that are so very, very important.

LADY CAROLINE: But you have not told us yet what the reward of the Ideal Man is to be.

MRS ALLONBY: His reward? Oh, infinite expectation. That is quite enough for him.

LADY STUTFIELD: But men are so terribly, terribly exacting, are they not?

MRS ALLONBY: That makes no matter. One should never surrender.

LADY STUTFIELD: Not even to the Ideal Man?

MRS ALLONBY: Certainly not to him. Unless, of course, one wants to grow tired of him.

LADY STUTFIELD: Oh! . . . Yes. I see that. It is very, very helpful. Do you think, Mrs Allonby, I shall ever meet the Ideal Man? Or are there more than one?

MRS ALLONBY: There are just four in London, Lady Stutfield.

LADY HUNSTANTON: Oh, my dear!

MRS ALLONBY (*going over to her*): What has happened? Do tell me.

LADY HUNSTANTON (*in a low voice*): I had completely forgotten that the American young lady has been in the room all the time. I am afraid some of this clever talk may have shocked her a little.

MRS ALLONBY: Ah, that will do her so much good!

LADY HUNSTANTON: Let us hope she didn't understand much. I think I had better go over and talk to her. (*Rises and goes across to Hester Worsley.*) Well, dear Miss Worsley. (*Sitting down beside her.*) How quiet you have been in your nice little corner all this time! I suppose you have been reading a book? There are so many books here in the library.

HESTER: No, I have been listening to the conversation.

LADY HUNSTANTON: You mustn't believe everything that was said, you know, dear.

HESTER: I didn't believe any of it.

LADY HUNSTANTON: That is quite right, dear.

HESTER (*continuing*): I couldn't believe that any women could really hold such views of life as I have heard to-night from some of your guests. (*An awkward pause.*)

LADY HUNSTANTON: I hear you have such pleasant society in America. Quite like our own in places, my son wrote to me.

HESTER: There are cliques in America as elsewhere, Lady Hunstanton. But true American society consists simply of all the good women and good men we have in our country.

LADY HUNSTANTON: What a sensible system, and I dare say quite pleasant, too. I am afraid in England we have too many artificial social barriers. We don't see as much as we should of the middle and lower classes.

HESTER: In America we have no lower classes.

LADY HUNSTANTON: Really? What a very strange arrangement!

MRS ALLONBY: What is that dreadful girl talking about?

LADY STUTFIELD: She is painfully natural, is she not?

LADY CAROLINE: There are a great many things you haven't got in America, I am told, Miss Worsley. They say you have no ruins, and no curiosities.

MRS ALLONBY (*to Lady Stutfield*): What nonsense! They have their mothers and their manners.

HESTER: The English aristocracy supply us with our curiosities, Lady Caroline. They are sent over to us every summer, regularly, in the steamers, and propose to us the day after they land. As for ruins, we

are trying to build up something that will last longer than brick or
stone. (*Gets up to take her fan from table.*)

LADY HUNSTANTON: What is that dear? Ah, yes, an iron Exhibition, is it
not, at that place that has the curious name?

HESTER (*standing by table*): We are trying to build up life, Lady Hunstanton, on a better, truer, purer basis than life rests on here. This
sounds strange to you all, no doubt. How could it sound other than
strange? You rich people in England, you don't know how you are
living. How could you know? You shut out from your society the
gentle and the good. You laugh at the simple and the pure. Living,
as you all do, on others and by them, you sneer at self-sacrifice, and
if you throw bread to the poor, it is merely to keep them quiet for a
season. With all your pomp and wealth and art you don't know how
to live – you don't even know that. You love the beauty that you can
see and touch and handle, the beauty that you can destroy, and do
destroy, but of the unseen beauty of life, of the unseen beauty of a
higher life, you know nothing. You have lost life's secret. Oh, your
English society seems to me shallow, selfish, foolish. It has blinded its
eyes, and stopped its ears. It lies like a leper in purple. It sits like a
dead thing smeared with gold. It is all wrong, all wrong.

LADY STUTFIELD: I don't think one should know of these things. It is not
very, very nice, is it?

LADY HUNSTANTON: My dear Miss Worsley, I thought you liked English
society so much. You were such a success in it. And you were so much
admired by the best people. I quite forget what Lord Henry Weston
said of you – but it was most complimentary, and you know what an
authority he is on beauty.

HESTER: Lord Henry Weston! I remember him, Lady Hunstanton. A
man with a hideous smile and a hideous past. He is asked everywhere.
No dinner-party is complete without him. What of those whose ruin
is due to him? They are outcasts. They are nameless. If you met them
in the street you would turn your head away. I don't complain of
their punishment. Let all women who have sinned be punished.

*Mrs Arbuthnot enters from terrace behind in a cloak with a lace veil over
her head. She hears the last words and starts.*

LADY HUNSTANTON: My dear young lady!

HESTER: It is right that they should be punished, but don't let them be
the only ones to suffer. If a man and woman have sinned, let them
both go forth into the desert to love or loathe each other there. Let
them both be branded. Set a mark, if you wish, on each, but don't
punish the one and let the other go free. Don't have one law for men
and another for women. You are unjust to women in England. And
till you count what is a shame in a woman to be infamy in a man, you
will always be unjust, and Right, that pillar of fire, and Wrong, that
pillar of cloud, will be made dim to your eyes, or be not seen at all,
or if seen, not regarded.

LADY CAROLINE: Might I, dear Miss Worsley, as you are standing up, ask
you for my cotton that is just behind you? Thank you.

LADY HUNSTANTON: My dear Mrs Arbuthnot! I am so pleased you have come up. But I didn't hear you announced.

MRS ARBUTHNOT: Oh, I came straight in from the terrace, Lady Hunstanton, just as I was. You didn't tell me you had a party.

LADY HUNSTANTON: Not a party. Only a few guests who are staying in the house, and whom you must know. Allow me *(Tries to help her. Rings bell.)* Caroline, this is Mrs Arbuthnot, one of my sweetest friends. Lady Caroline Pontefract, Lady Stutfield, Mrs Allonby, and my young American friend, Miss Worsley, who has just been telling us all how wicked we are.

HESTER: I am afraid you think I spoke too strongly, Lady Hunstanton. But there are some things in England—

LADY HUNSTANTON: My dear young lady, there was a great deal of truth, I dare say, in what you said, and you looked very pretty while you said it, which is much more important, Lord Illingworth would tell us. The only point where I thought you were a little hard was about Lady Caroline's brother, about poor Lord Henry. He is really such good company.
Enter Footman.
Take Mrs Arbuthnot's things. *(Exit Footman with wraps.)*

HESTER: Lady Caroline, I had no idea it was your brother. I am sorry for the pain I must have caused you – I—

LADY CAROLINE: My dear Miss Worsley, the only part of your little speech, if I may so term it, with which I thoroughly agreed, was the part about my brother. Nothing that you could possibly say could be too bad for him. I regard Henry as infamous, absolutely infamous. But I am bound to state, as you were remarking, Jane, that he is excellent company, and he has one of the best cooks in London, and after a good dinner one can forgive anybody, even one's own relations.

LADY HUNSTANTON *(to Miss Worsley)*: Now, do come, dear, and make friends with Mrs Arbuthnot. She is one of the good, sweet, simple people you told us we never admitted into society. I am sorry to say Mrs Arbuthnot comes very rarely to me. But that is not my fault.

MRS ALLONBY: What a bore it is the men staying so long after dinner! I expect they are saying the most dreadful things about us.

LADY STUTFIELD: Do you really think so?

MRS ALLONBY: I am sure of it.

LADY STUTFIELD: How very, very horrid of them! Shall we go on to the terrace?

MRS ALLONBY: Oh, anything to get away from the dowagers and the dowdies. *(Rises and goes with Lady Stutfield to door L.C.)* We are only going to look at the stars, Lady Hunstanton.

LADY HUNSTANTON: You will find a great many, dear, a great many. But don't catch cold. *(To Mrs Arbuthnot)*: We shall all miss Gerald so much, dear Mrs Arbuthnot.

MRS ARBUTHNOT: But has Lord Illingworth really offered to make Gerald his secretary?

LADY HUNSTANTON: Oh, yes! He has been most charming about it. He has the highest possible opinion of your boy. You don't know Lord Illingworth, I believe, dear.

MRS ARBUTHNOT: I have never met him.

LADY HUNSTANTON: You know him by name, no doubt?

MRS ARBUTHNOT: I am afraid I don't. I live so much out of the world, and see so few people. I remember hearing years ago of an old Lord Illingworth who lived in Yorkshire, I think.

LADY HUNSTANTON: Ah, yes. That would be the last Earl but one. He was a very curious man. He wanted to marry beneath him. Or wouldn't, I believe. There was some scandal about it. The present Lord Illingworth is quite different. He is very distinguished. He does – well, he does nothing, which I am afraid our pretty American visitor here thinks very wrong of anybody, and I don't know that he cares much for the subjects in which you are so interested, dear Mrs Arbuthnot. Do you think, Caroline, that Lord Illingworth is interested in the Housing of the Poor?

LADY CAROLINE: I should fancy not at all, Jane.

LADY HUNSTANTON: We all have our different tastes, have we not? But Lord Illingworth has a very high position, and there is nothing he couldn't get if he chose to ask for it. Of course, he is comparatively a young man still, and he has only come to his title within – how long exactly is it, Caroline, since Lord Illingworth succeeded?

LADY CAROLINE: About four years, I think, Jane. I know it was the same year in which my brother had his last exposure in the evening newspapers.

LADY HUNSTANTON: Ah, I remember. That would be about four years ago. Of course, there were a great many people between the present Lord Illingworth and the title, Mrs Arbuthnot. There was – who was there, Caroline?

LADY CAROLINE: There was poor Margaret's baby. You remember how anxious she was to have a boy, and it was a boy, but it died, and her husband died shortly afterwards, and she married almost immediately, one of Lord Ascot's sons, who, I am told, beats her.

LADY HUNSTANTON: Ah, that is in the family dear, that is in the family. And there was also, I remember, a clergyman who wanted to be a lunatic, or a lunatic who wanted to be a clergyman, I forget which, but I know the Court of Chancery investigated the matter, and decided that he was quite sane. And I saw him afterwards at poor Lord Plumstead's with straws in his hair, or something very odd about him. I can't recall what. I often regret, Lady Caroline, that dear Lady Cecilia never lived to see her son get the title.

MRS ARBUTHNOT: Lady Cecilia?

LADY HUNSTANTON: Lord Illingworth's mother, dear Mrs Arbuthnot, was one of the Duchess of Jerningham's pretty daughters, and she married Sir Thomas Harford, who wasn't considered a very good match for her at the time, though he was said to be the handsomest man in London. I knew them all quite intimately, and both the sons, Arthur and George.

MRS ARBUTHNOT: It was the eldest son who succeeded, of course, Lady Hunstanton?

LADY HUNSTANTON: No dear, he was killed in the hunting field. Or was it fishing, Caroline? I forget. But George came in for everything. I always tell him that no younger son has ever had such good luck as he had.

MRS ARBUTHNOT: Lady Hunstanton, I want to speak to Gerald at once. Might I see him? Can he be sent for?

LADY HUNSTANTON: Certainly, dear. I will send one of the servants into the dining-room to fetch him. I don't know what keeps the gentlemen so long. (*Rings bell.*) When I knew Lord Illingworth first as plain George Harford, he was simply a very brilliant young man about town, with not a penny of money except what poor dear Lady Cecilia gave him. She was quite devoted to him. Chiefly, I fancy, because he was on bad terms with his father. Oh, here is the dear Archdeacon. (*To Servant*): It doesn't matter.

Enter Sir John and Doctor Daubeny. Sir John goes over to Lady Stutfield, Doctor Daubeny to Lady Hunstanton.

THE ARCHDEACON: Lord Illingworth has been most entertaining. I have never enjoyed myself more. (*Sees Mrs Arbuthnot.*) Ah, Mrs Arbuthnot.

LADY HUNSTANTON (*to Doctor Daubeny*): You see I have got Mrs Arbuthnot to come to me at last.

THE ARCHDEACON: That is a great honour, Lady Hunstanton. Mrs Daubeny will be quite jealous of you.

LADY HUNSTANTON: Ah, I am so sorry Mrs Daubeny could not come with you to-night. Headache as usual, I suppose.

THE ARCHDEACON: Yes, Lady Hunstanton; a perfect martyr. But she is happiest alone. She is happiest alone.

LADY CAROLINE (*to her husband*): John!

Sir John goes over to his wife. Doctor Daubeny talks to Lady Hunstanton and Mrs Arbuthnot.

Mrs Arbuthnot watches Lord Illingworth the whole time. He has passed across the room without noticing her, and approaches Mrs Allonby, who with Lady Stutfield is standing by the door looking on to the terrace.

LORD ILLINGWORTH: How is the most charming woman in the world?

MRS ALLONBY (*taking Lady Stutfield by the hand*): We are both quite well, thank you, Lord Illingworth. But what a short time you have been in the dining-room! It seems as if we had only just left.

LORD ILLINGWORTH: I was bored to death. Never opened my lips the whole time. Absolutely longing to come in to you.

MRS ALLONBY: You should have. The American girl has been giving us a lecture.

LORD ILLINGWORTH: Really? All Americans lecture, I believe. I suppose it is something in their climate. What did she lecture about?

MRS ALLONBY: Oh, Puritanism, of course.

LORD ILLINGWORTH: I am going to convert her, am I not? How long do you give me?

MRS ALLONBY: A week.

LORD ILLINGWORTH: A week is more than enough.
Enter Gerald and Lord Alfred.
GERALD (*going to Mrs Arbuthnot*): Dear mother!
MRS ARBUTHNOT: Gerald, I don't feel at all well. See me home, Gerald.
I shouldn't have come.
GERALD: I am so sorry, mother. Certainly. But you must know Lord
Illingworth first. (*Goes across room.*)
MRS ARBUTHNOT: Not to-night, Gerald.
GERALD: Lord Illingworth, I want you so much to know my mother.
LORD ILLINGWORTH: With the greatest pleasure. (*To Mrs Allonby*): I'll be
back in a moment. People's mothers always bore me to death. All
women become like their mothers. That is their tragedy.
MRS ALLONBY: No man does. That is his.
LORD ILLINGWORTH: What a delightful mood you are in to-night! (*Turns
round and goes across with Gerald to Mrs Arbuthnot. When he sees her, he
starts back in wonder. Then slowly his eyes turn towards Gerald.*)
GERALD: Mother, this is Lord Illingworth, who has offered to take me
as his private secretary. (*Mrs Arbuthnot bows coldly.*) It is a wonderful
opening for me, isn't it? I hope he won't be disappointed in me, that
is all. You'll thank Lord Illingworth, mother, won't you?
MRS ARBUTHNOT: Lord Illingworth is very good, I am sure, to interest
himself in you for the moment.
LORD ILLINGWORTH (*putting his hand on Gerald's shoulder*): Oh, Gerald and
I are great friends already, Mrs. . . . Arbuthnot.
MRS ARBUTHNOT: There can be nothing in common between you and my
son, Lord Illingworth.
GERALD: Dear mother, how can you say so? Of course, Lord Illingworth
is awfully clever and that sort of thing. There is nothing Lord
Illingworth doesn't know.
LORD ILLINGWORTH: My dear boy!
GERALD: He knows more about life than any one I have ever met. I feel
an awful duffer when I am with you, Lord Illingworth. Of course, I
have had so few advantages. I have not been to Eton or Oxford like
other chaps. But Lord Illingworth doesn't seem to mind that. He has
been awfully good to me, mother.
MRS ARBUTHNOT: Lord Illingworth may change his mind. He may not
really want you as his secretary.
GERALD: Mother!
MRS ARBUTHNOT: You must remember, as you said yourself, you have
had so few advantages.
MRS ALLONBY: Lord Illingworth, I want to speak to you for a moment.
Do come over.
LORD ILLINGWORTH: Will you excuse me, Mrs Arbuthnot? Now, don't let
your charming mother make any more difficulties, Gerald. The thing
is quite settled, isn't it?
GERALD: I hope so.
Lord Illingworth goes across to Mrs Allonby.
MRS ALLONBY: I thought you were never going to leave the lady in black
velvet.

LORD ILLINGWORTH: She is excessively handsome. (*Looks at Mrs Arbuthnot.*)

LADY HUNSTANTON: Caroline, shall we all make a move to the music-room? Miss Worsley is going to play. You'll come too, dear Mrs Arbuthnot, won't you? You don't know what a treat is in store for you. (*To Doctor Daubeny*): I must really take Miss Worsley down some afternoon to the rectory. I should so much like dear Mrs Daubeny to hear her on the violin. Ah, I forgot. Dear Mrs Daubeny's hearing is a little defective, is it not?

THE ARCHDEACON: Her deafness is a great privation to her. She can't even hear my sermons now. She reads them at home. But she has many resources in herself, many resources.

LADY HUNSTANTON: She reads a good deal, I suppose?

THE ARCHDEACON:: Just the very largest print. The eyesight is rapidly going. But she's never morbid, never morbid.

GERALD (*to Lord Illingworth*): Do speak to my mother, Lord Illingworth, before you go into the music-room. She seems to think, somehow, you don't mean what you said to me.

MRS ALLONBY: Aren't you coming?

LORD ILLINGWORTH: In a few minutes. Lady Hunstanton, if Mrs Arbuthnot would allow me, I would like to say a few words to her, and we will join you later on.

LADY HUNSTANTON: Ah, of course. You will have a great deal to say to her, and she will have a great deal to thank you for. It is not every son who gets such an offer, Mrs Arbuthnot. But I know you appreciate that, dear.

LADY CAROLINE: John!

LADY HUNSTANTON: Now, don't keep Mrs Arbuthnot too long, Lord Illingworth. We can't spare her.

Exit following the other guests. Sound of violin heard from music-room.

LORD ILLINGWORTH: So that is our son, Rachel! Well, I am very proud of him. He is a Harford, every inch of him. By the way, why Arbuthnot, Rachel?

MRS ARBUTHNOT: One name is as good as another, when one has no right to any name.

LORD ILLINGWORTH: I suppose so – but why Gerald?

MRS ARBUTHNOT: After a man whose heart I broke – after my father.

LORD ILLINGWORTH: Well, Rachel, what is over is over. All I have got to say now is that I am very, very much pleased with our boy. The world will know him merely as my private secretary, but to me he will be something very near, and very dear. It is a curious thing, Rachel; my life seemed to be quite complete. It was not so. It lacked something, it lacked a son. I have found my son now. I am glad I have found him.

MRS ARBUTHNOT: You have no right to claim him, or the smallest part of him. The boy is entirely mine, and shall remain mine.

LORD ILLINGWORTH: My dear Rachel, you have had him to yourself for over twenty years. Why not let me have him for a little now? He is quite as much mine as yours.

MRS ARBUTHNOT: Are you talking of the child you abandoned? Of the child who, as far as you are concerned, might have died of hunger and of want?

LORD ILLINGWORTH: You forget, Rachel, it was you who left me. It was not I who left you.

MRS ARBUTHNOT: I left you because you refused to give the child a name. Before my son was born, I implored you to marry me.

LORD ILLINGWORTH: I had no expectations then. And besides, Rachel, I wasn't much older than you were. I was only twenty-two. I was twenty-one, I believe, when the whole thing began in your father's garden.

MRS ARBUTHNOT: When a man is old enough to do wrong he should be old enough to do right also.

LORD ILLINGWORTH: My dear Rachel, intellectual generalities are always interesting, but generalities in morals mean absolutely nothing. As for saying I left our child to starve, that, of course, is untrue and silly. My mother offered you six hundred a year. But you wouldn't take anything. You simply disappeared, and carried the the child away with you.

MRS ARBUTHNOT: I wouldn't have accepted a penny from her. Your father was different. He told you, in my presence, when we were in Paris, that it was your duty to marry me.

LORD ILLINGWORTH: Oh, duty is what one expects from others, it is not what one does oneself. Of course, I was influenced by my mother. Every man is when he is young.

MRS ARBUTHNOT: I am glad to hear you say so. Gerald shall certainly not go away with you.

LORD ILLINGWORTH: What nonsense, Rachel!

MRS ARBUTHNOT: Do you think I would allow my son—

LORD ILLINGWORTH: Our son.

MRS ARBUTHNOT: My son – (*Lord Illingworth shrugs his shoulders*) – to go away with the man who spoiled my youth, who ruined my life, who has tainted every moment of my days? You don't realise what my past has been in suffering and in shame.

LORD ILLINGWORTH: My dear Rachel, I must candidly say that I think Gerald's future considerably more important than your past.

MRS ARBUTHNOT: Gerald cannot separate his future from my past.

LORD ILLINGWORTH: That is exactly what he should do. That is exactly what you should help him to do. What a typical woman you are! You talk sentimentally and you are thoroughly selfish the whole time. But don't let us have a scene. Rachel, I want you to look at this matter from the common-sense point of view, from the point of view of what is best for our son, leaving you and me out of the question. What is our son at present? An underpaid clerk in a small Provincial Bank in a third-rate English town. If you imagine he is quite happy in such a position, you are mistaken. He is thoroughly discontented.

MRS ARBUTHNOT: He was not discontented till he met you. You have made him so.

LORD ILLINGWORTH: Of course I made him so. Discontent is the first step in the progress of a man or a nation. But I did not leave him with a mere longing for things he could not get. No, I made him a charming offer. He jumped at it, I need hardly say. Any young man would. And now, simply because it turns out that I am the boy's own father and he my own son, you propose practically to ruin his career. That is to say, if I were a perfect stranger, you would allow Gerald to go away with me, but as he is my own flesh and blood you won't. How utterly illogical you are!

MRS ARBUTHNOT: I will not allow him to go.

LORD ILLINGWORTH: How can you prevent it? What excuse can you give to him for making him decline such an offer as mine? I won't tell him in what relations I stand to him, I need hardly say. But you daren't tell him. You know that. Look how you have brought him up.

MRS ARBUTHNOT: I have brought him up to be a good man.

LORD ILLINGWORTH: Quite so. And what is the result? You have educated him to be your judge if he ever finds you out. And a bitter, an unjust judge he will be to you. Don't be deceived, Rachel. Children begin by loving their parents. After a time they judge them. Rarely, if ever, do they forgive them.

MRS ARBUTHNOT: George, don't take my son away from me. I have had twenty years of sorrow, and I have only had one thing to love me, only one thing to love. You have had a life of joy, and pleasure, and success. You have been quite happy, you have never thought of us. There was no reason, according to your views of life, why you should have remembered us at all. Your meeting us was a mere accident, a horrible accident. Forget it. Don't come now, and rob me of – of all I have in the whole world. You are so rich in other things. Leave me the little vineyard of my life; leave me the walled-in garden and the well of water; the ewe-lamb God sent me, in pity or in wrath, oh! leave me that. George, don't take Gerald from me.

LORD ILLINGWORTH: Rachel, at the present moment you are not necessary to Gerald's career; I am. There is nothing more to be said on the subject.

MRS ARBUTHNOT: I will not let him go.

LORD ILLINGWORTH: Here is Gerald. He has a right to decide for himself.
Enter Gerald.

GERALD: Well, dear mother, I hope you have settled it all with Lord Illingworth?

MRS ARBUTHNOT: I have not, Gerald.

LORD ILLINGWORTH: Your mother seems not to like your coming with me, for some reason.

GERALD: Why, mother?

MRS ARBUTHNOT: I thought you were quite happy here with me, Gerald. I didn't know you were so anxious to leave me.

GERALD: Mother, how can you talk like that? Of course I have been quite happy with you. But a man can't stay always with his mother. No chap does. I want to make myself a position, to do something. I thought you would have been proud to see me Lord Illingworth's secretary.

MRS ARBUTHNOT: I do not think you would be suitable as a private secretary to Lord Illingworth. You have no qualifications.

LORD ILLINGWORTH: I don't wish to seem to interfere for a moment, Mrs Arbuthnot, but as far as your last objection is concerned, I surely am the best judge. And I can only tell you that your son has all the qualifications I had hoped for. He has more, in fact, than I had even thought of. Far more. (*Mrs Arbuthnot remains silent.*) Have you any other reason, Mrs Arbuthnot, why you don't wish your son to accept this post?

GERALD: Have you, mother? Do answer.

LORD ILLINGWORTH: If you have, Mrs Arbuthnot, pray, pray say it. We are quite by ourselves here. Whatever it is, I need not say I will not repeat it.

GERALD: Mother?

LORD ILLINGWORTH: If you would like to be alone with your son, I will leave you. You may have some other reason you don't wish me to hear.

MRS ARBUTHNOT: I have no other reason.

LORD ILLINGWORTH: Then, my dear boy, we may look on the thing as settled. Come, you and I will smoke a cigarette on the terrace together. And Mrs Arbuthnot, pray let me tell you, that I think you have acted very, very wisely.

Exit with Gerald. Mrs Arbuthnot is left alone. She stands immobile with a look of unutterable sorrow on her face.

ACT THREE

Scene: The Picture Gallery at Hunstanton. Door at back leading on to terrace. Lord Illingworth and Gerald, R.C. Lord Illingworth lolling on a sofa. Gerald in a chair.

LORD ILLINGWORTH: Thoroughly sensible woman, your mother, Gerald. I knew she would come round in the end.

GERALD: My mother is awfully conscientious, Lord Illingworth, and I know she doesn't think I am educated enough to be your secretary. She is perfectly right, too. I was fearfully idle when I was at school, and I couldn't pass an examination now to save my life.

LORD ILLINGWORTH: My dear Gerald, examinations are of no value whatsoever. If a man is a gentleman, he knows quite enough, and if he is not a gentleman, whatever he knows is bad for him.

GERALD: But I am so ignorant of the world, Lord Illingworth.

LORD ILLINGWORTH: Don't be afraid, Gerald. Remember that you've got on your side the most wonderful thing in the world – youth! There is nothing like youth. The middle-aged are mortgaged to Life. The old are in life's lumber-room. But youth is the Lord of Life. Youth has a kingdom waiting for it. Every one is born a king, and most people die in exile, like most kings. To win back my youth, Gerald, there is nothing I wouldn't do – except take exercise, get up early, or be a useful member of the community.

GERALD: But you don't call yourself old, Lord Illingworth?

LORD ILLINGWORTH: I am old enough to be your father, Gerald.

GERALD: I don't remember my father; he died years ago.

LORD ILLINGWORTH: So Lady Hunstanton told me.

GERALD: It is very curious, my mother never talks to me about my father. I sometimes think she must have married beneath her.

LORD ILLINGWORTH (*winces slightly*): Really? (*Goes over and puts his hand on Gerald's shoulder.*) You have missed not having a father, I suppose, Gerald?

GERALD: Oh, no; my mother has been so good to me. No one ever had such a mother as I have had.

LORD ILLINGWORTH: I am quite sure of that. Still, I should imagine that most mothers don't quite understand their sons. Don't realise, I mean, that a son has ambitions, a desire to see life, to make himself a name. After all, Gerald, you couldn't be expected to pass all your life in such a hole as Wrockley, could you?

GERALD: Oh, no! It would be dreadful!

LORD ILLINGWORTH: A mother's love is very touching, of course, but it is often curiously selfish. I mean, there is a good deal of selfishness in it.

GERALD (*slowly*): I suppose there is.

LORD ILLINGWORTH: Your mother is a thoroughly good woman. But good women have such limited views of life, their horizon is so small, their interests are so petty, aren't they?

GERALD: They are awfully interested, certainly, in things we don't care much about.

LORD ILLINGWORTH: I suppose your mother is very religious, and that sort of thing.

GERALD: Oh, yes, she's always going to church.

LORD ILLINGWORTH: Ah! she is not modern, and to be modern is the only thing worth being nowadays. You want to be modern, don't you, Gerald? You want to know life as it really is. Not to be put off with any old-fashioned theories about life. Well, what you have to do at present is simply to fit yourself for the best society. A man who can dominate a London dinner-table can dominate the world. The future belongs to the dandy. It is the exquisites who are going to rule.

GERALD: I should like to wear nice things awfully, but I have always been told that a man should not think so much about his clothes.

LORD ILLINGWORTH: People nowadays are so absolutely superficial that they don't understand the philosophy of the superficial. By the way, Gerald, you should learn how to tie your tie better. Sentiment is all very well for the buttonhole. But the essential thing for a necktie is style. A well-tied tie is the first serious step in life.

GERALD (*laughing*): I might be able to learn how to tie a tie, Lord Illingworth, but I should never be able to talk as you do. I don't know how to talk.

LORD ILLINGWORTH: Oh! talk to every woman as if you loved her, and to every man as if he bored you, and at the end of your first season you will have the reputation of possessing the most perfect social tact.

GERALD: But it is very difficult to get into society, isn't it?

LORD ILLINGWORTH: To get into the best society, nowadays, one has either to feed people, amuse people, or shock people – that is all!

GERALD: I suppose society is wonderfully delightful!

LORD ILLINGWORTH: To be in it is merely a bore. But to be out of it simply a tragedy. Society is a necessary thing. No man has any real success in this world unless he has got women to back him, and women rule society. If you have not got women on your side you are quite over. You might just as well be a barrister or a stockbroker, or a journalist at once.

GERALD: It is very difficult to understand women, is it not?

LORD ILLINGWORTH: You should never try to understand them. Women are pictures. Men are problems. If you want to know what a woman really means – which, by the way, is always a dangerous thing to do – look at her, don't listen to her.

GERALD: But women are awfully clever, aren't they?

LORD ILLINGWORTH: One should always tell them so. But, to the philosopher, my dear Gerald, women represent the triumph of matter over mind – just as men represent the triumph of mind over morals.

GERALD: How then can women have so much power as you say they have?

LORD ILLINGWORTH: The history of women is the history of the worst form of tyranny the world has ever known. The tyranny of the weak over the strong. It is the only tyranny that lasts.

GERALD: But haven't women got a refining influence?

LORD ILLINGWORTH: Nothing refines but the intellect.

GERALD: Still, there are many different kinds of women, aren't there?

LORD ILLINGWORTH: Only two kinds in society: the plain and the coloured.

GERALD: But there are good women in society, aren't there?

LORD ILLINGWORTH: Far too many.

GERALD: But do you think women shouldn't be good?

LORD ILLINGWORTH: One should never tell them so, they'd all become good at once. Women are a fascinatingly wilful sex. Every woman is a rebel, and usually in wild revolt against herself.

GERALD: You have never been married, Lord Illingworth, have you?

LORD ILLINGWORTH: Men marry because they are tired; women because they are curious. Both are disappointed.

GERALD: But don't you think one can be happy when one is married?

LORD ILLINGWORTH: Perfectly happy. But the happiness of a married man, my dear Gerald, depends on the people he has not married.

GERALD: But if one is in love?

LORD ILLINGWORTH: One should always be in love. That is the reason one should never marry.

GERALD: Love is a very wonderful thing, isn't it?

LORD ILLINGWORTH: When one is in love one begins by deceiving oneself.

And one ends by deceiving others. That is what the world calls a
romance. But a really *grande passion* is comparatively rare nowadays.
It is the privilege of people who have nothing to do. That is the one
use of the idle classes in a country, and the only possible explanation
of us Harfords.

GERALD: Harfords, Lord Illingworth?

LORD ILLINGWORTH: That is my family name. You should study the
Peerage, Gerald. It is the one book a young man about town should
know thoroughly, and it is the best thing in fiction the English have
ever done. And now, Gerald, you are going into a perfectly new life
with me, and I want you to know how to live. (*Mrs Arbuthnot appears
on terrace behind.*) For the world has been made by fools that wise men
should live in it!

Enter L.C. Lady Hunstanton and Doctor Daubeny.

LADY HUNSTANTON: Ah! here you are, dear Lord Illingworth. Well, I
suppose you have been telling our young friend, Gerald, what his
new duties are to be, and giving him a great deal of good advice over
a pleasant cigarette.

LORD ILLINGWORTH: I have been giving him the best of advice, Lady
Hunstanton, and the best of cigarettes.

LADY HUNSTANTON: I am so sorry I was not here to listen to you, but I
suppose I am too old now to learn. Except from you, dear Archdeacon,
when you are in your nice pulpit. But then I always know what you
are going to say, so I don't feel alarmed. (*Sees Mrs Arbuthnot.*) Ah!
dear Mrs Arbuthnot, do come and join us. Come, dear. (*Enter Mrs
Arbuthnot.*) Gerald has been having such a long talk with Lord Illingworth; I am sure you must feel very much flattered at the pleasant
way in which everything has turned out for him. Let us sit down.
(*They sit down.*) And how is your beautiful embroidery going on?

MRS ARBUTHNOT: I am always at work, Lady Hunstanton.

LADY HUNSTANTON: Mrs Daubeny embroiders a little, too, doesn't she?

THE ARCHDEACON: She was very deft with her needle once, quite a Dorcas.
But the gout has crippled her fingers a good deal. She has not touched
the tambour frame for nine or ten years. But she has many other
amusements. She is very much interested in her own health.

LADY HUNSTANTON: Ah! that is always a nice distraction, is it not? Now,
what are you talking about, Lord Illingworth? Do tell us.

LORD ILLINGWORTH: I was on the point of explaining to Gerald that the
world has always laughed at its own tragedies, that being the only
way in which it has been able to bear them. And that, consequently,
whatever the world has treated seriously belongs to the comedy side
of things.

LADY HUNSTANTON: Now I am quite out of my depth. I usually am when
Lord Illingworth says anything. And the Humane Society is most
careless. They never rescue me. I am left to sink. I have a dim idea,
dear Lord Illingworth, that you are always on the side of the sinners,
and I know I always try to be on the side of the saints, but that is as
far as I get. And after all, it may be merely the fancy of a drowning
person.

LORD ILLINGWORTH: The only difference between the saint and the sinner is that every saint has a past, and every sinner has a future.

LADY HUNSTANTON: Ah! that quite does for me. I haven't a word to say. You and I, dear Mrs Arbuthnot, are behind the age. We can't follow Lord Illingworth. Too much care was taken with our education, I am afraid. To have been well brought up is a great drawback nowadays. It shuts one out from so much.

MRS ARBUTHNOT: I should be sorry to follow Lord Illingworth in any of his opinions.

LADY HUNSTANTON: You are quite right, dear.

Gerald shrugs his shoulders and looks irritably over at his mother. Enter Lady Caroline.

LADY CAROLINE: Jane, have you seen John anywhere?

LADY HUNSTANTON: You needn't be anxious about him, dear. He is with Lady Stutfield; I saw them some time ago, in the Yellow Drawing-room. They seem quite happy together. You are not going, Caroline? Pray sit down.

LADY CAROLINE: I think I had better look after John.

Exit Lady Caroline.

LADY HUNSTANTON: It doesn't do to pay men so much attention. And Caroline has really nothing to be anxious about. Lady Stutfield is very sympathetic. She is just as sympathetic about one thing as she is about another. A beautiful nature.

Enter Sir John and Mrs Allonby

Ah! here is Sir John! And with Mrs Allonby too! I suppose it was Mrs Allonby I saw him with. Sir John, Caroline has been looking everywhere for you.

MRS ALLONBY: We have been waiting for her in the Music-room, dear Lady Hunstanton.

LADY HUNSTANTON: Ah! the Music-room, of course. I thought it was the Yellow Drawing-room, my memory is getting so defective. (*To the Archdeacon*) Mrs Daubeny has a wonderful memory, hasn't she?

THE ARCHDEACON: She used to be quite remarkable for her memory, but since her last attack she recalls chiefly the events of her early childhood. But she finds great pleasure in such retrospections, great pleasure.

Enter Lady Stutfield and Mr Kelvil.

LADY HUNSTANTON: Ah! dear Lady Stutfield! and what has Mr Kelvil been talking to you about?

LADY STUTFIELD: About Bimetallism, as well as I remember.

LADY HUNSTANTON: Bimetallism! Is that quite a nice subject? However, I know people discuss everything very freely nowadays. What did Sir John talk to you about, dear Mrs Allonby?

MRS ALLONBY: About Patagonia.

LADY HUNSTANTON: Really? What a remote topic! But very improving, I have no doubt.

MRS ALLONBY: He has been most interesting on the subject of Patagonia. Savages seem to have quite the same views as cultured people on almost all subjects. They are excessively advanced.

LADY HUNSTANTON: What do they do?

MRS ALLONBY: Apparently everything.

LADY HUNSTANTON: Well, it is very gratifying, dear Archdeacon, is it not, to find that Human Nature is permanently one. – On the whole, the world is the same world, is it not?

LORD ILLINGWORTH: The world is simply divided into two classes – those who believe the incredible, like the public – and those who do the improbable—

MRS ALLONBY: Like yourself?

LORD ILLINGWORTH: Yes; I am always astonishing myself. It is the only thing that makes life worth living.

LADY STUTFIELD: And what have you been doing lately that astonishes you?

LORD ILLINGWORTH: I have been discovering all kinds of beautiful qualities in my own nature.

MRS ALLONBY: Ah! don't become quite perfect all at once. Do it gradually!

LORD ILLINGWORTH: I don't intend to grow perfect at all. At least, I hope I shan't. It would be most inconvenient. Women love us for our defects. If we have enough of them, they will forgive us everything, even our gigantic intellects.

MRS ALLONBY: It is premature to ask us to forgive analysis. We forgive adoration; that is quite as much as should be expected from us.

Enter Lord Alfred. He joins Lady Stutfield.

LADY HUNSTANTON: Ah! we women should forgive everything, shouldn't we, dear Mrs Arbuthnot? I am sure you agree with me in that.

MRS ARBUTHNOT: I do not, Lady Hunstanton. I think there are many things women should never forgive.

LADY HUNSTANTON: What sort of things?

MRS ARBUTHNOT: The ruin of another woman's life. (*Moves slowly away to back of stage.*)

LADY HUNSTANTON: Ah! those things are very sad, no doubt, but I believe there are admirable homes where people of that kind are looked after and reformed, and I think on the whole that the secret of life is to take things very, very easily.

MRS ALLONBY: The secret of life is never to have an emotion that is unbecoming.

LADY STUTFIELD: The secret of life is to appreciate the pleasure of being terribly, terribly deceived.

KELVIL: The secret of life is to resist temptation, Lady Stutfield.

LORD ILLINGWORTH: There is no secret of life. Life's aim, if it has one, is simply to be always looking for temptations. There are not nearly enough. I sometimes pass a whole day without coming across a single one. It is quite dreadful. It makes one so nervous about the future.

LADY HUNSTANTON (*shakes her fan at him*): I don't know how it is, Lord Illingworth, but everything you have said to-day seems to me excessively immoral. It has been most interesting, listening to you.

LORD ILLINGWORTH: All thought is immoral. Its very essence is destruction. If you think of anything, you kill it. Nothing survives being thought of.

LADY HUNSTANTON: I don't understand a word, Lord Illingworth. But I have no doubt it is all quite true. Personally, I have very little to reproach myself with, on the score of thinking. I don't believe in women thinking too much. Women should think in moderation, as they should do all things in moderation.

LORD ILLINGWORTH: Moderation is a fatal thing, Lady Hunstanton. Nothing succeeds like excess.

LADY HUNSTANTON: I hope I shall remember that. It sounds an admirable maxim. But I'm beginning to forget everything. It's a great misfortune.

LORD ILLINGWORTH: It is one of your most fascinating qualities, Lady Hunstanton. No woman should have a memory. Memory in a woman is the beginning of dowdiness. One can always tell from a woman's bonnet whether she has got a memory or not.

LADY HUNSTANTON: How charming you are, dear Lord Illingworth. You always find out that one's most glaring fault is one's important virtue. You have the most comforting view of life.

Enter Farquhar.

FARQUHAR: Doctor Daubeny's carriage!

LADY HUNSTANTON: My dear Archdeacon! It is only half-past ten.

THE ARCHDEACON (*rising*): I am afraid I must go, Lady Hunstanton. Tuesday is always one of Mrs Daubeny's bad nights.

LADY HUNSTANTON (*rising*): Well, I won't keep you from her. (*Goes with him towards door.*) I have told Farquhar to put a brace of partridge into the carriage. Mrs Daubeny may fancy them.

THE ARCHDEACON: It is very kind of you, but Mrs Daubeny never touches solids now. Lives entirely on jellies. But she is wonderfully cheerful, wonderfully cheerful. She has nothing to complain of.

Exit with Lady Hunstanton.

MRS ALLONBY (*goes over to Lord Illingworth*): There is a beautiful moon to-night.

LORD ILLINGWORTH: Let us go and look at it. To look at anything that is inconstant is charming nowadays.

MRS ALLONBY: You have your looking-glass.

LORD ILLINGWORTH: It is unkind. It merely shows me my wrinkles.

MRS ALLONBY: Mine is better behaved. It never tells me the truth.

LORD ILLINGWORTH: Then it is in love with you.

Exeunt Sir John, Lady Stutfield, Mr Kelvil, and Lord Alfred.

GERALD (*to Lord Illingworth*): May I come too?

LORD ILLINGWORTH: Do, my dear boy. (*Moves towards door with Mrs Allonby and Gerald.*)

Lady Caroline enters, looks rapidly round and goes out in opposite direction to that taken by Sir John and Lady Stutfield.

MRS ARBUTHNOT: Gerald!

GERALD: What, mother!

Exit Lord Illingworth with Mrs Allonby.

MRS ARBUTHNOT: It is getting late. Let us go home.

GERALD: My dear mother. Do let us wait a little longer. Lord Illingworth is so delightful, and, by the way, mother, I have a great surprise for you. We are starting for India at the end of this month.

MRS ARBUTHNOT: Let us go home.

GERALD: If you really want to, of course, mother, but I must bid good-bye to Lord Illingworth first. I'll be back in five minutes. (*Exit*)

MRS ARBUTHNOT: Let him leave me if he chooses, but not with him – not with him! I couldn't bear it. (*Walks up and down.*)
Enter Hester.

HESTER: What a lovely night it is, Mrs Arbuthnot.

MRS ARBUTHNOT: Is it?

HESTER: Mrs Arbuthnot, I wish you would let us be friends. You are so different from the other women here. When you came into the Drawing-room this evening, somehow you brought with you a sense of what is good and pure in life. I had been foolish. There are things that are right to say, but that may be said at the wrong time and to the wrong people.

MRS ARBUTHNOT: I heard what you said. I agree with it, Miss Worsley.

HESTER: I didn't know you had heard it. But I knew you would agree with me. A woman who has sinned should be punished, shouldn't she?

MRS ARBUTHNOT: Yes.

HESTER: She shouldn't be allowed to come into the society of good men and women?

MRS ARBUTHNOT: She should not.

HESTER: And the man should be punished in the same way?

MRS ARBUTHNOT: In the same way. And the children, if there are children, in the same way also?

HESTER: Yes, it is right that the sins of the parents should be visited on the children. It is a just law. It is God's law.

MRS ARBUTHNOT: It is one of God's terrible laws. (*Moves away to fireplace.*)

HESTER: You are distressed about your son leaving you, Mrs Arbuthnot?

MRS ARBUTHNOT: Yes.

HESTER: Do you like him going away with Lord Illingworth? Of course there is position, no doubt, and money, but position and money are not everything, are they?

MRS ARBUTHNOT: They are nothing; they bring misery.

HESTER: Then why do you let your son go with him?

MRS ARBUTHNOT: He wishes it himself.

HESTER: But if you asked him he would stay, would he not?

MRS ARBUTHNOT: He has set his heart on going.

HESTER: He couldn't refuse you anything. He loves you too much. Ask him to stay. Let me send him to you. He is on the terrace at this moment with Lord Illingworth. I heard them laughing together as I passed through the Music-room.

MRS ARBUTHNOT: Don't trouble, Miss Worsley, I can wait. It is of no consequence.

HESTER: No, I'll tell him you want him. Do – do ask him to stay.
Exit Hester.

MRS ARBUTHNOT: He won't come – I know he won't come.
Enter Lady Caroline. She looks round anxiously. Enter Gerald.
LADY CAROLINE: Mr Arbuthnot, may I ask you is Sir John anywhere on the terrace?
GERALD: No, Lady Caroline, he is not on the terrace.
LADY CAROLINE: It is very curious. It is time for him to retire.
Exit Lady Caroline.
GERALD: Dear mother, I am afraid I kept you waiting. I forgot all about it. I am so happy to-night, mother; I have never been so happy.
MRS ARBUTHNOT: At the prospect of going away?
GERALD: Don't put it like that, mother. Of course I am sorry to leave you. Why, you are the best mother in the whole world. But after all, as Lord Illingworth says, it is impossible to live in such a place as Wrockley. You don't mind it. But I'm ambitious; I want something more than that. I want to have a career. I want to do something that will make you proud of me, and Lord Illingworth is going to help me. He is going to do everything for me.
MRS ARBUTHNOT: Gerald, don't go away with Lord Illingworth. I implore you not to. Gerald, I beg you!
GERALD: Mother, how changeable you are! You don't seem to know your own mind for a single moment. An hour and a half ago in the Drawing-room you agreed to the whole thing; now you turn round and make objections, and try to force me to give up my one chance in life. Yes, my one chance. You don't suppose that men like Lord Illingworth are to be found every day, do you, mother? It is very strange that when I have had such a wonderful piece of good luck, the one person to put difficulties in my way should be my own mother. Besides, you know, mother, I love Hester Worsley. Who could help loving her? I love her more than I ever have told you, far more. And if I had a position, if I had prospects, I could – I could ask her . . . Don't you understand now, mother, what it means to me to be Lord Illingworth's secretary? To start like that is to find a career ready for one – before one – waiting for one. If I were Lord Illingworth's secretary I could ask Hester to be my wife. As a wretched bank clerk with a hundred a year it would be an impertinence.
MRS ARBUTHNOT: I fear you need have no hopes of Miss Worsley. I know her views on life. She has just told them to me. (*A pause.*)
GERALD: Then I have my ambition left, at any rate. That is something – I am glad I have that! You have always tried to crush my ambition, mother – haven't you? You have told me that the world is a wicked place, that success is not worth having, that society is shallow, and all that sort of thing – well, I don't believe it, mother. I think the world must be delightful. I think society must be exquisite. I think success is a thing worth having. You have been wrong in all that you taught me, mother, quite wrong. Lord Illingworth is a successful man. He is a fashionable man. He is a man who lives in the world and for it. Well, I would give anything to be just like Lord Illingworth.
MRS ARBUTHNOT: I would sooner see you dead.

GERALD: Mother, what is your objection to Lord Illingworth? Tell me – tell me right out. What is it?

MRS ARBUTHNOT: He is a bad man.

GERALD: In what way bad? I don't understand what you mean.

MRS ARBUTHNOT: I will tell you.

GERALD: I suppose you think him bad, because he doesn't believe the same things as you do. Well, men are different from women, mother. It is natural that they should have different views.

MRS ARBUTHNOT: It is not what Lord Illingworth believes, or what he does not believe, that makes him bad. It is what he is.

GERALD: Mother, is it something you know of him? Something you actually know?

MRS ARBUTHNOT: It is something I know.

GERALD: Something you are quite sure of?

MRS ARBUTHNOT: Quite sure of.

GERALD: How long have you known it?

MRS ARBUTHNOT: For twenty years.

GERALD: Is it fair to go back twenty years in any man's career? And what have you or I to do with Lord Illingworth's early life? What business is it of ours?

MRS ARBUTHNOT: What this man has been, he is now, and will be always.

GERALD: Mother, tell me what Lord Illingworth did? If he did anything shameful, I will not go away with him. Surely you know me well enough for that?

MRS ARBUTHNOT: Gerald, come near to me. Quite close to me, as you used to do when you were a little boy, when you were mother's own boy. (*Gerald sits down beside his mother. She runs her fingers through his hair, and strokes his hands.*) Gerald, there was a girl once, she was very young, she was little over eighteen at the time. George Harford – that was Lord Illingworth's name then – George Harford met her. She knew nothing about life. He – knew everything. He made this girl love him. He made her love so much that she left her father's house with him one morning. She loved him so much, and he had promised to marry her! He had solemnly promised to marry her, and she had believed him. She was very young, and – and ignorant of what life really is. But he put the marriage off from week to week, and month to month. – She trusted in him all the while. She loved him. – Before her child was born – for she had a child – she implored him for the child's sake to marry her, that the child might have a name, that her sin might not be visited on the child, who was innocent. He refused. After the child was born she left him, taking the child away, and her life was ruined, and her soul ruined, and all that was sweet, and good, and pure in her ruined also. She suffered terribly – she suffers now. She will always suffer. For her there is no joy, no peace, no atonement. She is a woman who drags a chain like a guilty thing. She is a woman who wears a mask, like a thing that is a leper. The fire cannot purify her. The waters cannot quench her anguish. Nothing can heal her! no anodyne can give her sleep! no poppies

forgetfulness! She is lost! She is a lost soul! That is why I call Lord Illingworth
a bad man. That is why I don't want my boy to be with him.

GERALD: My dear mother, it all sounds very tragic, of course. But I dare say
the girl was just as much to blame as Lord Illingworth was. – After all,
would a really nice girl, a girl with any nice feelings at all, go away from
her home with a man to whom she was not married, and live with him as
his wife? No nice girl would.

MRS ARBUTHNOT (*after a pause*): Gerald, I withdraw all my objections. You are
at liberty to go away with Lord Illingworth, when and where you choose.

GERALD: Dear mother, I knew you wouldn't stand in my way. You are the best
woman God ever made. And, as for Lord Illingworth, I don't believe he
is capable of anything infamous or base, I can't believe it of him – I can't.

HESTER (*outside*): Let me go! Let me go!

Enter Hester in terror, and rushes over to Gerald and flings herself in his arms.

HESTER: Oh! save me – save me from him!

GERALD: From whom?

HESTER: He has insulted me! Horribly insulted me! Save me!

GERALD: Who? Who has dared—?

*Lord Illingworth enters at back of stage. Hester breaks from Gerald's arms and
points to him.*

GERALD (*he is quite beside himself with rage and indignation*): Lord Illingworth,
you have insulted the purest thing on God's earth, a thing as pure as my
own mother. You have insulted the woman I love most in the world with
my own mother. As there is a God in Heaven, I will kill you!

MRS ARBUTHNOT (*rushing across and catching hold of him*): No! no!

GERALD (*thrusting her back*): Don't hold me, mother. Don't hold me – I'll kill
him!

MRS ARBUTHNOT: Gerald!

GERALD: Let me go, I say!

MRS ARBUTHNOT: Stop, Gerald, stop! He is your own father!

*Gerald clutches his mother's hands and looks into her face. She sinks slowly on the
ground in shame. Hester steals towards the door. Lord Illingworth frowns and bites
his lip. After a time Gerald raises his mother up, puts his arm round her, and leads
her from the room.*

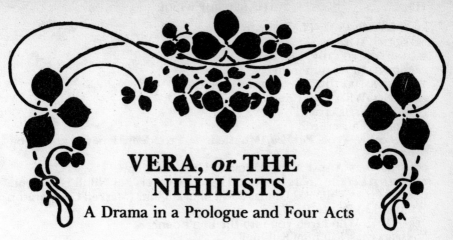

VERA, or THE NIHILISTS

A Drama in a Prologue and Four Acts

Persons in the play

IVAN THE CZAR
PRINCE PAUL MARALOFFSKI, Prime
  Minister of Russia
PRINCE PETROVITCH
COUNT ROUVALOFF

MARQUIS DE POIVRARD
BARON RAFF
GENERAL KOTEMKIN
A PAGE
COLONEL OF THE GUARD

Nihilists

PETER TCHERNAVITCH, President
  of the Nihilists
MICHAEL
ALEXIS IVANACIEVITCH, known as
  a Student of Medicine

PROFESSOR MARFA
VERA SABOUROFF
SOLDIERS, CONSPIRATORS,
ETC.

When her brother is sent to the Siberian mines for belonging to the Nihilists, a revolutionary group, Vera Sabouroff vows to avenge him, and goes to Moscow to join the same group. Alexis, the young Czarevitch, is himself a Nihilist and his execution has just been ordered when his father the Czar who, under the influence of Prime Minister Prince Paul Maraloffski, has become a tyrant, is assassinated ...

ACT THREE

Man in yellow dress, with drawn sword, at the door.

PASSWORD OUTSIDE. Vae tyrannis.
ANSWER. Vae victis (*repeated three times*).
  Enter Conspirators, who form a semicircle, masked and cloaked.
PRESIDENT: What hour is it?

FIRST CONSPIRATOR: The hour to strike.

PRESIDENT: What day?

SECOND CONSPIRATOR: The day of Marat.

PRESIDENT: In what month?

THIRD CONSPIRATOR: The months of liberty.

PRESIDENT: What is our duty?

FOURTH CONSPIRATOR: To obey.

PRESIDENT: Our creed?

FIFTH CONSPIRATOR: *Parbleu*, Monsieur le President, I never knew you had one.

CONSPIRATORS: A spy! A spy! Unmask! Unmask! A spy!

PRESIDENT: Let the doors be shut. There are others but Nihilists present.

CONSPIRATORS: Unmask! Unmask! Kill him! kill him! (Masked Conspirator unmasks.) Prince Paul!

VERA: *Devil!* Who lured you into the lion's den?

CONSPIRATORS: Kill him! Kill him!

PRINCE PAUL: *En vérité*, Messieurs, you are not over-hospitable in your welcome.

VERA: Welcome! What welcome should we give you but the dagger or the noose?

PRINCE PAUL: I had no idea really that the Nihilists were so exclusive. Let me assure you that if I had not always had an *entrée* to the very best society, and the very worst conspiracies, I could never have been Prime Minister in Russia.

VERA: The tiger cannot change its nature, nor the snake lose its venom; but are you turned a lover of the people?

PRINCE PAUL: *Mon Dieu, non, Mademoiselle!* I would much sooner talk scandal in a drawing-room than treason in a cellar. Besides, I hate the common mob, who smell of garlic, smoke bad tobacco, get up early, and dine off one dish.

PRESIDENT: What have you to gain, then, by a revolution?

PRINCE PAUL: *Mon ami*, I have nothing else to lose. That scatterbrained boy, this new Czar, has banished me.

VERA: To Siberia?

PRINCE PAUL: No, to Paris. He has confiscated my estates, robbed me of my office and my cook. I have nothing left but my decorations. I am here for revenge.

PRESIDENT: Then you have a right to be one of us. We also meet daily for revenge.

PRINCE PAUL: You want money, of course. No one ever joins a conspiracy who has any. Here. (*Throws money on table.*) You have so many spies that I should think you want information. Well, you will find me the best-informed man in Russia on the abuses of our Government. I made them nearly all myself.

VERA: President, I don't trust this man. He has done us too much harm in Russia to let him go in safety.

PRINCE PAUL: Believe me, Mademoiselle, you are wrong. I will be a most valuable addition to your circle; and as for you, gentlemen, if I had not thought that you would be useful to me I shouldn't have risked my neck among you, or dined an hour earlier than usual so as to be in time.

PRESIDENT: Ay, if he had wanted to spy on us, Vera, he wouldn't have come himself.

PRINCE PAUL (*aside*): No; I should have sent my best friend.

PRESIDENT: Besides, Vera, he is just the man to give us the information we want about some business we have in hand to-night.

VERA: Be it so if you wish it.

PRESIDENT: Brothers, is it your will that Prince Paul Maraloffski be admitted, and take the oath of the Nihilist?

CONSPIRATORS: It is! It is!

PRESIDENT (*holding out dagger and a paper*): Prince Paul, the dagger or the oath?

PRINCE PAUL (*smiles sardonically*): I would sooner annihilate than be annihilated. (*Takes paper.*)

PRESIDENT: Remember: Betray us, and as long as earth holds poison or steel, as long as men can strike or women betray, you shall not escape vengeance. The Nihilists never forget their friends, or forgive their enemies.

PRINCE PAUL: Really? I did not think you were so civilised.

VERA (*pacing up and down behind*): Why is he not here? He will not keep the crown. I know him well.

PRESIDENT: Sign. (*Prince Paul signs.*) You said you thought we had no creed. You were wrong. Read it!

VERA: This is a dangerous thing, President. What can we do with this man?

PRESIDENT: We can use him. He is of value to us to-night and to-morrow.

VERA: Perhaps there will be no morrow for any of us; but we have given him our word: he is safer here than ever he was in his palace.

PRINCE PAUL (*reading*): 'The rights of humanity'! In the old times men carried out their rights for themselves as they lived, but nowadays every baby seems born with a social manifesto in its mouth much bigger than itself. 'Nature is not a temple, but a workshop: we demand the right to labour.' Ah, I shall surrender my own rights in that respect.

VERA (*pacing up and down behind*): Oh, will he never come? Will he never come?

PRINCE PAUL: 'The family as subversive of true socialistic and communal unity is to be annihilated.' Yes, President, I agree completely with Article 5. A family is a terrible incumbrance, especially when one is not married. (*Three knocks at the door.*)

VERA: Alexis at last!

PASSWORD: Vae tyrannis!

ANSWER: Vae victis! (*Enter Michael Stroganoff.*)

PRESIDENT: Michael, the regicide! Brothers, let us do honour to a man who has killed a king.

VERA (*aside*): Oh, he will come yet!

PRESIDENT: Michael, you have saved Russia.

MICHAEL: Ay, Russia was free for a moment when the tyrant fell, but the sun of liberty has set again like that false dawn which cheats our eyes in autumn.

PRESIDENT: The dread night of tyranny is not yet past for Russia.

MICHAEL (*clutching his knife*): One more blow, and the end is come indeed.

VERA (*aside*): One more blow! What does he mean? Oh, impossible! but why is he not with us? Alexis! Alexis! why are you not here?

PRESIDENT: But how did you escape, Michael? They said you had been seized.

MICHAEL: I was dressed in the uniform of the Imperial Guard. The Colonel on duty was a brother, and gave me the password. I drove through the troops in safety with it, and, thanks to my good horse, reached the walls before the gates were closed.

PRESIDENT: What a chance his coming out on the balcony was!

MICHAEL: A chance? There is no such thing as chance. It was God's finger led him there.

PRESIDENT: And where have you been these three days?

MICHAEL: Hiding in the house of the priest Nicholas at the cross-roads.

PRESIDENT: Nicholas is an honest man.

MICHAEL: Ay, honest enough for a priest. I am here now for vengeance on a traitor!

VERA (*aside*): O God, will he never come? Alexis! why are you not here? you cannot have turned traitor!

MICHAEL (*seeing Prince Paul*): Prince Paul Maraloffski here! By St George, a lucky capture! This must have been Vera's doing. She is the only one who could have lured that serpent into the trap.

PRESIDENT: Prince Paul has just taken the oath.

VERA: Alexis, the Czar, has banished him from Russia.

MICHAEL: Bah! A blind to cheat us. We will keep Prince Paul here, and find some office for him in our reign of terror. He is well accustomed by this time to bloody work.

PRINCE PAUL (*approaching Michael*): That was a long shot of yours, *mon camarade*.

MICHAEL: I have had a good deal of practice shooting, since I have been a boy, off Your Highness's wild boars.

PRINCE PAUL: Are my gamekeepers like moles, then, always asleep?

MICHAEL: No, Prince. I am one of them: but, like you, I am fond of robbing what I am put to watch.

PRESIDENT: This must be a new atmosphere for you, Prince Paul. We speak the truth to one another here.

PRINCE PAUL: How misleading you must find it! You have an odd medley here, President.

PRESIDENT: You recognise a good many friends, I dare say?

PRINCE PAUL: Yes, there is always more brass than brains in an aristocracy.

PRESIDENT: But you are here yourself?

PRINCE PAUL: I? As I cannot be a Prime Minister, I must be a Nihilist. There is no alternative.

VERA: O God, will he never come? The hand is on the stroke of the hour. Will he never come?

MICHAEL (*aside*): President, you know what we have to do? 'Tis but a sorry hunter who leaves the wolf cub alive to avenge his father. How are we to get at this boy? It must be to-night. To-morrow he will be throwing some sop of reform to the people, and it will be too late for a republic.

PRINCE PAUL: You are quite right. Good kings are the only dangerous enemies that modern democracy has and when he has begun by banishing me you may be sure he intends to be a patriot.

MICHAEL: I am sick of patriot kings; what Russia needs is a Republic.

PRINCE PAUL: Messieurs, I have brought you two documents which I think will interest you – the proclamation this young Czar intends publishing to-morrow, and a plan of the Winter Palace, where he sleeps to-night. (*Hands papers.*)

VERA: I dare not ask them what they are plotting about. Oh, why is Alexis not here?

PRESIDENT: Prince, this is most valuable information. Michael, you were right. If it is not to-night it will be too late. Read that.

MICHAEL: Ah! A loaf of bread flung to a starving nation. A lie to cheat the people. (*Tears it up.*) It must be to-night. I do not believe him. Would he have kept his crown had he loved the people? But how are we to get at him, and shall we who could not bear the scorpions of the father suffer the whips of the son? – no; whatever is, must be destroyed: whatever is, is wrong.

PRINCE PAUL: The key of the private door in the street. (*Hands key.*)

PRESIDENT: Prince, we are in your debt.

PRINCE PAUL (*smiling*): The normal condition of the Nihilists.

MICHAEL: Ay, but we are paying our debts off with interest now. Two Emperors in one week. That will make the balance straight. We would have thrown in a Prime Minister if you had not come.

PRINCE PAUL: Ah, I am sorry you told me. It robs my visit of all its picturesqueness and adventure. I thought I was perilling my head by coming here, and you tell me I have saved it. One is sure to be disappointed if one tries to get romance out of modern life.

MICHAEL: It is not so romantic a thing to lose one's head, Prince Paul.

PRINCE PAUL: No, but it must often be very dull to keep it. Don't you find that sometimes? (*Clock strikes six.*)

VERA (*sinking into a seat*): Oh, it is past the hour! It is past the hour!

MICHAEL (*to President*): Remember to-morrow will be too late.

PRESIDENT: Brothers, it is full time. Which of us is absent?

CONSPIRATORS: Alexis! Alexis!

PRESIDENT: Michael, read Rule 7.

MICHAEL: 'When any brother shall have disobeyed a summons to be present, the president shall inquire if there is anything alleged against him.'

PRESIDENT: Is there anything against our brother Alexis?

CONSPIRATORS: He wears a crown! He wears a crown!

PRESIDENT: Michael, read Article 7 of the Code of Revolution.

MICHAEL: 'Between the Nihilists and all men who wear crowns above their fellows, there is war to the death.'

PRESIDENT: Brothers, what say you? Is Alexis, the Czar, guilty or not?

OMNES: He is guilty!

PRESIDENT: What shall the penalty be?

OMNES: Death!

PRESIDENT: Let the lots be prepared; it shall be to-night.

PRINCE PAUL: Ah, this is really interesting! I was getting afraid conspiracies were as dull as courts are.

PROFESSOR MARFA: My forte is more in writing pamphlets than in taking shots. Still a regicide has always a place in history.

MICHAEL: If your pistol is as harmless as your pen, this young tyrant will have a long life.

PRINCE PAUL: You ought to remember, too, Professor, that if you were seized, as you probably would be, and hung, as you certainly would be, there would be nobody left to read your own articles.

PRESIDENT: Brothers, are you ready?

VERA (*starting up*): Not yet! Not yet! I have a word to say.

MICHAEL (*aside*): Plague take her! I knew it would come to this.

VERA: This boy has been our brother. Night after night he has perilled his own life to come here. Night after night, when every street was filled with spies, every house with traitors. Delicately nurtured like a king's son, he has dwelt among us.

PRESIDENT: Ay! under a false name. He lied to us at the beginning. He lies to us now at the end.

VERA: I swear he is true. There is not a man here who does not owe him his life a thousand times. When the bloodhounds were on us that night, who saved us from arrest, torture, flogging, death, but he ye seek to kill? –

MICHAEL: To kill all tyrants is our mission!

VERA: He is no tyrant. I know him well! He loves the people.

PRESIDENT: We know him too; he is a traitor.

VERA: A traitor! Three days ago he could have betrayed every man of you here, and the gibbet would have been your doom. He gave you all your lives once. Give him a little time – a week, a month, a few days; but now! – O God, not now!

CONSPIRATORS (*brandishing daggers*): To-night! to-night! to-night!

VERA: Peace, you gorged adders! peace!

MICHAEL: What, are we not here to annihilate? Shall we not keep our oath?

VERA: Your oath! your oath! Greedy that you are of gain, every man's hand lusting for his neighbour's pelf, every heart set on pillage and rapine; who, of ye all, if the crown were set on his head, would give an empire up for the mob to scramble for? The people are not yet fit for a republic in Russia.

PRESIDENT: Every nation is fit for a republic.

MICHAEL: The man is a tyrant.

VERA: A tyrant! Hath he not dismissed his evil counsellors? That ill-omened raven of his father's life hath had his wings clipped and his claws pared, and comes to us croaking for revenge. Oh, have mercy on him! Give him a week to live!

PRESIDENT: Vera, pleading for a king!

VERA (*proudly*): I plead not for a king, but for a brother.

MICHAEL: For a traitor to his oath, a coward who should have flung the purple back to the fools that gave it him. No, Vera, no. The brood of men is not yet dead, nor the dull earth grown sick of childbearing. No crowned man in Russia shall pollute God's air by living.

PRESIDENT: You bade us try you once. We have tried you, and you are found wanting.

MICHAEL: Vera, I am not blind; I know your secret. You love this boy, this young prince with his pretty face, his curled hair, his soft white hands. Fool that you are, dupe of a lying tongue, do you know what he would have done to you, this boy you think loved you? He would have made you his mistress, used your body at his pleasure, thrown you away when he was wearied of you; you, the priestess of liberty, the flame of revolution, the torch of democracy.

VERA: What he would have done to me matters little. To the people, at least, he will be true. He loves the people; at least, he loves liberty.

PRESIDENT: So, he would play the citizen-king, would he, while we starve? Would flatter us with sweet speeches, would cheat us with promises like his father, would lie to us as his whole race have lied.

MICHAEL: And you whose very name made every despot tremble for his life, you, Vera Sabouroff, you would betray liberty for a lover and the people for a paramour!

CONSPIRATORS: Traitress! Draw the lots: draw the lots!

VERA: In thy throat thou liest, Michael! I love him not. He loves me not.

MICHAEL: You love him not? Shall he not die then?

VERA (*with an effort, clenching her hands*): Ay, it is right that he should die. He hath broken his oath. There should be no crowned man in Europe. Have I not sworn it. To be strong our new republic should be drunk with the blood of kings. He hath broken his oath. As the father died so let the son die too. Yet not to-night, not to-night. Russia, that hath borne her centuries of wrong, can wait a week for liberty. Give him a week.

PRESIDENT: We will have none of you! Begone from us to this boy you love.

MICHAEL: Though I find him in your arms I shall kill him.

CONSPIRATORS: To-night! To-night!

MICHAEL (*holding up his hand*): A moment! I have something to say. (*Approaches Vera; speaks very slowly.*) Vera Sabouroff, have you forgotten your brother? (*Pauses to see effect; Vera starts.*) Have you forgotten that young face, pale with famine; those young limbs twisted with torture; the iron chains they made him walk in? What week of liberty did they give him? What pity did they show him for a day? (*Vera falls in a chair.*) Oh! you could talk glibly enough then of vengeance, glibly enough of liberty. When you said you would come to Moscow, your old father caught you by the knees and begged you not to leave him to die childless and alone. I seem to hear his cries still ringing in my ears, but you were as deaf to him as the rocks on the roadside. You left your father that night, and three weeks after he died of a broken heart. You wrote to me to follow you here. I did so; first because I loved you; but you soon cured me of that; whatever gentle feeling, whatever pity, whatever love, whatever humanity was in my heart you withered up and destroyed, as the canker worm eats the corn. You bade me cast out love from my breast as a vile thing, you turned my hand to iron, and my heart to stone; you told me to live for freedom and revenge. I have done so. But you, what have you done?

VERA: Let the lots be drawn! (*Conspirators applaud.*)

PRINCE PAUL (*aside*): Ah, the Grand Duke will come to the throne sooner than he expected. He is sure to make a good king under my guidance. He is so cruel to animals, and never keeps his word.

MICHAEL: Now you are yourself at last, Vera.

VERA (*standing motionless in the middle*): The lots, I say, the lots! I am no woman now. My blood seems turned to gall; my heart is as cold as steel is; my hand shall be more deadly. From the desert and the tomb the voice of my prisoned brother cries aloud, and bids me strike one blow for liberty. The lots, I say, the lots!

PRESIDENT: Are ready. Michael, you have the right to draw first: you are a regicide.

VERA: O God, into my hands! Into my hands! (*They draw the lots from a bowl surmounted by a skull.*)

PRESIDENT: Open your lots.

VERA (*opening her lot*): The lot is mine! See, the bloody sign upon it! Dmitri, my brother, you shall have your revenge now.

PRESIDENT: Vera Sabouroff, you are chosen to be a regicide. God has been good to you. The dagger or the poison? (*Offers her dagger and vial.*)

VERA: I can trust my hand better with the dagger; it never fails. (*Takes dagger.*) I shall stab him to the heart, as he has stabbed me. Traitor, to leave us for a ribbon, a gaud, a bauble, to lie to me every day he came here, to forget us in an hour. Michael was right, he loved me not, nor the people either. Methinks that if I was a mother and bore a man-child, I would poison my breast against him, lest he might grow to a traitor or to a king. (*Prince Paul whispers to the President.*)

PRESIDENT: Ay, Prince Paul, that is the best way. Vera, the Czar sleeps to-night in his own room in the north wing of the palace. Here is a key of the private door in the street. The password of the guards will be given to you. His own servants will be drugged. You will find him alone.

VERA: It is well. I shall not fail.

PRESIDENT: We will wait outside in the Place Saint Isaac, under the window. As the clock strikes twelve from the tower of St Nicholas you will give us the sign that the dog is dead.

VERA: And what shall the sign be?

PRESIDENT: You are to throw us out the bloody dagger.

MICHAEL: Dripping with the traitor's life.

PRESIDENT: Else we shall know that you have been seized, and we will burst our way in, drag you from his guards.

MICHAEL: And kill him in the midst of them.

PRESIDENT: Michael, you will lead us?

MICHAEL: Ay, I shall lead you. See that your hand fails you not, Vera Sabouroff.

VERA: Fool, is it so hard a thing to kill one's enemy?

PRINCE PAUL (*aside*): This is the ninth conspiracy I have been in in Russia. They always end in a *voyage en Siberie* for my friends and a new decoration for myself.

MICHAEL: It is your last conspiracy, Prince.

PRESIDENT: At twelve o'clock, the bloody dagger.

VERA: Ay, red with the blood of that false heart. I shall not forget it. (*Standing in middle of stage.*) To strangle whatever nature is in me, neither to love nor to be loved, neither to pity nor to be pitied. Ay! it is an oath, an oath. Methinks the spirit of Charlotte Corday has entered my soul now. I shall carve my name on the world, and be ranked among the great heroines. Ay! the spirit of Charlotte Corday beats in each petty vein, and nerves my woman's hand to strike, as I have nerved my woman's heart to hate. Though he laugh in his dreams I shall not falter. Though he sleep peacefully I shall not miss my blow. Be glad, my brother, in your stifled cell; be glad and laugh to-night. To-night this new fledged Czar shall post with bloody feet to hell, and greet his father there! This Czar! O traitor, liar, false to his oath, false to me! To play the patriot among us, and now to wear a crown; to sell us, like Judas, for thirty silver pieces, to betray us with a kiss! (*With more passion.*) O Liberty, O mighty mother of eternal time, thy robe is purple with the blood of those who have died for thee! Thy throne is the Calvary of the people, thy crown the crown of thorns. O crucified mother, the despot has driven a nail through thy right hand, and the tyrant through thy left! Thy feet are pierced with their iron. When thou wert athirst thou calledst on the priests for water, and they gave thee bitter drink. They thrust a sword into thy side. They mocked thee in thine agony of age on age. Here, on thy altar, O Liberty, do I dedicate myself to thy service; do with me as thou wilt! (*Brandishing the dagger.*) The end has come now, and by thy sacred wounds, O crucified mother, O Liberty, I swear that Russia shall be saved!

THE DUCHESS OF PADUA

The persons of the play

SIMONE GESSO, Duke of Padua
BEATRICE, his Wife
ANDREAS POLLAJUOLO, Cardinal
  of Padua
MAFFIO PETRUCCI ⎫ Gentlemen of
JEPPO VITELLOZZO ⎬ the Duke's
TADDEO BARDI ⎭ Household
GUIDO FERRANTI, a Young Man
ASCANIO CRISTOFANO, his Friend

COUNT MORANZONE, an Old Man
BERNARDO CAVALCANTI, Lord Justice
  of Padua
HUGO, the Headsman
LUCY, a Tire Woman
SERVANTS, CITIZENS, SOLDIERS,
  MONKS, FALCONERS with their hawks
  and dogs, etc.

Time: *The latter half of the sixteenth century.*

Guido Ferranti has sworn to murder the Duke of Padua in revenge for his own father's death. He is employed in the Duke's household and only awaits a signal from Lord Moranzone to do the deed. But Guido and the Duke's wife have fallen in love. When he tells her that he must never see her again, she resolves to kill herself…

ACT THREE

Scene: A large corridor in the Ducal Palace: a window (L.C.) looks out on a view of Padua by moonlight: a staircase (R.C.) leads up to a door with a portière of crimson velvet, with the Duke's arms embroidered in gold on it: on the lowest step of the staircase a figure draped in black is sitting: the hall is lit by an iron cresset filled with burning tow: thunder and lightning outside: the time is night.

  Enter Guido through the window.
GUIDO: The wind is rising: how my ladder shook!
  I thought that every gust would break the cords!
  Looks out at the city.
  Christ! What a night:
  Great thunder in the heavens, and wild lightnings
  Striking from pinnacle to pinnacle

Across the city, till the dim houses seem
To shudder and to shake as each new glare
Dashes adown the street.
Passes across the stage to foot of staircase.
Ah! who art thou
That sittest on the stair, like unto Death
Waiting a guilty soul? (*A pause.*)
Canst thou not speak?
Or has this storm laid palsy on your tongue,
And chilled your utterance? Get from my path,
For I have certain business in yon chamber,
Which I must do alone.
The figure rises and takes off his mask.
MORANZONE: Guido Ferranti,
Thy murdered father laughs for joy to-night.
GUIDO (*confusedly*): What, art thou here?
MORANZONE: Ay, waiting for your coming.
GUIDO (*looking away from him*): I did not think to see you, but am glad,
That thou mayest know the very thing I mean to do.
MORANZONE: First, I would have you know my well-laid plans;
Listen: I have set horses at the gate
Which leads to Parma: when thou hast done thy business
We will ride hence, and by to-morrow night
If our good horses fail not by the way
Parma will see us coming; I have advised
Many old friends of your great father there,
Who have prepared the citizens for revolt.
With money, and with golden promises,
The which we need not keep, I have bought over
Many that stand by this usurping Duke.
As for the soldiers, they, the Duke being dead,
Will fling allegiance to the winds, so thou
Shalt sit again within thy father's palace,
As Parma's rightful lord.
GUIDO: It cannot be.
MORANZONE: Nay, but it shall.
GUIDO: Listen, Lord Moranzone,
I am resolved not to kill this man.
MORANZONE: Surely my ears are traitors, speak again:
It cannot be but age has dulled my powers,
I am an old man now: what did you say?
You said that with that dagger in your belt
You would avenge your father's bloody murder;
Did you not say that?
GUIDO: No, my lord, I said
I was resolved not to kill the Duke.
MORANZONE: You said not that; it is my senses mock me;
Or else this midnight air o'ercharged with storm

Alters your message in the giving it.

GUIDO: Nay, you heard rightly; I'll not kill this man.

MORANZONE: What of thine oath, thou traitor, what of thine oath?

GUIDO: I am resolved not to keep that oath.

MORANZONE: What of thy murdered father?

GUIDO: Dost thou think
My father would be glad to see me coming,
This old man's blood still hot upon mine hands?

MORANZONE: Ay! he would laugh for joy.

GUIDO: I do not think so,
There is better knowledge in the other world;
Vengeance is God's, let God himself revenge.

MORANZONE: Thou art God's minister of vengeance.

GUIDO: No!
God hath no minister but his own hand.
I will not kill this man.

MORANZONE: Why are you here,
If not to kill him, then?

GUIDO: Lord Moranzone,
I purpose to ascend to the Duke's chamber,
And as he lies asleep lay on his breast
The dagger and this writing; when he awakes
Then he will know who held him in his power
And slew him not: this is the noblest vengeance
Which I can take.

MORANZONE: You will not slay him?

GUIDO: No.

MORANZONE: Ignoble son of a noble father,
Who sufferest this man who sold that father
To live an hour.

GUIDO: 'Twas thou that hindered me;
I would have killed him in the open square,
The day I saw him first.

MORANZONE: It was not yet time;
Now it is time, and, like some green-faced girl,
Thou pratest of forgiveness.

GUIDO: No! revenge:
The right revenge my father's son should take.

MORANZONE: O wretched father, thus again betrayed,
And by thine own son too! You are a coward,
Take out the knife, get to the Duke's chamber,
And bring me back his heart upon the blade.
When he is dead, then you can talk to me
Of noble vengeances.

GUIDO: Upon thine honour,
And by the love thou bearest my father's name,
Dost thou think my father, that great gentleman,
That generous soldier, that most chivalrous lord,

Would have crept at night-time, like a common thief,
And stabbed an old man sleeping in his bed,
However he had wronged him: tell me that.
MORANZONE (*after some hesitation*): You have sworn an oath, see that you
keep that oath.
Boy do you think I do not know your secret,
Your traffic with the Duchess?
GUIDO: Silence, liar!
The very moon in heaven is not more chaste,
Nor the white stars so pure.
MORANZONE: And yet, you love her;
Weak fool, to let love in upon your life,
Save as a plaything.
GUIDO: You do well to talk:
Within your veins, old man, the pulse of youth
Throbs with no ardour. Your eyes full of rheum
Have against Beauty closed their filmy doors,
And your clogged ears, losing their natural sense,
Have shut you from the music of the world.
You talk of love! You know not what it is.
MORANZONE: Oh, in my time, boy, I have walked i' the moon.
Swore I would live on kisses and on blisses,
Swore I would die for love, and did not die,
Wrote love bad verses; ay, and sung them badly,
Like all true lovers: Oh, I have done the tricks!
I know the partings and the chamberings;
We are all animals at best, and love
Is merely passion with a holy name.
GUIDO: Now then I know you have not loved at all.
Love is the sacrament of life; it sets
Virtue where virtue was not; cleanses men
Of all the vile pollutions of this world;
It is the fire which purges gold from dross,
It is the fan which winnows wheat from chaff,
It is the spring which in some wintry soil
Makes innocence to blossom like a rose.
The days are over when God walked with men,
But Love, which is His image, holds His place.
When a man loves a woman, then he knows
God's secret, and the secret of the world.
There is no house so lowly or so mean,
Which, if their hearts be pure who live in it,
Love will not enter; but if bloody murder
Knock at the Palace gate and is let in,
Love like a wounded thing creeps out and dies.
This is the punishment God sets on sin
The wicked cannot love.
A groan comes from the Duke's chamber.

Ah! What is that?
Do you not hear? 'Twas nothing.
So I think
That it is woman's mission by their love
To save the souls of men: and loving her,
My Lady, my white Beatrice, I begin
To see a nobler and a holier vengeance
In letting this man live, than doth reside
In bloody deeds o' night, stabs in the dark,
And young hands clutching at a palsied throat.
It was, I think, for love's sake that Lord Christ,
Who was indeed himself incarnate Love,
Bade every man forgive his enemy.
MORANZONE (*sneeringly*): That was in Palestine, not Padua;
And said for saints: I have to do with men.
GUIDO: It was for all time said.
MORANZONE: And your white Duchess,
What will she do to thank you? Will she not come,
And put her cheek to yours, and fondle you,
For having left her lord to plague her life?
GUIDO: Alas, I will not see her face again.
'Tis but twelve hours since I parted from her,
So suddenly, and with such violent passion,
That she has shut her heart against me now;
No, I will never see her.
MORANZONE: What will you do?
GUIDO: After that I have laid the dagger there,
Get hence to-night from Padua.
MORANZONE: And then?
GUIDO: I will take service with the Doge at Venice,
And bid him pack me straightway to the wars,
In Holy Land against the Infidel;
And there I will, being now sick of life,
Throw that poor life against some desperate spear.
A groan from the Duke's chamber again.
Did you not hear a voice?
MORANZONE: I always hear,
From the dim confines of some sepulchre,
A voice that cries for vengeance: We waste time,
It will be morning soon; are you resolved
You will not kill the Duke?
GUIDO: I am resolved.
MORANZONE: Guido Ferranti, in that chamber yonder
There lies the man who sold your father's life,
And gave him to the hangman's murderous hands.
There does he sleep: you have your father's dagger;
Will you not kill him?
GUIDO: No, I will not kill him.

MORANZONE: O wretched father, lying unavenged.

GUIDO: More wretched were thy son a murderer.

MORANZONE: Why, what is life?

GUIDO: I do not know, my lord,
I did not give it, and I dare not take it.

MORANZONE: I do not thank God often; but I think
I thank him now that I have got no son!
And you, what bastard blood flows in your veins
That when you have your enemy in your grasp
You let him go! I would that I had left you
With the dull hinds that reared you.

GUIDO: Better perhaps
That you had done so! May be better still
I'd not been born to this distressful world.

MORANZONE: Farewell!

GUIDO: Farewell! Some day, Lord Moranzone,
You will understand my vengeance.

MORANZONE: Never, boy.
Gets out of window and exit by rope ladder.

GUIDO: Father, I think thou knowest my resolve,
And with this nobler vengeance are content.
Father, I think in letting this man live
That I am doing what you would have done.
Father, I know not if a human voice
Can pierce the iron gateway of the dead,
Or if the dead are set in ignorance
Of what we do, or do not, for their sakes.
And yet I feel a presence in the air,
There is a shadow standing at my side,
And ghostly kisses seem to touch my lips,
And leave them holier.
Kneels down.
O father, if 'tis thou,
Canst thou not burst through the decrees of death,
And in corporeal semblance show thyself,
That I may touch thy hand!
No, there is nothing.
Rises.
'Tis the night that cheats us with its phantoms,
And, like a puppet-master, makes us think
That things are real which are not. It grows late.
Now must I do my business.
Pulls out a letter from his doublet and reads it.
When he wakes,
And sees this letter, and the dagger with it,
Will he not have some loathing for his life,
Repent, perchance, and lead a better life,
Or will he mock because a young man spared

His natural enemy? I do not care,
Father, it is your bidding that I do,
Your bidding, and the bidding of my love
Which teaches me to know you are as you are.
*Ascends staircase stealthily, and just as he reaches out his hand to draw back
the curtain the Duchess appears all in white. Guido starts back.*
DUCHESS: Guido! what do you here so late?
GUIDO: O white and spotless angel of my life,
Sure thou hast come from Heaven with a message
That mercy is more noble than revenge?
DUCHESS: Ay! I do pray for mercy earnestly.
GUIDO: O father, now I know I do your bidding,
For hand in hand with Mercy, like a God,
Has Love come forth to meet me on the way.
DUCHESS: I felt you would come back to me again,
Although you left me very cruelly:
Why did you leave me? Nay, that matters not,
For I can hold you now, and feel your heart
Beat against mine with little throbs of love:
Our hearts are two caged birds, trying to kiss
Across their cages' bars: but the time goes,
It will be morning in an hour or so;
Let us get horses;: I must post to Venice,
They will not think of looking for me there.
GUIDO: Love, I will follow you across the world.
DUCHESS: But are you sure you love me?
GUIDO: Is the lark
Sure that it loves the dawn that bids it sing?
DUCHESS: Could nothing ever change you?
GUIDO: Nothing ever:
The shipman's needle is not set more sure
Than I am to the lodestone of your love.
DUCHESS: There is no barrier between us now.
GUIDO: None, love, nor shall be.
DUCHESS: I have seen to that.
GUIDO: Tarry here for me.
DUCHESS: No, you are not going?
You will not leave me as you did before?
GUIDO: I will return within a moment's space,
But first I must repair to the Duke's chamber,
And leave this letter and this dagger there,
That when he wakes—
DUCHESS: When who wakes?
GUIDO: Why, the Duke.
DUCHESS: He will not wake again.
GUIDO: What, is he dead?
DUCHESS: Ay! he is dead.
GUIDO: O God! how wonderful

Are all Thy secret ways! Who would have said
That on this very night, when I had yielded
Into Thy hands the vengeance that is Thine,
Thou with Thy finger should have touched the man,
And bade him come before Thy judgment seat.
DUCHESS: I have just killed him.
GUIDO (*in horror*): Oh!
DUCHESS: He was asleep;
Come closer, love, and I will tell you all.
Kiss me upon the mouth, and I will tell you.
You will not kiss me now? – well, you will kiss me
When I have told you how I killed the Duke.
After you left me with such bitter words,
Feeling my life went lame without your love,
I had resolved to kill myself to-night.
About an hour ago I waked from sleep,
And took my dagger from beneath my pillow,
Where I had hidden it to serve my need,
And drew it from the sheath, and felt the edge,
And thought of you, and how I loved you, Guido,
And turned to fall upon it, when I marked
The old man sleeping, full of years and sin;
There lay he muttering curses in his sleep.
And as I looked upon his evil face
Suddenly like a flame there flashed across me,
There is the barrier which Guido spoke of:
You said there lay a barrier between us,
What barrier but he? –
I hardly know
What happened, bur a steaming mist of blood
Rose up between us two.
GUIDO: O horrible!
DUCHESS: You would have said so had you seen that mist:
And then the air rained blood and then he groaned,
And then he groaned no more! I only heard
The dripping of the blood upon the floor.
GUIDO: Enough, enough.
DUCHESS: Will you not kiss me now?
Do you remember saying that women's love
Turns men to angels? well, the love of man
Turns women into martyrs; for its sake
We do or suffer anything.
GUIDO: O God!
DUCHESS: Will you not speak?
GUIDO: I cannot speak at all.
DUCHESS: This is the knife with which I killed the Duke.
I did not think he would have bled so much,
But I can wash my hands in water after;

Can I not wash my hands? Ay, but my soul?
Let us not talk of this! Let us go hence:
Is not the barrier broken down between us?
What would you more? Come, it is almost morning.
Puts her hand on Guido's.
GUIDO (*breaking from her*): O damned saint! O angel fresh from Hell!
What bloody devil tempted thee to this!
That thou hast killed thy husband, that is nothing –
Hell was already gaping for his soul –
But thou hast murdered Love, and in its place
Hast set a horrible and bloodstained thing,
Whose very breath breeds pestilence and plague,
And strangles Love.
DUCHESS (*in amazed wonder*): I did it all for you.
I would not have you do it, had you willed it,
For I would keep you without blot or stain,
A thing unblemished, unassailed, untarnished.
Men do not know what women do for love.
Have I not wrecked my soul for your dear sake,
Here and hereafter?
Oh be kind to me,
I did it all for you.
GUIDO: No, do not touch me,
Between us lies a thin red stream of blood,
I dare not look across it: when you stabbed him
You stabbed Love with a sharp knife to the heart.
We cannot meet again.
DUCHESS (*wringing her hands*): For you! For you!
I did it all for you: have you forgotten?
You said there was a barrier between us;
That barrier lies now i' the upper chamber
Upset, overthrown, beaten, and battered down,
And will not part us ever.
GUIDO: No, you mistook:
Sin was the barrier, you have raised it up;
Crime was the barrier, you have set it there.
The barrier was murder, and your hand
Has builded it so high it shuts out Heaven,
It shuts out God.
DUCHESS: I did it all for you;
You dare not leave me now; nay, Guido, listen.
Get horses ready, we will fly to-night.
The past is a bad dream, we will forget it:
Before us lies the future: will we not have
Sweet days of love beneath our vines and laugh? –
No, no, we will not laugh, but, when we weep,
Well, we will weep together; I will serve you
Like a poor housewife, like a common slave;

I will be very meek and very gentle:
You do not know me.
GUIDO: Nay, I know you now;
Get hence, I say, out of my sight.
DUCHESS (*pacing up and down*): O God,
How I have loved this man!
GUIDO: You never loved me.
Had it been so, Love would have stopped your hand,
Nor suffered you to stain his holy shrine,
Where none can enter but the innocent.
DUCHESS: These are but words, words, words.
GUIDO: Get hence, I pray:
How could we sit together at Love's table?
You have poured poison in the sacred wine,
And Murder dips his fingers in the sop.
Rather than this I had died a thousand deaths.
DUCHESS: I having done it, die a thousand deaths.
GUIDO: It is not death but life that you should fear.
DUCHESS (*throws herself on her knees*): Then slay me now! I have spilt blood
to-night,
You shall spill more, so we go hand in hand
To heaven or to hell. Draw your sword, Guido,
And traffic quickly for my life with Death,
Who is grown greedy of such merchandise.
Quick, let your soul go chambering in my heart,
It will but find its master's image there.
Nay, if you will not slay me with your sword,
Bid me to fall upon this reeking knife,
And I will do it.
GUIDO (*wresting knife from her*): Give it to me, I say.
O God, your very hands are wet with blood!
This place is Hell, I cannot tarry here.
DUCHESS: Will you not raise me up before you go,
Or must I like a beggar keep my knees?
GUIDO: I pray you let me see your face no more.
DUCHESS: Better for me I had not seen your face.
O think it was for you I killed this man.
Guido recoils: she seizes his hands as she kneels.
Nay, Guido, listen for a while:
Until you came to Padua I lived
Wretched indeed, but with no murderous thought,
Very submissive to a cruel Lord,
Very obedient to unjust commands,
As pure I think as any gentle girl
Who now would turn in horror from my hands –
You came: ah! Guido, the first kindly words
I ever heard since I had come from France
Were from your lips: well, well, that is no matter.

You came, and in the passion of your eyes
I read love's meaning, everything you said
Touched my dumb soul to music, and you seemed
Fair as that young Saint Michael on the wall
In Santa Croce, where we go and pray.
I wonder will I ever pray again?
Well, you were fair, and in your boyish face
The morning seemed to lighten, so I loved you.
And yet I did not tell you of my love.
'Twas you who sought me out, knelt at my feet
As I kneel now at yours, and with sweet vows
Whose music seems to linger in my ears,
Swore that you loved me, and I trusted you.
I think there are many women in the world
Who had they been unto this vile Duke mated,
Chained to his side, as the poor galley slave
Is to a leper chained, – ay! many women
Who would have tempted you to kill the man.
I did not.
Yet I know that had I done so,
I had not been thus humbled in the dust.
Stands up.
But you have loved me very faithfully.
After a pause approaches him timidly.
I do not think you understand me, Guido:
It was for your sake that I wrought this deed
Whose horror now chills my young blood to ice,
For your sake only (*Stretching out her arm.*)
Will you not speak to me?
Love me a little: in my girlish life
I have been starved for love, and kindliness
Has passed me by.
GUIDO: I dare not look at you:
You come to me with too pronounced a favour,
Get to your tirewomen.
DUCHESS: Ay, there it is!
There speaks the man! yet had you come to me
With any heavy sin upon your soul,
Some murder done for hire, not for love,
Why, I had sat and watched at your bedside
All through the night-time, lest Remorse might come
And pour his poisons in your ear, and so
Keep you from sleeping! Sure it is the guilty,
Who, being very wretched, need love most.
GUIDO: There is no love where there is any guilt.
DUCHESS: No love where there is any guilt! O God,
How differently do we love from men!
There is many a woman here in Padua,

Some workman's wife, or ruder artisan's,
Whose husband spends the wages of the week
In a coarse revel, or a tavern brawl,
And reeling home late on the Saturday night,
Finds his wife sitting by a fireless hearth,
Trying to hush the child who cries for hunger,
And then sets to and beats his wife because
The child is hungry, and the fire black.
Yet the wife loves him! and will rise next day
With some red bruise across a careworn face,
And sweep the house, and do the common service,
And try and smile, and only be too glad
If he does not beat her a second time
Before her child! – that is how women love.
A pause: Guido says nothing.
Do you say nothing? Oh be kind to me
While yet I know the summer of my days.
I think you will not drive me from your side.
Where have I got to go if you reject me?—
You for whose sake this hand has murdered life,
You for whose sake my soul has wrecked itself
Beyond all hope of pardon.

GUIDO: Get thee gone:
The dead man is a ghost, and our love too,
Flits like a ghost about its desolate tomb,
And wanders through this charnel house, and weeps
That when you slew your lord you slew it also.
Do you not see?

DUCHESS: I see when men love women
They give them but a little of their lives,
But women when they love give everything;
I see that, Guido, now.

GUIDO: Away, away,
And come not back till you have waked your dead.

DUCHESS: I would to God that I could wake the dead
Put vision in the glazèd eyes, and give
The tongue its natural utterance, and bid
The heart to beat again; that cannot be:
For what is done, is done: and what is dead
Is dead for ever: the fire cannot warm him:
The winter cannot hurt him with its snows;
Something has gone from him; if you call him now,
He will not answer; if you mock him now,
He will not laugh; and if you stab him now
He will not bleed.
I would that I could wake him!
O God, put back the sun a little space,
And from the roll of time blot out to-night,

And bid it not have been! put back the sun,
And make me what I was an hour ago!
No, no, time will not stop anything,
Nor the sun stay its courses, though Repentance
Calling it back grow hoarse; but you, my love,
Have you no word of pity even for me?
O Guido, Guido, will you not kiss me once?
Drive me not to some desperate resolve:
Women grow mad when they are treated thus:
Will you not kiss me once?

GUIDO (*holding up knife*): I will not kiss you
Until the blood grows dry upon this knife,
And not even then.

DUCHESS: Dear Christ! how little pity
We women get in this untimely world;
Men lure us to some dreadful precipice,
And, when we fall, they leave us.

GUIDO (*wildly*): Back to your dead!

DUCHESS (*going up the stairs*): Why, then I will be gone!
and may you find
More mercy than you showed to me to-night!

GUIDO: Let me find mercy when I go at night
And do foul murder.

DUCHESS (*coming down a few steps*): Murder did you say?
Murder is hungry, and still cries for more,
And Death, his brother, is not satisfied,
But walks the house, and will not go away,
Unless he has a comrade! Tarry, Death,
For I will give thee a most faithful lackey
To travel with thee! Murder, call no more,
For thou shalt eat thy fill.
There is a storm
Will break upon this house before the morning,
So horrible, that the white moon already
Turns grey and sick with terror, the low wind
Goes moaning round the house, and the high stars
Run madly through the vaulted firmament,
As though the night wept tears of liquid fire
For what the day shall look upon. O weep,
Thou lamentable heaven! Weep thy fill!
Though sorrow like a cataract drench the fields,
And make the earth one bitter lake of tears,
It would not be enough.
A peal of thunder.
Do you not hear,
There is artillery in the Heaven to-night.
Vengeance is wakened up, and has unloosed
His dogs upon the world, and in this matter

Which lies between us two, let him who draws
The thunder on his head beware the ruin
Which the forked flame brings after.
A flash of lightning followed by a peal of thunder.
GUIDO: Away! away!
  *Exit the Duchess, who as she lifts the crimson curtain looks back for a moment
at Guido, but he makes no sign. More thunder.*
Now is life fallen in ashes at my feet.
And noble self-slain; and in its place
Crept murder with its silent bloody feet.
And she who wrought it – Oh! and yet she loved me,
And for my sake did do this dreadful thing.
I have been cruel to her: Beatrice!
Beatrice, I say, come back.
Begins to ascend staircase, when the noise of Soldiers is heard.
Ah! what is that?
Torches ablaze, and noise of hurrying feet.
Pray God they have not seized her.
Noise grows louder.
 Beatrice!
There is yet time to escape. Come down, come out!
The voice of the Duchess outside: This way went he, the man who slew
my lord.
*Down the staircase come hurrying a confused body of Soldiers; Guido is not
seen at first, till the Duchess surrounded by Servants carrying torches appears
at the top of the staircase, and points to Guido, who is seized at once, one of
the Soldiers dragging the knife from his hand and showing it to the Captain
of the Guard in sight of the audience. Tableau.*

AN IDEAL HUSBAND

The persons of the play

THE EARL OF CAVERSHAM, K.G.
VISCOUNT GORING, his son
SIR ROBERT CHILTERN, Bart.,
  Under-Secretary for Foreign Affairs
VICOMTE DE NANJAC, Attaché at
  French Embassy in London
MR MONTFORT
MASON, Butler to Sir Robert Chiltern

LADY CHILTERN
LADY MARKBY
THE COUNTESS OF BASILDON
MRS MARCHMONT
MISS MABEL CHILTERN, Sir
  Robert Chiltern's sister
MRS CHEVELEY
PHIPPS, Lord Goring's servant
JAMES AND HAROLD, Footmen

Time: *the present*; Place: *London. . Sir Robert Chiltern is being blackmailed by the unscrupulous Mrs Cheveley . He confides in his friend, Lord Goring ...*

ACT TWO

LORD GORING: My dear Robert, it's a very awkward business, very awkward indeed. You should have told your wife the whole thing. Secrets from other people's wives are a necessary luxury in modern life. So, at least, I am always told at the club by people who are bald enough to know better. But no man should have a secret from his own wife. She invariably finds it out. Women have a wonderful instinct about things. They can discover everything except the obvious.

SIR ROBERT CHILTERN: Arthur, I couldn't tell my wife. When could I have told her? Not last night. It would have made a lifelong separation between us, and I would have lost the love of the one woman in the world I worship, of the only woman who had ever stirred love within me. Last night it would have been quite impossible. She would have turned from me in horror ... in horror and in contempt.

LORD GORING: Is Lady Chiltern as perfect as all that?

SIR ROBERT CHILTERN: Yes; my wife is as perfect as all that.

LORD GORING (*taking off his left-hand glove*): What a pity! I beg your pardon, my dear fellow, I didn't quite mean that. But if what you tell me is true, I should like to have a serious talk about life with Lady Chiltern.

SIR ROBERT CHILTERN: It would be quite useless.

LORD GORING: May I try?

SIR ROBERT CHILTERN: Yes; but nothing could make her alter her views.

LORD GORING: Well, at the worst it would simply be a psychological experiment.

SIR ROBERT CHILTERN: All such experiments are terribly dangerous.

LORD GORING: Everything is dangerous, my dear fellow. If it wasn't so, life wouldn't be worth living . . . Well, I am bound to say that I think you should have told her years ago.

SIR ROBERT CHILTERN: When? When we were engaged? Do you think she would have married me if she had known that the origin of my fortune is such as it is, the basis of my career such as it is, and that I had done a thing that I suppose most men would call shameful and dishonourable?

LORD GORING (*slowly*): Yes; most men would call it ugly names. There is no doubt of that.

SIR ROBERT CHILTERN (*bitterly*): Men who every day do something of the same kind themselves. Men who, each one of them, have worse secrets in their own lives.

LORD GORING: That is the reason they are so pleased to find out other people's secrets. It distracts public attention from their own.

SIR ROBERT CHILTERN: And, after all, whom did I wrong by what I did? No one.

LORD GORING (*looking at him steadily*): Except yourself, Robert.

SIR ROBERT CHILTERN (*after a pause*): Of course I had private information about a certain transaction contemplated by the Government of the day, and I acted on it. Private information is practically the source of every large modern fortune.

LORD GORING (*tapping his boot with his cane*): And public scandal invariably the result.

SIR ROBERT CHILTERN (*pacing up and down the room*): Arthur, do you think that what I did nearly eighteen years ago should be brought up against me now? Do you think it fair that a man's whole career should be ruined for a fault done in one's boyhood almost? I was twenty-two at the time, and I had the double misfortune of being well-born and poor, two unforgivable things nowadays. Is it fair that the folly, the sin of one's youth, if men choose to call it a sin, should wreck a life like mine, should place me in the pillory, should shatter all that I have worked for, all that I have built up? Is it fair, Arthur?

LORD GORING: Life is never fair, Robert. And perhaps it is a good thing for most of us that it is not.

SIR ROBERT CHILTERN: Every man of ambition has to fight his century with its own weapons. What this century worships is wealth. The God of this century is wealth. To succeed one must have wealth. At all costs one must have wealth.

LORD GORING: You underrate yourself, Robert. Believe me, without your wealth you could have succeeded just as well.

SIR ROBERT CHILTERN: When I was old, perhaps. When I had lost my passion for power, or could not use it. When I was tired, worn out, disappointed. I wanted my success when I was young. Youth is the time for success. I couldn't wait.

LORD GORING: Well, you certainly have had your successes while you are still young. No one in our day has had such a brilliant success. Under-Secretary for Foreign Affairs at the age of forty – that's good enough for any one, I should think.

SIR ROBERT CHILTERN: And if it is all taken away from me now? If I lose everything over a horrible scandal? If I am hounded from public life?

LORD GORING: Robert, how could you have sold yourself for money?

SIR ROBERT CHILTERN (*excitedly*): I did not sell myself for money. I bought success at a great price. That is all.

LORD GORING (*gravely*): Yes; you certainly paid a great price for it. But what first made you think of doing such a thing?

SIR ROBERT CHILTERN: Baron Arnheim.

LORD GORING: Damned scoundrel!

SIR ROBERT CHILTERN: No; he was a man of a most subtle and refined intellect. A man of culture, charm, and distinction. One of the most intellectual men I ever met.

LORD GORING: Ah! I prefer a gentlemanly fool any day. There is more to be said for stupidity than people imagine. Personally, I have a great admiration for stupidity. It is a sort of fellow-feeling, I suppose. But how did he do it? Tell me the whole thing.

SIR ROBERT CHILTERN (*throws himself into an arm-chair by the writing-table*): One night after dinner at Lord Radley's the Baron began talking about success in modern life as something that one could reduce to an absolutely definite science. With that wonderfully fascinating quiet voice of his he expounded to us the most terrible of all philosophies, the philosophy of power, preached to us the most marvellous of all gospels, the gospel of gold. I think he saw the effect he had produced on me, for some days afterwards he wrote and asked me to come and see him. He was living then in Park Lane, in the house Lord Woolcomb has now. I remember so well how, with a strange smile on his pale, curved lips, he led me through his wonderful picture gallery, showed me his tapestries, his enamels, his jewels, his carved ivories, made me wonder at the strange loveliness of the luxury in which he lived; and then told me that luxury was nothing but a background, a painted scene in a play, and that power, power over other men, power over the world, was the one thing worth having, the one supreme pleasure worth knowing, the one joy one never tired of, and that in our century only the rich possessed it.

LORD GORING (*with great deliberation*): A thoroughly shallow creed.

SIR ROBERT CHILTERN (*rising*): I didn't think so then. I don't think so now. Wealth has given me enormous power. It gave me at the very outset of my life freedom, and freedom is everything. You have never been poor, and never known what ambition is. You cannot understand what a wonderful chance the Baron gave me. Such a chance as few men get.

LORD GORING: Fortunately for them, if one is to judge by results. But tell me definitely, how did the Baron finally persuade you to – well, to do what you did?

SIR ROBERT CHILTERN: When I was going away he said to me that if I ever could give him any private information of real value he would make me a very rich man. I was dazed at the prospect he held out to me, and my ambition and my desire for power at that time boundless. Six weeks later certain private documents passed through my hands.

LORD GORING (*keeping his eyes steadily fixed on the carpet*): State documents?

SIR ROBERT CHILTERN: Yes.

Lord Goring sighs, then passes his hand across his forehead and looks up.

LORD GORING: I had no idea that you, of all men in the world, could have been so weak, Robert, as to yield to such a temptation as Baron Arnheim held out to you.

SIR ROBERT CHILTERN: Weak? Oh, I am sick of hearing that phrase. Sick of using it about others. Weak! Do you really think, Arthur, that it is weakness that yields to temptation? I tell you that there are terrible temptations that it requires strength, strength and courage, to yield to. To stake all one's life on a single moment, to risk everything on one throw, whether the stake be power or pleasure, I care not – there is no weakness in that. There is a horrible, a terrible courage. I had that courage. I sat down the same afternoon and wrote Baron Arnheim the letter this woman now holds. He made three-quarters of a million over the transaction.

LORD GORING: And you?

SIR ROBERT CHILTERN: I received from the Baron £110,000.

LORD GORING: You were worth more, Robert.

SIR ROBERT CHILTERN: No; that money gave me exactly what I wanted, power over others. I went into the House immediately. The Baron advised me in finance from time to time. Before five years I had almost trebled my fortune. Since then everything that I have touched has turned out a success. In all things connected with money I have had a luck so extraordinary that sometimes it has made me almost afraid. I remember having read somewhere, in some strange book, that when the gods wish to punish us they answer our prayers.

LORD GORING: But tell me, Robert, did you never suffer any regret for what you had done?

SIR ROBERT CHILTERN: No. I felt that I had fought the century with its own weapons, and won.

LORD GORING (*sadly*): You thought you had won.

SIR ROBERT CHILTERN: I thought so. (*After a long pause*): Arthur, do you despise me for what I have told you?

LORD GORING (*with deep feeling in his voice*): I am very sorry for you, Robert, very sorry indeed.

SIR ROBERT CHILTERN: I don't say that I suffered any remorse. I didn't. Not remorse in the ordinary, rather silly sense of the word. But I have paid conscience money many times. I had a wild hope that I might disarm destiny. The sum Baron Arnheim gave me I have distributed twice over in public charities since then.

LORD GORING (*looking up*): In public charities? Dear me! what a lot of harm you must have done, Robert!

SIR ROBERT CHILTERN: Oh, don't say that, Arthur; don't talk like that!

LORD GORING: Never mind what I say, Robert! I am always saying what I shouldn't say. In fact, I usually say what I really think. A great mistake nowadays. It makes one so liable to be understood. As regards this dreadful business, I will help you in whatever way I can. Of course you know that.

SIR ROBERT CHILTERN: Thank you, Arthur, thank you. But what is to be done? What can be done?

LORD GORING (*leaning back with his hands in his pockets*): Well, the English can't stand a man who is always saying he is in the right, but they are very fond of a man who admits that he has been in the wrong. It is one of the best things in them. However, in your case, Robert, a confession would not do. The money, if you will allow me to say so, is . . . awkward. Besides, if you did make a clean breast of the whole affair, you would never be able to talk morality again. And in England a man who can't talk morality twice a week to a large, popular, immoral audience is quite over as a serious politician. There would be nothing left for him as a profession except Botany or the Church. A confession would be of no use. It would ruin you.

SIR ROBERT CHILTERN: It would ruin me. Arthur, the only thing for me to do now is to fight the thing out.

LORD GORING (*rising from his chair*): I was waiting for you to say that, Robert. It is the only thing to do now. And you must begin by telling your wife the whole story.

SIR ROBERT CHILTERN: That I will not do.

LORD GORING: Robert, believe me, you are wrong.

SIR ROBERT CHILTERN: I couldn't do it. It would kill her love for me. And now about this woman, this Mrs Cheveley. How can I defend myself against her? You knew her before, Arthur, apparently.

LORD GORING: Yes.

SIR ROBERT CHILTERN: Did you know her well?

LORD GORING (*arranging his necktie*): So little that I got engaged to be married to her once, when I was staying at the Tenbys'. The affair lasted for three days . . . nearly.

SIR ROBERT CHILTERN: Why was it broken off?

LORD GORING (*airily*): Oh, I forget. At least, it makes no matter. By the way, have you tried her with money? She used to be confoundedly fond of money.

SIR ROBERT CHILTERN: I offered her any sum she wanted. She refused.

LORD GORING: Then the marvellous gospel of gold breaks down sometimes. The rich can't do everything, after all.

SIR ROBERT CHILTERN: Not everything. I suppose you are right. Arthur, I feel that public disgrace is in store for me. I feel certain of it. I never knew what terror was before. I know it now. It is as if a hand of ice were laid upon one's heart. It is as if one's heart were beating itself to death in some empty hollow.

LORD GORING (*striking the table*): Robert, you must fight her. You must fight her.

SIR ROBERT CHILTERN: But how?

LORD GORING: I can't tell you how at present. I have not the smallest idea. But every one has some weak point. There is some flaw in each one of us. (*Strolls over to the fireplace and looks at himself in the glass.*) My father tells me that even I have faults. Perhaps I have. I don't know.

SIR ROBERT CHILTERN: In defending myself against Mrs Cheveley I have a right to use any weapon I can find, have I not?

LORD GORING (*still looking in the glass*): In your place I don't think I should have the smallest scruple in doing so. She is thoroughly well able to take care of herself.

SIR ROBERT CHILTERN (*sits down at the table and takes a pen in his hand*): Well, I shall send a cipher telegram to the Embassy at Vienna, to inquire if there is anything known against her. There may be some secret scandal she might be afraid of.

LORD GORING (*settling his buttonhole*): Oh, I should fancy Mrs. Cheveley is one of those very modern women of our time who find a new scandal as becoming as a new bonnet, and air them both in the Park every afternoon at five-thirty. I am sure she adores scandals, and that the sorrow of her life at present is that she can't manage to have enough of them.

SIR ROBERT CHILTERN (*writing*): Why do you say that?

LORD GORING (*turning round*): Well, she wore far too much rouge last night, and not quite enough clothes. That is always a sign of despair in a woman.

SIR ROBERT CHILTERN (*striking a bell*): But it is worth while my wiring to Vienna, is it not?

LORD GORING: It is always worth while asking a question, though it is not always worth while answering one.

Enter Mason.

SIR ROBERT CHILTERN: Is Mr Trafford in his room?

MASON: Yes, Sir Robert.

SIR ROBERT CHILTERN (*puts what he has written into an envelope, which he then carefully closes*): Tell him to have this sent off in cipher at once. There must not be a moment's delay.

MASON: Yes, Sir Robert.

SIR ROBERT CHILTERN: Oh! just give that back to me again.

Writes something on the envelope. Mason then goes out with the letter.

SIR ROBERT CHILTERN: She must have had some curious hold over Baron Arnheim. I wonder what it was.

LORD GORING (*smiling*): I wonder.

SIR ROBERT CHILTERN: I will fight her to the death, as long as my wife knows nothing.

LORD GORING (*strongly*): Oh, fight in any case – in any case.

SIR ROBERT CHILTERN (*with a gesture of despair*): If my wife found out, there would be little left to fight for. Well, as soon as I hear from Vienna,

I shall let you know the result. It is a chance, just a chance, but I believe in it. And as I fought the age with its own weapons, I will fight her with her weapons. It is only fair, and she looks like a woman with a past, doesn't she?

LORD GORING: Most pretty women do. But there is a fashion in pasts just as there is a fashion in frocks. Perhaps Mrs Cheveley's past is merely a slightly *décolleté* one, and they are excessively popular nowadays. Besides, my dear Robert, I should not build too high hopes of frightening Mrs Cheveley. I should not fancy Mrs Cheveley is a woman who would be easily frightened. She has survived all her creditors, and she shows wonderful presence of mind.

SIR ROBERT CHILTERN: Oh! I live on hopes now. I clutch at every chance. I feel like a man on a ship that is sinking. The water is round my feet, and the very air is bitter with storm. Hush! I hear my wife's voice.
Enter Lady Chiltern in walking dress.

LADY CHILTERN: Good-afternoon, Lord Goring.

LORD GORING: Good-afternoon, Lady Chiltern! Have you been in the Park?

LADY CHILTERN: No; I have just come from the Woman's Liberal Association, where, by the way, Robert, your name was received with loud applause, and now I have come in to have my tea. (*To* Lord Goring): You will wait and have some tea, won't you?

LORD GORING: I'll wait for a short time, thanks.

LADY CHILTERN: I will be back in a moment. I am only going to take my hat off.

LORD GORING (*in his most earnest manner*): Oh! please don't. It is so pretty. One of the prettiest hats I ever saw. I hope the Woman's Liberal Association received it with loud applause.

LADY CHILTERN (*with a smile*): We have much more important work to do than look at each other's bonnets, Lord Goring.

LORD GORING: Really? What sort of work?

LADY CHILTERN: Oh! dull, useful, delightful things, Factory Acts, Female Inspectors, the Eight Hours' Bill, the Parliamentary Franchise. . . . Everything, in fact, that you would find thoroughly uninteresting.

LORD GORING: And never bonnets?

LADY CHILTERN (*with mock indignation*): Never bonnets, never!
Lady Chiltern goes out through the door leading to her boudoir.

SIR ROBERT CHILTERN (*takes Lord Goring's hand*): You have been a good friend to me, Arthur, a thoroughly good friend.

LORD GORING: I don't know that I have been able to do much for you, Robert, as yet. In fact, I have not been able to do anything for you, as far as I can see. I am thoroughly disappointed with myself.

SIR ROBERT CHILTERN: You have enabled me to tell you the truth. That is something. The truth has always stifled me.

LORD GORING: Ah! the truth is a thing I get rid of as soon as possible! Bad habit, by the way. Makes one very unpopular at the club . . . with the older members. They call it being conceited. Perhaps it is.

SIR ROBERT CHILTERN: I would to God that I had been able to tell the

truth ... to live the truth. Ah! that is the great thing in life, to live
the truth. (*Sighs, and goes towards the door.*) I'll see you soon again,
Arthur, shan't I?

LORD GORING: Certainly. Whenever you like. I'm going to look in at the
Bachelors' Ball to-night, unless I find something better to do. But I'll
come round to-morrow morning. If you should want me to-night by
any chance, send round a note to Curzon Street.

SIR ROBERT CHILTERN: Thank you.

As he reaches the door, Lady Chiltern enters from her boudoir.

LADY CHILTERN: You are not going, Robert?

SIR ROBERT CHILTERN: I have some letters to write, dear.

LADY CHILTERN (*going to him*): You work too hard, Robert. You seem
never to think of yourself, and you are looking so tired.

SIR ROBERT CHILTERN: It is nothing, dear, nothing. (*He kisses her and goes
out.*)

LADY CHILTERN (*to* Lord Goring): Do sit down. I am so glad you have
called. I want to talk to you about ... well, not about bonnets, or the
Woman's Liberal Association. You take far too much interest in the
first subject, and not nearly enough in the second.

LORD GORING: You want to talk to me about Mrs Cheveley?

LADY CHILTERN: Yes. You have guessed it. After you left last night I
found out that what she had said was really true. Of course I made
Robert write her a letter at once, withdrawing his promise.

LORD GORING: So he gave me to understand.

LADY CHILTERN: To have kept it would have been the first stain on a
career that has been stainless always. Robert must be above reproach.
He is not like other men. He cannot afford to do what other men do.
(*She looks at Lord Goring, who remains silent.*) Don't you agree with me?
You are Robert's greatest friend. You are our greatest friend, Lord
Goring. No one, except myself, knows Robert better than you do.
He has no secrets from me, and I don't think he has any from you.

LORD GORING: He certainly has no secrets from me. At least I don't think
so.

LADY CHILTERN: Then am I not right in my estimate of him? I know I am
right. But speak to me frankly.

LORD GORING (*looking straight at her*): Quite frankly?

LADY CHILTERN: Surely. You have nothing to conceal, have you?

LORD GORING: Nothing. But, my dear Lady Chiltern, I think, if you will
allow me to say so, that in practical life—

LADY CHILTERN (*smiling*): Of which you know so little, Lord Goring—

LORD GORING: Of which I know nothing by experience, though I know
something by observation. I think that in practical life there is
something about success, actual success, that is a little unscrupulous,
something about ambition that is unscrupulous always. Once a man
has set his heart and soul on getting to a certain point, if he has to
climb the crag, he climbs the crag; if he has to walk in the mire—

LADY CHILTERN: Well?

LORD GORING: He walks in the mire. Of course I am only talking generally
about life.

LADY CHILTERN (*gravely*): I hope so. Why do you look at me so strangely, Lord Goring?

LORD GORING: Lady Chiltern, I have sometimes thought that . . . perhaps you are a little hard in some of your views on life. I think that . . . often you don't make sufficient allowances. In every nature there are elements of weakness, or worse than weakness. Supposing, for instance, that—that any public man, my father, or Lord Merton, or Robert, say, had, years ago, written some foolish letter some one. . . .

LADY CHILTERN: What do you mean by a foolish letter?

LORD GORING: A letter gravely compromising one's position. I am only putting an imaginary case.

LADY CHILTERN: Robert is as incapable of doing a foolish thing as he is of doing a wrong thing.

LORD GORING (*after a long pause*): Nobody is incapable of doing a foolish thing. Nobody is incapable of doing a wrong thing.

LADY CHILTERN: Are you a Pessimist? What will the other dandies say? They will all have to go into mourning.

LORD GORING (*rising*): No, Lady Chiltern, I am not a Pessimist. Indeed I am not sure that I quite know what pessimism really means. All I do know is that life cannot be understood without much charity, cannot be lived without much charity. It is love, and not German philosophy, that is the true explanation of this world, whatever may be the explanation of the next. And if you are ever in trouble, Lady Chiltern, trust me absolutely, and I will help you in every way I can. If you ever want me, come to me for my assistance, and you shall have it. Come at once to me.

LADY CHILTERN (*looking at him in surprise*): Lord Goring, you are talking quite seriously. I don't think I ever heard you talk seriously before.

LORD GORING (*laughing*): You must excuse me, Lady Chiltern. It won't occur again, if I can help it.

LADY CHILTERN: But I like you to be serious.

Enter Mabel Chiltern, in the most ravishing frock.

MABEL CHILTERN: Dear Gertrude, don't say such a dreadful thing to Lord Goring. Seriousness would be very unbecoming to him. Good-afternoon, Lord Goring! Pray be as trivial as you can.

LORD GORING: I should like to, Miss Mabel, but I am afraid I am . . . a little out of practice this morning; and besides, I have to be going now.

MABEL CHILTERN: Just when I have come in! What dreadful manners you have! I am sure you were very badly brought up.

LORD GORING: I was.

MABEL CHILTERN: I wish I had brought you up!

LORD GORING: I am so sorry you didn't.

MABEL CHILTERN: It is too late now, I suppose?

LORD GORING (*smiling*): I am not so sure.

MABEL CHILTERN: Will you ride to-morrow morning?

LORD GORING: Yes, at ten.

MABEL CHILTERN: Don't forget.

LORD GORING: Of course I shan't. By the way, Lady Chiltern, there is no list of your guests in *The Morning Post* of to-day. It has apparently been crowded out by the County Council, or the Lambeth Conference, or something equally boring. Could you let me have a list? I have a particular reason for asking you.

LADY CHILTERN: I am sure Mr Trafford will be able to give you one.

LORD GORING: Thanks, so much.

MABEL CHILTERN: Tommy is the most useful person in London.

LORD GORING (*turning to her*): And who is the most ornamental?

MABEL CHILTERN (*triumphantly*): I am.

LORD GORING: How clever of you to guess it! (*Takes up his hat and cane.*) Good-bye, Lady Chiltern! You will remember what I said to you, won't you?

LADY CHILTERN: Yes; but I don't know why you said it to me.

LORD GORING: I hardly know myself. Good-bye, Miss Mabel!

MABEL CHILTERN (*with a little moue of disappointment*): I wish you were not going. I have had four wonderful adventures this morning; four and a half, in fact. You might stop and listen to some of them.

LORD GORING: How very selfish of you to have four and a half! There won't be any left for me.

MABEL CHILTERN: I don't want you to have any. They would not be good for you.

LORD GORING: That is the first unkind thing you have ever said to me. How charmingly you said it! Ten to-morrow.

MABEL CHILTERN: Sharp.

LORD GORING: Quite sharp. But don't bring Mr Trafford.

MABEL CHILTERN (*with a little toss of her head*): Of course I shan't bring Tommy Trafford. Tommy Trafford is in great disgrace.

LORD GORING: I am delighted to hear it. (*Bows and goes out.*)

MABEL CHILTERN: Gertrude, I wish you would speak to Tommy Trafford.

LADY CHILTERN: What has poor Mr Trafford done this time? Robert says he is the best secretary he has ever had.

MABEL CHILTERN: Well, Tommy has proposed to me again. Tommy really does nothing but propose to me. He proposed to me last night in the Music-room, when I was quite unprotected, as there was an elaborate trio going on. I didn't dare to make the smallest repartee, I need hardly tell you. If I had, it would have stopped the music at once. Musical people are so absurdly unreasonable. They always want one to be perfectly dumb at the very moment when one is longing to be absolutely deaf. Then he proposed to me in broad daylight this morning, in front of that dreadful statue of Achilles. Really, the things that go on in front of that work of art are quite appalling. The police should interfere. At luncheon I saw by the glare in his eye that he was going to propose again, and I just managed to check him in time by assuring him that I was a bimetallist. Fortunately I don't know what bimetallism means. And I don't believe anybody else does either. But the observation crushed Tommy for ten minutes. He looked quite shocked. And then Tommy is so annoying in the way he proposes. If he proposed at the top of his voice, I should not mind so much. That might produce some effect on the public. But he does it in a horrid confidential way. When Tommy wants to be romantic he talks to one just like a doctor. I am very fond of Tommy, but his methods of proposing are quite out of date. I wish, Gertrude, you would speak to him, and tell him that once a week is quite often enough to propose to any one, and that it should always be done in a manner that attracts some attention.

LADY CHILTERN: Dear Mabel, don't talk like that. Besides, Robert thinks very highly of Mr Trafford. He believes he has a brilliant future before him.

MABEL CHILTERN: Oh! I wouldn't marry a man with a future before him for anything under the sun.

LADY CHILTERN: Mabel!

MABEL CHILTERN: I know, dear. You married a man with a future, didn't you! But then Robert was a genius, and you have a noble, self-sacrificing character. You can stand geniuses. I have no character at all, and Robert is the only genius I could ever bear. As a rule, I think they are quite impossible. Geniuses talk so much, don't they? Such a bad habit! And they are always thinking about themselves, when I want them to be thinking about me. I must go round now and rehearse at Lady Basildon's. You remember, we are having tableaux, don't you? The Triumph of something. I don't know what! I hope it will be triumph of me. Only triumph I am really interested in at present. (*Kisses Lady Chiltern and goes out; then comes running back.*) Oh, Gertrude, do you know who is coming to see you? That dreadful Mrs Cheveley, in a most lovely gown. Did you ask her?

LADY CHILTERN (*rising*): Mrs Cheveley! Coming to see me? Impossible!

MABEL CHILTERN: I assure you she is coming upstairs, as large as life and not nearly so natural.

LADY CHILTERN: You need not wait, Mabel. Remember, Lady Basildon is expecting you.

MABEL CHILTERN: Oh! I must shake hands with Lady Markby. She is delightful. I love being scolded by her.

Enter Mason

MASON: Lady Markby. Mrs Cheveley.

Enter Lady Markby and Mrs Cheveley.

LADY CHILTERN (*advancing to meet them*): Dear Lady Markby, how nice of you to come and see me! (*Shakes hands with her, and bows somewhat distantly to Mrs Cheveley.*) Won't you sit down, Mrs Cheveley?

MRS CHEVELEY: Thanks. Isn't that Miss Chiltern? I should like so much to know her.

LADY CHILTERN: Mabel, Mrs Cheveley wishes to know you. (*Mabel Chiltern gives a little nod.*)

MRS CHEVELEY (*sitting down*): I thought your frock so charming, last night, Miss Chiltern So simple and . . . suitable.

MABEL CHILTERN: Really? I must tell my dressmaker. It will be such a surprise to her. Good-bye, Lady Markby!

LADY MARKBY: Going already?

MABEL CHILTERN: I am so sorry but I am obliged to. I am just off to rehearsal. I have got to stand on my head in some tableaux.

LADY MARKBY: On your head, child? Oh! I hope not. I believe it is most unhealthy. (*Takes a seat on the sofa next Lady Chiltern.*)

MABEL CHILTERN: But it is for an excellent charity; in aid of the Undeserving, the only people I am really interested in. I am the secretary, and Tommy Trafford is treasurer.

MRS CHEVELEY: And what is Lord Goring?

MABEL CHILTERN: Oh! Lord Goring is president.

MRS CHEVELEY: The post should suit him admirably, unless he has deteriorated since I knew him first.

LADY MARKBY (*reflecting*): You are remarkably modern, Mabel. A little too modern, perhaps. Nothing is so dangerous as being too modern. One is apt to grow old-fashioned quite suddenly. I have known many instances of it.

MABEL CHILTERN: What a dreadful prospect!

LADY MARKBY: Ah! my dear, you need not be nervous. You will always be as pretty as possible. That is the best fashion there is, and the only fashion that England succeeds in setting.

MABEL CHILTERN (*with a curtsey*): Thank you so much, Lady Markby, for England . . . and myself. (*Goes out.*)

LADY MARKBY (*turning to Lady Chiltern*): Dear Gertrude, we just called to know if Mrs Cheveley's diamond brooch has been found.

LADY CHILTERN: Here?

MRS CHEVELEY: Yes. I missed it when I got back to Claridge's, and I thought I might possibly have dropped it here.

LADY CHILTERN: I have heard nothing about it. But I will send for the butler and ask. (*Touches the bell.*)

MRS CHEVELEY: Oh, pray don't trouble, Lady Chiltern. I dare say I lost it at the Opera, before we came on here.

LADY MARKBY: Ah yes, I suppose it must have been at the Opera. The fact is, we all scramble and jostle so much nowadays that I wonder we have anything at all left on us at the end of an evening. I know myself that, when I am coming back from the Drawing-room, I always feel as if I hadn't a shred on me, except a small shred of decent reputation, just enough to prevent the lower classes making painful observations through the windows of the carriage. The fact is that our Society is terribly over-populated. Really, some one should arrange a proper scheme of assisted emigration. It would do a great deal of good.

MRS CHEVELEY: I quite agree with you, Lady Markby. It is nearly six years since I have been in London for the Season, and I must say Society has become dreadfully mixed. One sees the oddest people everywhere.

LADY MARKBY: That is quite true, dear. But one needn't know them. I'm sure I don't know half the people who come to my house. Indeed, from all I hear, I shouldn't like to.

Enter Mason.

LADY CHILTERN: What sort of brooch was it that you lost, Mrs Cheveley?

MRS CHEVELEY: A diamond snake brooch with a ruby, a rather large ruby.

LADY MARKBY: I thought you said there was a sapphire on the head, dear?

MRS CHEVELEY (*smiling*): No. Lady Markby – a ruby.

LADY MARKBY (*nodding her head*): And very becoming, I am quite sure.

LADY CHILTERN: Has a ruby and diamond brooch been found in any of the rooms this morning, Mason?

MASON: No, my lady.

MRS CHEVELEY: It really is of no consequence, Lady Chiltern. I am so sorry to have put you to any inconvenience.

LADY CHILTERN (*coldly*): Oh, it has been no inconvenience. That will do, Mason. You can bring tea. (*Exit Mason.*)

LADY MARKBY: Well, I must say it is most annoying to lose anything. I remember once at Bath, years ago, losing in the Pump Room an exceedingly handsome cameo bracelet that Sir John had given me. I don't think he has ever given me anything since, I am sorry to say. He has sadly degenerated. Really, this horrid House of Commons quite ruins our husbands for us. I think the Lower House by far the greatest blow to a happy married life that there has been since that terrible thing called the Higher Education of Women was invented.

LADY CHILTERN: Ah! It is heresy to say that in this house, Lady Markby. Robert is a great champion of the Higher Education of Woman, and so, I am afraid, am I.

MRS CHEVELEY: The higher education of men is what I should like to see. Men need it so sadly.

LADY MARKBY: They do, dear. But I am afraid such a scheme would be quite unpractical. I don't think man has much capacity for development. He has got as far as he can, and that is not far, is it? With regard to women, well, dear Gertrude, you belong to the younger generation, and I am sure it is all right if you approve of it. In my time, of course, we were taught not to understand anything. That was the old system, and wonderfully interesting it was. I assure you that the amount of things I and my poor dear sister were taught not to understand was quite extraordinary. But modern women understand everything, I am told.

MRS CHEVELEY: Except their husbands. That is the one thing the modern woman never understands.

LADY MARKBY: And a very good thing too, dear, I dare say. It might break up many a happy home if they did. Not yours, I need hardly say, Gertrude. You have married a pattern husband. I wish I could say as much for myself. But since Sir John has taken to attending the debates regularly, which he never used to do in the good old days, his language has become quite impossible. He always seems to think that he is addressing the House, and consequently whenever he discusses the state of the agricultural labourer, or the Welsh Church, or something quite improper of that kind, I am obliged to send all the servants out of the room. It is not pleasant to see one's own butler, who has been with one for twenty-three years, actually blushing at the sideboard, and the footmen making contortions in corners like persons in circuses. I assure you my life will be quite ruined unless they send John at once to the Upper House. He won't take any interest in politics then, will he? The House of Lords is so sensible. An assembly of gentlemen. But in his present state, Sir John is really a great trial. Why, this morning before breakfast was half over, he stood up on the hearth-rug, put his hands in his pockets, and appealed to the country at the top of his voice. I left the table as soon as I had my second cup of tea, I need.hardly say. But his violent language could be heard all over the house! I trust, Gertrude, that Sir Robert is not like that?

LADY CHILTERN: But I am very much interested in politics, Lady Markby. I love to hear Robert talk about them.

LADY MARKBY: Well, I hope he is not as devoted to Blue Books as Sir John is. I don't think they can be quite improving reading for any one.

MRS CHEVELEY (*languidly*): I have never read a Blue Book. I prefer books . . . in yellow covers.

LADY MARKBY (*genially unconscious*): Yellow is a gayer colour, is it not? I used to wear yellow a good deal in my early days, and would do so now if Sir John was not so painfully personal in his observations, and a man on the question of dress is always ridiculous, is he not?

MRS CHEVELEY: Oh, no! I think men are the only authorities on dress.

LADY MARKBY: Really? One wouldn't way so from the sort of hats they wear? Would one?

The butler enters, followed by the footman. Tea is set on a small table close to Lady Chiltern.

LADY CHILTERN: May I give you some tea, Mrs Cheveley?

MRS CHEVELEY: Thanks. (*The butler hands Mrs Cheveley a cup of tea on a salver.*)

LADY CHILTERN: Some tea, Lady Markby?

LADY MARKBY: No thanks, dear. (*The servants go out.*) The fact is, I have promised to go round for ten minutes to see poor Lady Brancaster, who is in very great trouble. Her daughter, quite a well-brought-up girl, too, has actually become engaged to be married to a curate in Shropshire. It is very sad, very sad indeed. I can't understand this modern mania for curates. In my time we girls saw them, of course, running about the place like rabbits. But we never took any notice of them, I need hardly say. But I am told that nowadays country society is quite honeycombed with them. I think it most irreligious. And then the eldest son has quarrelled with his father, and it is said that when they meet at the club Lord Brancaster always hides himself behind the money article in *The Times*. However, I believe that is quite a common occurrence nowadays and that they have to take in extra copies of *The Times* at all the clubs in St James's Street; there are so many sons who won't have anything to do with their fathers, and so many fathers who won't speak to their sons. I think myself, it is very much to be regretted.

MRS CHEVELEY: So do I. Fathers have so much to learn from their sons nowadays.

LADY MARKBY: Really, dear? What?

MRS CHEVELEY: The art of living. The only really Fine Art we have produced in modern times.

LADY MARKBY (*shaking her head*): Ah! I am afraid Lord Brancaster knew a good deal about that. More than his poor wife ever did. (*Turning to Lady Chiltern*): You know Lady Brancaster, don't you, dear?

LADY CHILTERN: Just slightly. She was staying at Langton last autumn, when we were there.

LADY MARKBY: Well, like all stout women, she looks the very picture of happiness, as no doubt you noticed. But there are many tragedies in her family, besides this affair of the curate. Her own sister, Mrs Jekyll, had a most unhappy life; through no fault of her own, I am sorry to say. She ultimately was so broken-hearted that she went into a convent, or on to the operatic stage, I forget which. No; I think it was decorative art-needlework she took up. I know she had lost all sense of pleasure in life. (*Rising*): And now, Gertrude, if you will allow me, I shall leave Mrs Cheveley in your charge and call back for her in a quarter of an hour. Or perhaps, dear Mrs Cheveley, you wouldn't mind waiting in the carriage while I am with Lady Brancaster. As I intend it to be a visit of condolence, I shan't stay long.

MRS CHEVELEY (*rising*): I don't mind waiting in the carriage at all, provided there is somebody to look at one.

LADY MARKBY: Well, I hear the curate is always prowling about the house.

MRS CHEVELEY: I am afraid I am not fond of girl friends.

LADY CHILTERN (*rising*): Oh, I hope Mrs Cheveley will stay here a little. I should like to have a few minutes' conversation with her.

MRS CHEVELEY: How very kind of you, Lady Chiltern! Believe me, nothing would give me greater pleasure.

LADY MARKBY: Ah, no doubt you both have many pleasant reminiscenses of your schooldays to talk over together. Good-bye, dear Gertrude! Shall I see you at Lady Bonar's to-night? She has discovered a wonderful new genius. He does . . . nothing at all, I believe. That is a great comfort, is it not?

LADY CHILTERN: Robert and I are dining at home by ourselves to-night, and I don't think I shall go anywhere afterwards. Robert, of course, will have to be in the House. But there is nothing interesting on.

LADY MARKBY: Dining at home by yourselves? Is that quite prudent? Ah, I forgot, your husband is an exception. Mine is the general rule, and nothing ages a woman so rapidly as having married the general rule. *Exit Lady Markby.*

MRS CHEVELEY: Wonderful woman, Lady Markby, isn't she? Talks more and says less than anybody I ever met. She is made to be a public speaker. Much more so than her husband, though he is a typical Englishman, always dull and usually violent.

LADY CHILTERN (*makes no answer, but remains standing. There is a pause. Then the eyes of the two women meet. Lady Chiltern looks stern and pale. Mrs Cheveley seems rather amused*): Mrs Cheveley, I think it is right to tell you quite frankly that, had I known who you really were, I should not have invited you to my house last night.

MRS CHEVELEY (*with an impertinent smile*): Really?

LADY CHILTERN: I could not have done so.

MRS CHEVELEY: I see that after all these years you have not changed a bit, Gertrude.

LADY CHILTERN: I never change.

MRS CHEVELEY (*elevating her eyebrows*): Then life has taught you nothing?

LADY CHILTERN: It has taught me that a person who has once been guilty of a dishonest and dishonourable action may be guilty of it a second time, and should be shunned.

MRS CHEVELEY: Would you apply that rule to every one?

LADY CHILTERN: Yes, to every one, without exception.

MRS CHEVELEY: Then I am sorry for you, Gertrude, very sorry for you.

LADY CHILTERN: You see now, I am sure, that for many reasons any further acquaintance between us during your stay in London is quite impossible?

MRS CHEVELEY (*leaning back in her chair*): Do you know, Gertrude, I don't mind your talking morality a bit. Morality is simply the attitude we adopt towards people whom we personally dislike. You dislike me. I am quite aware of that. And I have always detested you. And yet I have come here to do you a service.

LADY CHILTERN (*contemptuously*): Like the service you wished to render my husband last night, I suppose. Thank heaven, I saved him from that.

MRS CHEVELEY (*starting to her feet*): It was you who made him write that insolent letter to me? It was you who made him break his promise?

LADY CHILTERN: Yes.

MRS CHEVELEY: Then you must make him keep it. I give you till to-morrow morning – no more. If by that time your husband does not solemnly bind himself to help me in this great scheme in which I am interested—

LADY CHILTERN: This fraudulent speculation—

MRS CHEVELEY: Call it what you choose. I hold your husband in the hollow of my hand, and if you are wise you will make him do what I tell him.

LADY CHILTERN (*rising and going towards her*): You are impertinent. What has my husband to do with you? With a woman like you?

MRS CHEVELEY (*with a bitter laugh*): In this world like meets with like. It is because your husband is himself fraudulent and dishonest that we pair so well together. Between you and him there are chasms. He and I are closer than friends. We are enemies linked together. The same sin binds us.

LADY CHILTERN: How dare you class my husband with yourself? How dare you threaten him or me? Leave my house. You are unfit to enter it. *Sir Robert Chiltern enters from behind. He hears his wife's last words, and sees to whom they are addressed. He grows deadly pale.*

MRS CHEVELEY: Your house! A house bought with the price of dishonour. A house, everything in which has been paid for by fraud. (*Turns round and sees Sir Robert Chiltern.*) Ask him what the origin of his fortune is! Get him to tell you how he sold to a stockbroker a Cabinet secret. Learn from him to what you owe your position.

LADY CHILTERN: It is not true! Robert! It is not true!

MRS CHEVELEY (*pointing at him with outstretched finger*): Look at him! Can he deny it! Does he dare to?

SIR ROBERT CHILTERN: Go! Go at once. You have done your worst now.

MRS CHEVELEY: My worst? I have not yet finished with you, with either of you. I give you both till to-morrow at noon. If by then you don't do what I bid you to do, the whole world shall know the origin of Robert Chiltern.

Sir Robert Chiltern strikes the bell. Enter Mason.

SIR ROBERT CHILTERN: Show Mrs Cheveley out.

Mrs Cheveley starts; then bows with somewhat exaggerated politeness to Lady Chiltern, who makes no sign of response. As she passes by Sir Robert Chiltern, who is standing close to the door, she pauses for a moment and looks him straight in the face. She then goes out, followed by the servant, who closes the door after him. The husband and wife are left alone. Lady Chiltern stands like some one in a dreadful dream. Then she turns round and looks at her husband. She looks at him with strange eyes, as though she was seeing him for the first time.

LADY CHILTERN: You sold a Cabinet secret for money! You began your life with fraud! You built up your career on dishonour! Oh, tell me it is not true! Lie to me! Lie to me! Tell me it is not true.

SIR ROBERT CHILTERN: What this woman said is quite true. But, Gertrude, listen to me. You don't realise how I was tempted. Let me tell you the whole thing. (*Goes towards her.*)

LADY CHILTERN: Don't come near me. Don't touch me. I feel as if you had soiled me for ever. Oh! what a mask you have been wearing all these years! A horrible painted mask! You sold yourself for money. Oh! a common thief were better. You put yourself up to sale to the highest bidder! You were bought in the market. You lied to the whole world. And yet you will not lie to me.

SIR ROBERT CHILTERN (*rushing towards her*): Gertrude! Gertrude!

LADY CHILTERN (*thrusting him back with outstretched hands*): No, don't speak! Say nothing! Your voice wakes terrible memories – memories of things that made me love you – memories of words that made me love you – memories that now are horrible to me. And how I worshipped you! You were to me something apart from common life, a thing pure, noble, honest, without stain. The world seemed to me finer because you were in it, and goodness more real because you lived. And now – oh, when I think that I made of a man like you my ideal! the ideal of my life!

SIR ROBERT CHILTERN: There was your mistake. There was your error. The error all women commit. Why can't you women love us, faults and all? Why do you place us on monstrous pedestals? We have all feet of clay, women as well as men; but when we men love women, we love them knowing their weaknesses, their follies, their imperfections, love them all the more, it may be, for that reason. It is not the perfect, but the imperfect, who have need of love. It is when we are wounded by our own hands, or by the hands of others, that love should come to cure us – else what use is love at all? All sins, except a sin against itself, Love should forgive. All lives, save loveless lives, true Love should pardon. A man's love is like that. It is wider, larger, more human than a woman's. Women think that they are making ideals of men. What they are making of us are false idols merely. You made your false idol of me, and I had not the courage to come down, show you my wounds, tell you my weaknesses. I was afraid that I might lose your love, as I have lost it now. And so, last night you ruined my life for me – yes, ruined it! What this woman asked of me was nothing compared to what she offered to me. She offered security, peace, stability. The sin of my youth, that I had thought was buried, rose up in front of me, hideous, horrible, with its hands at my throat. I could have killed it for ever, sent it back into its tomb, destroyed its record, burned the one witness against me. You prevented me. No one but you, you know it. And now what is there before me but public disgrace, ruin, terrible shame, the mockery of the world, a lonely dishonoured life, a lonely dishonoured death, it may be, some day? Let women make no more ideals of men! let them not put them on altars and bow before them or they may ruin other lives as completely as you – you whom I have so wildly loved – have ruined mine!

He passes from the room. Lady Chiltern rushes towards him, but the door is closed when she reaches it. Pale with anguish, bewildered, helpless, she sways like a plant in the water. Her hands, outstretched, seem to tremble in the air like blossoms in the wind. Then she flings herself down beside a sofa and buries her face. Her sobs are like the sobs of a child.

ACT THREE

Scene: The Library in Lord Goring's house in Curzon Street. An Adam room. On the right is the door leading into the Hall. On the left, the door of the Smoking-room. A pair of folding doors at the back open into the Drawing-room. The fire is lit. Phipps, the butler, is arranging some newspapers on the writing-table. The distinction of Phipps is his impassivity. He has been termed by enthusiasts the Ideal Butler. The Sphinx is not so incommunicable. He is a mask with a manner. Of his intellectual or emotional life, history knows nothing. He represents the dominance of form.

Enter Lord Goring in evening dress with a buttonhole. He is wearing a silk hat and Inverness cape. White-gloved, he carries a Louis Seize cane. His are all the delicate fopperies of Fashion. One sees that he stands in immediate relation to modern life, makes it indeed, and so masters it. He is the first well-dressed philosopher in the history of thought.

LORD GORING: Got my second buttonhole for me, Phipps?
PHIPPS: Yes, my lord. (*Takes his hat, cane, and cape, and presents new buttonhole on salver.*)

LORD GORING: Rather distinguished thing, Phipps. I am the only person of the smallest importance in London at present who wears a buttonhole.

PHIPPS: Yes, my lord. I have observed that.

LORD GORING (*taking out old buttonhole*): You see, Phipps, Fashion is what one wears oneself. What is unfashionable is what other people wear.

PHIPPS: Yes, my lord.

LORD GORING: Just as vulgarity is simply the conduct of other people.

PHIPPS: Yes, my lord.

LORD GORING (*putting in new buttonhole*): And falsehoods the truths of other people.

PHIPPS: Yes, my lord.

LORD GORING: Other people are quite dreadful. The only possible society is oneself.

PHIPPS: Yes, my lord.

LORD GORING: To love oneself is the beginning of a lifelong romance, Phipps.

PHIPPS: Yes, my lord.

LORD GORING (*looking at himself in the glass*): Don't think I quite like this buttonhole, Phipps. Makes me look a little too old. Makes me almost in the prime of life, eh, Phipps?

PHIPPS: I don't observe any alteration in your lordship's appearance.

LORD GORING: You don't, Phipps?

PHIPPS: No, my lord.

LORD GORING: I am not quite sure. For the future a more trivial buttonhole, Phipps, on Thursday evenings.

PHIPPS: I will speak to the florist, my lord. She has had a loss in her family lately, which perhaps accounts for the lack of triviality your lordship complains of in the buttonhole.

LORD GORING: Extraordinary thing about the lower classes in England – they are always losing their relations.

PHIPPS: Yes, my lord! They are extremely fortunate in that respect.

LORD GORING (*turns round and looks at him. Phipps remains impassive*): Hum! Any letter, Phipps?

PHIPPS: Three, my lord. (*Hands letters on a salver.*)

LORD GORING (*takes letters*): Want my cab round in twenty minutes.

PHIPPS: Yes, my lord. (*Goes towards door.*)

LORD GORING (*holds up letter in pink envelope*): Ahem, Phipps, when did this letter arrive?

PHIPPS: It was brought by hand just after your lordship went to the club.

LORD GORING: That will do. (*Exit Phipps.*) Lady Chiltern's handwriting on Lady Chiltern's pink notepaper. That is rather curious. I thought Robert was to write. Wonder what Lady Chiltern has got to say to me? (*Sits at bureau and opens letter, and reads it.*) 'I want you, I trust you. I am coming to you. Gertrude.' (*Puts down the letter with a puzzled look. Then takes it up, and reads it again slowly.*) 'I want you. I trust you. I am coming to you.' She has found out everything! Poor woman! Poor woman! (*Pulls out watch and looks at it.*) But what an hour to call! Ten o'clock! I shall have to give up going to the Berkshires. However,

it is always nice to be expected, and not to arrive. I am not expected at the Bachelors', so I shall certainly go there. Well, I will make her stand by her husband. That is the only thing for any woman to do. It is the growth of the moral sense of women that makes marriage such a hopeless, one-sided institution. Ten o'clock. She should be here soon. I must tell Phipps I am not in to any one else. (*Goes towards the bell.*)
Enter Phipps.

PHIPPS: Lord Caversham.

LORD GORING: Oh, why will parents always appear at the wrong time? Some extraordinary mistake in nature, I suppose. (*Enter Lord Caversham.*) Delighted to see you, my dear father. (*Goes to meet him.*)

LORD CAVERSHAM: Take my cloak off.

LORD GORING: Is it worth while, father?

LORD CAVERSHAM: Of course it is worth while, sir. Which is the most comfortable chair?

LORD GORING: This one, father. It is the chair I use myself, when I have visitors.

LORD CAVERSHAM: Thank ye. No draught, I hope, in this room?

LORD GORING: No, father.

LORD CAVERSHAM (*sitting down*): Glad to hear it. Can't stand draughts. No draughts at home.

LORD GORING: Good many breezes, father.

LORD CAVERSHAM: Eh? Eh? Don't understand what you mean. Want to have a serious conversation with you, sir.

LORD GORING: My dear father! At this hour?

LORD CAVERSHAM: Well, sir, it is only ten o'clock. What is your objection to the hour? I think the hour is an admirable hour!

LORD GORING: Well, the fact is, father, this is not my day for talking seriously. I am very sorry, but it is not my day.

LORD CAVERSHAM: What do you mean, sir?

LORD GORING: During the Season, father, I only talk seriously on the first Tuesday in every month, from four to seven.

LORD CAVERSHAM: Well, make it Tuesday, sir, make it Tuesday.

LORD GORING: But it is after seven, father, and my doctor says I must not have any serious conversation after seven. It makes me talk in my sleep.

LORD CAVERSHAM: Talk in your sleep, sir? What does that matter? You are not married.

LORD GORING: No, father, I am not married.

LORD CAVERSHAM: Hum! That is what I have come to talk to you about, sir. You have got to get married, and at once. Why, when I was your age, sir, I had been an inconsolable widower for three months, and was already paying my addresses to your admirable mother. Damme, sir, it is your duty to get married. You can't be always living for pleasure. Every man of position is married nowadays. Bachelors are not fashionable any more. They are a damaged lot. Too much is known about them. You must get a wife, sir. Look where your friend

Robert Chiltern has got to by probity, hard work, and a sensible marriage with a good woman. Why don't you imitate him, sir? Why don't you take him for your model?

LORD GORING: I think I shall, father.

LORD CAVERSHAM: I wish you would, sir. Then I should be happy. At present I make your mother's life miserable on your account. You are heartless, sir, quite heartless.

LORD GORING: I hope not, father.

LORD CAVERSHAM: And it is high time for you to get married. You are thirty-four years of age, sir.

LORD GORING: Yes, father, but I only admit to thirty-two – thirty-one and a half when I have a really good buttonhole. This buttonhole is not . . . trivial enough.

LORD CAVERSHAM: I tell you you are thirty-four, sir. And there is a draught in your room, besides, which makes your conduct worse. Why did you tell me there was no draught, sir? I feel a draught, sir, I feel it distinctly.

LORD GORING: So do I, father. It is a dreadful draught. I will come and see you to-morrow, father. We can talk over anything you like. Let me help you on with your cloak, father.

LORD CAVERSHAM: No sir; I have called this evening for a definite purpose, and I am going to see it through at all costs to my health or yours. Put down my cloak, sir.

LORD GORING: Certainly, father. But let us go into another room. (*Rings bell.*) There is a dreadful draught here. (*Enter Phipps.*) Phipps, is there a good fire in the Smoking-room?

PHIPPS: Yes my Lord.

LORD GORING: Come in there, father. Your sneezes are quite heartrending.

LORD CAVERSHAM: Well, sir, I suppose I have a right to sneeze when I choose?

LORD GORING (*apologetically*): Quite so, father. I was merely expressing sympathy.

LORD CAVERSHAM: Oh, damn sympathy. There is a great deal too much of that sort of thing going on nowadays.

LORD GORING: I quite agree with you, father. If there was less sympathy in the world there would be less trouble in the world.

LORD CAVERSHAM (*going towards the Smoking-room*): That is a paradox, sir. I hate paradoxes.

LORD GORING: So do I, father. Everybody one meets is a paradox nowadays. It is a great bore. It makes society so obvious.

LORD CAVERSHAM (*turning round, and looking at his son beneath his bushy eyebrows*): Do you always really understand what you say, sir?

LORD GORING (*after some hesitation*): Yes, father, if I listen attentively.

LORD CAVERSHAM (*indignantly*): If you listen attentively! . . . Conceited young puppy!

Goes off grumbling into the Smoking-room. Phipps enters.

LORD GORING: Phipps, there is a lady coming to see me this evening on particular business. Show her into the Drawing-room when she arrives. You understand?

PHIPPS: Yes, my lord.

LORD GORING: It is a matter of the gravest importance, Phipps.

PHIPPS: I understand, my lord.

LORD GORING: No one else is to be admitted, under any circumstances.

PHIPPS: I understand, my lord. (*Bell rings.*)

LORD GORING: Ah! that is probably the lady. I shall see her myself.

Just as he is going towards the door Lord Caversham enters from the Smoking-room.

LORD CAVERSHAM: Well, sir? am I to wait attendance on you?

LORD GORING (*considerably perplexed*): In a moment, father. Do excuse me. (*Lord Caversham goes back.*) Well, remember my instructions, Phipps – into that room.

PHIPPS: Yes, my lord.

Lord Goring goes into the Smoking-room. Harold, the footman, shows Mrs Cheveley in. Lamia-like, she is in green and silver. She has a cloak of black satin, lined with dead rose-leaf silk.

HAROLD: What name, madam?

MRS CHEVELEY (*to Phipps, who advances towards her*): Is Lord Goring not here? I was told he was at home?

PHIPPS: His lordship is engaged at present with Lord Caversham, madam.

Turns a cold, glassy eye on Harold, who at once retires.

MRS CHEVELEY (*to herself*): How very filial!

PHIPPS: His lordship told me to ask you, madam, to be kind enough to wait in the Drawing-room for him. His lordship will come to you there.

MRS CHEVELEY (*with a look of surprise*): Lord Goring expects me?

PHIPPS: Yes, madam.

MRS CHEVELEY: Are you quite sure?

PHIPPS: His lordship told me that if a lady called I was to ask her to wait in the Drawing-room (*Goes to the door of the Drawing-room and opens it.*) His lordship's directions on the subject were very precise.

MRS CHEVELEY (*to herself*): How thoughtful of him! To expect the unexpected shows a thoroughly modern intellect. (*Goes towards the Drawing-room and looks in.*) Ugh! How dreary a bachelor's Drawing-room always looks. I shall have to alter this. (*Phipps brings the lamp from the writing table.*) No, I don't care for that lamp. It is far too glaring. Light some candles.

PHIPPS (*replaces lamp*): Certainly, madam.

MRS CHEVELEY: I hope the candles have very becoming shades.

PHIPPS: We have had no complaints about them, madam, as yet.

Passes into the Drawing-room and begins to light the candles.

MRS CHEVELEY (*to herself*): I wonder what woman he is waiting for to-night. It will be delightful to catch him. Men always look so silly when they are caught. And they are always being caught. (*Looks about room and approaches the writing-table.*) What a very interesting room! What a very interesting picture. Wonder what his correspondence is like.

(*Takes up letters.*) Oh, what a very uninteresting correspondence! Bills and cards, debts and dowagers! Who on earth writes to him on pink paper? How silly to write on pink paper! It looks like the beginning of a middle-class romance. Romance should never begin with senti-ment. It should begin with science and end with a settlement. (*Puts letter down, then takes it up again.*) I know that handwriting. That is Gertrude Chiltern's. I remember it perfectly. The ten commandments in every stroke of the pen, and the moral law all over the page. Wonder what Gertrude is writing to him about? Something horrid about me, I suppose. How I detest that woman! (*Reads it.*) 'I trust you. I want you. I am coming to you. Gertrude.' 'I trust you. I want you. I am coming to you.'

A look of triumph comes over her face. She is just about to steal the letter, when Phipps comes in.

PHIPPS: The candles in the Drawing-room are lit, madam, as you directed.

MRS CHEVELEY: Thank you. (*Rises hastily and slips the letter under a large silver-cased blotting-book that is lying on the table.*)

PHIPPS: I trust the shades will be to your liking, madam. They are the most becoming we have. They are the same as his lordship uses himself when he is dressing for dinner.

MRS CHEVELEY (*with a smile*): Then I am sure they will be perfectly right.

PHIPPS (*gravely*): Thank you, madam.

Mrs Cheveley goes into the Drawing-room. Phipps closes the door and retires. The door is then slowly opened, and Mrs Cheveley comes out and creeps stealthily towards the writing-table. Suddenly voices are heard from the Smoking-room. Mrs Cheveley grows pale, and stops. The voices grow louder, and she goes back into the Drawing room, biting her lip.

Enter Lord Goring and Lord Caversham.

LORD GORING (*expostulating*): My dear father, if I am to get married, surely you will allow me to choose the time, place and person? Particularly the person.

LORD CAVERSHAM (*testily*): That is a matter for me, sir. You would probably make a very poor choice. It is I who should be consulted, not you. There is property at stake. It is not a matter for affection. Affection comes later on in married life.

LORD GORING: Yes. In married life affection comes when people thoroughly dislike each other, father, doesn't it? (*Puts on Lord Caver-sham's cloak for him.*)

LORD CAVERSHAM: Certainly, sir. I mean certainly not, sir. You are talking very foolishly to-night. What I say is that marriage is a matter for common sense.

LORD GORING: But women who have common sense are so curiously plain, father, aren't they? Of course I only speak from hearsay.

LORD CAVERSHAM: No woman, plain or pretty, has any common sense at all, sir. Common sense is the privilege of our sex.

LORD GORING: Quite so. And we men are so self-sacrificing that we never use it, do we, father?

LORD CAVERSHAM: I use it, sir. I use nothing else.

LORD GORING: So my mother tells me.

LORD CAVERSHAM: It is the secret of your mother's happiness. You are very heartless, sir, very heartless.

LORD GORING: I hope not, father.

Goes out for a moment. then returns, looking put out, with Sir Robert Chiltern.

SIR ROBERT CHILTERN: My dear Arthur, what a piece of good luck meeting you on the doorstep! Your servant had just told me you were not at home. How extraordinary!

LORD GORING: The fact is, I am horribly busy to-night, Robert, and I gave orders I was not at home to any one. Even my father had a comparatively cold reception. He complained of a draught the whole time.

SIR ROBERT CHILTERN: Ah! you must be at home to me, Arthur. You are my best friend. Perhaps by to-morrow you will be my only friend. My wife has discovered everything.

LORD GORING: Ah! I guessed as much!

SIR ROBERT CHILTERN (*looking at him*): Really! How!

LORD GORING (*after some hesitation*): Oh, merely by something in the expression of your face as you came in. Who told her?

SIR ROBERT CHILTERN: Mrs Cheveley herself. And the woman I love knows that I began my career with an act of low dishonesty, that I built up my life upon sands of shame – that I sold, like a common huckster, the secret that had been intrusted to me as a man of honour. I thank heaven poor Lord Radley died without knowing that I betrayed him. I would to God I had died before I had been so horribly tempted, or had fallen so low. (*Burying his face in his hands.*)

LORD GORING (*after a pause*): You have heard nothing from Vienna yet, in answer to your wire?

SIR ROBERT CHILTERN (*looking up*): Yes; I got a telegram from the first secretary at eight o'clock to-night.

LORD GORING: Well?

SIR ROBERT CHILTERN: Nothing is absolutely known against her. On the contrary, she occupies a rather high position in society. It is a sort of open secret that Baron Arnheim left her the greater portion of his immense fortune. Beyond that I can learn nothing.

LORD GORING: She doesn't turn out to be a spy, then?

SIR ROBERT CHILTERN: Oh! spies are of no use nowadays. Their profession is over. The newspapers do their work instead.

LORD GORING: And thunderingly well they do it.

SIR ROBERT CHILTERN: Arthur, I am parched with thirst. May I ring for something? Some hock and seltzer?

LORD GORING: Certainly. Let me. (*Rings the bell.*)

SIR ROBERT CHILTERN: Thanks! I don't know what to do, Arthur, I don't know what to do, and you are my only friend. But what a friend you are – the one friend I can trust. I can trust you absolutely, can't I?

Enter Phipps.

LORD GORING: My dear Robert, of course. (*To Phipps*): Bring some hock and seltzer.

PHIPPS: Yes, my lord.

LORD GORING: And Phipps!

PHIPPS: Yes, my lord.

LORD GORING: Will you excuse me for a moment, Robert? I want to give some directions to my servant.

SIR ROBERT CHILTERN: Certainly.

LORD GORING: When that lady calls, tell her that I am not expected home this evening. Tell her that I have been suddenly called out of town. You understand?

PHIPPS: The lady is in that room, my lord. You told me to show her into that room, my lord.

LORD GORING: You did perfectly right. (*Exit Phipps.*) What a mess I am in. No; I think I shall get through it. I'll give her a lecture through the door. Awkward thing to manage, though.

SIR ROBERT CHILTERN: Arthur, tell me what I should do. My life seems to have crumbled about me. I am a ship without a rudder in a night without a star.

LORD GORING: Robert, you love your wife, don't you?

SIR ROBERT CHILTERN: I love her more than anything in the world. I used to think ambition the great thing. It is not. Love is the great thing in the world. There is nothing but love and I love her. But I am defamed in her eyes. I am ignoble in her eyes. There is a wide gulf between us now. She has found me out, Arthur, she has found me out.

LORD GORING: Has she never in her life done some folly – some indiscretion – that she should not forgive your sin?

SIR ROBERT CHILTERN: My wife! Never! She does not know what weakness or temptation is. I am of clay like other men. She stands apart as good women do – pitiless in her perfection – cold and stern and without mercy. But I love her, Arthur. We are childless, and I have no one else to love, no one else to love me. Perhaps if God had sent us children she might have been kinder to me. But God has given us a lonely house. And she has cut my heart in two. Don't let us talk of it. I was brutal to her this evening. But I suppose when sinners talk to saints they are brutal always. I said to her things that were hideously true, on my side, from my standpoint, from the standpoint of men. But don't let us talk of that.

LORD GORING: Your wife will forgive you. Perhaps at this moment she is forgiving you. She loves you, Robert. Why should she not forgive?

SIR ROBERT CHILTERN: God grant it! God grant it! (*Buries his face in his hands.*) But there is something more I have to tell you, Arthur.
Enter Phipps with drinks.

PHIPPS (*hands hock and seltzer to Sir Robert Chiltern*): Hock and seltzer, sir.

SIR ROBERT CHILTERN: Thank you.

LORD GORING: Is your carriage here, Robert?

SIR ROBERT CHILTERN: No; I walked from the club.

LORD GORING: Sir Robert will take my cab, Phipps.

PHIPPS: Yes, my lord.

Exit.

LORD GORING: Robert, you don't mind my sending you away?

SIR ROBERT CHILTERN: Arthur, you must let me stay for five minutes. I have made up my mind what I am going to do to-night in the House. The debate on the Argentine Canal is to begin at eleven. (*A chair falls in the Drawing-room.*) What is that!

LORD GORING: Nothing.

SIR ROBERT CHILTERN: I heard a chair fall in the next room. Some one has been listening.

LORD GORING: No, no; there is no one there.

SIR ROBERT CHILTERN: There is some one. There are lights in the room, and the door is ajar. Some one has been listening to every secret of my life. Arthur, what does this mean?

LORD GORING: Robert, you are excited, unnerved. I tell you there is no one in that room. Sit down, Robert.

SIR ROBERT CHILTERN: Do you give me your word that there is no one there?

LORD GORING: Yes.

SIR ROBERT CHILTERN: Your word of honour? (*Sits down.*)

LORD GORING: Yes.

SIR ROBERT CHILTERN (*rises*): Arthur, let me see for myself.

LORD GORING: No, no.

SIR ROBERT CHILTERN: If there is no one there why should I not look in that room? Arthur, you must let me go into that room and satisfy myself. Let me know that no eavesdropper has heard my life's secret. Arthur, you don't realise what I am going through.

LORD GORING: Robert, this must stop. I have told you that there is no one in that room – that is enough.

SIR ROBERT CHILTERN (*rushes to the door of the room*): It is not enough. I insist on going into this room. You have told me there is no one there, so what reason can you have for refusing me?

LORD GORING: For God's sake, don't! There is some one there. Some one whom you must not see.

SIR ROBERT CHILTERN: Ah, I thought so!

LORD GORING: I forbid you to enter that room.

SIR ROBERT CHILTERN: Stand back. My life is at stake. And I don't care who is there. I will know who it is to whom I have told my secret and my shame. (*Enters room.*)

LORD GORING: Great heavens! his own wife!

Sir Robert Chiltern comes back, with a look of scorn and anger on his face.

SIR ROBERT CHILTERN: What explanation have you to give for the presence of that woman here?

LORD GORING: Robert, I swear to you on my honour that that lady is stainless and guiltless of all offence towards you.

SIR ROBERT CHILTERN: She is vile, an infamous thing!

LORD GORING: Don't say that, Robert! It was for your sake she came here. It was to try and save you she came here. She loves you and no one else.

SIR ROBERT CHILTERN: You are mad. What have I to do with her intrigues with you? Let her remain your mistress! You are well suited to each other. She, corrupt and shameful – you, false as a friend, treacherous as an enemy even—

LORD GORING: It is not true, Robert. Before heaven, it is not true. In her presence and in yours I will explain all.

SIR ROBERT CHILTERN: Let me pass, sir. You have lied enough upon your word of honour.

Sir Robert Chiltern goes out. Lord Goring rushes to the door of the Drawing-room, when Mrs Cheveley comes out, looking radiant and much amused.

MRS CHEVELEY (*with a mock curtsey*): Good-evening, Lord Goring!

LORD GORING: Mrs Cheveley! Great heavens . . . May I ask what were you doing in my Drawing-room?

MRS CHEVELEY: Merely listening. I have a perfect passion for listening through keyholes. One always hears such wonderful things through them.

LORD GORING: Doesn't that sound rather like tempting Providence?

MRS CHEVELEY: Oh! surely Providence can resist temptation by this time. (*Makes a sign to him to take her cloak off, which he does.*)

LORD GORING: I am glad you have called. I am going to give you some good advice.

MRS CHEVELEY: Oh! pray don't. One should never give a woman anything that she can't wear in the evening.

LORD GORING: I see you are quite as wilful as you used to be.

MRS CHEVELEY: Far more! I have greatly improved. I have had more experience.

LORD GORING: Too much experience is a dangerous thing. Pray have a cigarette. Half the pretty women in London smoke cigarettes. Personally I prefer the other half.

MRS CHEVELEY: Thanks. I never smoke. My dressmaker wouldn't like it, and a woman's first duty in life is to her dressmaker, isn't it? What the second duty is, no one has as yet discovered.

LORD GORING: You have come here to sell me Robert Chiltern's letter, haven't you?

MRS CHEVELEY: To offer it to you on conditions! How did you guess that?

LORD GORING: Because you haven't mentioned the subject. Have you got it with you?

MRS CHEVELEY (*sitting down*): Oh, no! A well-made dress has no pockets.

LORD GORING: What is your price for it?

MRS CHEVELEY: How absurdly English you are! The English think that a cheque-book can solve every problem in life. Why, my dear Arthur, I have very much more money than you have, and quite as much as Robert Chiltern has got hold of. Money is not what I want.

LORD GORING: What do you want then, Mrs Cheveley?

MRS CHEVELEY: Why don't you call me Laura?

LORD GORING: I don't like the name.

MRS CHEVELEY: You used to adore it.

LORD GORING: Yes; that's why. (*Mrs Cheveley motions to him to sit down beside her. He smiles, and does so.*)

MRS CHEVELEY: Arthur, you loved me once.

LORD GORING: Yes.

MRS CHEVELEY: And you asked me to be your wife.

LORD GORING: That was the natural result of my loving you.

MRS CHEVELEY: And you threw me over because you saw, or said you saw, poor old Lord Mortlake trying to have a violent flirtation with me in the Conservatory at Tenby.

LORD GORING: I am under the impression that my lawyer settled that matter with you on certain terms . . . dictated by yourself.

MRS CHEVELEY: At that time I was poor; you were rich.

LORD GORING: Quite so. That is why you pretended to love me.

MRS CHEVELEY (*shrugging her shoulders*): Poor old Lord Mortlake, who had only two topics of conversation, his gout and his wife! I never could quite make out which of the two he was talking about. He used the most horrible language about them both. Well, you were silly, Arthur. Why, Lord Mortlake was never anything more to me than an amusement. One of those utterly tedious amusements one only finds at an English country house on an English country Sunday. I don't think any one at all morally responsible for what he or she does at an English country house.

LORD GORING: Yes. I know lots of people think that.

MRS CHEVELEY: I loved you, Arthur.

LORD GORING: My dear Mrs Cheveley, you have always been far too clever to know anything about love.

MRS CHEVELEY: I did love you. And you loved me. You know you loved me; and love is a very wonderful thing. I suppose that when a man has once loved a woman, he will do anything for her, except continue to love her? (*Puts her hand on his.*)

LORD GORING (*taking his hand away quietly*): Yes; except that.

MRS CHEVELEY (*after a pause*): I am tired of living abroad. I want to come back to London. I want to have a charming house here. I want to have a salon. If one could only teach the English how to talk, and the Irish how to listen, society here would be quite civilised. Besides, I have arrived at the romantic stage. When I saw you last night at the Chilterns', I knew you were the only person I had ever cared for, if I ever have cared for anybody, Arthur. And so, on the morning of the day you marry me, I will give you Robert Chiltern's letter. That is my offer. I will give it to you now, if you promise to marry me.

LORD GORING: Now?

MRS CHEVELEY (*smiling*): To-morrow.

LORD GORING: Are you really serious?

MRS CHEVELEY: Yes, quite serious.

LORD GORING: I should make you a very bad husband.

MRS CHEVELEY: I don't mind bad husbands. I have had two. They amused me immensely.

LORD GORING: You mean that you amused yourself immensely, don't you?

MRS CHEVELEY: What do you know about my married life?

LORD GORING: Nothing; but I can read it like a book.

MRS CHEVELEY: What book?

LORD GORING (*rising*): The Book of Numbers.

MRS CHEVELEY: Do you think it is quite charming of you to be so rude to a woman in your own house?

LORD GORING: In the case of very fascinating women, sex is a challenge, not a defence.

MRS CHEVELEY: I suppose that is meant for a compliment. My dear Arthur, women are never disarmed by compliments. Men always are. That is the difference between the two sexes.

LORD GORING: Women are never disarmed by anything, as far as I know them.

MRS CHEVELEY (*after a pause*): Then you are going to allow your greatest friend, Robert Chiltern, to be ruined, rather than marry some one who really has considerable attractions left. I thought you would have risen to some great height of self-sacrifice, Arthur. I think you should. And the rest of your life you could spend in contemplating your own perfections.

LORD GORING: Oh! I do that as it is. And self-sacrifice is a thing that should be put down by law. It is so demoralising to the people for whom one sacrifices oneself. They always go to the bad.

MRS CHEVELEY: As if anything could demoralise Robert Chiltern! You seem to forget that I know his real character.

LORD GORING: What you know about him is not his real character. It was an act of folly done in his youth, dishonourable, I admit, shameful, I admit, unworthy of him, I admit, and therefore . . . not his true character.

MRS CHEVELEY: How you men stand up for each other!

LORD GORING: How you women war against each other!

MRS CHEVELEY (*bitterly*): I only war against one woman, against Gertrude Chiltern. I hate her. I hate her now more than ever.

LORD GORING: Because you have brought a real tragedy into her life, I suppose.

MRS CHEVELEY (*with a sneer*): Oh, there is only one real tragedy in a woman's life. The fact that her past is always her lover, and her future invariably her husband.

LORD GORING: Lady Chiltern knows nothing of the kind of life to which you are alluding.

MRS CHEVELEY: A woman whose size in gloves is seven and three-quarters never knows much about anything. You know Gertrude has always worn seven and three-quarters? That is one of the reasons why there was never any moral sympathy between us. . . . Well, Arthur, I suppose this romantic interview may be regarded as at an end. You admit it was romantic, don't you? For the privilege of being your wife I was ready to surrender a great prize, the climax of my diplomatic career. You decline. Very well. If Sir Robert doesn't uphold my Argentine scheme, I expose him. *Voilà tout.*

LORD GORING: You mustn't do that. It would be vile, horrible, infamous.

MRS CHEVELEY (*shrugging her shoulders*): Oh, don't use big words. They mean so little. It is a commercial transaction. That is all. There is no good mixing up sentimentality in it. I offered to sell Robert Chiltern a certain thing. If he won't pay me my price, he will have to pay the world a greater price. There is no more to be said. I must go. Goodbye. Won't you shake hands?

LORD GORING: With you? No. Your transaction with Robert Chiltern may pass as a loathsome commercial transaction of a loathsome commercial age; but you seem to have forgotten that you came here to-night to talk of love, you whose lips desecrated the word love, you to whom the thing is a book closely sealed, went this afternoon to the house of one of the most noble and gentle women in the world to degrade her husband in her eyes, to try and kill her love for him, to put poison in her heart, and bitterness in her life, to break her idol, and, it may be, spoil her soul. That I cannot forgive you. That was horrible. For that there can be no forgiveness.

MRS CHEVELEY: Arthur, you are unjust to me. Believe me, you are quite unjust to me. I didn't go to taunt Gertrude at all. I had no idea of doing anything of the kind when I entered. I called with Lady Markby simply to ask whether an ornament, a jewel, that I lost somewhere last night, had been found at the Chilterns'. If you don't believe me, you can ask Lady Markby. She will tell you it is true. The scene that occurred happened after Lady Markby had left, and was really forced on me by Gertrude's rudeness and sneers. I called, oh! – a little out of malice if you like – but really to ask if a diamond brooch of mine had been found. That was the origin of the whole thing.

LORD GORING: A diamond snake-brooch with a ruby?

MRS CHEVELEY: Yes. How do you know?

LORD GORING: Because it is found. In point of fact, I found it myself, and stupidly forgot to tell the butler anything about it as I was leaving. (*Goes over to the writing-table and pulls out the drawers.*) It is in this drawer. No, that one, This is the brooch, isn't it? (*Holds up the brooch.*)

MRS CHEVELEY: Yes. I am so glad to get it back. It was . . . a present.

LORD GORING: Won't you wear it?

MRS CHEVELEY: Certainly, if you pin it in. (*Lord Goring suddenly clasps it on her arm.*) Why do you put it on as a bracelet? I never knew it could be worn as a bracelet.

LORD GORING: Really?

MRS CHEVELEY (*holding out her handsome arm*): No; but it looks very well on me as a bracelet doesn't it?

LORD GORING: Yes; much better than when I saw it last.

MRS CHEVELEY: When did you see it last?

LORD GORING (*calmly*): Oh, ten years ago, on Lady Berkshire, from whom you stole it.

MRS CHEVELEY (*starting*): What do you mean?

LORD GORING: I mean that you stole that ornament from my cousin, Mary Berkshire, to whom I gave it when she was married. Suspicion fell on a wretched servant, who was sent away in disgrace. I recognised it last night. I determined to say nothing about it till I had found the thief. I have found the thief now, and I have heard her own confession.

MRS CHEVELEY (*tossing her head*): It is not true.

LORD GORING: You know it is true. Why, thief is written across your face at this moment.

MRS CHEVELEY: I will deny the whole affair from beginning to end. I will say that I have never seen this wretched thing, that it was never in my possession.

Mrs Cheveley tries to get the bracelet off her arm, but fails. Lord Goring looks on amused. Her thin fingers tear at the jewel to no purpose. A curse breaks from her.

LORD GORING: The drawback of stealing a thing, Mrs Cheveley, is that one never knows how wonderful the thing that one steals is. You can't get that bracelet off, unless you know where the spring is. And I see you don't know where the spring is. It is rather difficult to find.

MRS CHEVELEY: You brute! You coward! (*She tries again to unclasp the bracelet, but fails.*)

LORD GORING: Oh! don't use big words. They mean so little.

MRS CHEVELEY (*again tears at the bracelet in a paroxysm of rage, with inarticulate sounds. Then stops, and looks at Lord Goring*): What are you going to do?

LORD GORING: I am going to ring for my servant. He is an admirable servant. Always comes in the moment one rings for him. When he comes I will tell him to fetch the police.

MRS CHEVELEY (*trembling*): The police? What for?

LORD GORING: To-morrow the Berkshires will prosecute you. That is what the police are for.

MRS CHEVELEY (*is now in an agony of physical terror. Her face is distorted. Her mouth awry. A mask has fallen from her. She is, for the moment, dreadful to look at*): Don't do that. I will do anything you want. Anything in the world you want.

LORD GORING: Give me Robert Chiltern's letter.

MRS CHEVELEY: Stop! Stop! Let me have time to think.

LORD GORING: Give me Robert Chiltern's letter.

MRS CHEVELEY: I have not got it with me. I will give it to you to-morrow.

LORD GORING: You know you are lying. Give it to me at once. (*Mrs Cheveley pulls the letter out, and hands it to him. She is horribly pale.*) This is it?

MRS CHEVELEY (*in a hoarse voice*): Yes.

LORD GORING (*takes the letter, examines it, sighs, and burns it over the lamp*): For so well-dressed a woman, Mrs Cheveley, you have moments of admirable common sense. I congratulate you.

MRS CHEVELEY (*catches sight of Lady Chiltern's letter, the cover of which is just showing from under the blotting-book*): Please get me a glass of water.

LORD GORING: Certainly. (*Goes to the corner of the room and pours out a glass of water. While his back is turned, Mrs Cheveley steals Lady Chiltern's letter. When Lord Goring returns with the glass she refuses it with a gesture.*)

MRS CHEVELEY: Thank you. Will you help me on with my cloak?

LORD GORING: With pleasure. (*Puts her cloak on.*)

MRS CHEVELEY: Thanks. I am never going to try to harm Robert Chiltern again.

LORD GORING: Fortunately you have not the chance, Mrs Cheveley.

MRS CHEVELEY: Well, even if I had the chance, I wouldn't. On the contrary, I am going to render him a great service.

LORD GORING: I am charmed to hear it. It is a reformation.

MRS CHEVELEY: Yes. I can't bear so upright a gentleman, so honourable an English gentleman, being so shamefully deceived and so—

LORD GORING: Well?

MRS CHEVELEY: I find that somehow Gertrude Chiltern's dying speech and confession has strayed into my pocket.

LORD GORING: What do you mean?

MRS CHEVELEY (*with a bitter note of triumph in her voice*): I mean that I am going to send Robert Chiltern the love-letter his wife wrote to you to-night.

LORD GORING: Love-letter?

MRS CHEVELEY (*laughing*): 'I want you. I trust you. I am coming to you. Gertrude.'

Lord Goring rushes to the bureau and takes up the envelope, finds it empty, and turns round.

LORD GORING: You wretched woman, must you always be thieving? Give me back that letter. I'll take it from you by force. You shall not leave my room till I have got it.

He rushes towards her, but Mrs Cheveley at once puts her hand on the electric bell that is on the table. The bell sounds with shrill reverberations, and Phipps enters.

MRS CHEVELEY (*after a pause*): Lord Goring merely rang that you should show me out. Good-night, Lord Goring!

Goes out followed by Phipps. Her face is illumined with evil triumph. There is joy in her eyes. Youth seems to have come back to her. Her last glance is like a swift arrow. Lord Goring bites his lip, and lights a cigarette.

THE IMPORTANCE
OF BEING EARNEST

The persons of the play

JOHN WORTHING, J.P.
ALGERNON MONCRIEFF
REV. CANON CHASUBLE, D.D.
MERRIMAN, Butler

LADY BRACKNELL
HON. GWENDOLEN FAIRFAX
CECILY CARDEW
MISS PRISM, Governess
LANE, Manservant

The scenes of the play

ACT I. *Algernon Moncrieff's flat in Half-Moon Street, W.*
ACT II. *The garden at the Manor House, Woolton*
ACT III. *Drawing-room of the Manor House, Woolton*

Time: *the present;* Place: *London and Hertfordshire*

ACT ONE

Scene: Morning-room in Algernon's flat in Half-Moon Street. The room is luxuriously and artistically furnished. The sound of a piano is heard in the adjoining room. Lane is arranging afternoon tea on the table, and after the music has ceased Algernon enters.

ALGERNON: Did you hear what I was playing, Lane?

LANE: I didn't think it polite to listen, sir.

ALGERNON: I'm sorry for that, for your sake. I don't play accurately – any one can play accurately – but I play with wonderful expression. As far as the piano is concerned, sentiment is my forte. I keep science for Life.

LANE: Yes, sir.

ALGERNON: And, speaking of the science of Life, have you got the cucumber sandwiches cut for Lady Bracknell?

LANE: Yes, sir. (*Hands them on a salver.*)

ALGERNON (*Inspects them, takes two, and sits down on the sofa*): Oh! . . . by the way, Lane, I see from your book that on Thursday night, when Lord Shoreman and Mr Worthing were dining with me, eight bottles of champagne are entered as having been consumed.

LANE: Yes, sir; eight bottles and a pint.

ALGERNON: Why is it that at a bachelor's establishment the servants invariably drink the champagne? I ask merely for information.

LANE: I attribute it to the superior quality of the wine, sir. I have often observed that in married households the champagne is rarely of a first-rate brand.

ALGERNON: Good heavens! Is marriage so demoralising as that?

LANE: I believe it *is* a very pleasant state, sir. I have had very little experience of it myself up to the moment. I have only been married once. That was in consequence of a misunderstanding between myself and a young person.

ALGERNON (*languidly*): I don't know that I am much interested in your family life, Lane.

LANE: No, sir it is not a very interesting subject. I never think of it myself.

ALGERNON: Very natural, I am sure. That will do, Lane, thank you.

LANE: Thank you, sir.

Lane goes out.

ALGERNON: Lane's views on marriage seem somewhat lax. Really, if the lower orders don't set us a good example, what on earth is the use of them? They seem, as a class, to have absolutely no sense of moral responsibility.

Enter Lane.

LANE: Mr Ernest Worthing.

Enter Jack. Lane goes out.

ALGERNON: How are you, my dear Ernest? What brings you up to town?

JACK: Oh, pleasure, pleasure! What else should bring one anywhere? Eating as usual, I see, Algy!

ALGERNON (*stiffly*): I believe it is customary in good society to take some slight refreshment at five o'clock. Where have you been since last Thursday?

JACK (*sitting down on the sofa*): In the country.

ALGERNON: What on earth do you do there?

JACK (*pulling off his gloves*): When one is in town one amuses oneself. When one is in the country one amuses other people. It is excessively boring.

ALGERNON: And who are the people you amuse?

JACK (*airily*): Oh, neighbours, neighbours.

ALGERNON: Got nice neighbours in your part of Shropshire?

JACK: Perfectly horrid! Never speak to one of them.

ALGERNON: How immensely you must amuse them! (*Goes over and takes sandwich.*) By the way, Shropshire is your county, is it not?

JACK: Eh? Shropshire? Yes, of course. Hullo! Why all these cups? Why cucumber sandwiches? Why such reckless extravagance in one so young? Who is coming to tea?

ALGERNON: Oh! merely Aunt Augusta and Gwendolen.

JACK: How perfectly delightful!

ALGERNON: Yes, that is all very well; but I am afraid Aunt Augusta won't quite approve of your being here.

JACK: May I ask why?

ALGERNON: My dear fellow, the way you flirt with Gwendolen is perfectly disgraceful. It is almost as ba ! as the way Gwendolen flirts with you.

JACK: I am in love with Gwendolen. I have come up to town expressly to propose to her.

ALGERNON: I thought you had come up for pleasure? . . . I call that business.

JACK: How utterly unromantic you are!

ALGERNON: I really don't see anything romantic in proposing. It is very romantic to be in love. But there is nothing romantic about a definite proposal. Why, one may be accepted. One usually is, I believe. Then the excitement is all over. The very essence of romance is uncertainty. If ever I get married, I'll certainly try to forget the fact.

JACK: I have no doubt about that, dear Algy. The Divorce Court was specially invented for people whose memories are so curiously constituted.   ·

ALGERNON: Oh! there is no use speculating on that subject. Divorces are made in Heaven—(*Jack puts out his hand to take a sandwich. Algernon at once interferes.*) Please don't touch the cucumber sandwiches. They are ordered specially for Aunt Augusta. (*Takes one and eats it.*)

JACK: Well, you have been eating them all the time.

ALGERNON: That is quite a different matter. She is my aunt. (*Takes plate from below.*) Have some bread and butter. The bread and butter is for Gwendolen. Gwendolen is devoted to bread and butter.

JACK (*advancing to table and helping himself*): And very good bread and butter it is too.

ALGERNON: Well, my dear fellow, you need not eat as if you were going to eat it all. You behave as if you were married to her already. You are not married to her already, and I don't think you ever will be.

JACK: Why on earth do you say that?

ALGERNON: Well, in the first place girls never marry the men they flirt with. Girls don't think it right.

JACK: Oh, that is nonsense!

ALGERNON: It isn't. It is a great truth. It accounts for the extraordinary number of bachelors that one sees all over the place. In the second place, I don't give my consent.

JACK: Your consent!

ALGERNON: My dear fellow, Gwendolen is my first cousin. And before I allow you to marry her, you will have to clear up the whole question of Cecily. (*Rings bell.*)

JACK: Cecily! What on earth do you mean? What do you mean, Algy, by Cecily! I don't know any one of the name of Cecily.

Enter Lane.

ALGERNON: Bring me that cigarette case Mr Worthing left in the Smoking-room the last time he dined here.

LANE: Yes, sir.

Lane goes out.

JACK: Do you mean to say you have had my cigarette case all this time? I wish to goodness you had let me know. I have been writing frantic letters to Scotland Yard about it. I was very nearly offering a large reward.

ALGERNON: Well, I wish you would offer one. I happen to be more than usually hard up.

JACK: There is no good offering a large reward now that the thing is found.

Enter Lane with the cigarette case on a salver. Algernon takes it at once. Lane goes out.

ALGERNON: I think that is rather mean of you, Ernest, I must say. (*Opens case and examines it.*) However, it makes no matter, for, now that I look at the inscription inside, I find that the thing isn't yours after all.

JACK: Of course it's mine (*Moving to him.*) You have seen me with it a hundred times, and you have no right whatsoever to read what is written inside. It is a very ungentlemanly thing to read a private cigarette case.

ALGERNON: Oh! it is absurd to have a hard and fast rule about what one should read and what one shouldn't. More than half of modern culture depends on what one shouldn't read.

JACK: I am quite aware of the fact, and I don't propose to discuss modern culture. It isn't the sort of thing one should talk of in private. I simply want my cigarette case back.

ALGERNON: Yes; but this isn't your cigarette case. This cigarette case is a present from some one of the name of Cecily, and you said you didn't know any one of that name.

JACK: Well, if you want to know, Cecily happens to be my aunt.

ALGERNON: Your aunt!

JACK: Yes. Charming old lady she is, too. Lives at Tunbridge Wells. Just give it back to me, Algy.

ALGERNON (*retreating to back of sofa*): But why does she call herself little Cecily if she is your aunt and lives at Tunbridge Wells? (*Reading.*) 'From little Cecily with her fondest love.'

JACK (*moving to sofa and kneeling upon it*): My dear fellow, what on earth is there in that? Some aunts are tall, some aunts are not tall. That is a matter that surely an aunt may be allowed to decide for herself. You seem to think that every aunt should be exactly like your aunt! That is absurd! For Heaven's sake give me back my cigarette case. (*Follows Algernon round the room.*)

ALGERNON: Yes. But why does your aunt call you her uncle? 'From little Cecily, with her fondest love to her dear Uncle Jack.' There is no objection, I admit, to an aunt being a small aunt, but why an aunt, no matter what her size may be, should call her own nephew her uncle, I can't quite make out. Besides, your name isn't Jack at all; it is Ernest.

JACK: It isn't Ernest; it's Jack.

ALGERNON: You have always told me it was Ernest. I have introduced you to every one as Ernest. You answer to the name of Ernest. You look as if your name was Ernest. You are the most earnest-looking person I ever saw in my life. It is perfectly absurd your saying that your name isn't Ernest. It's on your cards. Here is one of them. (*Taking it from case.*) 'Mr Ernest Worthing, B.4, The Albany.' I'll keep this as a proof that your name is Ernest if ever you attempt to deny it to me, or to Gwendolen, or to any one else. (*Puts the card in his pocket.*)

JACK: Well, my name is Ernest in town and Jack in the country, and the cigarette case was given to me in the country.

ALGERNON: Yes, but that does not account for the fact that your small Aunt Cecily, who lives at Tunbridge Wells, calls you her dear Uncle. Come, old boy, you had much better have the thing out at once.

JACK: My dear Algy, you talk exactly as if you were a dentist. It is very vulgar to talk like a dentist when one isn't a dentist. It produces a false impression.

ALGERNON: Well, that is exactly what dentists always do. Now, go on! Tell me the whole thing. I may mention that I have always suspected you of being a confirmed and secret Bunburyist; and I am quite sure of it now.

JACK: Bunburyist? What on earth do you mean by a Bunburyist?

ALGERNON: I'll reveal to you the meaning of that incomparable expression as soon as you are kind enough to inform me why you are Ernest in town and Jack in the country.

JACK: Well, produce my cigarette case first.

ALGERNON: Here it is. (*Hands cigarette case.*) Now produce your explanation, and pray make it improbable. (*Sits on sofa.*)

JACK: My dear fellow, there is nothing improbable about my explanation at all. In fact, it's perfectly ordinary. Old Mr Thomas Cardew, who adopted me when I was a little boy, made me in his will guardian to his grand-daughter, Miss Cecily Cardew. Cecily, who addresses me as her uncle from motives of respect that you could not possibly appreciate, lives at my place in the country under the charge of her admirable governess, Miss Prism.

ALGERNON: Where is that place in the country, by the way?

JACK: That is nothing to you, dear boy. You are not going to be invited. . . . I may tell you candidly that the place is not in Shropshire.

ALGERNON: I suspected that, my dear fellow! I have Bunburyed all over Shropshire on two separate occasions. Now, go on. Why are you Ernest in town and Jack in the country?

JACK: My dear Algy, I don't know whether you will be able to understand my real motives. You are hardly serious enough. When one is placed in the position of guardian, one has to adopt a very high moral tone on all subjects. It's one's duty to do so. And as a high moral tone can hardly be said to conduce very much to either one's health or one's happiness, in order to get up to town I have always pretended to have a younger brother of the name of Ernest, who lives in the Albany, and gets into the most dreadful scrapes. That, my dear Algy, is the whole truth pure and simple.

ALGERNON: The truth is rarely pure and never simple. Modern life would be very tedious if it were either, and modern literature a complete impossibility!

JACK: That wouldn't be at all a bad thing.

ALGERNON: Literary criticism is not your forte, my dear fellow. Don't try it. You should leave that to people who haven't been at a University. They do it so well in the daily papers. What you really are is a Bunburyist. I was quite right in saying you were a Bunburyist. You are one of the most advanced Bunburyists I know.

JACK: What on earth do you mean?

ALGERNON: You have invented a very useful younger brother called Ernest, in order that you may be able to come up to town as often as you like. I have invented an invaluable permanent invalid called Bunbury, in order that I may be able to go down into the country whenever I choose. Bunbury is perfectly invaluable. If it wasn't for Bunbury's extraordinarily bad health, for instance, I wouldn't be able to dine with you at Willis's to-night, for I have been really engaged to Aunt Augusta for more than a week.

JACK: I haven't asked you to dine with me anywhere to-night.

ALGERNON: I know. You are absolutely careless about sending out invitations. It is very foolish of you. Nothing annoys people so much as not receiving invitations.

JACK: You had much better dine with your Aunt Augusta.

ALGERNON: I haven't the smallest intention of doing anything of the kind. To begin with, I dined there on Monday, and once a week is quite enough to dine with one's own relations. In the second place, whenever I do dine there I am always treated as a member of the family, and sent down with either no woman at all, or two. In the third place, I know perfectly well whom she will place me next to, to-night. She will place me next Mary Farquhar, who always flirts with her own husband across the dinner-table. That is not very pleasant. Indeed, it is not even decent . . . and that sort of thing is enormously on the increase. The amount of women in London who flirt with their own husbands is perfectly scandalous. It looks so bad. It is simply washing one's clean linen in public. Besides, now that I know you to be a confirmed Bunburyist I naturally want to talk to you about Bunburying. I want to tell you the rules.

JACK: I'm not a Bunburyist at all. If Gwendolen accepts me, I am going to kill my brother, indeed I think I'll kill him in any case. Cecily is a little too much interested in him. It is rather a bore. So I am going to get rid of Ernest. And I strongly advise you to do the same with Mr . . . with your invalid friend who has the absurd name.

ALGERNON: Nothing will induce me to part with Bunbury, and if you ever get married, which seems to me extremely problematic, you will be very glad to know Bunbury. A man who marries without knowing Bunbury has a very tedious time of it.

JACK: That is nonsense. If I marry a charming girl like Gwendolen, and she is the only girl I ever saw in my life that I would marry, I certainly don't want to know Bunbury.

ALGERNON: Then your wife will. You don't seem to realise, that in married life three is company and two is none.

JACK (*sententiously*): That, my dear young friend, is the theory that the corrupt French Drama has been propounding for the last fifty years.

ALGERNON: Yes; and that the happy English home has proved in half the time.

JACK: For heaven's sake, don't try to be cynical. It's perfectly easy to be cynical.

ALGERNON: My dear fellow, it isn't easy to be anything nowadays. There's such a lot of beastly competition about. (*The sound of an electric bell is heard.*) Ah! that must be Aunt Augusta. Only relatives, or creditors, ever ring in that Wagnerian manner. Now, if I get her out of the way for ten minutes, so that you can have an opportunity for proposing to Gwendolen, may I dine with you to-night at Willis's?

JACK: I suppose so, if you want to.

ALGERNON: Yes, but you must be serious about it. I hate people who are not serious about meals. It is so shallow of them.
Enter Lane.

LANE: Lady Bracknell and Miss Fairfax.
Algernon goes forward to meet them. Enter Lady Bracknell and Gwendolen.

LADY BRACKNELL: Good-afternoon, dear Algernon, I hope you are behaving very well.

ALGERNON: I'm feeling very well, Aunt Augusta.

LADY BRACKNELL: That's not quite the same thing. In fact the two things rarely go together. (*Sees Jack and bows with icy coldness.*)

ALGERNON (*to* Gwendolen): Dear me, you are smart!

GWENDOLEN: I am always smart! Am I not, Mr Worthing?

JACK: You're quite perfect, Miss Fairfax.

GWENDOLEN: Oh! I hope I am not that. It would leave no room for developments, and I intend to develop in many directions. (*Gwendolen and Jack sit down together in the corner.*)

LADY BRACKNELL: I'm sorry if we are a little late, Algernon, but I was obliged to call on dear Lady Harbury. I hadn't been there since her poor husband's death. I never saw a woman so altered; she looks quite twenty years younger. And now I'll have a cup of tea, and one of those nice cucumber sandwiches you promised me.

ALGERNON: Certainly, Aunt Augusta. (*Goes over to tea-table.*)

LADY BRACKNELL: Won't you come and sit here, Gwendolen?

GWENDOLEN: Thanks, mamma, I'm quite comfortable where I am.

ALGERNON (*picking up empty plate in horror*): Good heavens! Lane! Why are there no cucumber sandwiches? I ordered them specially.

LANE (*gravely*): There were no cucumbers in the market this morning, sir. I went down twice.

ALGERNON: No cucumbers!

LANE: No, sir. Not even for ready money.

ALGERNON: That will do, Lane, thank you.

LANE: Thank you, sir. (*Goes out.*)

ALGERNON: I am greatly distressed, Aunt Augusta, about there being no cucumbers, not even for ready money.

LADY BRACKNELL: It really makes no matter, Algernon. I had some crumpets with Lady Harbury, who seems to be living entirely for pleasure now.

ALGERNON: I hear her hair has turned quite gold from grief.

LADY BRACKNELL: It certainly has changed its colour. From what cause I, of course, cannot say. (*Algernon crosses and hands tea.*) Thank you. I've quite a treat for you to-night, Algernon. I am going to send you down with Mary Farquhar. She is such a nice woman, and so attentive to her husband. It's delightful to watch them.

ALGERNON: I am afraid, Aunt Augusta, I shall have to give up the pleasure of dining with you to-night after all.

LADY BRACKNELL (*frowning*): I hope not, Algernon. It would put my table completely out. Your uncle would have to dine upstairs. Fortunately he is accustomed to that.

ALGERNON: It is a great bore, and, I need hardly say, a terrible disappointment to me, but the fact is I have just had a telegram to say that my poor friend Bunbury is very ill again. (*Exchanges glances with Jack.*) They seem to think I should be with him.

LADY BRACKNELL: It is very strange. This Mr Bunbury seems to suffer from curiously bad health.

ALGERNON: Yes; poor Bunbury is a dreadful invalid.

LADY BRACKNELL: Well, I must say, Algernon, that I think it is high time that Mr Bunbury made up his mind whether he was going to live or to die. This shilly-shallying with the question is absurd. Nor do I in any way approve of the modern sympathy with invalids. I consider it morbid. Illness of any kind is hardly a thing to be encouraged in others. Health is the primary duty of life. I am always telling that to your poor uncle, but he never seems to take much notice . . . as far as any improvement in his ailment goes. I should be much obliged if you would ask Mr Bunbury, from me, to be kind enough not to have a relapse on Saturday, for I rely on you to arrange my music for me. It is my last reception, and one wants something that will encourage conversation, particularly at the end of the season when every one has practically said whatever they had to say, which, in most cases, was probably not much.

ALGERNON: I'll speak to Bunbury, Aunt Augusta, if he is still conscious, and I think I can promise you he'll be all right by Saturday. Of course the music is a great difficulty. You see, if one plays good music, people don't listen, and if one plays bad music people don't talk. But I'll run over the programme I've drawn out, if you will kindly come into the next room for a moment.

LADY BRACKNELL: Thank you, Algernon. It is very thoughtful of you. (*Rising and following Algernon.*) I'm sure the programme will be delightful, after a few expurgations. French songs I cannot possibly allow. People always seem to think that they are improper, and either look shocked, which is vulgar, or laugh, which is worse. But German sounds a thoroughly respectable language, and indeed, I believe is so. Gwendolen, you will accompany me.

GWENDOLEN: Certainly, mamma.

Lady Bracknell and Algernon go into the Music-room. Gwendolen remains behind.

JACK: Charming day it has been, Miss Fairfax.

GWENDOLEN: Pray don't talk to me about the weather, Mr Worthing. Whenever people talk to me about the weather, I always feel quite certain that they mean something else. And that makes me so nervous.

JACK: I do mean something else.

GWENDOLEN: I thought so. In fact, I am never wrong.

JACK: And I would like to be allowed to take advantage of Lady Bracknell's temporary absence . . .

GWENDOLEN: I would certainly advise you to do so. Mamma has a way of coming back suddenly into a room that I have often had to speak to her about.

JACK (*nervously*): Miss Fairfax, ever since I met you I have admired you more than any girl . . . I have ever met since . . . I met you.

GWENDOLEN: Yes, I am quite well aware of the fact. And I often wish that in public, at any rate, you had been more demonstrative. For me you have always had an irresistible fascination. Even before I met you I was far from indifferent to you. (*Jack looks at her in amazement.*) We live, as I hope you know, Mr Worthing, in an age of ideals. The fact is constantly mentioned in the more expensive monthly magazines, and has now reached the provincial pulpits, I am told; and my ideal has always been to love some one of the name of Ernest. There is something in that name that inspires absolute confidence. The moment Algernon first mentioned to me that he had a friend called Ernest, I knew I was destined to love you.

JACK: You really love me, Gwendolen?

GWENDOLEN: Passionately!

JACK: Darling! You don't know how happy you've made me.

GWENDOLEN: My own Ernest!

JACK: But you don't really mean to say that you couldn't love me if my name wasn't Ernest?

GWENDOLEN: But your name is Ernest.

JACK: Yes, I know it is. But supposing it was something else? Do you mean to say you couldn't love me then?

GWENDOLEN (*glibly*): Ah! that is clearly a metaphysical speculation, and like most metaphysical speculations has very little reference at all to the actual facts of real life, as we know them.

JACK: Personally, darling, to speak quite candidly, I don't much care about the name of Ernest. . . . I don't think the name suits me at all.

GWENDOLEN: It suits you perfectly. It is a divine name. It has a music of its own. It produces vibrations.

JACK: Well, really, Gwendolen, I must say that I think there are lots of other much nicer names. I think Jack, for instance, a charming name.

GWENDOLEN: Jack? . . . No, there is very little music in the name Jack, if any at all, indeed. It does not thrill. It produces absolutely no vibrations. . . . I have known several Jacks, and they all, without exception, were more than usually plain. Besides, Jack is a notorious domesticity for John! And I pity any woman who is married to a man called John. She would probably never be allowed to know the entrancing pleasure of a single moment's solitude. The only really safe name is Ernest.

JACK: Gwendolen, I must get christened at once – I mean we must get married at once. There is no time to be lost.

GWENDOLEN: Married, Mr Worthing?

JACK (astounded): Well . . . surely. You know that I love you, and you led me to believe, Miss Fairfax, that you were not absolutely indifferent to me.

GWENDOLEN: I adore you. But you haven't proposed to me yet. Nothing has been said at all about marriage. The subject has not even been touched on.

JACK: Well . . . may I propose to you now?

GWENDOLEN: I think it would be an admirable opportunity. And to spare you any possible disappointment, Mr Worthing, I think it only fair to tell you quite frankly beforehand that I am fully determined to accept you.

JACK: Gwendolen!

GWENDOLEN: Yes, Mr Worthing, what have you got to say to me?

JACK: You know what I have got to say to you.

GWENDOLEN: Yes, but you don't say it.

JACK: Gwendolen, will you marry me? (Goes on his knees.)

GWENDOLEN: Of course I will, darling. How long you have been about it! I am afraid you have had very little experience in how to propose.

JACK: My own one, I have never loved any one in the world but you.

GWENDOLEN: Yes, but men often propose for practice. I know my brother Gerald does. All my girl-friends tell me so. What wonderfully blue eyes you have, Ernest! They are quite, quite blue. I hope you will always look at me just like that, especially when there are other people present.

Enter Lady Bracknell.

LADY BRACKNELL: Mr Worthing! Rise, sir, from this semi-recumbent posture. It is most indecorous.

GWENDOLEN: Mamma! (*He tries to rise; she restrains him.*) I must beg you to retire. This is no place for you. Besides, Mr Worthing has not quite finished yet.

LADY BRACKNELL: Finished what, may I ask?

GWENDOLEN: I am engaged to Mr Worthing, mamma. (*They rise together.*)

LADY BRACKNELL: Pardon me, you are not engaged to any one. When you do become engaged to some one, I, or your father, should his health permit him, will inform you of the fact. An engagement should come on a young girl as a surprise, pleasant or unpleasant, as the case may be. It is hardly a matter that she could be allowed to arrange for

herself. . . . And now I have a few questions to put to you, Mr
Worthing. While I am making these inquiries, you, Gwendolen, will
wait for me below in the carriage.

GWENDOLEN (*reproachfully*): Mamma!

LADY BRACKNELL: In the carriage, Gwendolen! (*Gwendolen goes to the door.
She and Jack blow kisses to each other behind Lady Bracknell's back. Lady
Bracknell looks vaguely about as if she could not understand what the noise
was. Finally turns round.*) Gwendolen, the carriage!

GWENDOLEN: Yes, mamma. (*Goes out, looking back at Jack.*)

LADY BRACKNELL (*sitting down*): You can take a seat, Mr Worthing.
Looks in her pocket for note-book and pencil.

JACK: Thank you, Lady Bracknell, I prefer standing.

LADY BRACKNELL (*pencil and note-book in hand*): I feel bound to tell you
that you are not down on my list of eligible young men, although I
have the same list as the dear Duchess of Bolton has. We work
together, in fact. However, I am quite ready to enter your name,
should your answers be what a really affectionate mother requires.
Do you smoke?

JACK: Well, yes, I must admit I smoke.

LADY BRACKNELL: I am glad to hear it. A man should have an occupation
of some kind. There are far too many idle men in London as it is.
How old are you?

JACK: Twenty-nine.

LADY BRACKNELL: A very good age to be married at. I have always been
of opinion that a man who desires to get married should know either
everything or nothing. Which do you know?

JACK (*after some hesitation*): I know nothing, Lady Bracknell.

LADY BRACKNELL: I am pleased to hear it. I do not approve of anything
that tampers with natural ignorance. Ignorance is like a delicate
exotic fruit; touch it and the bloom is gone. The whole theory of
modern education is radically unsound. Fortunately in England, at
any rate, education produces no effect whatsoever. If it did, it would
prove a serious danger to the upper classes, and probably lead to acts
of violence in Grosvenor Square. What is your income?

JACK: Between seven and eight thousand a year.

LADY BRACKNELL (*makes a note in her book*): In land, or in investments?

JACK: In investments, chiefly.

LADY BRACKNELL: That is satisfactory. What between the duties expected
of one during one's lifetime, and the duties exacted from one after
one's death, land has ceased to be either a profit or a pleasure. It
gives one position, and prevents one from keeping it up. That's all
that can be said about land.

JACK: I have a country house with some land, of course, attached to it,
about fifteen hundred acres, I believe; but I don't depend on that for
my real income. In fact, as far as I can make out, the poachers are
the only people who make anything out of it.

LADY BRACKNELL: A country house! How many bedrooms? Well, that
point can be cleared up afterwards. You have a town house, I hope?

A girl with a simple, unspoiled nature, like Gwendolen, could hardly be expected to reside in the country.

JACK: Well, I own a house in Belgrave Square, but it is let by the year to Lady Bloxham. Of course, I can get it back whenever I like, at six months' notice.

LADY BRACKNELL: Lady Bloxham? I don't know her.

JACK: Oh, she goes about very little. She is a lady considerably advanced in years.

LADY BRACKNELL: Ah, nowadays that is no guarantee of respectability of character. What number in Belgrave Square?

JACK: 149.

LADY BRACKNELL (*shaking her head*): The unfashionable side. I thought there was something. However, that could easily be altered.

JACK: Do you mean the fashion, or the side?

LADY BRACKNELL (*sternly*): Both, if necessary, I presume. What are your politics?

JACK: Well, I am afraid I really have none. I am a Liberal Unionist.

LADY BRACKNELL: Oh, they count as Tories. They dine with us. Or come in the evening, at any rate. Now to minor matters. Are your parents living?

JACK: I have lost both my parents.

LADY BRACKNELL: To lose one parent, Mr Worthing, may be regarded as a misfortune; to lose both looks like carelessness. Who was your father? He was evidently a man of some wealth. Was he born in what the Radical papers call the purple of commerce, or did he rise from the ranks of the aristocracy?

JACK: I am afraid I really don't know. The fact is, Lady Bracknell, I said I had lost my parents. It would be nearer the truth to say that my parents seem to have lost me. . . . I don't actually know who I am by birth. I was . . . well, I was found.

LADY BRACKNELL: Found!

JACK: The late Mr Thomas Cardew, an old gentleman of a very charitable and kindly disposition, found me, and gave me the name of Worthing, because he happened to have a first-class ticket for Worthing in his pocket at the time. Worthing is a place in Sussex. It is a seaside resort.

LADY BRACKNELL: Where did the charitable gentleman who had a first-class ticket for this seaside resort find you?

JACK (*gravely*): In a hand-bag.

LADY BRACKNELL: A hand-bag?

JACK (*very seriously*): Yes, Lady Bracknell. I was in a hand-bag – a somewhat large, black leather hand-bag, with handles to it – an ordinary hand-bag in fact.

LADY BRACKNELL: In what locality did this Mr James, or Thomas, Cardew come across this ordinary hand-bag?

JACK: In the cloak-room at Victoria Station. It was given to him in mistake for his own.

LADY BRACKNELL: The cloak-room at Victoria Station?

JACK: Yes. The Brighton line.

LADY BRACKNELL: The line is immaterial. Mr Worthing, I confess I feel somewhat bewildered by what you have just told me. To be born, or at any rate bred, in a hand-bag, whether it had handles or not, seems to me to display a contempt for the ordinary decencies of family life that reminds one of the worst excesses of the French Revolution. And I presume you know what that unfortunate movement led to? As for the particular locality in which the hand-bag was found, a cloak-room at a railway station might serve to conceal a social indiscretion – has probably, indeed, been used for that purpose before now – but it could hardly be regarded as an assured basis for a recognised position in good society.

JACK: May I ask you then what you would advise me to do? I need hardly say I would do anything in the world to ensure Gwendolen's happiness.

LADY BRACKNELL: I would strongly advise you, Mr Worthing, to try and acquire some relations as soon as possible, and to make a definite effort to produce at any rate one parent, of either sex, before the season is quite over.

JACK: Well, I don't see how I could possibly manage to do that. I can produce the hand-bag at any moment. It is in my dressing-room at home. I really think that should satisfy you, Lady Bracknell.

LADY BRACKNELL: Me, sir! What has it to do with me? You can hardly imagine that I and Lord Bracknell would dream of allowing our only daughter – a girl brought up with the utmost care – to marry into a cloak-room, and form an alliance with a parcel. Good-morning, Mr Worthing!

Lady Bracknell sweeps out in majestic indignation.

JACK: Good-morning! (*Algernon, from the other room, strikes up the Wedding March. Jack looks perfectly furious, and goes to the door.*) For goodness' sake don't play that ghastly tune, Algy! How idiotic you are!

The music stops and Algernon enters cheerily.

ALGERNON: Didn't it go off all right, old boy? You don't mean to say Gwendolen refused you? I know it is a way she has. She is always refusing people. I think it is most ill-natured of her.

JACK: Oh, Gwendolen is as right as a trivet. As far as she is concerned, we are engaged. Her mother is perfectly unbearable. Never met such a Gorgon. . . . I don't really know what a Gorgon is like but I am quite sure that Lady Bracknell is one. In any case, she is a monster, without being a myth, which is rather unfair. . . . I beg your pardon, Algy, I suppose I shouldn't talk about your own aunt in that way before you.

ALGERNON: My dear boy, I love hearing my relations abused. It is the only thing that makes me put up with them at all. Relations are simply a tedious pack of people, who haven't got the remotest knowledge of how to live, nor the smallest instinct about when to die.

JACK: Oh, that is nonsense!

ALGERNON: It isn't!

JACK: Well, I won't argue about the matter. You always want to argue about things.

ALGERNON: That is exactly what things were originally made for.

JACK: Upon my word, if I thought that, I'd shoot myself. . . . (*A pause.*) You don't think there is any chance of Gwendolen becoming like her mother in about a hundred and fifty years, do you, Algy?

ALGERNON: All women become like their mothers. That is their tragedy. No man does. That's his.

JACK: Is that clever?

ALGERNON: It is perfectly phrased! And quite as true as any observation in civilised life should be.

JACK: I am sick to death of cleverness. Everybody is clever nowadays. You can't go anywhere without meeting clever people. The thing has become an absolute public nuisance. I wish to goodness we had a few fools left.

ALGERNON: We have.

JACK: I should extremely like to meet them. What do they talk about?

ALGERNON: The fools? Oh! about the clever people of course.

JACK: What fools.

ALGERNON: By the way, did you tell Gwendolen the truth about your being Ernest in town, and Jack in the country?

JACK (*in a very patronising manner*): My dear fellow, the truth isn't quite the sort of thing one tells to a nice, sweet, refined girl. What extraordinary ideas you have about the way to behave to a woman!

ALGERNON: The only way to behave to a woman is to make love to her, if she is pretty, and to some one else, if she is plain.

JACK: Oh, that is nonsense.

ALGERNON: What about your brother? What about the profligate Ernest?

JACK: Oh, before the end of the week I shall have got rid of him. I'll say he died in Paris of apoplexy. Lots of people die of apoplexy, quite suddenly, don't they?

ALGERNON: Yes, but it's hereditary, my dear fellow. It's a sort of thing that runs in families. You had much better say a severe chill.

JACK: You are sure a severe chill isn't hereditary, or anything of that kind?

ALGERNON: Of course it isn't!

JACK: Very well, then. My poor brother Ernest is carried off suddenly, in Paris, by a severe chill. That gets rid of him.

ALGERNON: But I thought you said that . . . Miss Cardew was a little too much interested in your poor brother Ernest? Won't she feel his loss a good deal?

JACK: Oh, that is all right. Cecily is not a silly romantic girl, I am glad to say. She has got a capital appetite, goes long walks, and pays no attention at all to her lessons.

ALGERNON: I would rather like to see Cecily.

JACK: I will take very good care you never do. She is excessively pretty, and she is only just eighteen.

ALGERNON: Have you told Gwendolen yet that you have an excessively pretty ward who is only just eighteen?

JACK: Oh! one doesn't blurt these things out to people. Cecily and

Gwendolen are perfectly certain to be extremely great friends. I'll bet you anything you like that half an hour after they have met, they will be calling each other sister.

ALGERNON: Women only do that when they have called each other a lot of other things first. Now, my dear boy, if we want to get a good table at Willis's, we really must go and dress. Do you know it is nearly seven?

JACK (*irritably*): Oh! it always is nearly seven.

ALGERNON: Well, I'm hungry.

JACK: I never knew you when you weren't. . . .

ALGERNON: What shall we do after dinner? Go to a theatre?

JACK: Oh, no! I loathe listening.

ALGERNON: Well, let us go to the Club?

JACK: Oh, no! I hate talking.

ALGERNON: Well, we might trot round to the Empire at ten?

JACK: Oh, no! I can't bear looking at things. It is so silly.

ALGERNON: Well, what shall we do?

JACK: Nothing!

ALGERNON: It is awfully hard work doing nothing. However, I don't mind hard work where there is no definite object of any kind.

Enter Lane.

LANE: Miss Fairfax.

Enter Gwendolen. Lane goes out.

ALGERNON: Gwendolen, upon my word!

GWENDOLEN: Algy, kindly turn your back. I have something very particular to say to Mr Worthing.

ALGERNON: Really, Gwendolen, I don't think I can allow this at all.

GWENDOLEN: Algy, you always adopt a strictly immoral attitude towards life. You are not quite old enough to do that. (*Algernon retires to the fireplace.*)

JACK: My own darling.

GWENDOLEN: Ernest, we may never be married. From the expression on mamma's face I fear we never shall. Few parents nowadays pay any regard to what their children say to them. The old-fashioned respect for the young is fast dying out. Whatever influence I ever had over mamma, I lost at the age of three. But although she may prevent us from becoming man and wife, and I may marry some one else, and marry often, nothing that she can possibly do can alter my eternal devotion to you.

JACK: Dear Gwendolen!

GWENDOLEN: The story of your romantic origin, as related to me by mamma, with unpleasing comments, has naturally stirred the deeper fibres of my nature. Your Christian name has an irresistible fascination. The simplicity of your character makes you exquisitely incomprehensible to me. Your town address at the Albany I have. What is your address in the country?

JACK: The Manor House, Woolton, Hertfordshire.

Algernon, who has been carefully listening, smiles to himself, and writes the address on his shirt-cuff. Then picks up the Railway Guide.

GWENDOLEN: There is a good postal service, I suppose? It may be necessary to do something desperate. That, of course, will require serious consideration. I will communicate with you daily.

JACK: My own one!

GWENDOLEN: How long do you remain in town?

JACK: Till Monday.

GWENDOLEN: Good! Algy, you may turn round now.

ALGERNON: Thanks, I've turned round already.

GWENDOLEN: You may also ring the bell.

JACK: You will let me see you to your carriage, my own darling?

GWENDOLEN: Certainly.

JACK (*To Lane, who now enters*): I will see Miss Fairfax out.

LANE: Yes, sir. (*Jack and Gwendolen go off.*)
Lane presents several letters on a salver to Algernon. It is to be surmised that they are bills, as Algernon, after looking at the envelopes, tears them up.

ALGERNON: A glass of sherry, Lane.

LANE: Yes, sir.

ALGERNON: To-morrow, Lane, I'm going Bunburying.

LANE: Yes, sir.

ALGERNON: I shall probably not be back till Monday. You can put up my dress clothes, my smoking jacket, and all the Bunbury suits . . .

LANE: Yes, sir. (*Handing sherry.*)

ALGERNON: I hope to-morrow will be a fine day, Lane.

LANE: It never is, sir.

ALGERNON: Lane, you're a perfect pessimist.

LANE: I do my best to give satisfaction, sir.
Enter Jack. Lane goes off.

JACK: There's a sensible, intellectual girl! the only girl I ever cared for in my life. (*Algernon is laughing immoderately.*) What on earth are you so amused at?

ALGERNON: Oh, I'm a little anxious about poor Bunbury, that is all.

JACK: If you don't take care, your friend Bunbury will get you into a serious scrape some day.

ALGERNON: I love scrapes. They are the only things that are never serious.

JACK: Oh, that's nonsense, Algy. You never talk anything but nonsense.

ALGERNON: Nobody ever does.
Jack looks indignantly at him and leaves the room. Algernon lights a cigarette, reads his shirt-cuff, and smiles.

ACT TWO

Scene: Garden at the Manor House. A flight of grey stone steps leads up to the house. The garden, an old-fashioned one, full of roses. Time of year, July. Basket chairs, and a table covered with books, are set under a large yew-tree.

Miss Prism discovered seated at the table. Cecily is at the back watering flowers.

MISS PRISM (*calling*): Cecily, Cecily! Surely such a utilitarian occupation as the watering of flowers is rather Moulton's duty than yours? Especially at a moment when intellectual pleasures await you. Your German grammar is on the table. Pray open it at page fifteen. We will repeat yesterday's lesson.

CECILY (*coming over very slowly*): But I don't like German. It isn't at all a becoming language. I know perfectly well that I look quite plain after my German lesson.

MISS PRISM: Child, you know how anxious your guardian is that you should improve yourself in every way. He laid particular stress on your German, as he was leaving for town yesterday. Indeed, he always lays stress on your German when he is leaving for town.

CECILY: Dear Uncle Jack is so very serious! Sometimes he is so serious that I think he cannot be quite well.

MISS PRISM (*drawing herself up*): Your guardian enjoys the best of health, and his gravity of demeanour is especially to be commended in one so comparatively young as he is. I know no one who has a higher sense of duty and responsibility.

CECILY: I suppose that is why he often looks a little bored when we three are together.

MISS PRISM: Cecily! I am surprised at you. Mr Worthing has many troubles in his life. Idle merriment and triviality would be out of place in his conversation. You must remember his constant anxiety about that unfortunate young man his brother.

CECILY: I wish Uncle Jack would allow that unfortunate young man, his brother, to come down here sometimes. We might have a good influence over him, Miss Prism. I am sure you certainly would. You know German, and geology, and things of that kind influence a man very much. (*Cecily begins to write in her diary.*)

MISS PRISM (*shaking her head*): I do not think that even I could produce any effect on a character that according to his own brother's admission is irretrievably weak and vacillating. Indeed I am not sure that I would desire to reclaim him. I am not in favour of this modern mania for turning bad people into good people at a moment's notice. As a man sows so let him reap. You must put away your diary, Cecily. I really don't see why you should keep a diary at all.

CECILY: I keep a diary in order to enter the wonderful secrets of my life. If I didn't write them down, I should probably forget all about them.

MISS PRISM: Memory, my dear Cecily, is the diary that we all carry about with us.

CECILY: Yes, but it usually chronicles the things that have never happened, and couldn't possibly have happened. I believe that Memory is responsible for nearly all the three-volume novels that Mudie sends us.

MISS PRISM: Do not speak slightingly of the three-volume novel, Cecily. I wrote one myself in earlier days.

CECILY: Did you really, Miss Prism? How wonderfully clever you are! I hope it did not end happily? I don't like novels that end happily. They depress me so much.

MISS PRISM: The good ended happily, and the bad unhappily. That is what Fiction means.

CECILY: I suppose so. But it seems very unfair. And was your novel ever published?

MISS PRISM: Alas! no. The manuscript was abandoned. (*Cecily starts.*) I use the word in the sense of lost or mislaid. To your work, child, these speculations are profitless.

CECILY (*smiling*): But I see Dr Chasuble coming up through the garden.

MISS PRISM (*rising and advancing*): Dr Chasuble! This is indeed a pleasure. *Enter Canon Chasuble.*

CHASUBLE: And how are we this morning? Miss Prism, you are, I trust, well?

CECILY: Miss Prism has just been complaining of a slight headache. I think it would do her so much good to have a short stroll with you in the Park, Dr Chasuble.

MISS PRISM: Cecily, I have not mentioned anything about a headache.

CECILY: No, dear Miss Prism, I know that, but I felt instinctively that you had a headache. Indeed I was thinking about that, and not about my German lesson, when the Rector came in.

CHASUBLE: I hope, Cecily, you are not inattentive.

CECILY: Oh, I am afraid I am.

CHASUBLE: That is strange. Were I fortunate enough to be Miss Prism's pupil, I would hang upon her lips. (*Miss Prism glares.*) I spoke metaphorically. – My metaphor was drawn from bees. Ahem! Mr Worthing, I suppose, has not returned from town yet?

MISS PRISM: We do not expect him till Monday afternoon.

CHASUBLE: Ah yes, he usually likes to spend his Sunday in London. He is not one of those whose sole aim is enjoyment, as, by all accounts, that unfortunate young man his brother seems to be. But I must not disturb Egeria and her pupil any longer.

MISS PRISM: Egeria? My name is Laetitia, Doctor.

CHASUBLE (*bowing*): A classical allusion merely, drawn from the Pagan authors. I shall see you both no doubt at Evensong?

MISS PRISM: I think, dear Doctor, I will have a stroll with you. I find I have a headache after all, and a walk might do it good.

CHASUBLE: With pleasure, Miss Prism, with pleasure. We might go as far as the schools and back.

MISS PRISM: That would be delightful. Cecily, you will read your Political Economy in my absence. The chapter on the Fall of the Rupee you may omit. It is somewhat too sensational. Even these metallic problems have their melodramatic side.
Goes down the garden with Dr Chasuble.

CECILY (*picks up books and throws them back on table*): Horrid Political Economy! Horrid Geography! Horrid, horrid German!
Enter Merriman with a card on a salver.

288THE BEDSIDE WILDE

MERRIMAN: Mr Ernest Worthing has just driven over from the station. He has brought his luggage with him.

CECILY (*takes the card and reads it*): 'Mr Ernest Worthing, B.4, The Albany, W.' Uncle Jack's brother! Did you tell him Mr Worthing was in town?

MERRIMAN: Yes, Miss. He seemed very much disappointed. I mentioned that you and Miss Prism were in the garden. He said he was anxious to speak to you privately for a moment.

CECILY: Ask Mr Ernest Worthing to come here. I suppose you had better talk to the housekeeper about a room for him.

MERRIMAN: Yes, Miss.

Merriman goes off.

CECILY: I have never met any really wicked person before. I feel rather frightened. I am so afraid he will look just like every one else.

Enter Algernon, very gay and debonair.

He does!

ALGERNON (*raising his hat*): You are my little cousin Cecily, I'm sure.

CECILY: You are under some strange mistake. I am not little. In fact, I believe I am more than usually tall for my age. (*Algernon is rather taken aback.*) But I am your cousin Cecily. You, I see from your card, are Uncle Jack's brother, my cousin Ernest, my wicked cousin Ernest.

ALGERNON: Oh! I am not really wicked at all, cousin Cecily. You mustn't think that I am wicked.

CECILY: If you are not, then you have certainly been deceiving us all in a very inexcusable manner. I hope you have not been leading a double life, pretending to be wicked and being really good all the time. That would be hypocrisy.

ALGERNON (*looks at her in amazement*): Oh! Of course I have been rather reckless.

CECILY: I am glad to hear it.

ALGERNON: In fact, now you mention the subject, I have been very bad in my own small way.

CECILY: I don't think you should be so proud of that, though I am sure it must have been very pleasant.

ALGERNON: It is much pleasanter being here with you.

CECILY: I can't understand how you are here at all. Uncle Jack won't be back till Monday afternoon.

ALGERNON: That is a great disappointment. I am obliged to go up by the first train on Monday morning. I have a business appointment that I am anxious . . . to miss!

CECILY: Couldn't you miss it anywhere but in London?

ALGERNON: No: the appointment is in London.

CECILY: Well, I know, of course, how important it is not to keep a business engagement, if one wants to retain any sense of the beauty of life, but still I think you had better wait till Uncle Jack arrives. I know he wants to speak to you about your emigrating.

ALGERNON: About my what?

CECILY: Your emigrating. He has gone up to buy your outfit.

ALGERNON: I certainly wouldn't let Jack buy my outfit. He has no taste in neckties at all.

CECILY: I don't think you will require neckties. Uncle Jack is sending you to Australia.

ALGERNON: Australia! I'd sooner die.

CECILY: Well, he said at dinner on Wednesday night, that you would have to choose between this world, the next world, and Australia.

ALGERNON: Oh, well! The accounts I have received of Australia and the next world, are not particularly encouraging. This world is good enough for me, cousin Cecily.

CECILY: Yes, but are you good enough for it?

ALGERNON: I'm afraid I'm not that. That is why I want you to reform me. You might make that your mission, if you don't mind, cousin Cecily.

CECILY: I'm afraid I've no time, this afternoon.

ALGERNON: Well, would you mind my reforming myself this afternoon?

CECILY: It is rather Quixotic of you. But I think you should try.

ALGERNON: I will. I feel better already.

CECILY: You are looking a little worse.

ALGERNON: That is because I am hungry.

CECILY: How thoughtless of me. I should have remembered that when one is going to lead an entirely new life, one requires regular and wholesome meals. Won't you come in?

ALGERNON: Thank you. Might I have a buttonhole first? I never have any appetite unless I have a buttonhole first.

CECILY: A Maréchal Niel? (*Picks up scissors.*)

ALGERNON: No, I'd sooner have a pink rose.

CECILY: Why? (*Cuts a flower.*)

ALGERNON: Because you are like a pink rose, cousin Cecily.

CECILY: I don't think it can be right for you to talk to me like that. Miss Prism never says such things to me.

ALGERNON: Then Miss Prism is a short-sighted old lady. (*Cecily puts the rose in his buttonhole.*) You are the prettiest girl I ever saw.

CECILY: Miss Prism says that all good looks are a snare.

ALGERNON: They are a snare that every sensible man would like to be caught in.

CECILY: Oh, I don't think I would care to catch a sensible man. I shouldn't know what to talk to him about.

They pass into the house. Miss Prism and Dr Chasuble return.

MISS PRISM: You are too much alone, dear Dr Chasuble. You should get married. A misanthrope I can understand – a woman-thrope, never!

CHASUBLE (*with a scholar's shudder*): Believe me, I do not deserve so neologistic a phrase. The precept as well as the practice of the Primitive Church was distinctly against matrimony.

MISS PRISM (*sententiously*): That is obviously the reason why the Primitive Church has not lasted up to the present day. And you do not seem to realise, dear Doctor, that by persistently remaining single, a man converts himself into a permanent public temptation. Men should be more careful; this very celibacy leads weaker vessels astray.

CHASUBLE: But is a man not equally attractive when married?

MISS PRISM: No married man is ever attractive except to his wife.

CHASUBLE: And often, I've been told, not even to her.

MISS PRISM: That depends on the intellectual sympathies of the woman. Maturity can always be depended on. Ripeness can be trusted. Young women are green. (*Dr Chasuble starts.*) I spoke horticulturally. My metaphor was drawn from fruit. But where is Cecily?

CHASUBLE: Perhaps she followed us to the schools.

Enter Jack slowly from the back of the garden. He is dressed in the deepest mourning, with crêpe hatband and black gloves.

MISS PRISM: Mr Worthing!

CHASUBLE: Mr Worthing?

MISS PRISM: This is indeed a surprise. We did not look for you till Monday afternoon.

JACK (*shakes Miss Prism's hand in a tragic manner*): I have returned sooner than I expected. Dr Chasuble, I hope you are well?

CHASUBLE: Dear Mr Worthing, I trust this garb of woe does not betoken some terrible calamity?

JACK: My brother.

MISS PRISM: More shameful debts and extravagance?

CHASUBLE: Still leading his life of pleasure?

JACK (*shaking his head*): Dead!

CHASUBLE: Your brother Ernest dead?

JACK: Quite dead.

MISS PRISM: What a lesson for him! I trust he will profit by it.

CHASUBLE: Mr Worthing, I offer you my sincere condolence. You have at least the consolation of knowing that you were always the most generous and forgiving of brothers.

JACK: Poor Ernest! He had many faults, but it is a sad, sad blow.

CHASUBLE: Very sad indeed. Were you with him at the end?

JACK: No he died abroad; in Paris, in fact. I had a telegram last night from the manager of the Grand Hotel.

CHASUBLE: Was the cause of death mentioned?

JACK: A severe chill, it seems.

MISS PRISM: As a man sows, so shall he reap.

CHASUBLE (*raising his hand*): Charity, dear Miss Prism, charity! None of us are perfect. I myself am peculiarly susceptible to draughts. Will the interment take place here?

JACK: No. He seems to have expressed a desire to be buried in Paris.

CHASUBLE: In Paris! (*Shakes his head.*) I fear that hardly points to any very serious state of mind at the last. You would no doubt wish to make some slight allusion to this tragic domestic affliction next Sunday. (*Jack presses his hand convulsively.*) My sermon on the meaning of the manna in the wilderness can be adapted to almost any occasion, joyful, or, as in the present case, distressing. (*All sigh.*) I have preached it at harvest celebrations, christenings, confirmations, on days of humiliation and festal days. The last time I delivered it was in the Cathedral, as a charity sermon on behalf of the Society for the Prevention of Discontent among the Upper Orders. The Bishop, who was present, was much struck by some of the analogies I drew.

JACK: Ah! that reminds me, you mentioned christenings, I think, Dr Chasuble? I suppose you know how to christen all right? (*Dr Chasuble looks astounded.*) I mean, of course, you are continually christening, aren't you?

MISS PRISM: It is, I regret to say, one of the Rector's most constant duties in this parish. I have often spoken to the poorer classes on the subject. But they don't seem to know what thrift is.

CHASUBLE: But is there any particular infant in whom you are interested, Mr Worthing? Your brother was, I believe, unmarried, was he not?

JACK: Oh yes.

MISS PRISM (*bitterly*): People who live entirely for pleasure usually are.

JACK: But it is not for any child, dear Doctor. I am very fond of children. No! the fact is, I would like to be christened myself, this afternoon, if you have nothing better to do.

CHASUBLE: But surely, Mr Worthing, you have been christened already?

JACK: I don't remember anything about it.

CHASUBLE: But have you any grave doubts on the subject?

JACK: I certainly intend to have. Of course I don't know if the thing would bother you in any way, or if you think I am a little too old now.

CHASUBLE: Not at all. The sprinkling, and, indeed, the immersion of adults is a perfectly canonical practice.

JACK: Immersion!

CHASUBLE: You need have no apprehensions. Sprinkling is all that is necessary, or indeed I think advisable. Our weather is so changeable. At what hour would you wish the ceremony performed?

JACK: Oh, I might trot round about five if that would suit you.

CHASUBLE: Perfectly, perfectly! In fact, I have two similar ceremonies to perform at that time. A case of twins that occurred recently in one of the outlying cottages on your own estate. Poor Jenkins the carter, a most hard-working man.

JACK: Oh! I don't see much fun in being christened along with other babies. It would be childish. Would half-past five do?

CHASUBLE: Admirably! Admirably! (*Takes our watch.*) And now, dear Mr Worthing, I will not intrude any longer into a house of sorrow. I would merely beg you not to be too much bowed down by grief. What seem to us bitter trials are often blessings in disguise.

MISS PRISM: This seems to me a blessing of an extremely obvious kind.
Enter Cecily from the house.

CECILY: Uncle Jack! Oh, I am pleased to see you back. But what horrid clothes you have got on! Do go and change them.

MISS PRISM: Cecily!

CHASUBLE: My child! my child! (*Cecily goes towards Jack; he kisses her brow in a melancholy manner.*)

CECILY: What is the matter, Uncle Jack? Do look happy! You look as if you had toothache, and I have got such a surprise for you. Who do you think is in the Dining-room? Your brother!

JACK: Who?

POEMS

HUMANITAD

It is full winter now: the trees are bare,
   Save where the cattle huddle from the cold
Beneath the pine, for it doth never wear
   The Autumn's gaudy livery whose gold
Her jealous brother pilfers, but is true
To the green doublet; bitter is the wind, as though it blew

From Saturn's cave; a few thin wisps of hay
   Lie on the sharp black hedges, where the wain
Dragged the sweet pillage of a summer's day
   From the low meadows up the narrow lane;
Upon the half-thawed snow the bleating sheep
Press close against the hurdles, and the shivering house-
      dogs creep

From the shut stable to the frozen stream
   And back again disconsolate, and miss
The bawling shepherds and the noisy team;
   And overhead in circling listlessness
The cawing rooks whirl round the frosted stack,
Or crowd the dripping boughs; and in the fen the icepools
      crack

Where the gaunt bittern stalks among the reeds
   And flaps his wings, and stretches back his neck,
And hoots to see the moon; across the meads
   Limps the poor frightened hare, a little speck;
And a stray seamew with its fretful cry
Flits like a sudden drift of snow against the dull grey sky.

Full winter: and the lusty goodman brings
   His load of faggots from the chilly byre,
And stamps his feet upon the hearth, and flings
   The sappy billets on the waning fire,
And laughs to see the sudden lightening scare
His children at their play; and yet, – the Spring is in the
      air.

Already the slim crocus stirs the snow,
   And soon yon blanchèd fields will bloom again
With nodding cowslips for some lad to mow,
   For with the first warm kisses of the rain

The winter's icy sorrow breaks to tears,
And the brown thrushes mate, and with bright eyes the
    rabbit peers

From the dark warren where the fir-cones lie,
    And treads one snowdrop under foot, and runs
Over the mossy knoll, and blackbirds fly
    Across our path at evening, and the suns
Stay longer with us; ah! how good to see
Grass-girdled Spring in all her joy of laughing greenery

Dance through the hedges till the early rose,
    (That sweet repentance of the thorny brier!)
Burst from its sheathèd emerald and disclose
    The little quivering disk of golden fire
Which the bees know so well, for with it come
Pale boy's-love, sops-in-wine, and daffodillies all in bloom.

Then up and down the field the sower goes,
    While close behind the laughing younker scares
With shrilly whoop the black and thievish crows,
    And then the chestnut-tree its glory wears,
And on the grass the creamy blossom falls
In odorous excess, and faint half-whispered madrigals

Steal from the bluebells' nodding carillons
    Each breezy morn, and then white jessamine,
That star of its own heaven, snap-dragons
    With lolling crimson tongues, and eglantine
In dusty velvets clad usurp the bed
And woodland empery, and when the lingering rose hath
    shed

Red leaf by leaf its folded panoply,
    And pansies closed their purple-lidded eyes,
Chrysanthemums from gilded argosy
    Unload their gaudy scentless merchandise,
And violets getting overbold withdraw
From their shy nooks, and scarlet berries dot the leafless
    haw.

O happy field! and O thrice happy tree!
    Soon will your queen in daisy-flowered smock
And crown of flower-de-luce trip down the lea,
    Soon will the lazy shepherds drive their flock
Back to the pasture by the pool, and soon

Through the green leaves will float the hum of murmuring
    bees at noon.

Soon will the glade be bright with bellamour,
    The flower which wantons love, and those sweet nuns
Vale-lilies in their snowy vestiture
    Will tell their beaded pearls, and carnations
With mitred dusky leaves will scent the wind,
And straggling traveller's-joy each hedge with yellow stars
    will bind.

Dear Bride of Nature and most bounteous Spring!
    That canst give increase to the sweet-breath'd kine,
And to the kid its little horns, and bring
    The soft and silky blossoms to the vine,
Where is that old nepenthe which of yore
Man got from poppy root and glossy-berried mandragore!

There was a time when any common bird
    Could make me sing in unison, a time
When all the strings of boyish life were stirred
    To quick response or more melodious rhyme
By every forest idyll; – do I change?
Or rather doth some evil thing through thy fair pleasaunce
    range?

Nay, nay, thou art the same: 'tis I who seek
    To vex with sighs thy simple solitude,
And because fruitless tears bedew my cheek
    Would have thee weep with me in brotherhood;
Fool! shall each wronged and restless spirit dare
To taint such wine with the salt poison of his own despair!

Thou art the same: 'tis I whose wretched soul
    Takes discontent to be its paramour,
And gives its kingdom to the rude control
    Of what should be its servitor, – for sure
Wisdom is somewhere, though the stormy sea
Contain it not, and the huge deep answer ''Tis not in me.'

To burn with one clear flame, to stand erect
    In natural honour, not to bend the knee
In profitless prostrations whose effect
    Is by itself condemned, what alchemy
Can teach me this? what herb Medea brewed
Will bring the unexultant peace of essence not subdued?

The minor chord which ends the harmony,

And for its answering brother waits in vain
Sobbing for incompleted melody,
    Dies a Swan's death; but I the heir of pain,
A silent Memnon with blank lidless eyes,
Wait for the light and music of those suns which never rise.

The quenched-out torch, the lonely cypress-gloom,
    The little dust stored in the narrow urn,
The gentle XAIPE* of the Attic tomb, –
    Were not these better far than to return
To my old fitful restless malady,
Or spend my days within the voiceless cave of misery?

Nay! for perchance that poppy-crownèd God
    Is like the watcher by a sick man's bed
Who talks of sleep but gives it not; his rod
    Hath lost its virtue, and, when all is said,
Death is too rude, too obvious a key
To solve one single secret in a life's philosophy.

And Love! that noble madness, whose august
    And inextinguishable might can slay
The soul with honied drugs, – alas! I must
    From such sweet ruin play the runaway,
Although too constant memory never can
Forget the archèd splendour of those brows Olympian

Which for a little season made my youth
    So soft a swoon of exquisite indolence
That all the chiding of more prudent Truth
    Seemed the thin voice of jealousy, – O Hence
Thou huntress deadlier than Artemis!
Go seek some other quarry! for of thy too perilous bliss

My lips have drunk enough, – no more, no more, –
    Though Love himself should turn his gilded prow
Back to the troubled waters of this shore
    Where I am wrecked and stranded, even now
The chariot wheels of passion sweep too near,
Hence! Hence! I pass into a life more barren, more austere.

More barren – ay, those arms will never lean
    Down through the trellised vines and draw my soul
In sweet reluctance through the tangled green;
    Some other head must wear that aureole,
For I am Hers who loves not any man

*Translation: Farewell.

Whose white and stainless bosom bears the sign Gorgonian.

Let Venus go and chuck her dainty page,
    And kiss his mouth, and toss his curly hair,
With net and spear and hunting equipage
    Let young Adonis to his tryst repair,
But me her fond and subtle-fashioned spell
Delights no more, though I could win her dearest citadel.

Ay, though I were that laughing shepherd boy
    Who from Mount Ida saw the little cloud
Pass over Tenedos and lofty Troy
    And knew the coming of the Queen, and bowed
In wonder at her feet, not for the sake
Of a new Helen would I bid her hand the apple take.

Then rise supreme Athena argent-limbed!
    And, if my lips be music-less, inspire
At least my life: was not thy glory hymned
    By One who gave to thee his sword and lyre
Like Æschylos at well-fought Marathon,
And died to show that Milton's England still could bear a
    son!

And yet I cannot tread the Portico
    And live without desire, fear and pain,
Or nurture that wise calm which long ago
    The grave Athenian master taught to men,
Self-poised, self-centred, and self-comforted,
To watch the world's vain phantasies go by with unbowed
    head.

Alas! that serene brow, those eloquent lips,
    Those eyes that mirrored all eternity,
Rest in their own Colonos, an eclipse
    Hath come on Wisdom, and Mnemosyne
Is childless; in the night which she had made
For lofty secure flight Athena's owl itself hath strayed.

Nor much with Science do I care to climb,
    Although by strange and subtle witchery
She draw the moon from heaven; the Muse of Time
    Unrolls her gorgeous-coloured tapestry
To no less eager eyes; often indeed
In the great epic of Polymnia's scroll I love to read

How Asia sent her myriad hosts to war
    Against a little town, and panoplied

In gilded mail with jewelled scimitar,
   White-shielded, purple-crested, rode the Mede
Between the waving poplars and the sea
Which men call Artemisium, till he saw Thermopylae

Its steep ravine spanned by a narrow wall,
   And on the nearer side a little brood
Of careless lions holding festival!
   And stood amazèd at such hardihood,
And pitched his tent upon the reedy shore,
And stayed two days to wonder, and then crept at midnight
   o'er

Some unfrequented height, and coming down
   The autumn forests treacherously slew
What Sparta held most dear and was the crown
   Of far Eurotas, and passed on, nor knew
How God had staked an evil net for him
In the small bay at Salamis, – and yet, the page grows dim,

Its cadenced Greek delights me not, I feel
   With such a goodly time too out of tune
To love it much: for like the Dials wheel
   That from its blinded darkness strikes the noon
Yet never sees the sun, so do my eyes
Restlessly follow that which from my cheated vision flies.

O for one grand unselfish simple life
   To teach us what is Wisdom! speak ye hills
Of lone Helvellyn, for this note of strife
   Shunned your untroubled crags and crystal rills,
Where is that spirit which living blamelessly
Yet dared to kiss the smitten mouth of his own century!

Speak ye Rydalian laurels! where is He
   Whose gentle head ye sheltered, that pure soul
Whose gracious days of uncrowned majesty
   Through lowliest conduct touched the lofty goal
Where Love and Duty mingle! Him at least
The most high Laws were glad of, He had sat at Wisdom's
   feast,

But we are Learning's changelings, know by rote
   The clarion watchword of each Grecian school
And follow none, the flawless sword which smote
   The pagan Hydra is an effete tool
Which we ourselves have blunted, what man now

Shall scale the august ancient heights and to old Reverence
   bow?

One such indeed I saw, but, Ichabod!
   Gone is that last dear son of Italy,
Who being man died for the sake of God,
   And whose un-risen bones sleep peacefully,
O guard him, guard him well, my Giotto's tower,
Thou marble lily of the lily town! let not the lour

Of the rude tempest vex his slumber, or
   The Arno with its tawny troubled gold
O'er-leap its marge, no mightier conqueror
   Clomb the high Capitol in the days of old
When Rome was indeed Rome, for Liberty
Walked like a Bride beside him, at which sight pale Mystery

Fled shrieking to her farthest sombrest cell
   With an old man who grabbled rusty keys,
Fled shuddering, for that immemorial knell
   With which oblivion buries dynasties
Swept like a wounded eagle on the blast,
As to the holy heart of Rome the great triumvir passed.

He knew the holiest heart and heights of Rome,
   He drave the base wolf from the lion's lair,
And now lies dead by that empyreal dome
   Which overtops Valdarno hung in air
By Brunelleschi – O Melpomene
Breathe through thy melancholy pipe the sweetest
   threnody!

Breathe through the tragic stops such melodies
   That Joy's self may grow jealous, and the Nine
Forget awhile their discreet emperies,
   Mourning for him who on Rome's lordliest shrine
Lit for men's lives the light of Marathon,
And bare to sun-forgotten fields the fire of the sun!

O guard him, guard him well, my Giotto's tower,
   Let some young Florentine each eventide
Bring coronals of that enchanted flower
   Which the dim woods of Vallombrosa hide,
And deck the marble tomb wherein he lies
Whose soul is as some mighty orb unseen of mortal eyes.

Some mighty orb whose cycled wanderings,
   Being tempest-driven to the farthest rim

Where Chaos meets Creation and the wings
  Of the eternal chanting Cherubim
Are pavilioned on Nothing, passed away
Into a moonless void, – and yet, though he is dust and clay,

He is not dead, the immemorial Fates
  Forbid it, and the closing shears refrain,
Lift up your heads ye everlasting gates!
  Ye argent clarions, sound a loftier strain!
For the vile thing he hated lurks within
Its sombre house, alone with God and memories of sin.

Still what avails it that she sought her cave
  That murderous mother of red harlotries?
At Munich on the marble architrave
  The Grecian boys die smiling, but the seas
Which wash Ægina fret in loneliness
Not mirroring their beauty, so our lives grow colourless

For lack of our ideals, if one star
  Flame torch-like in the heavens the unjust
Swift daylight kills it, and no trump of war
  Can wake to passionate voice the silent dust
Which was Mazzini once! rich Niobe
For all her stony sorrows hath her sons, but Italy!

What Easter Day shall make her children rise,
  Who were not Gods yet suffered? what sure feet
Shall find their grave-clothes folded? what clear eyes
  Shall see them bodily? O it were meet
To roll the stone from off the sepulchre
And kiss the bleeding roses of their wounds, in love of Her

Our Italy! our mother visible!
  Most blessed among nations and most sad,
For whose dear sake the young Calabrian fell
  That day at Aspromonte and was glad
That in an age when God was bought and sold
One man could die for Liberty! but we, burnt out and cold,

See Honour smitten on the cheek and gyves
  Bind the sweet feet of Mercy: Poverty
Creeps through our sunless lanes and with sharp knives
  Cuts the warm throats of children stealthily,
And no word said: – O we are wretched men
Unworthy of our great inheritance! where is the pen

Of austere Milton? where the mighty sword

Which slew its master righteously? the years
Have lost their ancient leader, and no word
   Breaks from the voiceless tripod on our ears:
While as a ruined mother in some spasm
Bears a base child and loathes it, so our best enthusiasm

Genders unlawful children, Anarchy
   Freedom's own Judas, the vile prodigal
Licence who steals the gold of Liberty
   And yet has nothing, Ignorance the real
One Fratricide since Cain, Envy the asp
That stings itself to anguish, Avarice whose palsied grasp

Is in its extent stiffened, moneyed Greed
   For whose dull appetite men waste away
Amid the whirr of wheels and are the seed
   Of things which slay their sower, these each day
Sees rife in England, and the gentle feet
Of Beauty tread no more the stones of each unlovely street.

What even Cromwell spared is desecrated
   By weed and worm, left to the stormy play
Of wind and beating snow, or renovated
   By more destructful hands: Time's worst decay
Will wreathe its ruins with some loveliness,
But these new Vandals can but make a rainproof
    barrenness.

Where is that Art which bade the Angels sing
   Through Lincoln's lofty choir, till the air
Seems from such marble harmonies to ring
   With sweeter song than common lips can dare
To draw from actual reed? ah! where is now
The cunning hand which made the flowering hawthorn
    branches bow

For Southwell's arch, and carved the House of One
   Who loved the lilies of the field with all
Our dearest English flowers? the same sun
   Rises for us: the seasons natural
Weave the same tapestry of green and grey:
The unchanged hills are with us: but that Spirit hath passed
    away.

And yet perchance it may be better so,
   For Tyranny is an incestuous Queen,
Murder her brother is her bedfellow,
   And the Plague chambers with her: in obscene

And bloody paths her treacherous feet are set;
Better the empty desert and a soul inviolate!

For gentle brotherhood, the harmony
    Of living in the healthful air, the swift
Clean beauty of strong limbs when men are free
    And women chaste, these are the things which lift
Our souls up more than even Agnolo's
Gaunt blinded Sibyl poring o'er the scroll of human woes,

Or Titian's little maiden on the stair
    White as her own sweet lily and as tall,
Or Mona Lisa smiling through her hair, –
    Ah! somehow life is bigger after all
Than any painted Angel, could we see
The God that is within us! The old Greek serenity

Which curbs the passion of that level line
    Or marble youths, who with untroubled eyes
And chastened limbs ride round Athena's shrine
    And mirror her divine economies,
And balanced symmetry what in man
Would else wage ceaseless warfare, – this at least within
        the span

Between our mother's kisses and the grave
    Might so inform our lives, that we could win
Such mighty empires that from her cave
    Temptation would grow hoarse, and pallid Sin
Would walk ashamed of his adulteries,
And Passion creep from out the House of Lust with startled
        eyes.

To make the Body and the Spirit one
    With all right things, till no thing live in vain
From morn to noon, but in sweet unison
    With every pulse of flesh and throb of brain
The soul in flawless essence high enthroned,
Against all outer vain attack invincibly bastioned,

Mark with serene impartiality
    The strife of things, and yet be comforted,
Knowing that by the chain causality
    All separate existences are wed
Into one supreme whole, whose utterance
Is joy, or holier praise! ah! surely this were governance

Of Life in most august omnipresence,

Through which the rational intellect would find
In passion its expression, and mere sense,
  Ignoble else, lend fire to the mind,
And being joined with it in harmony ·
More mystical than that which binds the stars planetary,

Strike from their several tones one octave chord
  Whose cadence being measureless would fly
Through all the circling spheres, then to its Lord
  Return refreshed with its new empery
And more exultant power, – this indeed
  Could we but reach it were to find the last, the perfect
    creed.

Ah! It was easy when the world was young
  To keep one's life free and inviolate,
From our sad lips another song is rung,
  By our hands our heads are desecrate,
Wanderers in drear exile, and dispossessed
Of what should be our own, we can but feed on wild unrest.

Somehow, the grace, the bloom of things has flown,
  And of all men we are most wretched who
Must live each other's lives and not our own
  For very pity's sake and then undo
All that we lived for – it was otherwise
When soul and body seemed to blend in mystic symphonies.

But we have left those gentle haunts to pass
  With weary feet to the new Calvary,
Where we behold, as one who in a glass
  Sees his own face, self-slain Humanity,
And in the dumb reproach of that sad gaze
Learn what an awful phantom the red hand of man can
    raise.

O smitten mouth! O forehead crowned with thorn!
  O chalice of all common miseries!
Thou for our sakes that loved thee not hast borne
  An agony of endless centuries,
And we were vain and ignorant nor knew
That when we stabbed thy heart it was our own real hearts
    we slew.

Being ourselves the sowers and the seeds,
  The night that covers and the lights that fade,
The spear that pierces and the side that bleeds,

The lips betraying and the life betrayed;
The deep hath calm: the moon hath rest: but we
Lords of the natural world are yet our own dread enemy.

Is this the end of all that primal force
    Which, in its changes being still the same,
From eyeless Chaos cleft its upward course,
    Through ravenous seas and whirling rocks and flame,
Till the suns met in heaven and began
Their cycles, and the morning stars sang, and the Word
        was Man!

Nay, nay, we are but crucified, and though
    The bloody sweat falls from our brows like rain,
Loosen the nails – we shall come down I know,
    Staunch the red wounds – we shall be whole again,
No need have we of hyssop-laden rod,
That which is purely human, that is Godlike, that is God.

VITA NUOVA

I stood by the unvintageable sea
    Till the wet waves drenched face and hair with spray;
    The long red fires of the dying day
Burned in the west; the wind piped drearily;
And to the land the clamorous gulls did flee:
    'Alas!' I cried, 'my life is full of pain,
    And who can garner fruit or golden grain
From these waste fields which travel ceaselessly!'
My nets gaped wide with many a break and flaw,
    Nathless I threw them as my final cast
    Into the sea, and waited for the end.
When lo! a sudden glory! and I saw
    The argent splendour of white limbs ascend,
    And in that joy forgot my tortured past.

THE BALLAD OF READING GAOL

I

He did not wear his scarlet coat,
    For blood and wine are red,
And blood and wine were on his hands
    When they found him with the dead,
The poor dead woman whom he loved,
    And murdered in her bed.

He walked amongst the Trial Men
    In a suit of shabby grey;
A cricket cap was on his head,
    And his step seemed light and gay;
But I never saw a man who looked
    So wistfully at the day.

I never saw a man who looked
    With such a wistful eye
Upon that little tent of blue
    Which prisoners call the sky,
And at every drifting cloud that went
    With sails of silver by.

I walked, with other souls in pain,
    Within another ring,
And was wondering if the man had done
    A great or little thing,
When a voice behind me whispered low,
    That fellow's got to swing.

Dear Christ! The very prison walls
    Suddenly seemed to reel,
And the sky above my head became
    Like a casque of scorching steel;
And, though I was a soul in pain,
    My pain I could not feel.

I only knew what hunted thought
    Quickened his step, and why
He looked upon the garish day
    With such a wistful eye;
The man had killed the thing he loved,
    And so he had to die.

*

Yet each man kills the thing he loves,
  By each let this be heard,
Some do it with a bitter look,
  Some with a flattering word,
The coward does it with a kiss,
  The brave man with a sword!

Some kill their love when they are young,
  And some when they are old;
Some strangle with the hands of Lust,
  Some with the hands of Gold:
The kindest use a knife, because
  The dead so soon grow cold.

Some love too little, some too long,
  Some sell, and others buy;
Some do the deed with many tears,
  And some without a sigh:
For each man kills the thing he loves,
  Yet each man does not die.

He does not die a death of shame
  On a day of dark disgrace,
Nor have a noose about his neck,
  Nor a cloth upon his face,
Nor drop feet foremost through the floor
  Into an empty space.

He does not sit with silent men
  Who watch him night and day;
Who watch him when he tries to weep,
  And when he tries to pray;
Who watch him lest himself should rob
  The prison of its prey.

He does not wake at dawn to see
  Dread figures throng his room,
The shivering Chaplain robed in white,
  The Sheriff stern with gloom,
And the Governor all in shiny black,
  With the yellow face of Doom.

He does not rise in piteous haste
  To put on convict-clothes,
While some coarse-mouthed Doctor gloats, and
    notes
  Each new and nerve-twitched pose,
Fingering a watch whose little ticks
  Are like horrible hammer-blows.

He does not feel that sickening thirst
   That sands one's throat, before
The hangman with his gardener's gloves
   Comes through the padded door,
And binds one with three leathern thongs,
   That the throat may thirst no more.

He does not bend his head to hear
   The Burial Office read,
Nor, while the anguish of his soul
   Tells him he is not dead,
Cross his own coffin, as he moves
   Into the hideous shed.

He does not stare upon the air
   Through a little roof of glass:
He does not pray with lips of clay
   For his agony to pass;
Nor feel upon his shuddering cheek
   The kiss of Caiaphas.

II

Six weeks the guardsman walked the yard,
   In the suit of shabby grey:
His cricket cap was on his head,
   And his step seemed light and gay,
But I never saw a man who looked
   So wistfully at the day.

I never saw a man who looked
   With such a wistful eye
Upon that little tent of blue
   Which prisoners call the sky,
And at every wandering cloud that trailed
   Its ravelled fleeces by.

He did not wring his hands, as do
   Those witless men who dare
To try to rear the changeling Hope
   In the cave of black Despair:
He only looked upon the sun,
   And drank the morning air.

He did not wring his hands nor weep,
   Nor did he peek or pine,
But he drank the air as though it held
   Some healthful anodyne;
With open mouth he drank the sun
   As though it had been wine!

And I and all the souls in pain,
  Who tramped the other ring,
Forgot if we ourselves had done
  A great or little thing,
And watched with gaze of dull amaze
  The man who had to swing.

For strange it was to see him pass
  With a step so light and gay,
And strange it was to see him look
  So wistfully at the day,
And strange it was to think that he
  Had such a debt to pay.

For oak and elm have pleasant leaves
  That in the spring-time shoot;
But grim to see is the gallows-tree,
  With its adder-bitten root,
And, green or dry, a man must die
  Before it bears its fruit!

The loftiest place is that seat of grace
  For which all worldlings try:
But who would stand in hempen band
  Upon a scaffold high,
And through a murderer's collar take
  His last look at the sky?

It is sweet to dance to violins
  When Love and Life are fair:
To dance to flutes, to dance to lutes
  Is delicate and rare:
But it is not sweet with nimble feet
  To dance upon the air!

So with curious eyes and sick surmise
  We watched him day by day,
And wondered if each one of us
  Would end the self-same way,
For none can tell to what red Hell
  His sightless soul may stray.

At last the dead man walked no more
  Amongst the Trial Men,
And I knew that he was standing up
  In the black dock's dreadful pen,
And that never would I see his face
  For weal or woe again.

Like two doomed ships that pass in storm
 We had crossed each other's way:
But we made no sign, we said no word,
 We had no word to say;
For we did not meet in the holy night,
 But in the shameful day.

A prison wall was round us both,
 Two outcast men we were:
The world had thrust us from its heart,
 And God from out His care:
 And the iron gin that waits for Sin
  Had caught us in its snare.

III

In Debtor's Yard the stones are hard,
 And the dripping wall is high,
So it was there he took the air
 Beneath the leaden sky,
And by each side a Warder walked,
 For fear the man might die.

Or else he sat with those who watched
 His anguish night and day;
Who watched him when he rose to weep,
 And when he crouched to pray;
Who watched him lest himself should rob
 Their scaffold of its prey.

The Governor was strong upon
 The Regulations Act:
The Doctor said that Death was but
 A scientific fact:
And twice a day the Chaplain called,
 And left a little tract.

And twice a day he smoked his pipe,
 And drank his quart of beer:
His soul was resolute, and held
 No hiding-place for fear;
He often said that he was glad
 The hangman's day was near.

But why he said so strange a thing
 No warder dared to ask:
For he to whom a watcher's doom
 Is given as his task,
Must set a lock upon his lips
 And make his face a mask.

Or else he might be moved, and try
  To comfort or console:
And what should Human Pity do
  Pent up in Murderer's Hole?
What word of grace in such a place
  Could help a brother's soul?

With slouch and swing around the ring
  We trod the Fools' Parade!
We did not care: we knew we were
  The Devil's Own Brigade:
And shaven head and feet of lead
  Make a merry masquerade.

We tore the tarry rope to shreds
  With blunt and bleeding nails;
We rubbed the doors, and scrubbed the floors,
  And cleaned the shining rails:
And, rank by rank, we soaped the plank,
  And clattered with the pails.

We sewed the sacks, we broke the stones,
  We turned the dusty drill:
We banged the tins, and bawled the hymns,
  And sweated on the mill:
But in the heart of every man
  Terror was lying still.

So still it lay that every day
  Crawled like a weed-clogged wave:
And we forgot the bitter lot
  That waits for fool and knave,
Till once, as we tramped in from work,
  We passed an open grave.

With yawning mouth the yellow hole
  Gaped for a living thing;
The very mud cried out for blood
  To the thirsty asphalte ring:
And we knew that ere one dawn grew fair
  Some prisoner had to swing.

Right in we went, with soul intent
  On Death and Dread and Doom:
The hangman, with his little bag,
  Went shuffling though the gloom:
And I trembled as I groped my way
  Into my numbered tomb.

That night the empty corridors
  Were full of forms of Fear,
And up and down the iron town
  Stole feet we could not hear,
And through the bars that hide the stars
  White faces seemed to peer.

He lay as one who lies and dreams
  In a pleasant meadow-land,
The watchers watched him as he slept,
  And could not understand
How one could sleep so sweet a sleep
  With a hangman close at hand.

But there is no sleep when men must weep
  Who never yet have wept:
So we – the fool, the fraud, the knave –
  That endless vigil kept,
And through each brain on hands of pain
  Another's terror crept.

Alas! it is a fearful thing
  To feel another's guilt!
For, right, within, the Sword of Sin
  Pierced to its poisoned hilt,
And as molten lead were the tears we shed
  For the blood we had not spilt.

The warders with their shoes of felt
  Crept by each padlocked door,
And peeped and saw, with eyes of awe,
  Grey figures on the floor,
And wondered why men knelt to pray
  Who never prayed before.

All through the night we knelt and prayed,
  Mad mourners of a corse!
The troubled plumes of midnight shook
  The plumes upon a hearse:
And bitter wine upon a sponge
  Was the savour of Remorse.

*

The grey cock crew, the red cock crew,
  But never came the day:
And crooked shapes of Terror crouched,
  In the corners where we lay:
And each evil sprite that walks by night
  Before us seemed to play.

They glided past, they glided fast,
　　Like travellers through a mist:
They mocked the moon in a rigadoon
　　Of delicate turn and twist,
And with formal pace and loathsome grace
　　The phantoms kept their tryst.

With mop and mow, we saw them go,
　　Slim shadows hand in hand:
About, about, in ghostly rout
　　They trod a saraband:
And the damned grotesques made arabesques,
　　Like the wind upon the sand!

With the pirouettes of marionettes,
　　They tripped on pointed tread:
But with flutes of Fear they filled the ear,
　　As their grisly masque they led,
And loud they sang, and long they sang,
　　For they sang to wake the dead.

'Oho!' they cried, 'The world is wide,
　　But fettered limbs go lame!
And once, or twice, to throw the dice
　　Is a gentlemanly game,
But he does not win who plays with Sin
　　In the secret House of Shame.'

No things of air these antics were,
　　That frolicked with such glee:
To men whose lives were held in gyves,
　　And whose feet might not go free,
Ah! wounds of Christ! they were living things
　　Most terrible to see.

Around, around, they waltzed and wound;
　　Some wheeled in smirking pairs;
With the mincing step of a demirep
　　Some sidled up the stairs:
And with subtle sneer, and fawning leer,
　　Each helped us at our prayers.

The morning wind began to moan,
　　But still the night went on:
Through its giant loom the web of gloom
　　Crept till each thread was spun:
And, as we prayed, we grew afraid
　　Of the Justice of the Sun.

The moaning wind went wandering round
  The weeping prison-wall:
Till like a wheel of turning steel
  We felt the minutes crawl:
O moaning wind! what had we done
  To have such a seneschal?

At last I saw the shadowed bars,
  Like a lattice wrought in lead,
Move right across the whitewashed wall
  That faced my three-plank bed,
And I knew that somewhere in the world
  God's dreadful dawn was red.

At six o'clock we cleaned our cells,
  At seven all was still,
But the sough and swing of a mighty wing
  The prison seemed to fill,
For the Lord of Death with icy breath
  Had entered in to kill.

He did not pass in purple pomp,
  Nor ride a moon-white steed.
Three yards of cord and a sliding board
  Are all the gallows' need:
So with rope of shame the Herald came
  To do the secret deed.

We were as men who through a fen
  Of filthy darkness grope:
We did not dare to breathe a prayer,
  Or to give our anguish scope:
Something was dead in each of us,
  And what was dead was Hope.

For Man's grim Justice goes its way,
  And will not swerve aside:
It slays the weak, it slays the strong,
  It has a deadly stride:
With iron heel it slays the strong,
  The monstrous parricide!

We waited for the stroke of eight:
  Each tongue was thick with thirst:
For the stroke of eight is the stroke of Fate
  That makes a man accursed,
And Fate will use a running noose
  For the best man and the worst.

We had no other thing to do,
   Save to wait for the sign to come:
So, like things of stone in a valley lone,
   Quiet we sat and dumb:
But each man's heart beat thick and quick,
   Like a madman on a drum!

With sudden shock the prison-clock
   Smote on the shivering air,
And from all the gaol rose up a wail
   Of impotent despair,
Like the sound that frightened marshes hear
   From some leper in his lair.

And as one sees most fearful things
   In the crystal of a dream,
We saw the greasy hempen rope
   Hooked to the blackened beam,
And heard the prayer the hangman's snare
   Strangled into a scream.

And all the woe that moved him so
   That he gave that bitter cry,
And the wild regrets, and the bloody sweats,
   None knew so well as I:
For he who lives more lives than one
   More deaths than one must die.

IV

There is no chapel on the day
   On which they hang a man:
The Chaplain's heart is far too sick,
   Or his face is far too wan,
Or there is that written in his eyes
   Which none should look upon.

So they kept us close till nigh on noon,
   And then they rang the bell,
And the warders with their jingling keys
   Opened each listening cell,
And down the iron stair we tramped,
   Each from his separate Hell.

Out into God's sweet air we went,
   But not in wonted way,
For this man's face was white with fear,
   And that man's face was grey,
And I never saw sad men who looked
   So wistfully at the day.

I never saw sad men who looked
  With such a wistful eye
Upon that little tent of blue
  We prisoners called the sky,
And at every happy cloud that passed
  In such strange freedom by.

But there were those amongst us all
  Who walked with downcast head,
And knew that, had each got his due,
  They should have died instead:
He had but killed a thing that lived,
  Whilst they had killed the dead.

For he who sins a second time
  Wakes a dead soul to pain,
And draws it from its spotted shroud,
  And makes it bleed again,
And makes it bleed great gouts of blood,
  And makes it bleed in vain!

*

Like ape or clown, in monstrous garb
  With crooked arrows starred,
Silently we went round and round
  The slippery asphalte yard;
Silently we went round and round,
  And no man spoke a word.

Silently we went round and round,
  And through each hollow mind
The Memory of dreadful things
  Rushed like a dreadful wind,
And Horror stalked before each man,
  And Terror crept behind.

The warders strutted up and down,
  And watched their herd of brutes,
Their uniforms were spick and span,
  And they wore their Sunday suits,
But we knew the work they had been at,
  By the quicklime on their boots.

For where a grave had opened wide,
  There was no grave at all:
Only a stretch of mud and sand
  By the hideous prison-wall,
And a little heap of burning lime,
  That the man should have his pall.

For he has a pall, this wretched man,
  Such as few men can claim:
Deep down below a prison-yard,
  Naked for greater shame,
He lies, with fetters on each foot,
  Wrapt in a sheet of flame!

And all the while the burning lime
  Eats flesh and bone away,
It eats the brittle bone by night,
  And the soft flesh by day,
It eats the flesh and bone by turns,
  But it eats the heart alway.

                    *

For three long years they will not sow
  Or root or seedling there:
For three long years the unblessed spot
  Will sterile be and bare,
And look upon the wondering sky
  With unreproachful stare.

They think a murderer's heart would taint
  Each simple seed they sow.
It is not true! God's kindly earth
  Is kindlier than men know,
And the red rose would but blow more red,
  The white rose whiter blow.

Out of his mouth a red, red rose!
  Out of his heart a white!
For who can say by what strange way,
  Christ brings His will to light,
Since the barren staff the pilgrim bore
  Bloomed in the great Pope's sight?

But neither milk-white rose nor red
  May bloom in prison-air;
The shard, the pebble, and the flint,
  Are what they give us there:
For flowers have been known to heal
  A common man's despair.

So never will wine-red rose or white,
  Petal by petal, fall
On that stretch of mud and sand that lies
  By the hideous prison-wall,
To tell the men who tramp the yard
  That God's Son died for all.

Yet though the hideous prison-wall
   Still hems him round and round,
And a spirit may not walk by night
   That is with fetters bound,
And a spirit may but weep that lies
   In such unholy ground.

He is at peace – this wretched man –
   At peace, or will be soon;
There is no thing to make him mad,
   Nor does Terror walk at noon,
For the lampless Earth in which he lies
   Has neither Sun nor Moon.

They hanged him as a beast is hanged!
   They did not even toll
A requiem that might have brought
   Rest to his startled soul,
But hurriedly they took him out,
   And hid him in a hole.

The warders stripped him of his clothes,
   And gave him to the flies:
They mocked the swollen purple throat,
   And the stark and staring eyes:
And with laughter loud they heaped the shroud
   In which the convict lies.

The Chaplain would not kneel to pray
   By his dishonoured grave:
Nor mark it with that blessed Cross
   That Christ for sinners gave,
Because the man was one of those
   Whom Christ came down to save.

Yet all is well; he has but passed
   To Life's appointed bourne:
And alien tears will fill for him
   Pity's long-broken urn,
For his mourners will be outcast men,
   And outcasts always mourn.

V

I know not whether Laws be right,
   Or whether Laws be wrong;
All that we know who lie in gaol
   Is that the wall is strong;
And that each day is like a year,
   A year whose days are long.

But this I know, that every Law
   That men hath made for Man,
Since first Man took his brother's life,
   And the sad world began,
But straws the wheat and saves the chaff
   With a most evil fan.

This too I know – and wise it were
   If each could know the same –
That every prison that men build
   Is built with bricks of shame,
And bound with bars lest Christ should see
   How men their brothers maim.

With bars they blur the gracious moon,
   And blind the goodly sun;
And they do well to hide their Hell,
   For in it things are done
That Son of God nor son of Man
   Ever should look upon!

                         *

The vilest deeds like poison weeds,
   Bloom well in prison-air;
It is only what is good in Man
   That wastes and withers there:
Pale Anguish keeps the heavy gate,
   And the Warder is Despair.

For they starve the little frightened child
   Till it weeps both night and day:
And they scourge the weak, and flog the fool,
   And gibe the old and grey,
And some grow mad, and all grow bad,
   And none a word may say.

Each narrow cell in which we dwell
   Is a foul and dark latrine,
And the fetid breath of living Death
   Chokes up each grated screen,
And all, but Lust, is turned to dust
   In Humanity's machine.

The brackish water that we drink
   Creeps with a loathsome slime,
And the bitter bread they weigh in scales
   Is full of chalk and lime,
And Sleep will not lie down, but walks
   Wild-eyed, and cries to Time.

*

But though lean Hunger and green Thirst
    Like asp with adder fight,
We have little care of prison fare,
    For what chills and kills outright
Is that every stone one lifts by day
    Becomes one's heart by night.

With midnight always in one's heart,
    And twilight in one's cell,
We turn the crank, or tear the rope,
    Each in his separate Hell,
And the silence is more awful far
    Than the sound of a brazen bell.

And never a human voice comes near
    To speak a gentle word:
And the eye that watches through the door
    Is pitiless and hard:
And by all forgot, we rot and rot,
    With soul and body marred.

And thus we rust Life's iron chain
    Degraded and alone:
And some men curse, and some men weep,
    And some men make no moan:
But God's eternal Laws are kind
    And break the heart of stone.

And every human heart that breaks,
    In prison-cell or yard,
Is as that broken box that gave
    Its treasure to the Lord,
And filled the unclean leper's house
    With the scent of costliest nard.

Ah! happy they whose hearts can break
    And peace of pardon win!
How else may man make straight his plan
    And cleanse his soul from Sin?
How else but through a broken heart
    May Lord Christ enter in?

And he of the swollen purple throat,
    And the stark and staring eyes,
Waits for the holy hands that took
    The Thief to Paradise;
And a broken and a contrite heart
    The Lord will not despise.

The man in red who reads the Law
 Gave him three weeks of life,
Three little weeks in which to heal
 His soul of his soul's strife,
And cleanse from every blot of blood
 The hand that held the knife.

And with tears of blood he cleansed the hand,
 The hand that held the steel:
For only blood can wipe out blood,
 And only tears can heal:
And the crimson stain that was of Cain
 Became Christ's snow-white seal.

VI

In Reading gaol by Reading town
 There is a pit of shame,
And in it lies a wretched man
 Eaten by teeth of flame,
In a burning winding-sheet he lies,
 And his grave has got no name.

And there, till Christ call forth the dead,
 In silence let him lie:
No need to waste the foolish tear,
 Or heave the windy sigh:
The man had killed the thing he loved,
 And so he had to die.

And all men kill the thing they love,
 By all let this be heard,
Some do it with a bitter look,
 Some with a flattering word,
The coward does it with a kiss,
 The brave man with a sword!

SANTA DECCA

The Gods are dead: no longer do we bring
   To grey-eyed Pallas crowns of olive-leaves!
   Demeter's child no more hath tithe of sheaves,
And in the noon the careless shepherds sing,
For Pan is dead, and all the wantoning
   By secret glade and devious haunt is o'er:
   Young Hylas seeks the water-springs no more;
Great Pan is dead, and Mary's son is King.

And yet – perchance in this sea-trancèd isle,
   Chewing the bitter fruit of memory,
   Some God lies hidden in the asphodel.
Ah Love! if such there be, then it were well
   For us to fly his anger: nay, but see,
   The leaves are stirring: let us watch awhile.

THE GARDEN OF EROS

It is full summer now, the heart of June;
   Not yet the sunburnt reapers are a-stir
Upon the upland meadow where too soon
   Rich autumn time, the season's usurer,
Will lend his hoarded gold to all the trees,
And see his treasure scattered by the wild and spendthrift
    breeze.

Too soon indeed! yet here the daffodil,
   That love-child of the Spring, has lingered on
To vex the rose with jealousy, and still
   The harebell spreads her azure pavilion,
And like a strayed and wandering reveller
Abandoned of its brothers, whom long since June's
    messenger

The missel-thrush has frighted from the glade,
   One pale narcissus loiters fearfully

Close to a shadowy nook, where half afraid
    Of their own loveliness some violets lie
That will not look the gold sun in the face
For fear of too much splendour, – ah! methinks it is a place

Which should be trodden by Persephone
    When wearied of the flowerless fields of Dis!
Or danced on by the lads of Arcady!
    The hidden secret of eternal bliss
Known to the Grecian here a man might find,
Ah! you and I may find it now if Love and Sleep be kind.

There are the flowers which mourning Herakles
    Strewed on the tomb of Hylas, columbine,
Its white doves all a-flutter where the breeze
    Kissed them too harshly, the small celandine,
That yellow-kirtled chorister of eve,
And lilac lady-smock, – but let them bloom alone and leave

Yon spirèd hollyhock red-crocketed
    To sway its silent chimes, else must the bee,
Its little bellringer, go seek instead
    Some other pleasaunce; the anemone
That weeps at daybreak, like a silly girl
Before her love, and hardly lets the butterflies unfurl

Their painted wings beside it, – bid it pine
    In pale virginity; the winter snow
Will suit it better than those lips of thine
    Whose fires would but scorch it, rather go
And pluck that amorous flower which blooms alone,
Fed by the pander wind with dust of kisses not its own.

The trumpet-mouths of red convolvulus
    So dear to maidens, creamy meadow-sweet,
Whiter than Juno's throat and odorous
    As all Arabia, hyacinths the feet
    Of Huntress Dian would be loth to mar
For any dappled fawn, – pluck these, and those fond flowers
    which are

Fairer than what Queen Venus trod upon
    Beneath the pines of Ida, eucharis,
That morning star which does not dread the sun,
    And budding marjoram which but to kiss
Would sweeten Cytheraea's lips and make
Adonis jealous, – these for thy head, – and for thy girdle
    take

Yon curving spray of purple clematis
 Whose gorgeous dye outflames the Tyrian King,
And fox-gloves with their nodding chalices,
 But that one narciss which the startled Spring
Let from her kirtle fall when first she heard
In her own woods the wild tempestuous song of summer's
 bird,

Ah! leave it for a subtle memory
 Of those sweet tremulous days of rain and sun,
When April laughed between her tears to see
 The early primrose with shy footsteps run
From the gnarled oak-tree roots till all the wold,
Spite of its brown and trampled leaves, grew bright with
 shimmering gold.

Nay, pluck it too, it is not half so sweet
 As thou thyself, my soul's idolatry!
And when thou are a-wearied at thy feet
 Shall oxlips weave their brightest tapestry,
For thee the woodbine shall forget its pride
And veil its tangled whorls, and thou shalt walk on daisies
 pied.

And I will cut a reed by yonder spring
 And make the wood-gods jealous, and old Pan
Wonder what young intruder dares to sing
 In these still haunts, where never foot of man
Should tread at evening, lest he chance to spy
The marble limbs of Artemis and all her company.

And I will tell thee why the jacinth wears
 Such dread embroidery of dolorous moan,
And why the hapless nightingale forbears
 To sing her song at noon, but weeps alone
When the fleet swallow sleeps, and rich men feast,
And why the laurel trembles when she sees the lightening
 east.

And I will sing how sad Proserpina
 Unto a grave and gloomy Lord was wed,
And lure the silver-breasted Helena
 Back from the lotus meadows of the dead,
So shalt thou see that awful loveliness
For which two mighty Hosts met fearfully in war's abyss!

And then I'll pipe to thee that Grecian tale
 How Cynthia loves the lad Endymion,
And hidden in a grey and misty veil

Hies to the cliffs of Latmos once the Sun
Leaps from his ocean bed in fruitless chase
Of those pale flying feet which fade away in his embrace.

And if my flute can breathe sweet melody,
   We may behold Her face who long ago
Dwelt among men by the Aegean sea,
   And whose sad house with pillaged portico
And friezeless wall and columns toppled down
Looms o'er the ruins of that fair and violet cinctured town.

Spirit of Beauty! tarry still a-while,
   They are not dead, thine ancient votaries;
Some few there are to whom thy radiant smile
   Is better than a thousand victories,
Though all the nobly slain of Waterloo
Rise up in wrath against them! tarry still, there are a few

Who for thy sake would give their manlihood
   And consecrate their being, I at least
Have done so, made thy lips my daily food,
   And in thy temples found a goodlier feast
Than this starved age can give me, spite of all
Its new-found creeds so sceptical and so dogmatical.

Here not Cephissos, not Ilissos flows,
   The woods of white Colonos are not here,
On our bleak hills the olive never blows,
   No simple priest conducts his lowing steer
Up the steep marble way, nor through the town
Do laughing maidens bear to thee the crocus-flowered
   gown.

Yet tarry! for the boy who loved thee best,
   Whose very name should be a memory
To make thee linger, sleeps in silent rest
   Beneath the Roman walls, and melody,
Still mourns her sweetest lyre, none can play
The lute of Adonais, with his lips Song passed away.

Nay, when Keats died the Muses still had left
   One silver voice to sing his threnody,
But ah! too soon of it we were bereft
   When on that riven night and stormy sea
Panthea claimed her singer as her own,
And slew the mouth that praised her; since which time we
   walk alone,

Save for that fiery heart, that morning star
   Of re-arisen England, whose clear eye
Saw from our tottering throne and waste of war
   The grand Greek limbs of Young Democracy
Rise mightily like Hesperus and bring
The great Republic! him at least thy love hath taught to
     sing,

And he hath been with thee at Thessaly,
   And seen white Atalanta fleet of foot
In passionless and fierce virginity
   Hunting the tuskèd boar, his honied lute
Hath pierced the cavern of the hollow hill,
And Venus laughs to know one knee will bow before her
     still.

And he hath kissed the lips of Proserpine,
   And sung the Galilaean's requiem,
That wounded forehead dashed with blood and wine
   He hath discrowned, the Ancient Gods in him
Have found their last, most ardent worshipper,
And the new Sign grows grey and dim before its conqueror.

Spirit of Beauty! tarry with us still,
   It is not quenched the torch of poesy,
The star that shook above the Eastern hill
   Holds unassailed its argent armoury
From all the gathering gloom and fretful fight –
O tarry with us still! for through the long and common
     night,

Morris, our sweet and simple Chaucer's child,
   Dear heritor of Spenser's tuneful reed,
With soft and sylvan pipe has oft beguiled
   The weary soul of man in troublous need,
And from the far and flowerless fields of ice
Has brought fair flowers to make an earthly paradise.

We know them all, Gudrun the strong men's bride,
   Aslaug and Olafson we know them all,
How giant Grettir fought and Sigurd died,
   And what enchantment held the king in thrall
When lonely Brynhild wrestled with the powers
That war against all passion, ah! how oft through summer
     hours,

Long listless summer hours when the noon
   Being enamoured of a damask rose
Forgets to journey westward, till the moon

The pale usurper of its tribute grows
From a thin sickle to a silver shield
And chides its loitering car – how oft, in some cool grassy
    field

Far from the cricket-ground and noisy eight,
    At Bagley, where the rustling bluebells come
Almost before the blackbird finds a mate
    And overstay the swallow, and the hum
Of many murmuring bees flits through the leaves,
Have I lain poring on the dreamy tales his fancy weaves,

And through their unreal woes and mimic pain
    Wept for myself, and so was purified,
And in their simple mirth grew glad again;
    For as I sailed upon that pictured tide
The strength and splendour of the storm was mine
Without the storm's red ruin, for the singer is divine;

The little laugh of water falling down
    Is not so musical, the clammy gold
Close hoarded in the tiny waxen town
    Has less of sweetness in it, and the old
Half-withered reeds that waved in Arcady
Touched by his lips break forth again to fresher harmony.

Spirit of Beauty, tarry yet awhile!
    Although the cheating merchants of the mart
With iron roads profane our lovely isle,
    And break on whirling wheels the limbs of Art,
Ay! though the crowded factories beget
The blind-worm Ignorance that slays the soul, O tarry yet!

For one at least is there, – He bears his name
    From Dante and the seraph Gabriel, –
Whose double laurels burn with deathless flame
    To light thine altar; He too loves thee well,
Who saw old Merlin lured in Vivien's snare,
And the white feet of angels coming down the golden stair,

Loves thee so well, that all the World for him
    A gorgeous-coloured vestiture must wear,
And Sorrow take a purple diadem,
    Or else be no more Sorrow, and Despair
Gild its own thorns, and Pain, like Adon, be
Even in anguish beautiful; – such is the empery

Which Painters hold, and such the heritage
  This gentle solemn Spirit doth possess,
Being a better mirror of his age
  In all his pity, love, and weariness,
Than those who can but copy common things,
And leave the Soul unpainted with its mighty questionings.

But they are few, and all romance has flown,
  And men can prophesy about the sun,
And lecture on his arrows – how, alone,
  Through a waste void the soulless atoms run,
How far from each tree its weeping nymph has fled,
And that no more 'mid English reeds a Naiad shows her
    head.

Methinks these new Actaeons boast too soon
  That they have spied on beauty; what if we
Have analysed the rainbow, robbed the moon
  Of her most ancient, chastest mystery,
Shall I, the last Endymion, lose all hope
Because rude eyes peer at my mistress through a telescope!

What profit if this scientific age
  Burst through our gates with all its retinue
Of modern miracles! Can it assuage
  One lover's breaking heart? what can it do
To make one life more beautiful, one day
More godlike in its period? but now the age of Clay

Returns in horrid cycle, and the earth
  Hath borne again a noisy progeny
Of ignorant Titans, whose ungodly birth
  Hurls them against the august hierarchy
Which sat upon Olympus, to the Dust
They have appealed, and to that barren arbiter they must

Repair of judgment, let them, if they can,
  From Natural Warfare and insensate Chance,
Create the new Ideal rule for man!
  Methinks that was not my inheritance;
For I was nurtured otherwise, my soul
Passes from higher heights of life to a more supreme goal.

Lo! while we spake the earth did turn away
  Her visage from the God, and Hecate's boat
Rose silver-laden, till the jealous day
  Blew all its torches out: I did not note
The waning hours, to young Endymions

Time's palsied fingers count in vain his rosary of suns!

Mark how the yellow iris wearily
  Leans back its throat, as though it would be kissed
By its false chamberer, the dragon-fly,
  Who, like a blue vein on a girl's white wrist,
Sleeps on that snowy primrose of the night,
Which 'gins to flush with crimson shame, and die beneath
    the light.

Come let us go, against the pallid shield
  Of the wan sky the almond blossoms gleam,
The corncrake nested in the unmown field
  Answers its mate, across the misty stream
On fitful wing the startled curlews fly,
And in his sedgy bed the lark, for joy that Day is nigh,

Scatters the pearlèd dew from off the grass,
  In tremulous ecstasy to greet the sun,
Who soon in gilded panoply will pass
  Forth from yon orange-curtained pavilion
Hung in the burning east, see, the red rim
O'ertops the expectant hills! it is the God! for love of him

Already the shrill lark is out of sight,
  Flooding with waves of song this silent dell, –
Ah! there is something more in that bird's flight
  Than could be tested in a crucible! –
But the air freshens, let us go, why soon
The woodmen will be here; how we have lived this night
    of June!

REQUIESCAT

Tread lightly, she is near
  Under the snow,
Speak gently, she can hear
  The daisies grow.

All her bright golden hair
  Tarnished with rust,
She that was young and fair
  Fallen to dust.

Lily-like, white as snow,
   She hardly knew
She was a woman, so
   Sweetly she grew.

Coffin-board, heavy stone,
   Lie on her breast,
I vex my heart alone,
   She is at rest.

Peace, peace, she cannot hear
   Lyre or sonnet,
All my life's buried here,
   Heap earth upon it.

Avignon

SONNET ON APPROACHING ITALY

I reached the Alps: the soul within me burned,
   Italia, my Italia, at thy name:
   And when from out the mountain's heart I came
And saw the land for which my life had yearned,
I laughed as one who some great prize had earned:
   And musing on the marvel of thy fame
   I watched the day, till marked with wounds of flame
The turquoise sky to burnished gold was turned.
The pine-trees waved as waves a woman's hair,
   And in the orchards every twining spray
   Was breaking into flakes of blossoming foam:
But when I knew that far away at Rome
   In evil bonds a second Peter lay,
   I wept to see the land so very fair.

Turin

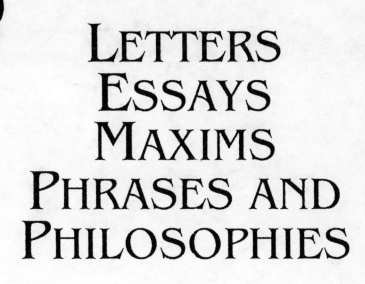

LETTERS
ESSAYS
MAXIMS
PHRASES AND
PHILOSOPHIES

A FEW MAXIMS FOR
THE INSTRUCTION OF THE
OVER-EDUCATED

Saturday Review

Education is an admirable thing. But it is well to remember from time to time that nothing that is worth knowing can be taught.

Public opinion exists only where there are no ideas.

The English are always degrading truths into facts. When a truth becomes a fact it loses all its intellectual value.

It is a very sad thing that nowadays there is so little useless information.

The only link between Literature and the Drama left to us in England at the present moment is the bill of the play.

In old days books were written by men of letters and read by the public. Nowadays books are written by the public and read by nobody.

Most women are so artificial that they have no sense of Art. Most men are so natural that they have no sense of Beauty.

Friendship is far more tragic than love. It lasts longer.

What is abnormal in Life stands in normal relations to Art. It is the only thing in Life that stands in normal relations to Art.

A subject that is beautiful in itself gives no suggestion to the artist. It lacks imperfection.

The only thing that the artist cannot see is the obvious. The only thing that the public can see is the obvious. The result is the Criticism of the Journalist.

Art is the only serious thing in the world. And the artist is the only person who is never serious.

To be really mediæval one should have no body. To be really modern one should have no soul. To be really Greek one should have no clothes.

Dandyism is the assertion of the absolute modernity of Beauty.

The only thing that can console one for being poor is extravagance. The only thing that can console one for being rich is economy.

One should never listen. To listen is a sign of indifference to one's hearers.

Even the disciple has his uses. He stands behind one's throne, and at the moment of one's triumph whispers in one's ear that, after all, one is immortal.

The criminal classes are so close to us that even the policeman can see them. They are so far away from us that only the poet can understand them.

Those whom the gods love grow young.

PEN, PENCIL AND POISON

A Study in Green

IT has constantly been made a subject of reproach against artists and men of letters that they are lacking in wholeness and completeness of nature. As a rule this must necessarily be so. That very concentration of vision and intensity of purpose which is the characteristic of the artistic temperament is in itself a mode of limitation. To those who are pre-occupied with the beauty of form nothing else seems of much importance. Yet there are many exceptions to this rule. Rubens served as ambassador, and Goethe as state councillor, and Milton as Latin secretary to Cromwell. Sophocles held civic office in his own city; the humorists, essayists, and novelists of modern America seem to desire nothing better than to become the diplomatic representatives of their country; and Charles Lamb's friend, Thomas Griffiths Wainewright, the subject of this brief memoir, though of an extremely artistic temperament, followed many masters other than art, being not merely a poet and a painter, an art-critic, an antiquarian, and a writer of prose, an amateur of beautiful things and a dilettante of things delightful, but also a forger of no mean or ordinary capabilities, and as a subtle and secret poisoner almost without rival in this or any age.

This remarkable man, so powerful with 'pen, pencil and poison', as a great poet of our own day has finely said of him, was born at Chiswick, in 1794. His father was the son of a distinguished solicitor of Gray's Inn and Hatton Garden. His mother was the daughter of the celebrated Dr Griffiths, the editor and founder of the *Monthly Review,* the partner in another literary speculation of Thomas Davis, that famous bookseller of whom Johnson said that he was not a bookseller, but 'a gentleman who dealt in books', the friend of Goldsmith and Wedgwood, and one of the most well-known men of his day. Mrs Wainewright died, in giving him birth, at the early age of twenty-one, and an obituary notice in the *Gentleman's Magazine* tells us of her 'amiable disposition and numerous accomplishments', and adds somewhat quaintly that 'she is supposed to have understood the writings of Mr Locke as well as perhaps any person of either sex now living'. His father did not long survive his young wife, and the little child seems to have been brought up by his grandfather, and, on the death of the latter in 1803, by his uncle, George Edward Griffiths, whom he subsequently poisoned. His boyhood was passed at Linden House, Turnham Green, one of those many fine Georgian mansions that have unfortunately disappeared before the inroads of the suburban builder, and to its lovely gardens and well-timbered park he owed that simple and impassioned love of nature which never left him all through his life, and which made him so peculiarly susceptible to the spiritual influences of Wordsworth's poetry. He went to school at Charles Burney's academy at Hammersmith. Mr Burney was the son of the historian of music, and the near kinsman of the artistic lad who was destined to turn out his most remarkable pupil. He seems to have been a man of a good deal of culture, and in after years Mr Wainewright often spoke of him with much affection as a philosopher, an archaeologist, and an admirable teacher, who, while he valued the intellectual side of education, did not forget the importance of early moral training. It was under Mr Burney that he first developed his talent as an artist, and Mr Hazlitt tells us that a drawing-book which he used at school is still extant, and displays great talent and natural feeling. Indeed, painting was the first art that fascinated him. It was not till much later that he sought to find expression by pen or poison.

Before this, however, he seems to have been carried away by boyish dreams of the romance and chivalry of a soldier's life, and to have become a young guardsman. But the reckless dissipated life of his companions failed to satisfy the refined artistic temperament of one who was made for other things. In a short time he wearied of the service. 'Art', he tells us, in words that still move many by their ardent sincerity and strange fervour, 'Art touched her renegade; by her pure and high influence the noisome mists were purged; my feelings, parched, hot, and tarnished, were renovated with cool, fresh bloom, simple, beautiful to the simple-hearted.' But Art was not the only cause of the change. 'The writings of Wordsworth', he goes on to say, 'did much towards calming the confusing whirl necessarily incident to sudden mutations. I wept over them tears of happiness and gratitude.' He accordingly left the army, with its rough barrack life and coarse mess-room tittle-tattle, and returned to Linden House, full of this new-born enthusiasm for culture. A severe illness, in which, to use his own words, he was 'broken like a vessel of clay', prostrated him for a time. His delicately strung organisation, however indifferent it might have been to inflicting pain on others, was itself most keenly sensitive to pain. He shrank from suffering as a thing that mars and maims human life, and seems to have wandered through that terrible valley of melancholia from which so many great, perhaps greater, spirits have never emerged. But he was young – only twenty-five years of age – and he soon passed out of the 'dead black waters', as he called them, into the larger air of humanistic culture. As he was recovering from the illness that had led him almost to the gates of death, he conceived the idea of taking up literature as an art. 'I said with John Woodvil,' he cries, 'it were a life of gods to dwell in such an element', to see and hear and write brave things:—

These high and gusty relishes of life
Have no allayings of mortality.

It is impossible not to feel that in this passage we have the utterance of a man who had a true passion for letters. 'To see and hear and write brave things,' this was his aim.

Scott, the editor of the *London Magazine,* struck by the young man's genius, or under the influence of the strange fascination that he exercised on every one who knew him, invited him to write a series of articles on artistic subjects, and under a series of fanciful pseudonyms he began to contribute to the literature of his day. *Janus Weathercock, Egomet Bonmot,* and *Van Vinkvooms,* were some of the grotesque masks under which he choose to hide his seriousness or to reveal his levity. A mask tells us more than a face. These disguises intensified his personality. In an incredibly short time he seems to have made his mark. Charles Lamb speaks of 'kind light-hearted Wainewright' whose prose is 'capital'. We hear of him entertaining Macready, John Forster, Maginn, Talfourd, Sir Wentworth Dilke the poet, John Clare, and others, at a *petit-dîner.** Like Disraeli he determined to startle the town as a dandy, and his beautiful rings, his antique cameo breast-pin, and his pale lemon-coloured kid gloves, were well known and indeed were regarded by Hazlitt as being the signs of a new manner in literature: while his rich curly hair, fine eyes, and exquisite white hands gave him the dangerous and delightful distinction of being different from others. There was something in him of Balzac's Lucien de Rubempré. At times he reminds us of Julien Sorel. De Quincey saw him once. It was at a dinner at Charles Lamb's. 'Amongst the company, all literary men, sat a murderer,' he tells us, and he goes on to describe how on that day he had been ill, and had hated the face of man and woman, and yet found himself looking with intellectual interest across the table at the young writer beneath whose affectations of manner there seemed to him to lie so much unaffected sensibility, and speculates on 'what sudden growth of another interest' would have changed his mood, had he known of what terrible sin the guest to whom Lamb paid so much attention was even then guilty.

His life-work falls naturally under the three heads suggested by Mr Swinburne, and it may be partly admitted that, if we set aside his achievements in the sphere of poison, what he has actually left to us hardly justifies his reputation.

But then it is only the Philistine who seeks to estimate a personality by the vulgar test of production. This young dandy sought to be somebody, rather than to do something. He recognised that Life itself is an art, and has its modes of style no less than the arts that seek to express it. Nor is his work without interest. We hear of William Blake stopping in the Royal Academy before one of his pictures and pronouncing it to be 'very fine'. His essays are prefiguring of much that has since been realised. He seems to have anticipated some of those accidents of modern culture that are regarded by many as true essentials. He writes about La Gioconda, and early French poets and the Italian Renaissance. He loves Greek gems, and Persian carpets, and

*Luncheon.

Elizabethan translations of *Cupid and Psyche*, and the *Hypnerotomachia*, and book-bindings, and early editions, and wide-margined proofs. He is keenly sensitive to the value of beautiful surroundings, and never wearies of describing to us the rooms in which he lived or would have liked to live. He had that curious love of green, which in individuals is always the sign of a subtle artistic temperament, and in nations is said to denote a laxity, if not a decadence of morals. Like Baudelaire he was extremely fond of cats, and with Gautier, he was fascinated by that 'sweet marble monster' of both sexes that we can still see at Florence and in the Louvre.

There is, of course, much in his descriptions, and his suggestions for decoration, that shows that he did not entirely free himself from the false taste of his time. But it is clear that he was one of the first to recognise what is, indeed, the very keynote of aesthetic eclecticism, I mean the true harmony of all really beautiful things irrespective of age or place, of school or manner. He saw that in decorating a room, which is to be, not a room for show, but a room to live in, we should never aim at any archaeological reconstruction of the past, nor burden ourselves with any fanciful necessity for historical accuracy. In this artistic perception he was perfectly right. All beautiful things belong to the same age.

And so, in his own library, as he describes it, we find the delicate fictile vase of the Greek, with its exquisitely painted figures and the faint ΚΛΛΟΣ* finely traced upon its side, and behind it hangs an engraving of the 'Delphic Sibyl' of Michael Angelo, or of the 'Pastoral' of Giorgione. Here is a bit of Florentine majolica, and here a rude lamp from some old Roman tomb. On the table lies a book of Hours, 'cased in a cover of solid silver gilt, wrought with quaint devices and studded with small brilliants and rubies', and close by it 'squats a little ugly monster, a Lar, perhaps, dug up in the sunny fields of corn-bearing Sicily'. Some dark antique bronzes contrast 'with the pale gleam of two noble *Christi Crucifixi*, one carved in ivory, the other moulded in wax.' He has his trays of Tassie's gems, his tiny Louis-Quatorze *bonbonnière*† with a miniature by Pettitot, his highly prized 'brown-biscuit teapots, filagree-worked', his citron morocco letter-case, and his 'pomona-green' chair.

One can fancy him lying there in the midst of his books and casts and engravings, a true virtuoso, a subtle connoisseur turning over his fine collection of Marc Antonios, and his Turner's 'Liber Studiorum', of which he was a warm admirer, or examining with a magnifier some of his antique gems and cameos, 'the head of Alexander on an onyx of two strata', or 'that superb *altissimo relievo* on cornelian, Jupiter Ægiochus'. He was always a great amateur of engravings, and gives some very useful suggestions as to the best means of forming a collection. Indeed, while fully appreciating modern art, he never lost sight of the importance of reproductions of the great master-pieces of the past, and all that he says about the value of plaster casts is quite admirable.

As an art-critic he concerned himself primarily with the complex impressions produced by a work of art, and certainly the first step in aesthetic criticism is to realise one's own impressions. He cared nothing for abstract discussions on the nature of the Beautiful, and the historical method, which

*Beautiful   †Chocolate Box.

has since yielded such rich fruit, did not belong to his day, but he never lost sight of the great truth that Art's first appeal is neither to the intellect nor to the emotions, but purely to the artistic temperament, and he more than once points out that this temperament, this 'taste', as he calls it, being unconsciously guided and made perfect by frequent contact with the best work, becomes in the end a form of right judgment. Of course there are fashions in art just as there are fashions in dress, and perhaps none of us can ever quite free ourselves from the influence of custom and the influence of novelty. He certainly could not, and he frankly acknowledges how difficult it is to form any fair estimate of contemporary work. But, on the whole, his taste was good and sound. He admired Turner and Constable at a time when they were not so much thought of as they are now, and saw that for the highest landscape art we require more than 'mere industry and accurate transcription.' Of Crome's 'Heath Scene near Norwich' he remarks that it shows 'how much a subtle observation of the elements, in their wild moods, does for a most uninteresting flat', and of the popular type of landscape of his day he says that it is 'simply an enumeration of hill and dale, stumps of trees, shrubs, water, meadows, cottages and houses; little more than topography, a kind of pictorial mapwork; in which rainbows, showers, mists, haloes, large beams shooting through rifted clouds, storms, starlight, all the most valuable materials of the real painter, are not.' He had a thorough dislike of what is obvious or commonplace in art, and while he was charmed to entertain Wilkie at dinner, he cared as little for Sir David's pictures as he did for Mr Crabbe's poems. With the imitative and realistic tendencies of his day he had no sympathy, and he tells us frankly that his great admiration for Fuseli was largely due to the fact that the little Swiss did not consider it necessary that an artist should paint only what he sees. The qualities that he sought for in a picture were composition, beauty and dignity of line, richness of colour, and imaginative power. Upon the other hand, he was not a doctrinaire. 'I hold that no work of art can be tried otherwise than by laws deduced from itself: whether or not it be consistent with itself is the question.' This is one of his excellent aphorisms. And in criticising painters so different as Landseer and Martin, Stothard and Etty, he shows that, to use a phrase now classical, he is trying 'to see the object as in itself it really is.'

However, as I pointed out before, he never feels quite at his ease in his criticisms of contemporary work. 'The present', he says, 'is about as agreeable a confusion to me as Ariosto on the first perusal…. Modern things dazzle me. I must look at them through Time's telescope. Elia complains that to him the merit of a MS. poem is uncertain; "print", as he excellently says, "settles it." Fifty years' toning does the same thing to a picture.' He is happier when he is writing about Watteau and Lancret, about Rubens and Giorgione, about Rembrandt, Corregio, and Michael Angelo; happiest of all when he is writing about Greek things. What is Gothic touched him very little, but classical art and the art of the Renaissance were always dear to him. He saw what our English school could gain from a study of Greek models, and never wearies of pointing out to the young student the artistic possibilities that lie dormant in Hellenic marbles and Hellenic methods of work. In his judgments on the great Italian Masters, says De Quincey, 'there seemed a tone of sincerity and of native sensibility, as in one who spoke for himself, and was not merely a copier from books.' The highest praise that we can give to him is that he tried to revive style as a conscious tradition. But he saw that no amount of art lectures or art congresses, or 'plans for advancing the fine arts', will ever produce this result. The people, he says very wisely, and in the true spirit of Toynbee Hall, must always have 'the best models constantly before their eyes.'

As is to be expected from one who was a painter, he is often extremely technical in his art criticisms. Of Tintoret's 'St. George delivering the Egyptian Princess from the Dragon', he remarks:—

> The robe of Sabra, warmly glazed with Prussian blue, is relieved from the pale greenish background by a vermilion scarf; and the full hues of both are beautifully echoed, as it were, in a lower key by the purple-lake coloured stuffs and bluish iron armour of the saint, besides an ample balance to the vivid azure drapery on the foreground in the indigo shades of the wild wood surrounding the castle.

And elsewhere he talks learnedly of 'a delicate Schiavone, various as a tulip-bed, with rich broken tints,' of 'a glowing portrait, remarkable for *morbidezza*,* by the scarce Moroni,' and of another picture being 'pulpy in the carnations'.

But, as a rule, he deals with his impressions of the work as an artistic whole, and tries to translate those impressions into words, to give, as it were, the literary equivalent for the imaginative and mental effect. He was one of the first to develop what has been called the art-literature of the nineteenth century, that form of literature which has found in Mr Ruskin and Mr Browning its two most perfect exponents. His description of Lancret's *Repas Italien*, in which 'a dark-haired girl, "amorous of mischief," lies on the daisy-powdered grass', is in some respects very charming. Here is his account of 'The Crucifixion,' by Rembrandt. It is extremely characteristic of his style:—

> Darkness – sooty, portentous darkness – shrouds the whole scene: only above the accursed wood, as if through a horrid rift in the murky ceiling, a rainy deluge – 'sleety-flaw, discoloured water' – streams down amain, spreading a grisly spectral light, even more horrible than that palpable night. Already the Earth pants thick and fast! the darkened Cross trembles! the winds are dropt – the air is stagnant – a muttering rumble growls underneath their feet, and some of that miserable crowd begin to fly down the hill. The horses snuff the coming terror, and become unmanageable through fear. The moment rapidly approaches when, nearly torn asunder by His own weight, fainting with loss of blood, which now runs in narrower rivulets from His slit veins, His temples and breast drowned in sweat and His black tongue parched with the fiery death-fever, Jesus cries, 'I thirst.' The deadly vinegar is elevated to Him.

*Delicateness.

His head sinks, and the sacred corpse 'swings senseless of the cross.'
A sheet of vermilion flame shoots sheer through the air and vanishes;
the rocks of Carmel and Lebanon cleave asunder; the sea rolls on high
from the sands its black weltering waves. Earth yawns, and the graves
give up their dwellers. The dead and the living are mingled together
in unnatural conjunction and hurry through the holy city. New prodi-
gies await them there. The veil of the temple – the unpierceable veil –
is rent asunder from top to bottom, and that dreaded recess containing
the Hebrew mysteries – the fatal ark with the tables and seven-branched
candelabrum – is disclosed by the light of unearthly flames to the
God-deserted multitude.

Rembrandt never *painted* this sketch, and he was quite right. It would
have lost nearly all its charms in losing that perplexing veil of indistinct-
ness which affords such ample range wherein the doubting imagination may speculate. At present it is like a thing in another world. A dark
gulf is betwixt us. It is not tangible by the body. We can only approach
it in the spirit.

In this passage, written, the author tells us, 'in awe and reverence', there
is much that is terrible, and very much that is quite horrible, but it is not
without a certain crude form of power, or, at any rate, a certain crude
violence of words, a quality which this age should highly appreciate, as it is
its chief defect. It is pleasanter, however, to pass to this description of Giulio
Romano's 'Cephalus and Procris':—

We should read Moschus's lament for Bion, the sweet shepherd, before
looking at this picture, or study the picture as a preparation for the
lament. We have nearly the same images in both. For either victim the
high groves and forest dells murmur; the flowers exhale sad perfume
from their buds; the nightingale mourns on the craggy lands, and the
swallow in the long-winding vales; 'the satyrs, too, and fauns dark-veiled
groan', and the fountain nymphs within the wood melt into tearful
waters. The sheep and goats leave their pasture; and oreads, 'who love
to scale the most inaccessible tops of all uprightest rocks', hurry down
from the song of their wind-courting pines; while the dryads bend from
the branches of the meeting trees, and the rivers moan for white
Procris, 'with many-sobbing streams'.

'Filling the far-seen ocean with a voice.'

The golden bees are silent on the thymy Hymettus; and the knelling
horn of Aurora's love no more shall scatter away the cold twilight on
the top of Hymettus. The foreground of our subject is a grassy sunburnt
bank, broken into swells and hollows like waves (a sort of land-break-
ers), rendered more uneven by many foot-tripping roots and stumps
of trees stocked untimely by the axe, which are again throwing out
light-green shoots. This bank rises rather suddenly on the right to a
clustering grove, penetrable to no star, at the entrance of which sits the

stunned Thessalian king, holding between his knees that ivory-bright body which was, but an instant agone, parting the rough boughs with her smooth forehead, and treading alike on thorns and flowers with jealously-stung foot – now helpless, heavy, void of all motion, save when the breeze lifts her thick hair in mockery.

From between the closely-neighboured boles astonished nymphs press forward with loud cries –

'And deerskin-vested satyrs, crowned with ivy twists, advance;
And put strange pity in their horned countenance.'

Laelaps lies beneath, and shows by his panting the rapid pace of death. On the other side of the group, Virtuous Love with 'vans dejected' holds forth the arrow to an approaching troop of sylvan people, fauns, rams, goats, satyrs, and satyr-mothers, pressing their children tighter with their fearful hands, who hurry along from the left in a sunken path between the foreground and a rocky wall, on whose lowest ridge a brook-guardian pours from her urn her grief-telling waters. Above and more remote than the Ephidryad, another female, rending her locks, appears among the vine-festooned pillars of an unshorn grove. The centre of the picture is filled by shady meadows, sinking down to a river-mouth; beyond is 'the vast strength of the ocean stream', from whose floor the extinguisher of stars, rosy Aurora, drives furiously up her brine-washed steeds to behold the death-pangs of her rival.

Were this description carefully re-written, it would be quite admirable. The conception of making a prose poem out of paint is excellent. Much of the best modern literature springs from the same aim. In a very ugly and sensible age, the arts borrow, not from life, but from each other.

His sympathies, too, were wonderfully varied. In everything connected with the stage, for instance, he was always extremely interested, and strongly upheld the necessity for archaeological accuracy in costume and scene-painting. 'In art,' he says in one of his essays, 'whatever is worth doing at all is worthy doing well'; and he points out that once we allow the intrusion of anachronisms, it becomes difficult to say where the line is to be drawn. In literature, again, like Lord Beaconsfield on a famous occasion, he was 'on the side of the angels'. He was one of the first to admire Keats and Shelley – 'the tremulously-sensitive and poetical Shelley', as he calls him. His admiration for Wordsworth was sincere and profound. He thoroughly appreciated William Blake. One of the best copies of the 'Songs of Innocence and Experience' that is now in existence was wrought specially for him. He loved Alain Chartier, and Ronsard, and the Elizabethan dramatists, and Chaucer and Chapman, and Petrarch. And to him all the arts were one. 'Our critics', he remarks with much wisdom, 'seem hardly aware of the identity of the primal seeds of poetry and painting, nor that any true advancement in the serious study of one art co-generates a proportionate perfection in the other'; and he says elsewhere that if a man who does not admire Michael

Angelo talks of his love for Milton, he is deceiving either himself or his listeners. To his fellow contributors in the *London Magazine* he was always most generous, and praises Barry Cornwall, Allan Cunningham, Hazlitt, Elton, and Leigh Hunt without anything of the malice of a friend. Some of his sketches of Charles Lamb are admirable in their way, and, with the art of the true comedian, borrow their style from their subject:—

What can I say of thee more than all know? that thou hadst the gaiety of a boy with the knowledge of a man: as gentle a heart as ever sent tears to the eyes.

How wittily would he mistake your meaning, and put in a conceit most seasonably out of season. His talk without affectation was compressed, like his beloved Elizabethans, even unto obscurity. Like grains of fine gold, his sentences would beat out into whole sheets. He had small mercy on spurious fame, and a caustic observation on the *fashion for men of genius* was a standing dish. Sir Thomas Browne was a 'bosom cronie' of his; so was Burton, and old Fuller. In his amorous vein he dallied with that peerless Duchess of many-folio odour; and with the heyday comedies of Beaumont and Fletcher he induced light dreams. He would deliver critical touches on these, like one inspired, but it was good to let him choose his own game; if another began even on the acknowledged pets he was liable to interrupt, or rather append, in a mode difficult to define, whether as misapprehensive or mischievous. One night at C——'s, the above dramatic partners were the temporary subject of chat. Mr. X. commended the passion and haughty style of a tragedy (I don't know which of them), but was instantly taken up by Elia, who told him '*That* was nothing; the lyrics were the high things – the lyrics!'

One side of his literary career deserves especial notice. Modern journalism may be said to owe almost as much to him as to any man of the early part of this century. He was the pioneer of Asiatic prose, and delighted in pictorial epithets and pompous exaggerations. To have a style so gorgeous that it conceals the subject is one of the highest achievements of an important and much admired school of Fleet Street leader-writers, and this school *Janus Weathercock* may be said to have invented. He also saw that it was quite easy by continued reiteration to make the public interested in his own personality, and in his purely journalistic articles this extraordinary young man tells the world what he had for dinner, where he gets his clothes, what wines he likes, and in what state of health he is, just as if he were writing weekly notes for some popular newspaper of our own time. This being the least valuable side of his work, is the one that has had the most obvious influence. A publicist, nowadays, is a man who bores the community with the details of the illegalities of his private life.

Like most artificial people, he had a great love of nature. 'I hold three things in high estimation,' he says somewhere: 'to sit lazily on an eminence that commands a rich prospect; to be shadowed by thick trees while the sun shines around me; and to enjoy solitude with the consciousness of neighbourhood. The country gives them all to me.' He writes about his wandering over fragrant furze and heath, repeating Collins's 'Ode to Evening', just to catch the fine quality of the moment; about smothering his face 'in a watery bed of cowslips, wet with May dews'; and about the pleasure of seeing the sweet-breathed kine 'pass slowly homeward through the twilight', and hearing 'the distant clank of the sheep-bell'. One phrase of his, 'the polyanthus glowed in its cold bed of earth, like a solitary picture of Giorgione on a dark oaken panel', is curiously characteristic of his temperament, and this passage is rather pretty in its way:—

> The short tender grass was covered with marguerites – 'such that men called *daisies* in our town' – thick as stars on a summer's night. The harsh caw of the busy rooks came pleasantly mellowed from a high dusky grove of elms at some distance off, and at intervals was heard the voice of a boy scaring away the birds from the newly-sown seeds. The blue depths were the colour of the darkest ultramarine; not a cloud streaked the calm aether; only round the horizon's edge streamed a light, warm film of misty vapour, against which the near village with its ancient stone church showed sharply out with blinding whiteness. I thought of Wordsworth's 'Lines written in March'.

However, we must not forget that the cultivated young man who penned these lines, and who was so susceptible to Wordsworthian influences, was also, as I said at the beginning of this memoir, one of the most subtle and secret poisoners of this or any age. How he first became fascinated by this strange sin he does not tell us, and the diary in which he carefully noted the results of his terrible experiments and the methods that he adopted, has unfortunately been lost to us. Even in later days, too, he was always reticent on the matter, and preferred to speak about 'The Excursion', and the 'Poems founded on the Affections'. There is no doubt, however, that the poison that he used was strychnine. In one of the beautiful rings of which he was so proud, and which served to show off the fine modelling of his delicate ivory hands, he used to carry crystals of the Indian *nux vomica*, a poison, one of his biographers tells us, 'nearly tasteless, difficult of discovery, and capable of almost infinite dilution.' His murders, says De Quincey, were more than were ever made known judicially. This is no doubt so, and some of them are worthy of mention. His first victim was his uncle, Mr Thomas Griffiths. He poisoned him in 1829 to gain possession of Linden House, a place to which he had always been very much attached. In the August of the next year he poisoned Mrs Abercrombie, his wife's mother, and in the following December he poisoned the lovely Helen Abercrombie, his sister-in-law. Why he murdered Mrs Abercrombie is not ascertained. It may have been for a caprice, or to quicken some hideous sense of power that was in him, or because she suspected something, or for no reason. But the murder of Helen Abercrombie was carried out by himself and his wife for the sake of a sum of about £18,000, for which they had insured her life in various offices. The circumstances were as follows. On the 12th of December, he and his wife and child came up to London from Linden House, and took lodgings at No. 12 Conduit Street,

Regent Street. With them were the two sisters, Helen and Madeleine Abercrombie. On the evening of the 14th they all went to the play, and at supper that night Helen sickened. The next day she was extremely ill, and Dr Locock, of Hanover Square, was called in to attend her. She lived till Monday, the 20th, when, after the doctor's morning visit, Mr and Mrs Wainewright brought her some poisoned jelly, and then went out for a walk. When they returned, Helen Abercrombie was dead. She was about twenty years of age, a tall graceful girl with fair hair. A very charming red-chalk drawing of her by her brother-in-law is still in existence, and shows how much his style as an artist was influenced by Sir Thomas Lawrence, a painter for whose work he had always entertained a great admiration. De Quincey says that Mrs Wainewright was not really privy to the murder. Let us hope that she was not. Sin should be solitary, and have no accomplices.

The insurance companies, suspecting the real facts of the case, declined to pay the policy on the technical ground of misrepresentation and want of interest, and with curious courage the poisoner entered an action in the Court of Chancery against the Imperial, it being agreed that one decision should govern all the cases. The trial, however, did not come on for five years, when, after one disagreement, a verdict was ultimately given in the companies' favour. The judge on the occasion was Lord Abinger. *Egomet Bonmot* was represented by Mr Erle and Sir William Follet, and the Attorney-General and Sir Frederick Pollock appeared for the other side. The plaintiff, unfortunately, was unable to be present at either of the trials. The refusal of the companies to give him the £18,000 had placed him in a position of most painful pecuniary embarrassment. Indeed, a few months after the murder of Helen Abercrombie, he had been actually arrested for debt in the streets of London while he was serenading the pretty daughter of one of his friends. This difficulty was got over at the time, but shortly afterwards he thought it better to go abroad till he could come to some practical arrangement with his creditors. He accordingly went to Boulogne on a visit to the father of the young lady in question, and while he was there induced him to insure his life with the Pelican Company for £3000. As soon as the necessary formalities had been gone through and the policy executed, he dropped some crystals of strychnine into his coffee as they sat together one evening after dinner. He himself did not gain any monetary advantage by doing this. His aim was simply to revenge himself on the first office that had refused to pay him the price of his sin. His friend died the next day in his presence, and he left Boulogne at once for a sketching tour through the most picturesque parts of Brittany, and was for a time the guest of an old French gentleman, who had a beautiful country house at St Omer. From this he moved to Paris, where he remained for several years, living in luxury, some say, while others talk of his 'skulking with poison in his pocket, and being dreaded by all who knew him.' In 1837 he returned to England privately. Some strange mad fascination brought him back. He followed a woman whom he loved.

It was the month of June, and he was staying at one of the hotels in Covent Garden. His sitting-room was on the ground floor, and he prudently kept the blinds down for fear of being seen. Thirteen years before, when he was making his fine collection of majolica and Marc Antonios, he had forged the names of his trustees to a power of attorney, which enabled him to get possession of some of the money which he had inherited from his mother, and had brought into marriage settlement. He knew that this forgery had been discovered, and that by returning to England he was imperilling his life. Yet he returned. Should one wonder? It was said that the woman was very beautiful. Besides, she did not love him.

It was by a mere accident that he was discovered. A noise in the street attracted his attention, and, in his artistic interest in modern life, he pushed aside the blind for a moment. Some one outside called out, 'That's Wainewright, the Bank-forger'. It was Forrester, the Bow Street runner.

On the 5th of July he was brought up at the Old Bailey. The following report of the proceedings appeared in the *Times*:—

Before Mr. Justice Vaughan and Mr. Baron Alderson, Thomas Griffiths Wainewright, aged forty-two, a man of gentlemanly appearance, wearing mustachios, was indicted for forging and uttering a certain power of attorney for £2259, with intent to defraud the Governor and Company of the Bank of England.

There were five indictments against the prisoner, to all of which he pleaded not guilty, when he was arraigned before Mr. Serjeant Arabin in the course of the morning. On being brought before the judges, however, he begged to be allowed to withdraw the former plea, and then pleaded guilty to two of the indictments which were not of a capital nature.

The counsel for the Bank having explained that there were three other indictments, but that the Bank did not desire to shed blood, the plea of guilty on the two minor charges was recorded and the prisoner at the close of the session sentenced by the Recorder to transportation for life.

He was taken back to Newgate, preparatory to his removal to the colonies. In a fanciful passage in one of his early essays he had fancied himself 'lying in Horsemonger Gaol under sentence of death', for having been unable to resist the temptation of stealing some Marc Antonios from the British Museum in order to complete his collection. The sentence now passed on him was to a man of his culture a form of death. He complained bitterly of it to his friends, and pointed out, with a good deal of reason, some people may fancy, that the money was practically his own, having come to him from his mother, and that the forgery, such as it was, had been committed thirteen years before, which, to use his own phrase, was at least a *circonstance attenuante*. The permanence of personality is a very subtle metaphysical problem, and certainly the English law solves the question in an extremely rough-and-ready manner. There is, however, something dramatic in the fact that this heavy punishment was inflicted on him for what, if we remember his fatal influence on the prose of modern journalism, was certainly not the worst of all his sins.

While he was in gaol, Dickens, Macready, and Hablot Browne came across him by chance. They had been going over the prisons of London, searching for artistic effects, and in Newgate they suddenly caught sight of Wainewright. He met them with a defiant stare, Forster tells us, but Macready was 'horrified to recognise a man familiarly known to him in former years and at whose table he had dined.'

Others had more curiosity, and his cell was for some time a kind of fashionable lounge. Many men of letters went down to visit their old literary comrade. But he was no longer the kind light-hearted Janus whom Charles Lamb admired. He seems to have grown quite cynical.

To the agent of an insurance company who was visiting him one afternoon, and thought he would improve the occasion by pointing out that, after all, crime was a bad speculation, he replied: 'Sir, you City men enter on your speculations, and take the chances of them. Some of your speculations succeed, some fail. Mine happen to have failed, yours happen to have succeeded. That is the only difference, sir, between my visitor and me. But, sir, I will tell you one thing in which I have succeeded to the last. I have been determined through life to hold the position of a gentleman. I have always done so. I do so still. It is the custom of this place that each of the inmates of a cell shall take his morning's turn of sweeping it out. I occupy a cell with a bricklayer and a sweep, but they never offer me the broom!' When a friend reproached him with the murder of Helen Abercrombie he shrugged his shoulders and said, 'Yes; it was a dreadful thing to do, but she had very thick ankles.'

From Newgate he was brought to the hulks at Portsmouth, and sent from there in the *Susan* to Van Diemen's Land along with three hundred other convicts. The voyage seems to have been most distasteful to him, and in a letter written to a friend he spoke bitterly about the ignominy of 'the companion of poets and artists' being compelled to associate with 'country bumpkins'. The phrase that he applies to his companions need not surprise us. Crime in England is rarely the result of sin. It is nearly always the result of starvation. There was probably no one on board in whom he would have found a sympathetic listener, or even a psychologically interesting nature.

His love of art, however, never deserted him. At Hobart Town he started a studio, and returned to sketching and portrait-painting, and his conversation and manners seem not to have lost their charm. Nor did he give up his habit of poisoning, and there are two cases on record in which he tried to make away with people who had offended him. But his hand seems to have lost its cunning. Both of his attempts were complete failures, and in 1844, being thoroughly dissatisfied with Tasmanian society, he presented a memorial to the governor of the settlement, Sir John Eardley Wilmot, praying for a ticket-of-leave. In it he speaks of himself as being 'tormented by ideas struggling for outward form and realisation, barred up from increase of knowledge, and deprived of the exercise of profitable or even of decorous speech.' His request, however, was refused, and the associate of Coleridge consoled himself by making those marvellous *Paradis Artificiels* whose secret is only known to the eaters of opium. In 1852 he died of apoplexy, his sole living companion being a cat, for which he had evinced an extraordinary affection.

His crimes seem to have had an important effect upon his art. They gave a strong personality to his style, a quality that his early work certainly lacked. In a note to the *Life of Dickens*, Forster mentions that in 1847 Lady Blessington received from her brother, Major Powell, who held a military appointment at Hobart Town, an oil portrait of a young lady from his clever brush; and it is said that 'he had contrived to put the expression of his own wickedness into the portrait of a nice, kind-hearted girl.' M Zola, in one of his novels, tells us of a young man who, having committed a murder, takes to art, and paints greenish impressionist portraits of perfectly respectable people, all of which bear a curious resemblance to his victim. The development of Mr Wainewright's style seems to me far more subtle and suggestive. One can fancy an intense personality being created out of sin.

This strange and fascinating figure that for a few years dazzled literary London, and made so brilliant a *début* in life and letters, is undoubtedly a most interesting study. Mr W. Carew Hazlitt, his latest biographer, to whom I am indebted for many of the facts contained in this memoir, and whose little book is, indeed, quite invaluable in its way, is of opinion that his love of art and nature was a mere pretence and assumption, and others have denied to him all literary power. This seems to me a shallow, or at least a mistaken, view. The fact of a man being a poisoner is nothing against his prose. The domestic virtues are not the true basis of art, though they may serve as an excellent advertisement for second-rate artists. It is possible that De Quincey exaggerated his critical powers, and I cannot help saying again that there is much in his published works that is too familiar, too common, too journalistic, in the bad sense of that bad word. Here and there he is distinctly vulgar in expression, and he is always lacking in the self-restraint of the true artist. But for some of his faults we must blame the time in which he lived, and, after all, prose that Charles Lamb thought 'capital' has no small historic interest. That he had a sincere love of art and nature seems to me quite certain. There is no essential incongruity between crime and culture. We cannot re-write the whole of history for the purpose of gratifying our moral sense of what should be.

Of course, he is far too close to our own time for us to be able to form any purely artistic judgment about him. It is impossible not to feel a strong prejudice against a man who might have poisoned Lord Tennyson, or Mr Gladstone, or the Master of Balliol. But had the man worn a costume and spoken a language different from our own, had he lived in imperial Rome, or at the time of the Italian Renaissance, or in Spain in the seventeenth century, or in any land or any century but this century and this land, we would be quite able to arrive at a perfectly unprejudiced estimate of his position and value. I know that there are many historians, or at least writers on historical subjects, who still think it necessary to apply moral judgments to history, and who distribute their praise or blame with the solemn complacency of a successful schoolmaster. This, however, is a foolish habit, and merely shows that the moral instinct can be brought to such a pitch of perfection that it will make its appearance wherever it is not required. Nobody with the true historical sense ever dreams of blaming Nero, or scolding Tiberius, or censuring Caesar Borgia. These personages have become like the puppets of a play. They may fill us with terror, or horror, or wonder, but they do not harm us. They are not in immediate relation to us. We have nothing to fear from them. They have passed into the sphere of art and science, and neither art nor science knows anything of moral approval or disapproval. And so it may be some day with Charles Lamb's friend. At present I feel that he is just a little too modern to be treated in that fine spirit of disinterested curiosity to which we owe so many charming studies of the great criminals of the Italian Renaissance from the pens of Mr John Addington Symonds, Miss A. Mary F. Robinson, Miss Vernon Lee, and other distinguished writers. However, Art has not forgotten him. He is the hero of Dickens's *Hunted Down*, the Varney of Bulwer's *Lucretia*; and it is gratifying to note that fiction has paid some homage to one who was so powerful with 'pen, pencil and poison'. To be suggestive for fiction is to be of more importance than a fact.

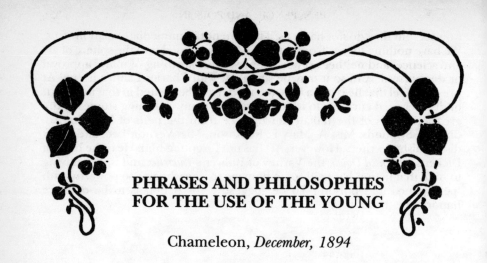

PHRASES AND PHILOSOPHIES
FOR THE USE OF THE YOUNG

Chameleon, *December, 1894*

The first duty in life is to be as artificial as possible. What the second duty is no one has as yet discovered.

Wickedness is a myth invented by good people to account for the curious attractiveness of others.

If the poor only had profiles there would be no difficulty in solving the problem of poverty.

Those who see any difference between soul and body have neither.

A really well-made buttonhole is the only link between Art and Nature.

Religions die when they are proved to be true. Science is the record of dead religions.

The well-bred contradict other people. The wise contradict themselves.

Nothing that actually occurs is of the smallest importance.

Dullness is the coming of age of seriousness.

In all unimportant matters, style, not sincerity, is the essential. In all important matters, style, not sincerity, is the essential.

If one tells the truth, one is sure, sooner or later, to be found out.

Pleasure is the only thing one should live for. Nothing ages like happiness.

It is only by not paying one's bills that one can hope to live in the memory of the commercial classes.

No crime is vulgar, but all vulgarity is crime. Vulgarity is the conduct of others.

Only the shallow know themselves.

Time is waste of money.

One should always be a little improbable.

There is a fatality about all good resolutions. They are invariably made too soon.

The only way to atone for being occasionally a little over-dressed is by being always absolutely over-educated.

To be premature is to be perfect.

Any preoccupation with ideas of what is right or wrong in conduct shows an arrested intellectual development.

Ambition is the last refuge of the failure.

A truth ceases to be true when more than one person believes in it.

In examinations the foolish ask questions that the wise cannot answer.

Greek dress was in its essence inartistic. Nothing should reveal the body but the body.

One should either be a work of art, or wear a work of art.

It is only the superficial qualities that last. Man's deeper nature is soon found out.

Industry is the root of all ugliness.

The ages live in history through their anachronisms.

It is only the gods who taste of death. Apollo has passed away, but Hyacinth, whom men say he slew, lives on. Nero and Narcissus are always with us.

The old believe everything: the middle-aged suspect everything: the young know everything.

The condition of perfection is idleness: the aim of perfection is youth.

Only the great masters of style ever succeed in being obscure.

There is something tragic about the enormous number of young men there are in England at the present moment who start life with perfect profiles, and end by adopting some useful profession.

To love oneself is the beginning of a life-long romance.

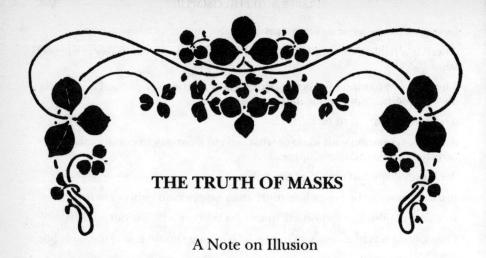

THE TRUTH OF MASKS

A Note on Illusion

IN many of the somewhat violent attacks that have recently been made on that splendour of mounting which now characterises our Shakespearian revivals in England, it seems to have been tacitly assumed by the critics that Shakespeare himself was more or less indifferent to the costumes of his actors, and that, could he see Mrs Langtry's production of *Antony and Cleopatra*, he would probably say that the play, and the play only, is the thing, and that everything else is leather and prunella. While as regards any historical accuracy in dress, Lord Lytton, in an article in the *Nineteenth Century*, has laid it down as a dogma of art that archaeology is entirely out of place in the presentation of any of Shakespeare's plays, and the attempt to introduce it one of the stupidest pedantries of an age of prigs.

Lord Lytton's position I shall examine later on; but as regards the theory that Shakespeare did not busy himself much about the costume-wardrobe of his theatre, anybody who cares to study Shakespeare's method will see that there is absolutely no dramatist of the French, English, or Athenian stage who relies so much for his illusionist effects on the dress of his actors as Shakespeare does himself.

Knowing how the artistic temperament is always fascinated by beauty of costume, he constantly introduces into his plays masques and dances, purely for the sake of the pleasure which they give the eye; and we have still his stage-directions for the three great processions in *Henry the Eighth*, directions which are characterised by the most extraordinary elaborateness of detail down to the collars of S.S. and the pearls in Anne Boleyn's hair. Indeed it would be quite easy for a modern manager to reproduce these pageants absolutely as Shakespeare had them designed; and so accurate were they that one of the court officials of the time, writing an account of the last performance of the play at the Globe Theatre to a friend, actually complains of their realistic character, notably of the production on the stage of the Knights of the Garter in the robes and insignia of the order as being calculated to bring ridicule on the real ceremonies; much in the same spirit in which the

French Government, some time ago, prohibited that delightful actor, M. Christian, from appearing in uniform, on the plea that it was prejudicial to the glory of the army that a colonel should be caricatured. And elsewhere the gorgeousness of apparel which distinguished the English stage under Shakespeare's influence was attacked by the contemporary critics, not as a rule, however, on the grounds of the democratic tendencies of realism, but usually on those moral grounds which are always the last refuge of people who have no sense of beauty.

The point, however, which I wish to emphasise is, not that Shakespeare appreciated the value of lovely costumes in adding picturesqueness to poetry, but that he saw how important costume is as a means of producing certain dramatic effects. Many of his plays, such as *Measure for Measure, Twelfth Night, The Two Gentlemen of Verona, All's Well that Ends Well, Cymbeline*, and others, depend for their illusion on the character of the various dresses worn by the hero or the heroine; the delightful scene in *Henry the Sixth*, on the modern miracles of healing by faith, loses all its point unless Gloster is in black and scarlet; and the *dénoûment* of the *Merry Wives of Windsor* hinges on the colour of Anne Page's gown. As for the uses Shakespeare makes of disguises the instances are almost numberless. Posthumous hides his passion under a peasant's garb, and Edgar his pride beneath an idiot's rags; Portia wears the apparel of a lawyer, and Rosalind is attired in 'all points as a man;' the cloak-bag of Pisanio changes Imogen to the youth Fidele; Jessica flees from her father's house in boy's dress, and Julia ties up her yellow hair in fantastic love-knots, and dons hose and doublet; Henry the Eighth woos his lady as a shepherd, and Romeo his as a pilgrim; Prince Hal and Poins appear first as footpads in buckram suits, and then in white aprons and leather jerkins as the waiters in a tavern: and as for Falstaff, does he not come on as a highwayman, as an old woman, as Herne the Hunter, and as the clothes going to the laundry?

Nor are the examples of the employment of costume as a mode of intensifying dramatic situation less numerous. After slaughter of Duncan, Macbeth appears in his night-gown as if aroused from sleep; Timon ends in rags the play he had begun in splendour; Richard flatters the London citizens in a suit of mean and shabby armour, and as soon as he has stepped in blood to the throne, marches through the streets in crown and George and Garter; the climax of *The Tempest* is reached when Prospero, throwing off his enchanter's robes, sends Ariel for his hat and rapier, and reveals himself as the great Italian Duke; the very Ghost in *Hamlet* changes his mystical apparel to produce different effects; and as for Juliet, a modern playwright would probably have laid her out in her shroud, and made the scene a scene of horror merely, but Shakespeare arrays her in rich and gorgeous raiment, whose loveliness makes the vault 'a feasting presence full of light,' turns the tomb into a bridal chamber, and gives the cue and motive for Romeo's speech of the triumph of Beauty over Death.

Even small details of dress, such as the colour of a major-domo's stockings, the pattern on a wife's handkerchief, the sleeve of a young soldier, and a fashionable woman's bonnets, become in Shakespeare's hands points of actual dramatic importance, and by some of them the action of the play in question is conditioned absolutely. Many other dramatists have availed themselves of costume as a method of expressing directly to the audience the character of a person on his entrance, though hardly so brilliantly as Shakespeare has done in the case of the dandy Parolles, whose dress, by the way, only an archaeologist can understand; the fun of a master and servant exchanging coats in presence of the audience, of shipwrecked sailors squabbling over the division of a lot of fine clothes, and of a tinker dressed up like a duke while he is in his cups, may be regarded as part of that great career which costume has always played in comedy from the time of Aristophanes down to Mr Gilbert; but nobody from the mere details of apparel and adornment has ever drawn such irony of contrast, such immediate and tragic effect, such pity and such pathos, as Shakespeare himself. Armed cap-à-pie, the dead King stalks on the battlements of Elsinore because all is not right with Denmark; Shylock's Jewish gaberdine is part of the stigma under which that wounded and embittered nature writhes; Arthur begging for his life can think of no better plea than the handkerchief he had given Hubert –

> Have you the heart! when your head did but ache,
> I knit my handkerchief about your brows,
> (The best I had, a princess wrought it me)
> And I did never ask it you again;

and Orlando's bloodstained napkin strikes the first sombre note in that exquisite woodland idyll, and shows us the depth of feeling that underlies Rosalind's fanciful wit and wilful jesting.

> Last night 'twas on my arm; I kissed it;
> I hope it be not gone to tell my lord
> That I kiss aught but he,

says Imogen, jesting on the loss of the bracelet which was already on its way to Rome to rob her of her husband's faith; the little Prince passing to the Tower plays with the dagger in his uncle's girdle; Duncan sends a ring to Lady Macbeth on the night of his own murder, and the ring of Portia turns the tragedy of the merchant into a wife's comedy. The great rebel York dies with a paper crown on his head; Hamlet's black suit is a kind of colour-motive in the piece, like the mourning of the Chimène in the *Cid*: and the climax of Antony's speech is the production of Cæsar's cloak: –

>   I remember
> The first time ever Cæsar put it on.
> 'Twas on a summer's evening, in his tent,
> The day he overcame the Nervii: –
> Look, in this place ran Cassius' dagger through:
> See what a rent the envious Casca made:
> Through this the well-beloved Brutus stabbed... .
> Kind souls, what, weep you when you but behold
> Our Cæsar's vesture wounded?

The flowers which Ophelia carries with her in her madness are as pathetic as the violets that blossom on a grave; the effect of Lear's wandering on the heath is intensified beyond words by his fantastic attire; and when Cloten, stung by the taunt of that simile which his sister draws from her husband's raiment, arrays himself in that husband's very garb to work upon her the deed of shame, we feel that there is nothing in the whole of modern French realism, nothing even in *Thérèse Raquin*, that masterpiece of horror, which for terrible and tragic significance can compare with this strange scene in *Cymbeline*.

In the actual dialogue also some of the most vivid passages are those suggested by costume. Rosalind's

> Dost thou think, though I am caparisoned like a man, I have a doublet and hose in my disposition?

Constance's

> Grief fills the place of my absent child,
> Stuffs out his vacant garments with his form;

and the quick sharp cry of Elizabeth –

> 'Ah! cut my lace asunder! – '

are only a few of the many examples one might quote. One of the finest effects I have ever seen on the stage was Salvini, in the last act of *Lear*, tearing the plume from Kent's cap and applying it to Cordelia's lips when he came to the line,

> This feather stirs; she lives!

Mr Booth, whose Lear had many noble qualities of passion, plucked, I remember, some fur from his archaeologically-incorrect ermine for the same business; but Salvini's was the finer effect of the two, as well as the truer. And those who saw Mr Irving in the last act of *Richard the Third* have not, I am sure, forgotten how much the agony and terror of his dream was intensified, by contrast, through the calm and quiet that preceded it, and the delivery of such lines as

> What, is my beaver easier than it was?
> And all my armour laid into my tent?
> Look that my staves be sound and not too heavy –

lines which had a double meaning for the audience, remembering the last words which Richard's mother called after him as he was marching to Bosworth: –

> Therefore take with thee my most grievous curse,

Which in the day of battle tire thee more
Than all the complete armour that thou wear'st.

As regards the resources which Shakespeare had at his disposal, it is to be remarked that, while he more than once complains of the smallness of the stage on which he has to produce big historical plays and of the want of scenery which obliges him to cut out many effective open-air incidents, he always writes as a dramatist who had at his disposal a most elaborate theatrical wardrobe, and who could rely on the actors taking pains about their make-up. Even now it is difficult to produce such a play as the *Comedy of Errors*; and to the picturesque accident of Miss Ellen Terry's brother resembling herself we owe the opportunity of seeing *Twelfth Night* adequately performed. Indeed, to put any play of Shakespeare's on the stage, absolutely as he himself wished it to be done, requires the services of a good property-man, a clever wig-maker, a costumier with a sense of colour and a knowledge of textures, a master of the methods of making-up, a fencing-master, a dancing-master, and an artist to direct personally the whole production. For he is most careful to tell us the dress and appearance of each character. 'Racine abhorre la réalité,' says Auguste Vacquerie somewhere; 'il ne daigne pas s'occuper de son costume. Si l'on s'en rapportait aux indications du poète, Agamemnon serait vêtu d'un sceptre et Achille d'une épée.'* But with Shakespeare it is very different. He gives us directions about the costumes of Perdita, Florizel, Autolycus, the Witches in *Macbeth*, and the apothecary in *Romeo and Juliet*, several elaborate descriptions of his fat knight, and a detailed account of the extraordinary garb in which Petruchio is to be married. Rosaline, he tells us, is tall, and is to carry a spear and a little dagger; Celia is smaller, and is to paint her face brown so as to look sunburnt. The children who play at fairies in Windsor Forest are to be dressed in white and green – a compliment, by the way, to Queen Elizabeth, whose favourite colours they were – and in white, with green garlands and gilded vizors, the angels are to come to Katherine in Kimbolton. Bottom is in home-spun, Lysander is distinguished from Oberon by his wearing an Athenian dress, and Launce has holes in his boots. The Duchess of Gloucester stands in a white sheet with her husband in mourning beside her. The motley of the Fool, the scarlet of the Cardinal, and the French lilies broidered on the English coats, are all made occasion for jest or taunt in the dialogue. We know the patterns on the Dauphin's armour and the Pucelle's sword, the crest on Warwick's helmet and the colour of Bardolph's nose. Portia has golden hair, Phœbe is black-haired, Orlando has chestnut curls, and Sir Andrew Aguecheek's hair hangs like flax on a distaff, and won't curl at all. Some of the characters are stout, some lean, some straight, some hunchbacked, some fair, some dark, and some are to blacken their faces. Lear has a white beard, Hamlet's father a grizzled, and Benedick is to shave his in the course of the play. Indeed, on the subject of stage beards Shakespeare is quite elaborate; tells us of the many different colours in use, and gives a hint to actors always to see that their own are properly tied on. There is a dance of reapers in rye-straw hats, and of rustics

---

*Racine hates reality. He disdains to worry about his attire. If you referred to the poet's own indications Agamemnon would be clad in a sceptre and Achilles in a sword.

in hairy coats like satyrs; a masque of Amazons, a masque of Russians, and a classical masque; several immortal scenes over a weaver in an ass's head, a riot over the colour of a coat which it takes the Lord Mayor of London to quell, and a scene between an infuriated husband and his wife's milliner about the slashing of a sleeve.

As for the metaphors Shakespeare draws from dress, and the aphorisms he makes on it, his hits at the costume of his age, particularly at the ridiculous size of the ladies' bonnets, and the many descriptions of the *mundus muliebris*,* from the song of Autolycus in the *Winter's Tale* down to the account of the Duchess of Milan's gown in *Much Ado About Nothing*, they are far too numerous to quote; though it may be worth while to remind people that the whole of the Philosophy of Clothes is to be found in Lear's scene with Edgar – a passage which has the advantage of brevity and style over the grotesque wisdom and somewhat mouthing metaphysics of *Sartor Resartus*. But I think that from what I have already said it is quite clear that Shakespeare was very much interested in costume. I do not mean in that shallow sense by which it has been concluded from his knowledge of deeds and daffodils that he was the Blackstone and Paxton of the Elizabethan age; but that he saw that costume could be made at once impressive of a certain effect on the audience and expressive of certain types of character, and is one of the essential factors of the means which a true illusionist has at his disposal. Indeed to him the deformed figure of Richard was of as much value as Juliet's loveliness; he sets the serge of the radical beside the silks of the lord, and sees the stage effects to be got from each; he has as much delight in Caliban as he has in Ariel, in rags as he has in cloth of gold, and recognises the artistic beauty of ugliness.

The difficulty Ducis felt about translating *Othello* in consequence of the importance given to such a vulgar thing as a handkerchief, and his attempt to soften its grossness by making the Moor reiterate 'Le bandeau!** le bandeau!' may be taken as an example of the difference between *la tragédie philosophique* and the drama of real life; and the introduction for the first time of the word *mouchoir*† at the Théâtre Français was an era in that romantic-realistic movement of which Hugo is the father and M. Zola the *enfant terrible*, just as the classicism of the earlier part of the century was emphasised by Talma's refusal to play Greek heroes any longer in a powdered periwig – one of the many instances, by the way, of that desire for archaeological accuracy in dress which has distinguished the great actors of our age.

In criticising the importance given to money in *La Comédie Humaine*, Théophile Gautier says that Balzac may claim to have invented a new hero in fiction, *le héros métallique*. Of Shakespeare it may be said he was the first to see the dramatic value of doublets, and that a climax may depend on a crinoline.

The burning of the Globe Theatre – an event due, by the way, to the results of the passion for illusion that distinguished Shakespeare's stage-management – has unfortunately robbed us of many important documents; but in the inventory, still in existence, of the costume-wardrobe of a London theatre in Shakespeare's time, there are mentioned particular costumes for cardinals,

*Woman's world.   **The veil.   †Handkerchief.

shepherds, kings, clowns, friars, and fools; green coats for Robin Hood's men, and a green gown for Maid Marian; a white and gold doublet for Henry the Fifth, and a robe for Longshanks; besides surplices, copes, damask gowns, gowns of cloth of gold and of cloth of silver, taffeta gowns, calico gowns, velvet coats, satin coats, frieze coats, jerkins of yellow leather and of black leather, red suits, grey suits, French Pierrot suits, a robe 'for to goo invisibell', which seems inexpensive at £3 10s., and four incomparable fardingales – all of which show a desire to give every character an appropriate dress. There are also entries of Spanish, Moorish and Danish costumes, of helmets, lances, painted shields, imperial crowns, and papal tiaras, as well as of costumes for Turkish Janissaries, Roman Senators, and all the gods and goddesses of Olympus, which evidence a good deal of archaeological research on the part of the manager of the theatre. It is true that there is a mention of a bodice for Eve, but probably the *donnée** of the play was after the Fall.

Indeed, anybody who cares to examine the age of Shakespeare will see that archaeology was one of its special characteristics. After that revival of the classical forms of architecture which was one of the notes of the Renaissance, and the printing at Venice and elsewhere of the masterpieces of Greek and Latin literature, had come naturally an interest in the ornamentation and costume of the antique world. Nor was it for the learning that they could acquire, but rather for the loveliness that they might create, that the artists studied these things. The curious objects that were being constantly brought to light by excavations were not left to moulder in a museum, for the contemplation of a callous curator, and the *ennui* of a policeman bored by the absence of crime. They were used as motives for the production of a new art, which was to be not beautiful merely, but also strange.

Infessura tells us that in 1485 some workmen digging on the Appian Way came across an old Roman sarcophagus inscribed with the name 'Julia, daughter of Claudius'. On opening the coffer they found within its marble womb the body of a beautiful girl of about fifteen years of age, preserved by the embalmer's skill from corruption and the decay of time. Her eyes were half open, her hair rippled round her in crisp curling gold, and from her lips and cheek the bloom of maidenhood had not yet departed. Borne back to the Capitol, she became at once the centre of a new cult, and from all parts of the city crowded pilgrims to worship at the wonderful shrine, till the Pope, fearing lest those who had found the secret of beauty in a Pagan tomb might forget what secrets Judæa's rough and rock-hewn sepulchre contained, had the body conveyed away by night, and in secret buried. Legend though it may be, yet the story is none the less valuable as showing us the attitude of the Renaissance towards the antique world. Archaeology to them was not a mere science for the antiquarian; it was a means by which they could touch the dry dust of antiquity into the very breath and beauty of life, and fill with the new wine of romanticism forms that else had been old and outworn. From the pulpit of Niccola Pisano down to Mantegna's 'Triumph of Cæsar', and the service Cellini designed for King Francis, the influence of this spirit can be traced; nor was it confined merely to the immobile arts – the arts of arrested movement – but its influence was to be seen also in the

*Motif.

great Græco-Roman masques which were the constant amusement of the gay courts of the time, and in the public pomps and processions with which the citizens of big commercial towns were wont to greet the princes that chanced to visit them; pageants, by the way, which were considered so important that large prints were made of them and published – a fact which is a proof of the general interest at the time in matters of such kind.

And this use of archaeology in shows, so far from being a bit of priggish pedantry, is in every way legitimate and beautiful. For the stage is not merely the meeting-place of all the arts, but is also the return of art to life. Sometimes in an archaeological novel the use of strange and obsolete terms seems to hide the reality beneath the learning, and I dare say that many of the readers of *Notre Dame de Paris* have been much puzzled over the meaning of such expressions as *la casaque à mahoitres, les voulgiers, le gallimard taché d'encre, les caraquiniers,** and the like; but with the stage how different it is! The ancient world wakes from its sleep, and history moves as a pageant before our eyes, without obliging us to have recourse to a dictionary or an encyclopaedia for the perfection of our enjoyment. Indeed, there is not the slightest necessity that the public should know the authorities for the mounting of any piece. From such materials, for instance, as the disk of Theodosius, materials with which the majority of people are probably not very familiar, Mr E. W. Godwin, one of the most artistic spirits of this century in England, created the marvellous loveliness of the first act of *Claudian,* and showed us the life of Byzantium in the fourth century, not by a dreary lecture and a set of grimy casts, not by a novel which requires a glossary to explain it, but by the visible presentation before us of all the glory of that great town. And while the costumes were true to the smallest points of colour and design, yet the details were not assigned that abnormal importance which they must necessarily be given in a piecemeal lecture, but were subordinated to the rules of lofty composition and the unity of artistic effect. Mr Symonds, speaking of that great picture of Mantegna's, now in Hampton Court, says that the artist has converted an antiquarian motive into a theme for melodies of line. The same could have been said with equal justice of Mr Godwin's scene. Only the foolish called it pedantry, only those who would neither look nor listen spoke of the passion of the play being killed by its paint. It was in reality a scene not merely perfect in its picturesqueness, but absolutely dramatic also, getting rid of any necessity for tedious descriptions, and showing us, by the colour and character of Claudian's dress, and the dress of his attendants, the whole nature and life of the man, from what school of philosophy he affected, down to what horses he backed on the turf.

And indeed archaeology is only really delightful when transfused into some form of art. I have no desire to underrate the services of laborious scholars, but I feel that the use Keats made of Lemprière's Dictionary is of far more value to us than Professor Max Müller's treatment of the same mythology as a disease of language. Better *Endymion* than any theory, however sound, or, as in the present instance, unsound, of an epidemic among adjectives! And who does not feel that the chief glory of Piranesi's book on Vases is that it gave Keats the suggestion for his 'Ode on a Grecian Urn'? Art,

---

*Tunic with padded sleeves, men with halberts, pen-box stained with ink, sailors of caracks.

and art only, can make archaeology beautiful; and the theatric art can use it most directly and most vividly, for it can combine in one exquisite presentation the illusion of actual life with the wonder of the unreal world. But the sixteenth century was not merely the age of Vitruvius; it was the age of Vecellio also. Every nation seems suddenly to have become interested in the dress of its neighbours. Europe began to investigate its own clothes, and the amount of books published on national costumes is quite extraordinary. At the beginning of the century the *Nuremberg Chronicle*, with its two thousand illustrations, reached its fifth edition, and before the century was over seventeen editions were published of Munster's *Cosmography*. Besides these two books there were also the works of Michael Colyns, of Hans Weigel, of Amman, and of Vecellio himself, all of them well illustrated, some of the drawings in Vecellio being probably from the hand of Titian.

Nor was it merely from books and treatises that they acquired their knowledge. The development of the habit of foreign travel, the increased commercial intercourse between countries, and the frequency of diplomatic missions, gave every nation many opportunities of studying the various forms of contemporary dress. After the departure from England, for instance, of the ambassadors from the Czar, the Sultan and the Prince of Morocco, Henry the Eighth and his friends gave several masques in the strange attire of their visitors. Later on London saw, perhaps too often, the sombre splendour of the Spanish Court, and to Elizabeth came envoys from all lands, whose dress, Shakespeare tells us, had an important influence on English costume.

And the interest was not confined merely to classical dress, or the dress of foreign nations; there was also a good deal of research, amongst theatrical people especially, into the ancient costume of England itself: and when Shakespeare, in the prologue to one of his plays, expresses his regret at being unable to produce helmets of the period, he is speaking as an Elizabethan manager and not merely as an Elizabethan poet. At Cambridge, for instance, during his day, a play of *Richard the Third* was performed, in which the actors were attired in real dresses of the time, procured from the great collection of historical costume in the Tower, which was always open to the inspection of managers, and sometimes placed at their disposal. And I cannot help thinking that this performance must have been far more artistic as regards costume, than Garrick's mounting of Shakespeare's own play on the subject, in which he himself appeared in a nondescript fancy dress, and everybody else in the costume of the time of George the Third, Richmond especially being much admired in the uniform of a young guardsman.

For what is the use to the stage of that archaeology which has so strangely terrified the critics, but that it, and it alone, can give us the architecture and apparel suitable to the time in which the action of the play passes? It enables us to see a Greek dressed like a Greek, and an Italian like an Italian; to enjoy the arcades of Venice and the balconies of Verona; and, if the play deals with any of the great eras in our country's history, to contemplate the age in its proper attire, and the king in his habit as he lived. And I wonder, by the way, what Lord Lytton would have said some time ago, at the Princess's Theatre, had the curtain risen on his father's Brutus reclining in a Queen Anne chair, attired in a flowing wig and a flowered dressing-gown, a costume which in the last century was considered peculiarly appropriate to an antique Roman! For in those halcyon days of the drama no archaeology troubled the stage, or distressed the critics, and our inartistic grandfathers sat peaceably in a stifling atmosphere of anachronisms, and beheld with the calm complacency of the age of prose an Iachimo in powder and patches, a Lear in lace ruffles, and a Lady Macbeth in a large crinoline. I can understand archaeology being attacked on the ground of its excessive realism, but to attack it as pedantic seems to be very much beside the mark. However, to attack it for any reason is foolish; one might just as well speak disrespectfully of the equator. For archaeology, being a science, is neither good nor bad, but a fact simply. Its value depends entirely on how it is used, and only an artist can use it. We look to the archaeologist for the materials, to the artist for the method.

In designing the scenery and costumes for any of Shakespeare's plays, the first thing the artist has to settle is the best date for the drama. This should be determined by the general spirit of the play, more than by any actual historical references which may occur in it. Most *Hamlets* I have seen were placed far too early. Hamlet is essentially a scholar of the Revival of Learning; and if the allusion to the recent invasion of England by the Danes puts it back to the ninth century, the use of foils brings it down much later. Once, however, that the date has been fixed, then the archaeologist is to supply us with the facts which the artist is to convert into effects.

It has been said that the anachronisms in the plays themselves show us that Shakespeare was indifferent to historical accuracy, and a great deal of capital has been made out of Hector's indiscreet quotation from Aristotle. Upon the other hand, the anachronisms are really few in number, and not very important, and, had Shakespeare's attention been drawn to them by a brother artist, he would probably have corrected them. For, though they can hardly be called blemishes, they are certainly not the great beauties of his work; or, at least, if they are, their anachronistic charm cannot be emphasised unless the play is accurately mounted according to its proper date. In looking at Shakespeare's plays as a whole, however, what is really remarkable is their extraordinary fidelity as regards his personages and his plots. Many of his *dramatis personæ* are people who actually existed, and some of them might have been seen in real life by a portion of his audience. Indeed the most violent attack that was made on Shakespeare in his time was for his supposed caricature of Lord Cobham. As for his plots, Shakespeare constantly draws them either from authentic history, or from the old ballads and traditions which served as history to the Elizabethan public, and which, even now, no scientific historian would dismiss as absolutely untrue. And not merely did he select fact instead of fancy as the basis of much of his imaginative work, but he always gives to each play the general character, the social atmosphere in a word, of the age in question. Stupidity he recognises as being one of the permanent characteristics of all European civilisations; so he sees no difference between a London mob of his own day and a Roman mob of pagan days, between a silly watchman in Messina and a silly Justice of the Peace in Windsor. But when he deals with higher characters, with those exceptions of each age which are so fine that they become its types, he gives them absolutely the stamp and seal of their time. Virgilia is one of those Roman wives on whose tomb was written *Domi mansit lanam fecit,** as surely as Juliet is the romantic girl of the Renaissance. He is even true to the characteristics of race. Hamlet has all the imagination and irresolution of the Northern nations, and the Princess Katharine is as entirely French as the heroine of *Divorçons*. Harry the Fifth is a pure Englishman, and Othello a true Moor.

Again when Shakespeare treats of the history of England from the fourteenth to the sixteenth centuries, it is wonderful how careful he is to have his facts perfectly right – indeed he follows Holinshed with curious fidelity. The incessant wars between France and England are described with extraordinary accuracy down to the names of the besieged towns, the ports of landing and embarkation, the sites and dates of the battles, the titles of the commanders on each side, and the lists of the killed and wounded. And as regards the Civil Wars of the Roses we have many elaborate genealogies of the seven sons of Edward the Third; the claims of the rival Houses of York and Lancaster to the throne are discussed at length; and if the English aristocracy will not read Shakespeare as a poet, they should certainly read him as a sort of early Peerage. There is hardly a single title in the Upper House, with the exception, of course, of the uninteresting titles assumed by the law lords, which does not appear in Shakespeare along with many details of family history, creditable and discreditable. Indeed, if it be really necessary that the School Board children should know about the Wars of the Roses, they could learn their lessons just as well out of Shakespeare as out of shilling primers, and learn them, I need not say, far more pleasurably. Even in Shakespeare's own day this use of his plays was recognised. 'The historical plays teach history to those who cannot read it in the chronicles,' says Heywood in a tract about the stage, and yet I am sure that sixteenth-century chronicles were much more delightful reading than nineteenth-century primers are.

Of course the æsthetic value of Shakespeare's plays does not, in the slightest degree, depend on their facts, but on their Truth, and Truth is independent of facts always, inventing or selecting them at pleasure. But still Shakespeare's use of facts is a most interesting part of his method of work, and shows us his attitude towards the stage, and his relations to the great art of illusion. Indeed he would have been very much surprised at any one classing his plays with 'fairy tales,' as Lord Lytton does; for one of his aims was to create for England a national historical drama, which should deal with incidents with which the public was well acquainted, and with heroes that lived in the memory of a people. Patriotism, I need hardly say, is not a necessary quality of art; but it means, for the artist, the substitution of a universal for an individual feeling, and for the public the presentation of a work of art in a most attractive and popular form. It is worth noticing that Shakespeare's first and last successes were both historical plays.

It may be asked, what has this to do with Shakespeare's attitude towards costume? I answer that a dramatist who laid such stress on historical accuracy of fact would have welcomed historical accuracy of costume as a most important adjunct to his illusionist method. And I have no hesitation in saying that he did so. The reference to helmets of the period in the prologue

*She stayed at home and spun.

to *Henry the Fifth* may be considered fanciful, though Shakespeare must have often seen

> The very casque
> That did affright the air at Agincourt,

where it still hangs in the dusky gloom of Westminster Abbey, along with the saddle of that 'imp of fame', and the dinted shield with its torn blue velvet lining and its tarnished lilies of gold; but the use of military tabards in *Henry the Sixth* is a bit of pure archaeology, as they were not worn in the sixteenth century; and the King's own tabard, I may mention, was still suspended over his tomb in St George's Chapel, Windsor, in Shakespeare's day. For, up to the time of the unfortunate triumph of the Philistines in 1645, the chapels and cathedrals of England were the great national museums of archaeology, and in them were kept the armour and attire of the heroes of English history. A good deal was, of course, preserved in the Tower, and even in Elizabeth's day tourists were brought there to see such curious relics of the past as Charles Brandon's huge lance, which is still, I believe, the admiration of our country visitors; but the cathedrals and churches were, as a rule, selected as the most suitable shrines for the reception of the historic antiquities. Canterbury can still show us the helm of the Black Prince, Westminster the robes of our kings, and in old St Paul's the very banner that had waved on Bosworth field was hung up by Richmond himself.

In fact, everywhere that Shakespeare turned in London, he saw the apparel and appurtenances of past ages, and it is impossible to doubt that he made use of his opportunities. The employment of lance and shield, for instance, in actual warfare, which is so frequent in his plays, is drawn from archaeology, and not from the military accoutrements of his day; and his general use of armour in battle was not a characteristic of his age, a time when it was rapidly disappearing before firearms. Again, the crest on Warwick's helmet, of which such a point is made in *Henry the Sixth*, is absolutely correct in a fifteenth-century play when crests were generally worn, but would not have been so in a play of Shakespeare's own time, when feathers and plumes had taken their place – a fashion which, as he tells us in *Henry the Eighth*, was borrowed from France. For the historical plays, then, we may be sure that archaeology was employed, and as for the others I feel certain that it was the case also. The appearance of Jupiter on his eagle, thunderbolt in hand, of Juno with her peacocks, and of Iris with her many-coloured bow; the Amazon masque and the masque of the Five Worthies, may all be regarded as archaeological; and the vision which Posthumous sees in prison of Sicilius Leonatus – 'an old man, attired like a warrior, leading an ancient matron' – is clearly so. Of the 'Athenian dress' by which Lysander is distinguished from Oberon I have already spoken; but one of the most marked instances is in the case of the dress of Coriolanus, for which Shakespeare goes directly to Plutarch. That historian, in his Life of the great Roman, tells us of the oak-wreath with which Caius Marcius was crowned, and of the curious kind of dress in which, according to ancient fashion, he had to canvass his electors; and on both of these points he enters into long disquisitions, investigating the origin and meaning of the old customs. Shakespeare, in the spirit of the true artist, accepts the facts of the antiquarian and converts them into dramatic and picturesque effects: indeed, the gown of humility, the 'wolvish gown', as Shakespeare calls it, is the central note of the play. There are other cases I might quote, but this one is quite sufficient for my purpose; and it is evident from it at any rate that, in mounting a play in the accurate costume of the time, according to the best authorities, we are carrying out Shakespeare's own wishes and method.

Even if it were not so, there is no more reason that we should continue any imperfections which may be supposed to have characterised Shakespeare's stage mounting than that we should have Juliet played by a young man, or give up the advantage of changeable scenery. A great work of dramatic art should not merely be made expressive of modern passion by means of the actor, but should be presented to us in the form most suitable to the modern spirit. Racine produced his Roman plays in Louis Quatorze dress on a stage crowded with spectators; but we require different conditions for the enjoyment of his art. Perfect accuracy of detail, for the sake of perfect illusion, is necessary for us. What we have to see is that the details are not allowed to usurp the principal place. They must be subordinate always to the general motive of the play. But subordination in art does not mean disregard of truth; it means conversion of fact into effect, and assigning to each detail its proper relative value.

Les petits détails d'histoire et de vie domestique (says Hugo) doivent être scrupuleusement étudiés et reproduits par la poète, mais uniquement comme des moyens d'accroître la réalité de l'ensemble, et de faire pénétrer jusque dans les coins les plus obscurs de l'œuvre cette vie générale et puissant au milieu de laquelle les personnages sont plus vrais, et les catastrophes, par conséquent, plus poignantes. Tout doit être subordonné à ce but. L'Homme sur le premier plan, le reste au fond.*

This passage is interesting as coming from the first great French dramatist who employed archaeology on the stage, and whose plays, though absolutely correct in detail, are known to all for their passion, not for their pedantry – for their life, not for their learning. It is true that he has made certain concessions in the case of the employment of curious or strange expressions. Ruy Blas talks of M. de Priego as 'sujet du roi' instead of 'noble du roi', and Angelo Malipieri speaks of 'la croix rouge' instead of 'la croix de gueules'.** But they are concessions made to the public, or rather to a section of it. 'J'en offre ici toute mes excuses aux spectateurs intelligents', he says in a note to one of the plays; 'espérons qu'un jour un seigneur vénitien pourra dire tout

*The little details of history and of domestic life must be scrupulously studied and reproduced by the poet, but solely as a means of adding to the reality of the whole and of instilling into the darkest corners of the work this general and powerful life, in the midst of which the characters are more real and the catastrophies, as a result, more poignant. Everything must be subordinated to this end. Man in the foreground – the rest in the background.
**The cross of gules.

bonnement sans péril son blason sur le théâtre. C'est un progrès qui viendra'.* And though the description of the crest is not couched in accurate language, still the crest itself was accurately right. It may, of course, be said that the public do not notice these things; upon the other hand, it should be remembered that Art has no other aim but her own perfection, and proceeds simply by her own laws, and that the play which Hamlet describes as being caviare to the general is a play he highly praises. Besides, in England at any rate, the public have undergone a transformation; there is far more appreciation of beauty now than there was a few years ago; and though they may not be familiar with the authorities and archaeological data for what is shown to them, still they enjoy whatever loveliness they look at. And this is the important thing. Better to take pleasure in a rose than to put its root under a microscope. Archaeological accuracy is merely a condition of illusionist stage effect; it is not its quality. And Lord Lytton's proposal that the dresses should merely be beautiful without being accurate is founded on a misapprehension of the nature of costume, and of its value on the stage. This value is twofold, picturesque and dramatic; the former depends on the colour of the dress, the latter on its design and character. But so inter-woven are the two that, whenever in our own day historical accuracy has been disregarded, and the various dresses in a play taken from different ages, the result has been that the stage has been turned into that chaos of costume, that caricature of the centuries, the Fancy Dress Ball, to the entire ruin of all dramatic and picturesque effect. For the dresses of one age do not artistically harmonise with the dresses of another; and, as far as dramatic value goes, to confuse the costumes is to confuse the play. Costume is a growth, an evolution, and a most important, perhaps the most important, sign of the manners, customs and mode of life of each century. The Puritan dislike of colour, adornment and grace in apparel was part of the great revolt of the middle classes against Beauty in the seventeenth century. A historian who disregarded it would give us a most inaccurate picture of the time, and a dramatist who did not avail himself of it would miss a most vital element in producing an illusionist effect. The effeminacy of dress that characterised the reign of Richard the Second was a constant theme of contemporary authors. Shakespeare, writing two hundred years after, makes the king's fondness for gay apparel and foreign fashions a point in the play, from John of Gaunt's reproaches down to Richard's own speech in the third act on his deposition from the throne. And that Shakespeare examined Richard's tomb in Westminster Abbey seems to me certain from York's speech: –

See, see, King Richard doth himself appear
As doth the blushing discontented sun
From out the fiery portal of the east,
When he perceives the envious clouds are bent
To dim his glory.

*I offer here all my apologies to intelligent spectators; let us hope that one day a Venetian nobleman will be able to mention quite simply and fearlessly his coat of arms on the stage. That improvement will come.

For we can still discern on the King's robe his favourite badge – the sun issuing from a cloud. In fact, in every age the social conditions are so exemplified in costume, that to produce a sixteenth-century play in fourteenth-century attire, or *vice versa*, would make the performance seem unreal because untrue. And, valuable as beauty of effect on the stage is, the highest beauty is not merely comparable with absolute accuracy of detail, but really dependent on it. To invent an entirely new costume is almost impossible except in burlesque or extravaganza, and as for combining the dress of different centuries into one, the experiment would be dangerous, and Shakespeare's opinion of the artistic value of such a medley may be gathered from his incessant satire of the Elizabethan dandies for imagining that they were well dressed because they got their doublets in Italy, their hats in Germany, and their hose in France. And it should be noted that the most lovely scenes that have been produced on our stage have been those that have been characterised by perfect accuracy, such as Mr and Mrs Bancroft's eighteenth-century revivals at the Haymarket, Mr Irving's superb production of *Much Ado About Nothing* and Mr Barrett's *Claudian*. Besides, and this is perhaps the most complete answer to Lord Lytton's theory, it must be remembered that neither in costume nor in dialogue is beauty the dramatist's primary aim at all. The true dramatist aims first at what is characteristic, and no more desires that all his personages should be beautifully attired than he desires that they should all have beautiful natures or speak beautiful English. The true dramatist, in fact, shows us life under the conditions of art, not art in the form of life. The Greek dress was the loveliest dress the world has ever seen, and the English dress of the last century one of the most monstrous; yet we cannot costume a play by Sheridan as we would costume a play by Sophokles. For, as Polonius says in his excellent lecture, a lecture to which I am glad to have the opportunity of expressing my obligations, one of the first qualities of apparel is its expressiveness. And the affected style of dress in the last century was the natural characteristic of a society of affected manners and affected conversation – a characteristic which the realistic dramatist will highly value down to the smallest detail of accuracy, and the materials for which he can get only from archaeology.

But it is not enough that a dress should be accurate; it must also be appropriate to the stature and appearance of the actor and to his supposed condition, as well as to his necessary action in the play. In Mr Hare's production of *As You Like It* at the St James's Theatre, for instance, the whole point of Orlando's complaint that he is brought up like a peasant, and not like a gentleman, was spoiled by the gorgeousness of his dress, and the splendid apparel worn by the banished Duke and his friends was quite out of place. Mr Lewis Wingfield's explanation that the sumptuary laws of the period necessitated their doing so, is, I am afraid, hardly sufficient. Outlaws, lurking in a forest and living by the chase, are not very likely to care much about ordinances of dress. They were probably attired like Robin Hood's men, to whom, indeed, they are compared in the course of the play. And that their dress was not that of wealthy noblemen may be seen by Orlando's words when he breaks in upon them. He mistakes them for robbers, and is amazed to find that they answer him in courteous and gentle terms. Lady

Archibald Campbell's production, under Mr E. W. Godwin's direction, of the same play in Coombe Wood was, as regards mounting, far more artistic. At least it seemed so to me. The Duke and his companions were dressed in serge tunics, leathern jerkins, high boots and gauntlets, and wore bycocket hats and hoods. And as they were playing in a real forest, they found, I am sure, their dresses extremely convenient. To every character in the play was given a perfectly appropriate attire, and the brown and green of their costumes harmonised exquisitely with the ferns through which they wandered, the trees beneath which they lay, and the lovely English landscape that surrounded the Pastoral Players. The perfect naturalness of the scene was due to the absolute accuracy and appropriateness of everything that was worn. Nor could archaeology have been put to a severer test, or come out of it more triumphantly. The whole production showed once for all that, unless a dress is archaeologically correct, and artistically appropriate, it always looks unreal, unnatural, and theatrical in the sense of artificial.

Nor, again, is it enough that there should be accurate and appropriate costumes of beautiful colours; there must be also beauty of colour on the stage as a whole, and as long as the background is painted by one artist, and the foreground figures independently designed by another, there is the danger of a want of harmony in the scene as a picture. For each scene the colour-scheme should be settled as absolutely as for the decoration of a room, and the textures which it is proposed to use should be mixed and re-mixed in every possible combination, and what is discordant removed. Then, as regards the particular kinds of colours, the stage is often too glaring, partly through the excessive use of hot, violent reds, and partly through the costumes looking too new. Shabbiness, which in modern life is merely the tendency of the lower orders towards tone, is not without its artistic value, and modern colours are often much improved by being a little faded. Blue also is too frequently used: it is not merely a dangerous colour to wear by gaslight, but it is really difficult in England to get a thoroughly good blue. The fine Chinese blue, which we all so much admire, takes two years to dye, and the English public will not wait so long for a colour. Peacock blue, of course, has been employed on the stage, notably at the Lyceum, with great advantage; but all attempts at a good light blue, or good dark blue, which I have seen have been failures. The value of black is hardly appreciated; it was used effectively by Mr Irving in *Hamlet* as the central note of a composition, but as a tone-giving neutral its importance is not recognised. And this is curious, considering the general colour of the dress of a century in which, as Baudelaire says, 'Nous célébrons tous quelque enterrement.'* The archaeologist of the future will probably point to this age as the time when the beauty of black was understood; but I hardly think that, as regards stage-mounting or house decoration, it really is. Its decorative value is, of course, the same as that of white or gold; it can separate and harmonise colours. In modern plays the black frock-coat of the hero becomes important in itself, and should be given a suitable background. But it rarely is. Indeed the only good background for a play in modern dress which I have ever seen was the dark grey and cream-white scene of the first act of the *Princesse Georges* in Mrs

*We are all dressed for a funeral.

Langtry's production. As a rule, the hero is smothered in *bric-à-brac* and palm-trees, lost in the gilded abyss of Louis Quatorze furniture, or reduced to a mere midge in the midst of marqueterie; whereas the background should always be kept as a background, and colour subordinated to effect. This, of course, can only be done when there is one single mind directing the whole production. The facts of art are diverse, but the essence of artistic effect is unity. Monarchy, Anarchy, and Republicanism may contend for the government of nations; but a theatre should be in the power of a cultured despot. There may be division of labour, but there must be no division of mind. Whoever understands the costume of an age understands of necessity its architecture and its surroundings also, and it is easy to see from the chairs of a century whether it was a century of crinolines or not. In fact, in art there is no specialism, and a really artistic production should bear the impress of one master, and one master only, who not merely should design and arrange everything, but should have complete control over the way in which each dress is to be worn.

Mademoiselle Mars, in the first production of *Hernani*, absolutely refused to call her lover '*Mon Lion!*' unless she was allowed to wear a little fashionable *toque* then much in vogue on the Boulevards; and many young ladies on our own stage insist to the present day on wearing stiff starched petticoats under Greek dresses, to the entire ruin of all delicacy of line and fold; but these wicked things should not be allowed. And there should be far more dress rehearsals than there are now. Actors such as Mr Forbes-Robertson, Mr Conway, Mr George Alexander, and others, not to mention older artists, can move with ease and elegance in the attire of any century; but there are not a few who seem dreadfully embarrassed about their hands if they have no side pockets, and who always wear their dresses as if they were costumes. Costumes, of course, they are to the designer; but dresses they should be to those that wear them. And it is time that a stop should be put to the idea, very prevalent on the stage, that the Greeks and Romans always went about bareheaded in the open air – a mistake the Elizabethan managers did not fall into, for they gave hoods as well as gowns to their Roman senators.

More dress rehearsals would also be of value in explaining to the actors that there is a form of gesture and movement that is not merely appropriate to each style of dress, but really conditioned by it. The extravagant use of the arms in the eighteenth century, for instance, was the necessary result of the large hoop, and the solemn dignity of Burleigh owed as much to his ruff as to his reason. Besides, until an actor is at home in his dress, he is not at home in his part.

Of the value of beautiful costume in creating an artistic temperament in the audience, and producing that joy in beauty for beauty's sake, without which the great masterpieces of art can never be understood, I will not here speak; though it is worth while to notice how Shakespeare appreciated that side of the question in the production of his tragedies, acting them always by artificial light, and in a theatre hung with black; but what I have tried to point out is that archaeology is not a pedantic method, but a method of artistic illusion, and that costume is a means of displaying character without description, and of producing dramatic situations and dramatic effects. And

I think it is a pity that so many critics should have set themselves to attack one of the most important movements on the modern stage before that movement has at all reached its proper perfection. That it will do so, however, I feel as certain as that we shall require from our dramatic critics in the future higher qualifications than that they can remember Macready or have seen Benjamin Webster; we shall require of them, indeed, that they cultivate a sense of beauty. *Pour être plus difficile, la tâche n'en est que plus glorieuse.** And if they will not encourage, at least they must not oppose, a movement of which Shakespeare of all dramatists would have most approved, for it has the illusion of truth for its method, and the illusion of beauty for its result. Not that I agree with everything that I have said in this essay. There is much with which I entirely disagree. The essay simply represents an artistic standpoint, and in æsthetic criticism attitude is everything. For in art there is no such thing as a universal truth. A Truth in art is that whose contradictory is also true. And just as it is only in art-criticism, and through it, that we can apprehend the Platonic theory of ideas, so it is only in art-criticism, and through it, that we can realise Hegel's system of contraries. The truths of metaphysics are the truths of masks.

*Because it is more difficult, the task is only more glorious for that.

TWO LETTERS TO THE *DAILY CHRONICLE*

The case of Warder Martin: some cruelties of prison life*

The Editor of the Daily Chronicle

SIR, – I learn with great regret, through the columns of your paper, that the warder Martin, of Reading Prison, has been dismissed by the Prison Commissioners for having given some sweet biscuits to a little hungry child. I saw the three children myself on the Monday preceding my release. They had just been convicted, and were standing in a row in the central hall in their prison dress, carrying their sheets under their arms previous to their being sent to the cells allotted to them. I happened to be passing along one of the galleries on my way to the reception room, where I was to have an interview with a friend. They were quite small children, the youngest – the one to whom the warder gave the biscuits – being a tiny little chap, for whom they had evidently been unable to find clothes small enough to fit. I had, of course, seen many children in prison during the two years during which I was myself confined. Wandsworth Prison especially contained always a large number of children. But the little child I saw on the afternoon of Monday the 17th, at Reading, was tinier than any one of them. I need not say how utterly distressed I was to see these children at Reading, for I knew the treatment in store for them. The cruelty that is practised by day and night on children in English prisons is incredible, except to those that have witnessed it and are aware of the brutality of the system.

* May 28, 1897.

People nowadays do not understand what cruelty is. They regard it as a sort of terrible mediæval passion, and connect it with the race of men like Eccelin da Romano, and others, to whom the deliberate infliction of pain gave a real madness of pleasure. But men of the stamp of Eccelin are merely abnormal types of perverted individualism. Ordinary cruelty is simply stupidity. It is the entire want of imagination. It is the result in our days of stereotyped systems, of hard-and-fast rules, and of stupidity. Wherever there is centralisation there is stupidity. What is inhuman in modern life is officialism. Authority is as destructive to those who exercise it as it is to those on whom it is exercised. It is the Prison Board, and the system that it carries out, that is the primary source of the cruelty that is exercised on a child in prison. The people who uphold the system have excellent intentions. Those who carry it out are humane in intention also. Responsibility is shifted on to the disciplinary regulations. It is supposed that because a thing is the rule it is right.

The present treatment of children is terrible, primarily from people not understanding the peculiar psychology of a child's nature. A child can understand a punishment inflicted by an individual, such as a parent or guardian, and bear it with a certain amount of acquiescence. What it cannot understand is a punishment inflicted by society. It cannot realise what society is. With grown people it is, of course, the reverse. Those of us who are either in prison or have been sent there, can understand, and do understand, what that collective force called society means, and whatever we may think of its methods or claims, we can force ourselves to accept it. Punishment inflicted on us by an individual, on the other hand, is a thing that no grown person endures, or is expected to endure.

The child consequently, being taken away from its parents by people whom it has never seen, and of whom it knows nothing, and finding itself in a lonely and unfamiliar cell, waited on by strange faces, and ordered about and punished by the representatives of a system that it cannot understand, becomes an immediate prey to the first and most prominent emotion produced by modern prison life – the emotion of terror. The terror of a child in prison is quite limitless. I remember once in Reading, as I was going out to exercise, seeing in the dimly lit cell right opposite my own a small boy. Two warders – not unkindly men – were talking to him, with some sternness apparently, or perhaps giving him some useful advice about his conduct. One was in the cell with him, the other was standing outside. The child's face was like a white wedge of sheer terror. There was in his eyes the terror of a hunted animal. The next morning I heard him at breakfast-time crying, and calling to be let out. His cry was for his parents. From time to time I could hear the deep voice of the warder on duty telling him to keep quiet. Yet he was not even convicted of whatever little offence he had been charged with. He was simply on remand. That I knew by his wearing his own clothes, which seemed neat enough. He was, however, wearing prison socks and shoes. This showed that he was a very poor boy, whose own shoes, if he had any, were in a bad state. Justices and magistrates, an entirely ignorant class as a rule, often remand children for a week, and then perhaps remit whatever sentence they are entitled to pass. They call this 'not sending a child to prison.' It is, of course, a stupid view on their part. To a little child, whether he is in prison on remand or after conviction, is not a subtlety of social position he can comprehend. To him the horrible thing is to be there at all. In the eyes of humanity it should be a horrible thing for him to be there at all.

This terror that seizes and dominates the child, as it seizes the grown man also, is of course intensified beyond power of expression by the solitary cellular system of our prisons. Every child is confined to its cell for twenty-three hours out of the twenty-four. This is the appalling thing. To shut up a child in a dimly lit cell, for twenty-three hours out of the twenty-four, is an example of the cruelty of stupidity. If an individual, parent or guardian, did this to a child, he would be severely punished. The Society for the Prevention of Cruelty to Children would take the matter up at once. There would be on all hands the utmost detestation of whomsoever had been guilty of such cruelty. A heavy sentence would, undoubtedly, follow conviction. But our own actual society does worse itself, and to the child to be so treated by a strange abstract force, of whose claims it has no cognisance, is much worse than it would be to receive the same treatment from its father or mother, or some one it knew. The inhuman treatment of a child is always inhuman, by whomsoever it is inflicted. But inhuman treatment by society is to the child the more terrible because there is no appeal. A parent or guardian can be moved, and let out a child from the dark lonely room in which it is confined. But a warder cannot. Most warders are very fond of children. But the system prohibits them from rendering the child any assistance. Should they do so, as Warder Martin did, they are dismissed.

The second thing from which a child suffers in prison is hunger. The food that is given to it consists of a piece of usually badly-baked prison bread and a tin of water for breakfast at half-past seven. At twelve o'clock it gets dinner, composed of a tin of coarse Indian meal stirabout; and at half-past five it gets a piece of dry bread and a tin of water for its supper. This diet in the case of a strong grown man is always productive of illness of some kind, chiefly, of course, diarrhoea, with its attendant weakness. In fact, in a big prison astringent medicines are served out regularly by the warders as a matter of course. In the case of a child, the child is, as a rule, incapable of eating the food at all. Any one who knows anything about children knows how easily a child's digestion is upset by a fit of crying, or trouble and mental distress of any kind. A child who has been crying all day long, and perhaps half the night, in a lonely dimly lit cell, and is preyed upon by terror, simply cannot eat food of this coarse, horrible kind. In the case of the little child to whom Warder Martin gave the biscuits, the child was crying with hunger on Tuesday morning, and utterly unable to eat the bread and water served to it for its breakfast. Martin went out after the breakfasts had been served, and bought the few sweet biscuits for the child rather than see it starving. It was a beautiful action on his part, and was so recognised by the child, who, utterly unconscious of the regulation of the Prison Board, told one of the senior warders how kind this junior warder had been to him. The result was, of course, a report and a dismissal.

I know Martin extremely well, and I was under his charge for the last seven weeks of my imprisonment. On his appointment at Reading he had charge

of Gallery C, in which I was confined, so I saw him constantly. I was struck by
the singular kindness and humanity of the way in which he spoke to me and
to the other prisoners. Kind words are much in prison, and a pleasant
'Good-morning' or 'Good-evening' will make one as happy as one can be in
a prison. He was always gentle and considerate. I happen to know another
case in which he showed great kindness to one of the prisoners, and I have
no hesitation in mentioning it. One of the most horrible things in prison is
the badness of the sanitary arrangements. No prisoner is allowed, under any
circumstances, to leave his cell after half-past five p.m. If, consequently, he
is suffering from diarrhoea, he has to use his cell as a latrine, and pass the
night in a most fetid and unwholesome atmosphere. Some days before my
release, Martin was going the rounds at half-past seven with one of the senior
warders for the purpose of collecting the oakum and tools of the prisoners.
A man just convicted, and suffering from violent diarrhoea in consequence
of the food, as is always the case, asked the senior warder to allow him to
empty the slops in his cell on account of the horrible odour of the cell and
the possibility of illness again in the night. The senior warder refused
absolutely; it was against the rules. The man had to pass the night in this
dreadful condition. Martin, however, rather than see this wretched man in
such a loathsome predicament, said he would empty the man's slops himself,
and did so. A warder emptying a prisoner's slops, is of course, against the
rules, but Martin did this act of kindness to the man out of the simple
humanity of his nature, and the man was naturally most grateful.

As regards the children, a great deal has been talked and written lately
about the contaminating influence of prison on young children. What is said
is quite true. A child is utterly contaminated by prison life. But the contaminating influence is not that of the prisoners. It is that of the whole prison
system – of the governor, the chaplain, the warders, the lonely cell, the
isolation, the revolting food, the rules of the Prison Commissioners, the
mode of discipline, as it is termed, of the life. Every care is taken to isolate a
child from the sight even of all prisoners over sixteen years of age. Children
sit behind a curtain in chapel, and are sent to take exercise in small sunless
yards – sometimes a stone-yard, sometimes a yard at the back of the mills –
rather than that they should see the elder prisoners at exercise. But the only
really humanising influence in prison is the influence of the prisoners. Their
cheerfulness under terrible circumstances, their sympathy for each other,
their humility, their gentleness, their pleasant smiles of greeting when they
meet each other, their complete acquiescence in their punishments, are all
quite wonderful, and I myself learned many sound lessons from them. I am
not proposing that the children should not sit behind a curtain in chapel,
or that they should take exercise in a corner of the common yard. I am merely
pointing out that the bad influence on children is not, and could never be,
that of the prisoners, but is, and will always remain, that of the prison system
itself. There is not a single man in Reading Gaol that would not gladly have
done the three children's punishment for them. When I saw them last it was
on the Tuesday following their conviction. I was taking exercise at half-past
eleven with about twelve other men, as the three children passed near us, in
charge of a warder, from the damp, dreary stone-yard in which they had been

at their exercise. I saw the greatest pity and sympathy in the eyes of my companions as they looked at them. Prisoners are, as a class, extremely kind and sympathetic to each other. Suffering and the community of suffering makes people kind, and day after day as I tramped the yard I used to feel with pleasure and comfort what Carlyle calls somewhere 'the silent rhythmic charm of human companionship.' In this, as in all other things, philanthropists and people of that kind are astray. It is not the prisoners who need reformation. It is the prisons.

Of course no child under fourteen years of age should be sent to prison at all. It is an absurdity, and, like many absurdities, of absolutely tragic results. If, however, they are to be sent to prison, during the daytime they should be in a workshop or schoolroom with a warder. At night they should sleep in a dormitory, with a night-warder to look after them. They should be allowed exercise for at least three hours a day. The dark, badly ventilated, ill-smelling prison cells are dreadful for a child, dreadful indeed for any one. One is always breathing bad air in prison. The food given to children should consist of tea and bread-and-butter and soup. Prison soup is very good and wholesome. A resolution of the House of Commons could settle the treatment of children in half an hour. I hope you will use your influence to have this done. The way that children are treated at present is really an outrage on humanity and common sense. It comes from stupidity.

Let me draw attention now to another terrible thing that goes on in English prisons, indeed in prisons all over the world where the system of silence and cellular confinement is practised. I refer to the large number of men who become insane or weak-minded in prison. In convict prisons this is, of course, quite common; but in ordinary gaols also, such as that I was confined in, it is to be found.

About three months ago I noticed amongst the prisoners who took exercise with me a young man who seemed to me to be silly or half-witted. Every prison, of course, has its half-witted clients, who return again and again, and may be said to live in the prison. But this young man struck me as being more than usually half-witted on account of his silly grin and idiotic laughter to himself, and the peculiar restlessness of his eternally twitching hands. He was noticed by all the other prisoners on account of the strangeness of his conduct. From time to time he did not appear at exercise, which showed me that he was being punished by confinement to his cell. Finally, I discovered that he was under observation, and being watched night and day by warders. When he did appear at exercise he always seemed hysterical, and used to walk round crying or laughing. At chapel he had to sit right under the observation of two warders, who carefully watched him all the time. Sometimes he would bury his head in his hands, an offence against the chapel regulations, and his head would be immediately struck up by a warder so that he should keep his eyes fixed permanently in the direction of the Communion-table. Sometimes he would cry – not making any disturbance – but with tears streaming down his face and an hysterical throbbing in the throat. Sometimes he would grin idiot-like to himself and make faces. He was on more than one occasion sent out of chapel to his cell, and of course he was continually punished. As the bench on which I used to sit in chapel was directly behind the bench at the end of which this unfortunate man was placed, I had full opportunity of observing him. I also saw him, of course, at exercise continually, and I saw that he was becoming insane, and was being treated as if he was shamming.

On Saturday week last I was in my cell at about one o'clock occupied in cleaning and polishing the tins I had been using for dinner. Suddenly I was startled by the prison silence being broken by the most horrible and revolting shrieks, or rather howls, for at first I thought some animal like a bull or a cow was being unskilfully slaughtered outside the prison walls. I soon realised, however, that the howls proceeded from the basement of the prison, and I knew that some wretched man was being flogged. I need not say how hideous and terrible it was for me, and I began to wonder who it was who was being punished in this revolting manner. Suddenly it dawned upon me that they might be flogging this unfortunate lunatic. My feelings on the subject need not be chronicled; they have nothing to do with the question.

The next day, Sunday 16th, I saw the poor fellow at exercise, his weak, ugly wretched face bloated by tears and hysteria almost beyond recognition. He walked in the centre ring along with the old men, the beggars, and the lame people, so that I was able to observe him the whole time. It was my last Sunday in prison, a perfectly lovely day, the finest day we had had the whole year, and there, in the beautiful sunlight, walked this poor creature – made once in the image of God – grinning like an ape, and making with his hands the most fantastic gestures, as though he was playing in the air on some invisible stringed instrument, or arranging and dealing counters in some curious game. All the while these hysterical tears, without which none of us ever saw him, were making soiled runnels on his white swollen face. The hideous and deliberate grace of his gestures made him like an antic. He was a living grotesque. The other prisoners all watched him, and not one of them smiled. Everybody knew what had happened to him, and that he was being driven insane – was insane already. After half an hour he was ordered in by the warder, and I suppose punished. At least he was not at exercise on Monday, though I think I caught sight of him at the corner of the stone-yard, walking in charge of a warder.

On the Tuesday – my last day in prison – I saw him at exercise. He was worse than before, and again was sent in. Since then I know nothing of him, but I found out from one of the prisoners who walked with me at exercise that he had had twenty-four lashes in the cookhouse on Saturday afternoon, by order of the visiting justices on the report of the doctor. The howls that had horrified us all were his.

This man is undoubtedly becoming insane. Prison doctors have no knowledge of mental disease of any kind. They are as a class ignorant men. The pathology of the mind is unknown to them. When a man grows insane, they treat him as shamming. They have him punished again and again. Naturally the man becomes worse. When ordinary punishments are exhausted, the doctor reports the case to the justices. The result is flogging. Of course the flogging is not done with a cat-of-nine-tails. It is what is called birching. The instrument is a rod; but the result on the wretched half-witted man may be imagined.

His number is, or was, A.2.11. I also managed to find out his name. It is Prince. Something should be done at once for him. He is a soldier, and his sentence is one of court-martial. The term is six months. Three have yet to run.

May I ask you to use your influence to have this case examined into, and to see that the lunatic prisoner is properly treated?

No report by the Medical Commissioners is of any avail. It is not to be trusted. The medical inspectors do not seem to understand the difference between idiocy and lunacy – between the entire absence of a function or organ and the disease of a function or organ. This man A.2.11 will, I have no doubt, be able to tell his name, the nature of his offence, the day of month, the date of the beginning of expiration of his sentence, and answer any ordinary simple question; but that his mind is diseased admits of no doubt. At present it is a horrible duel between himself and the doctor. The doctor is fighting for a theory. The man is fighting for his life. I am anxious that the man should win. But let the whole case be examined into by experts who understand brain diseases, and by people of humane feelings who have still some common sense and some pity. There is no reason that the sentimentalist should be asked to interfere. He always does harm.

The case is a special instance of the cruelty inseparable from a stupid system, for the present Governor of Reading is a man of gentle and humane character greatly liked and respected by all the prisoners. He was appointed in July last, and though he cannot alter the rules of the prison system, he has altered the spirit in which they used to be carried out under his predecessor. He is very popular with the prisoners and with the warders. Indeed he has quite altered the whole tone of the prison life. Upon the other hand, the system is, of course, beyond his reach as far as altering its rules is concerned. I have no doubt that he sees daily much of what he knows to be unjust, stupid and cruel. But his hands are tied. Of course I have no knowledge of his real views of the case of A.2.11, nor, indeed, of his views on our present system. I merely judge him by the complete change he brought about in Reading Prison. Under his predecessor the system was carried out with the greatest harshness and stupidity. – I remain, Sir, your obedient servant,

OSCAR WILDE.

May 27

Prison Reform*

The Editor of the Daily Chronicle

SIR, – I understand that the Home Secretary's Prison Reform Bill is to be read this week for the first or second time, and as your journal has been the one paper in England that has taken a real and vital interest in this important question, I hope that you will allow me, as one who has had long personal experience of life in an English gaol, to point out what reforms in our present stupid and barbarous system are urgently necessary.

From a leading article that appeared in your columns about a week ago, I learn that the chief reform proposed is an increase in the number of inspectors and official visitors that are to have access to our English prisons.

Such a reform as this is entirely useless. The reason is extremely simple. The inspectors and justices of the peace that visit prisons come there for the purpose of seeing that the prison regulations are duly carried out. They come for no other purpose, nor have they any power, even if they had the desire, to alter a single clause in the regulations. No prisoner has ever had the smallest relief, or attention, or care from any of the official visitors. The visitors arrive not to help the prisoners, but to see that the rules are carried out. Their object in coming is to ensure the enforcement of a foolish and inhuman code. And, as they must have some occupation, they take very good care to do it. A prisoner who has been allowed the smallest privilege dreads the arrival of the inspectors. And on the day of any prison inspection the prison officials are more than usually brutal to the prisoners. Their object is, of course, to show the splendid discipline they maintain.

The necessary reforms are very simple. They concern the needs of the body and the needs of the mind of each unfortunate prisoner.

With regard to the first, there are three permanent punishments authorised by law in English prisons:—

*March 24, 1898.

1. Hunger.
2. Insomnia.
3. Disease.

The food supplied to prisoners is entirely inadequate. Most of it is revolting in character. All of it is insufficient. Every prisoner suffers day and night from hunger. A certain amount of food is carefully weighed out ounce by ounce for each prisoner. It is just enough to sustain, not life exactly, but existence. But one is always racked by the pain and sickness of hunger.

The result of the food – which in most cases consists of weak gruel, suet, and water – is disease in the form of incessant diarrhoea. This malady, which ultimately with most prisoners becomes a permanent disease, is a recognised institution in every prison. At Wandsworth Prison, for instance – where I was confined for two months, till I had to be carried into hospital, where I remained for another two months – the warders go round twice or three times a day with astringent medicines, which they serve out to the prisoners as a matter of course. After about a week of such treatment it is unnecessary to say that the medicine produces no effect at all. The wretched prisoner is then left a prey to the most weakening, depressing, and humiliating malady that can be conceived: and if, as often happens, he fails from physical weakness to complete his required revolutions at the crank or the mill, he is reported for idleness, and punished with the greatest severity and brutality. Nor is this all.

Nothing can be worse than the sanitary arrangements of English prisons. In old days each cell was provided with a form of latrine. These latrines have now been suppressed. They exist no longer. A small tin vessel is supplied to each prisoner instead. Three times a day a prisoner is allowed to empty his slops. But he is not allowed to have access to the prison lavatories, except during the one hour when he is at exercise. And after five o'clock in the evening he is not allowed to leave his cell under any pretence, or for any reason. A man suffering from diarrhoea is consequently placed in a position so loathsome that it is unnecessary to dwell on it, that it would be unseemly to dwell on it. The misery and tortures that prisoners go through in consequence of the revolting sanitary arrangements are quite indescribable. And the foul air of the prison cells, increased by a system of ventilation that is utterly ineffective, and is so sickening and unwholesome that it is no uncommon thing for warders, when they come in the morning out of the fresh air and open and inspect each cell, to be violently sick. I have seen this myself on more than three occasions, and several of the warders have mentioned it to me as one of the disgusting things that their office entails on them.

The food supplied to prisoners should be adequate and wholesome. It should not be of such a character as to produce the incessant diarrhoea that, at first a malady, becomes a permanent disease.

The sanitary arrangements in English prisons should be entirely altered. Every prisoner should be allowed to have access to the lavatories when necessary, and to empty his slops when necessary. The present system of ventilation in each cell is utterly useless. The air comes through choked-up gratings, and through a small ventilator in the tiny barred window, which is

far too small, and too badly constructed, to admit any adequate amount of
fresh air. One is only allowed out of one's cell for one hour out of the
twenty-four that compose the long day, and so for twenty-three hours one is
breathing the foulest possible air.

With regard to the punishment of insomnia, it only exists in Chinese and
in English prisons. In China it is inflicted by placing the prisoner in a small
bamboo cage; in England by means of the plank bed. The object of the plank
bed is to produce insomnia. There is no other object in it, and it invariably
succeeds. And even when one is subsequently allowed a hard mattress, as
happens in the course of imprisonment, one still suffers from insomnia. For
sleep, like all wholesome things, is a habit. Every prisoner who has been on
a plank bed suffers from insomnia. It is a revolting and ignorant punishment.

With regard to the needs of the mind, I beg that you will allow me to say
something.

The present prison system seems almost to have for its aim the wrecking
and the destruction of the mental faculties. The production of insanity is, if
not its object, certainly its result. That is a well-ascertained fact. Its causes are
obvious. Deprived of books, of all human intercourse, isolated from every
humane and humanising influence, condemned to eternal silence, robbed
of all intercourse with the external world, treated like an unintelligent
animal, brutalised below the level of any of the brute creation, the wretched
man who is confined in an English prison can hardly escape becoming
insane. I do not wish to dwell on these horrors; still less to excite any
momentary sentimental interest in these matters. So I will merely, with your
permission, point out what should be done.

Every prisoner should have an adequate supply of good books. At present,
during the first three months of imprisonment, one is allowed no books at
all, except a Bible, Prayer-book, and hymn-book. After that one is allowed
one book a week. That is not merely inadequate, but the books that compose
an ordinary prison library are perfectly useless. They consist chiefly of
third-rate, badly written, religious books, so called, written apparently for
children, and utterly unsuitable for children or for any one else. Prisoners
should be encouraged to read, and should have whatever books they want
and the books should be well chosen. At present the selection of books is
made by the prison chaplain. Under the present system a prisoner is only
allowed to see his friends four times a year, for twenty minutes each time.
This is quite wrong. A prisoner should be allowed to see his friends once a
month, and for a reasonable time. The mode at present in vogue of exhib-
iting a prisoner to his friends should be altered. Under the present system
the prisoner is either locked up in a large iron cage or in a large wooden box
with a small aperture covered with wire netting, through which he is allowed
to peer. His friends are placed in a similar cage, some three or four feet
distant, and two warders stand between to listen to, and if they wish, stop or
interrupt the conversation, such as it may be. I propose that a prisoner should
be allowed to see his relatives or friends in a room. The present regulations
are inexpressibly revolting and harassing. A visit from (our) relatives or
friends is to every prisoner an intensification of humiliation and mental
distress. Many prisoners, rather than support such an ordeal, refuse to see

their friends at all. And I cannot say I am surprised. When one sees one's solicitor, one sees him in a room with a glass door on the other side of which stands the warder. When a man sees his wife and children, or his parents, or his friends, he should be allowed the same privilege. To be exhibited, like an ape, in a cage, to people who are fond of one, and of whom one is fond, is a needless and horrible degradation.

Every prisoner should be allowed to write and receive a letter at least once a month. At present one is allowed to write only four times a year. This is quite inadequate. One of the tragedies of prison life is that it turns a man's heart to stone. The feelings of natural affection, like all other feelings, require to be fed. They die easily of inanition. A brief letter, four times a year, is not enough to keep alive the gentler and more humane affections by which ultimately the nature is kept sensitive to any fine or beautiful influences that may heal a wrecked and ruined life.

The habit of mutilating and expurgating prisoners' letters should be stopped. At present, if a prisoner in a letter makes any complaint of the prison system, that portion of his letter is cut out with a pair of scissors. If, upon the other hand, he makes any complaint when he speaks to his friends through the bars of the cage, or the aperture of the wooden box, he is brutalised by the warders, and reported for punishment every week till his next visit comes round, by which time he is expected to have learned, not wisdom, but cunning, and one always learns that. It is one of the few things that one does learn in prison. Fortunately, the other things are, in some instances, of higher import.

If I may trespass for a little longer, may I say this? You suggested in your leading article that no prison chaplain should be allowed to have any care or employment outside the prison itself. But this is a matter of no moment. The prison chaplains are entirely useless. They are, as a class, well-meaning, but foolish, indeed silly men. They are of no help to any prisoner. Once every six weeks or so a key turns in the lock of one's cell door, and the chaplain enters. One stands, of course, at attention. He asks one whether one has been reading the Bible. One answers 'Yes' or 'No,' as the case may be. He then quotes a few texts, and goes out and locks the door. Sometimes he leaves a tract.

The officials who should not be allowed to hold any employment outside the prison, or to have any private practice, are the prison doctors. At present the prison doctors have usually if not always a large private practice, and hold appointments in other institutions. The consequence is that the health of the prisoners is entirely neglected, and the sanitary condition of the prison entirely overlooked. As a class, I regard, and have always from my earliest youth regarded, doctors as by far the most humane profession in the community. But I must make an exception for prison doctors. They are, as far as I came across them, and from what I saw of them in hospital and elsewhere, brutal in manner, coarse in temperament, and utterly indifferent to the health of the prisoners or their comfort. If prison doctors were prohibited from private practice they would be compelled to take some interest in the health and sanitary condition of the people under their charge. I have tried to indicate in my letter a few of the reforms necessary to our English prison system. They are simple, practical, and humane. They are, of course, only a beginning. But it is time that a beginning should be made, and it can only be started by a strong pressure of public opinion formularised in your powerful paper, and fostered by it.

But to make even these reforms effectual, much has to be done. And the first, and perhaps the most difficult task, is to humanise the governors of prisons, to civilise the warders and to Christianise the chaplains. – Yours, etc.,

THE AUTHOR OF THE 'BALLAD
OF READING GAOL.'

March 23.